PANDORA IN THE CRIMSON SHELL

GHOST URN

Original story:
Shirow Masamune
(in cooperation with Crossroad)

Manga: Rikudou Koushi

Art: Rin Hitotose

12

GHOST URN-CHARACTERS —— Main Characters

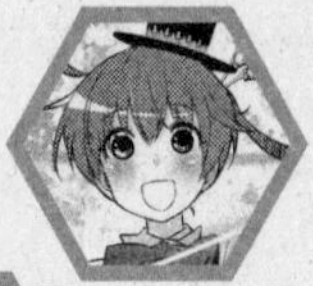

■ Nanakorobi Nene

A girl whose brain was implanted into an entirely artificial body after an accident when she was young. Nene has one of the few full-body prosthetics in the world!

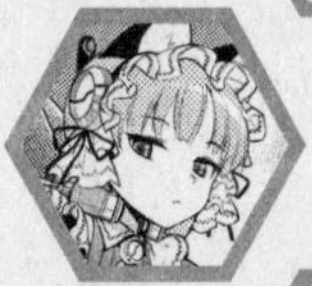

■ Clarion

A cat-eared girl wearing a maid uniform who initially accompanied Uzal. Like Nanakorobi Nene, Clarion has a full-body prosthetic...or does she? Clarion and Nene were brought together during the initial incident with Buer.

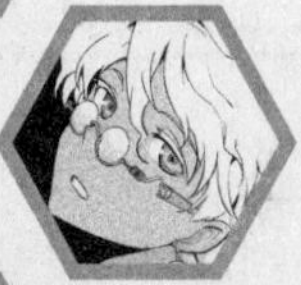

■ Uzal Delilah

The mysterious Uzal (real name: Sahar Schehera) is a well-known international businesswoman, but this brilliant scientist has plenty of secrets. She vanished during the chaos when Buer ran wild.

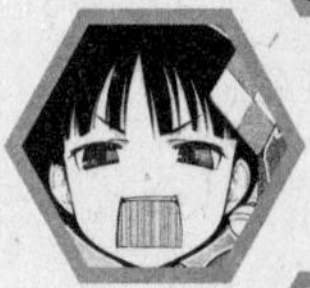

■ Korobase Takumi

Nene's mysterious aunt, and an acquaintance of Uzal's. She heads up the Korobase Foundation, which controls cybrain marketing, but has a pathological fear of people.

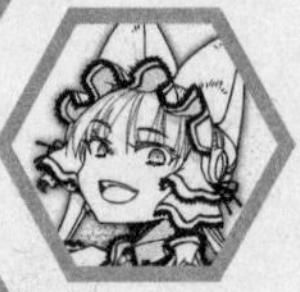

■ Phobos

The same model as Clarion: unit number Clarion 00 type 02. She now lives in the Korobase household with Nene and Clarion.

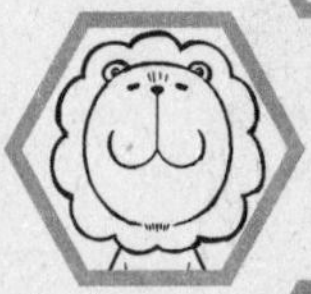

■ Massive boring machine Buer: Central Nervous Unit

The central control unit for the large multi-legged boring machine Buer, operating independently from the actual body and accompanying Nene and Clarion. This pompous-sounding entity provides a constant stream of perverted, leering commentary.

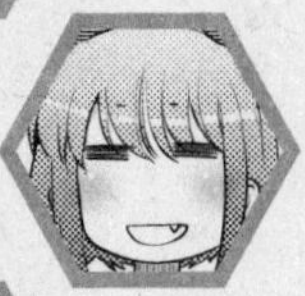

■ VlindXX XXXX

A perky, enthusiastic freelance reporter who dreams of taking her place among the top idols *and* the top reporters in the world! She's in feverish pursuit of her dream to dominate mass media, and dreams of romance with her bureau chief.

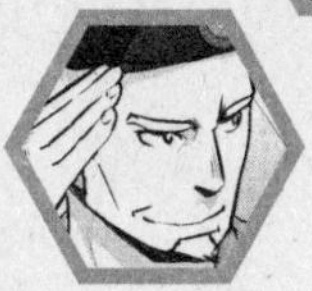

■ Captain Robert Altman

A captain with the Cenancle Defense Forces and a master of karate-style jujitsu. A passionate tough guy who loves justice and peace.

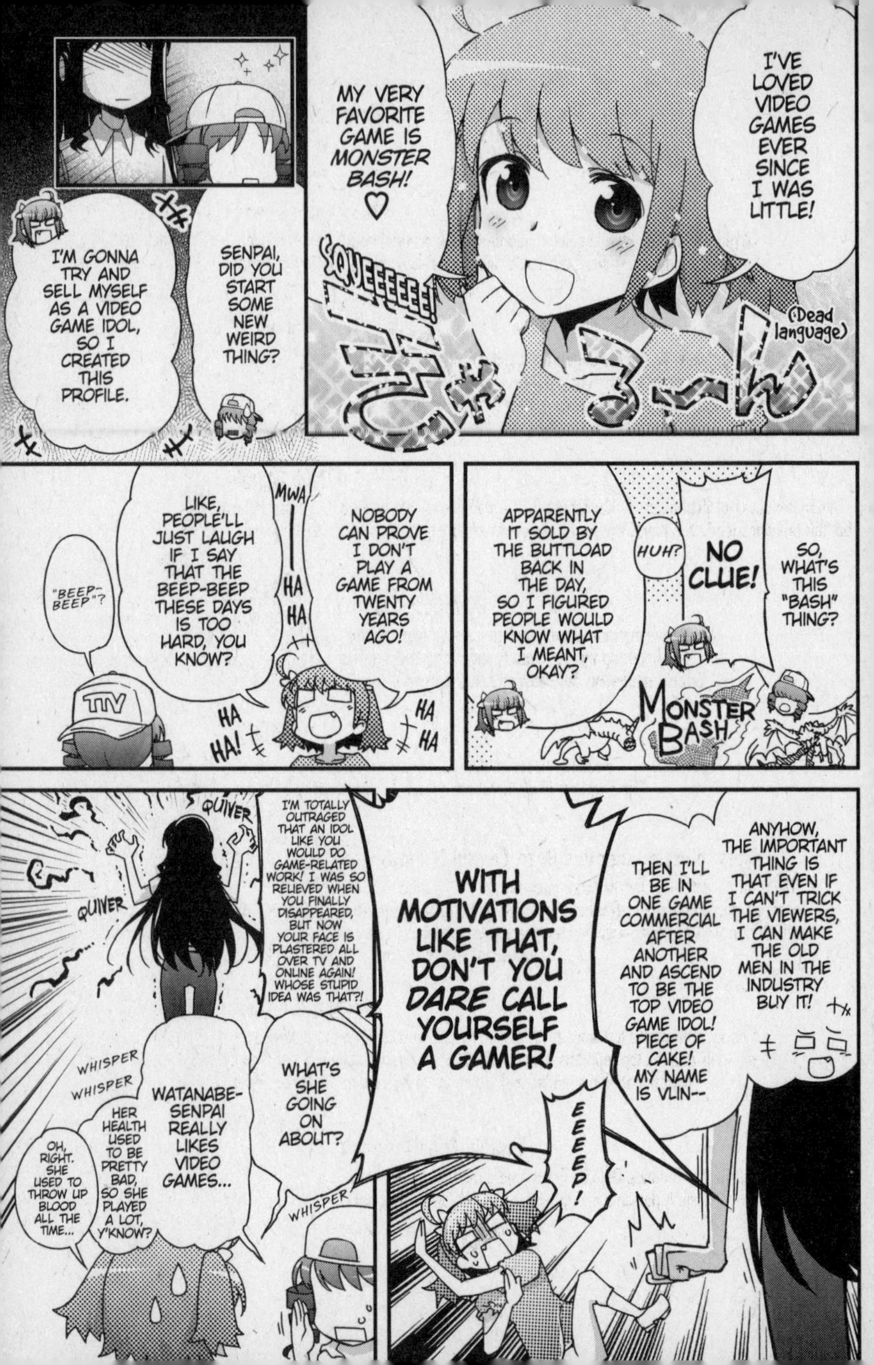
I'VE LOVED VIDEO GAMES EVER SINCE I WAS LITTLE!
MY VERY FAVORITE GAME IS MONSTER BASH! ♡
QYEEEEEE!
(Dead language)
SENPAI, DID YOU START SOME NEW WEIRD THING?
I'M GONNA TRY AND SELL MYSELF AS A VIDEO GAME IDOL, SO I CREATED THIS PROFILE.
SO, WHAT'S THIS "BASH" THING?
NO CLUE!
HUH?
APPARENTLY IT SOLD BY THE BUTTLOAD BACK IN THE DAY, SO I FIGURED PEOPLE WOULD KNOW WHAT I MEANT, OKAY?
MONSTER BASH
NOBODY CAN PROVE I DON'T PLAY A GAME FROM TWENTY YEARS AGO!
MWA HA HA
LIKE, PEOPLE'LL JUST LAUGH IF I SAY THAT THE BEEP-BEEP THESE DAYS IS TOO HARD, YOU KNOW?
"BEEP-BEEP"?
HA HA
HA HA!
TTV
ANYHOW, THE IMPORTANT THING IS THAT EVEN IF I CAN'T TRICK THE VIEWERS, I CAN MAKE THE OLD MEN IN THE INDUSTRY BUY IT!
THEN I'LL BE IN ONE GAME COMMERCIAL AFTER ANOTHER AND ASCEND TO BE THE TOP VIDEO GAME IDOL! PIECE OF CAKE! MY NAME IS VLIN--
WITH MOTIVATIONS LIKE THAT, DON'T YOU DARE CALL YOURSELF A GAMER!
EEEEP!
I'M TOTALLY OUTRAGED THAT AN IDOL LIKE YOU WOULD DO GAME-RELATED WORK! I WAS SO RELIEVED WHEN YOU FINALLY DISAPPEARED, BUT NOW YOUR FACE IS PLASTERED ALL OVER TV AND ONLINE AGAIN! WHOSE STUPID IDEA WAS THAT?!
QUIVER
QUIVER
WHAT'S SHE GOING ON ABOUT?
WATANABE-SENPAI REALLY LIKES VIDEO GAMES...
WHISPER
WHISPER
HER HEALTH USED TO BE PRETTY BAD, SO SHE PLAYED A LOT, Y'KNOW?
OH, RIGHT. SHE USED TO THROW UP BLOOD ALL THE TIME...
WHISPER

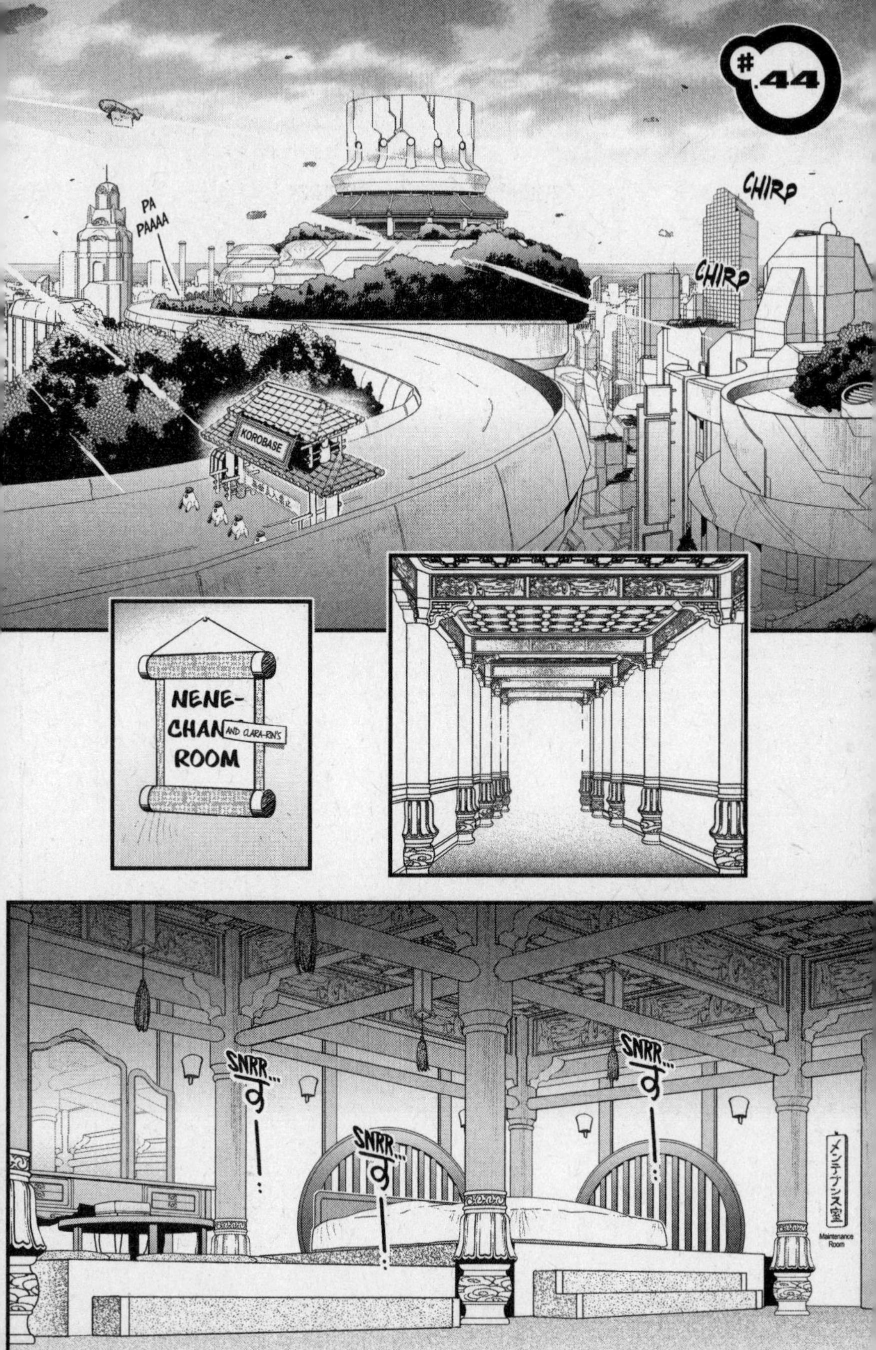

#.44
CHIRP
CHIRP
PA PAAAA
KOROBASE
NENE-CHAN AND CLARA-RIN'S ROOM
メンテナンス室
Maintenance Room
SNRR... す—...
SNRR... す—...
SNRR... す—...

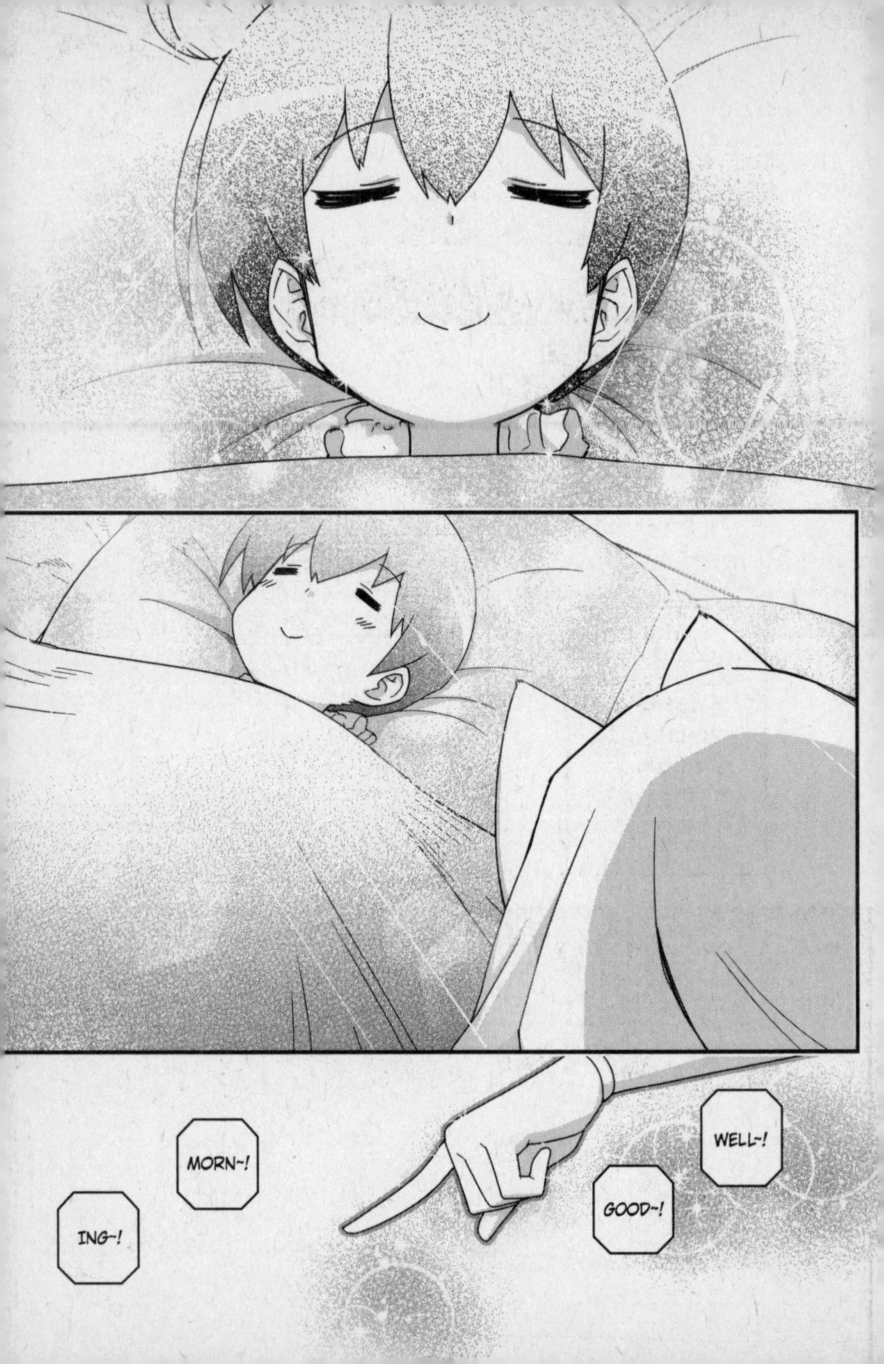
WELL~!
GOOD~!
MORN~!
ING~!

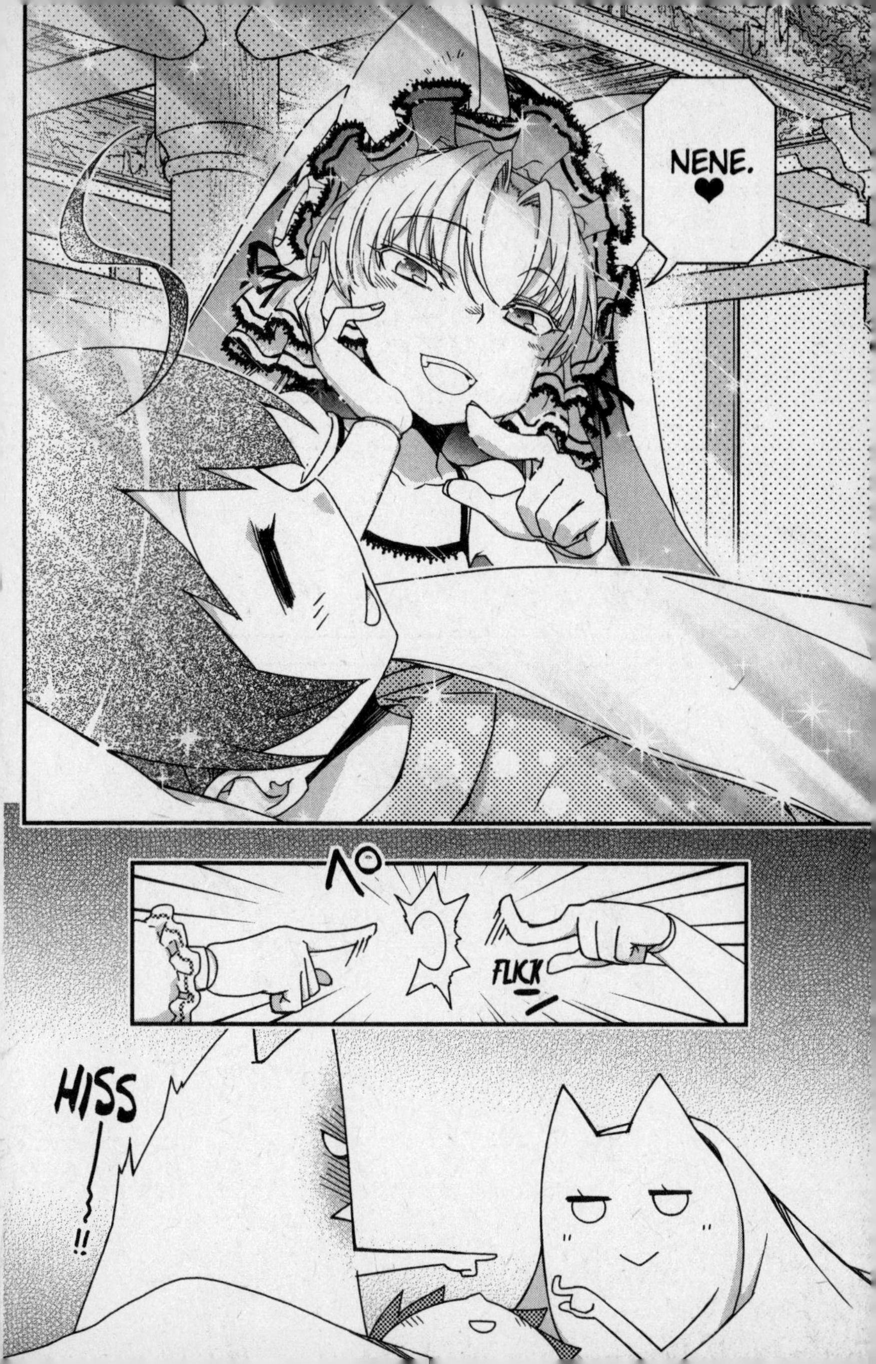
NENE. ❤
FLICK
HISS~!!

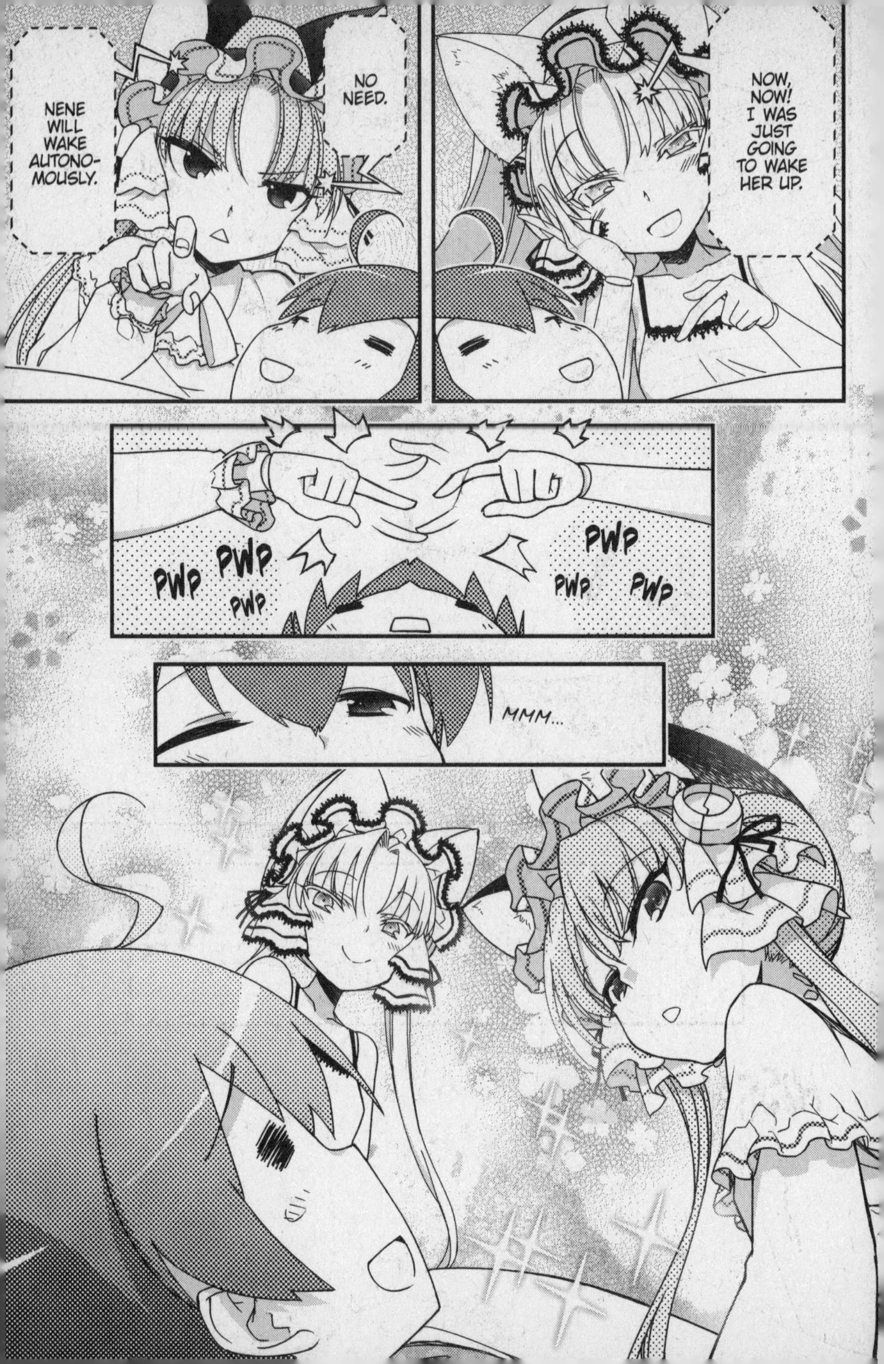
NOW, NOW! I WAS JUST GOING TO WAKE HER UP.
NO NEED.
NENE WILL WAKE AUTONO-MOUSLY.
PWP
PWP
PWP
PWP
PWP
PWP
MMM...

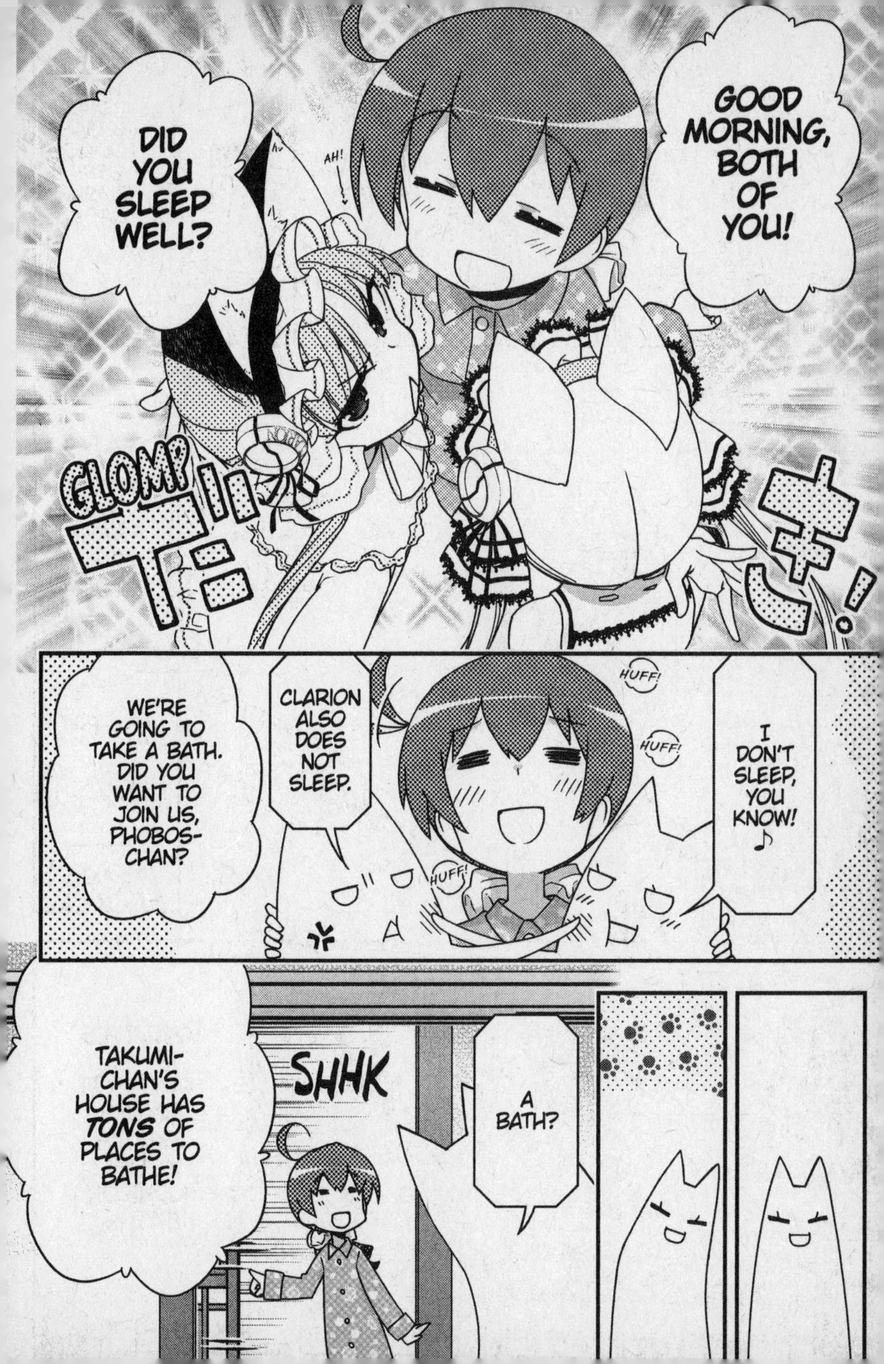
GOOD MORNING, BOTH OF YOU!
AH!
DID YOU SLEEP WELL?
GLOMP
HUFF!
I DON'T SLEEP, YOU KNOW! ♪
HUFF!
HUFF!
CLARION ALSO DOES NOT SLEEP.
WE'RE GOING TO TAKE A BATH. DID YOU WANT TO JOIN US, PHOBOS-CHAN?
A BATH?
SHHK
TAKUMI-CHAN'S HOUSE HAS *TONS* OF PLACES TO BATHE!

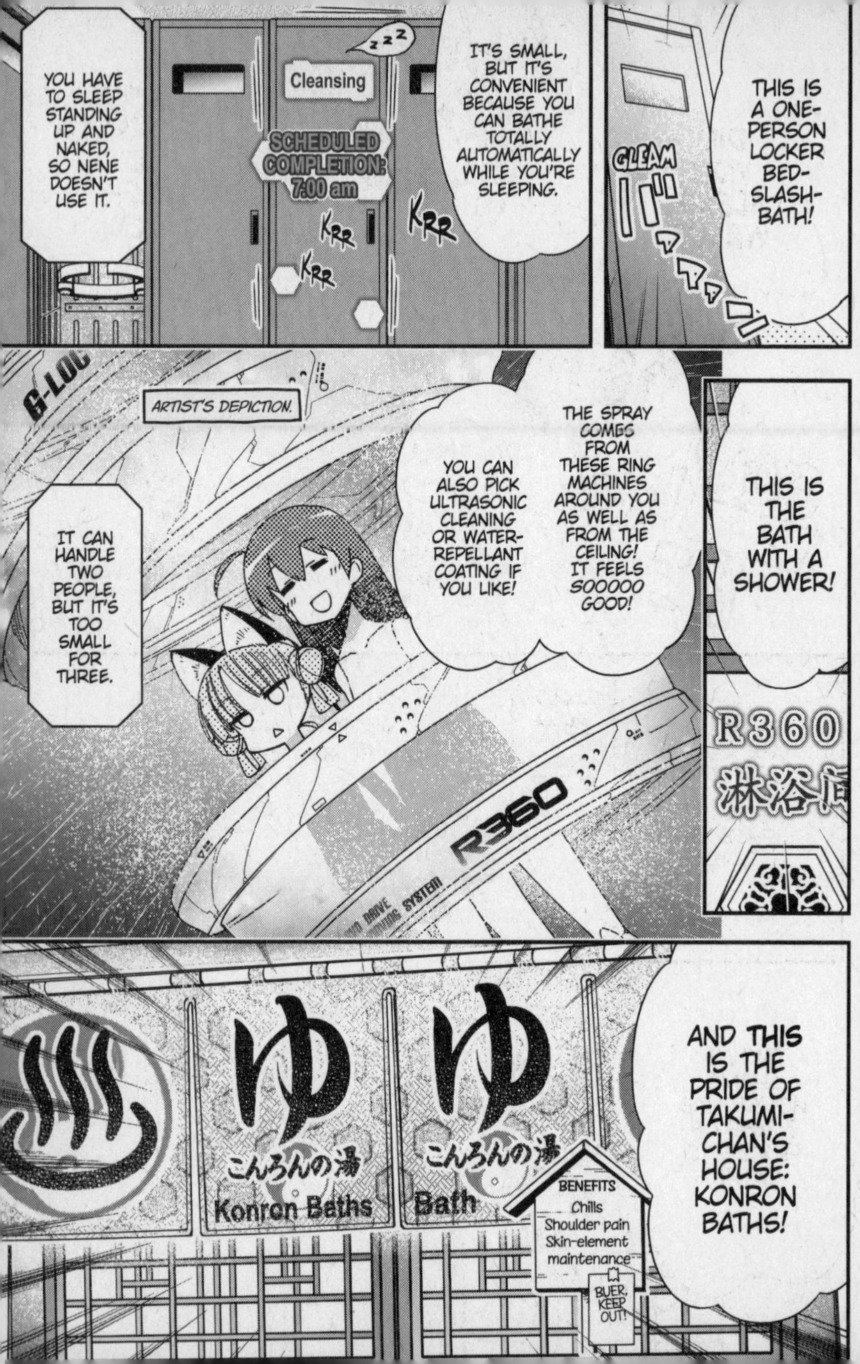
THIS IS A ONE-PERSON LOCKER BED-SLASH-BATH!
GLEAM
IT'S SMALL, BUT IT'S CONVENIENT BECAUSE YOU CAN BATHE TOTALLY AUTOMATICALLY WHILE YOU'RE SLEEPING.
ZZZ
Cleansing
SCHEDULED COMPLETION: 7:00 am
KRR
KRR
KRR
YOU HAVE TO SLEEP STANDING UP AND NAKED, SO NENE DOESN'T USE IT.
THIS IS THE BATH WITH A SHOWER!
R360
G-LOC
ARTIST'S DEPICTION.
THE SPRAY COMES FROM THESE RING MACHINES AROUND YOU AS WELL AS FROM THE CEILING! IT FEELS SOOOOO GOOD!
YOU CAN ALSO PICK ULTRASONIC CLEANING OR WATER-REPELLANT COATING IF YOU LIKE!
IT CAN HANDLE TWO PEOPLE, BUT IT'S TOO SMALL FOR THREE.
R360
AND THIS IS THE PRIDE OF TAKUMI-CHAN'S HOUSE: KONRON BATHS!
ゆ
こんろんの湯
Bath
ゆ
こんろんの湯
Konron Baths
BENEFITS
Chills
Shoulder pain
Skin-element maintenance
BUER, KEEP OUT!

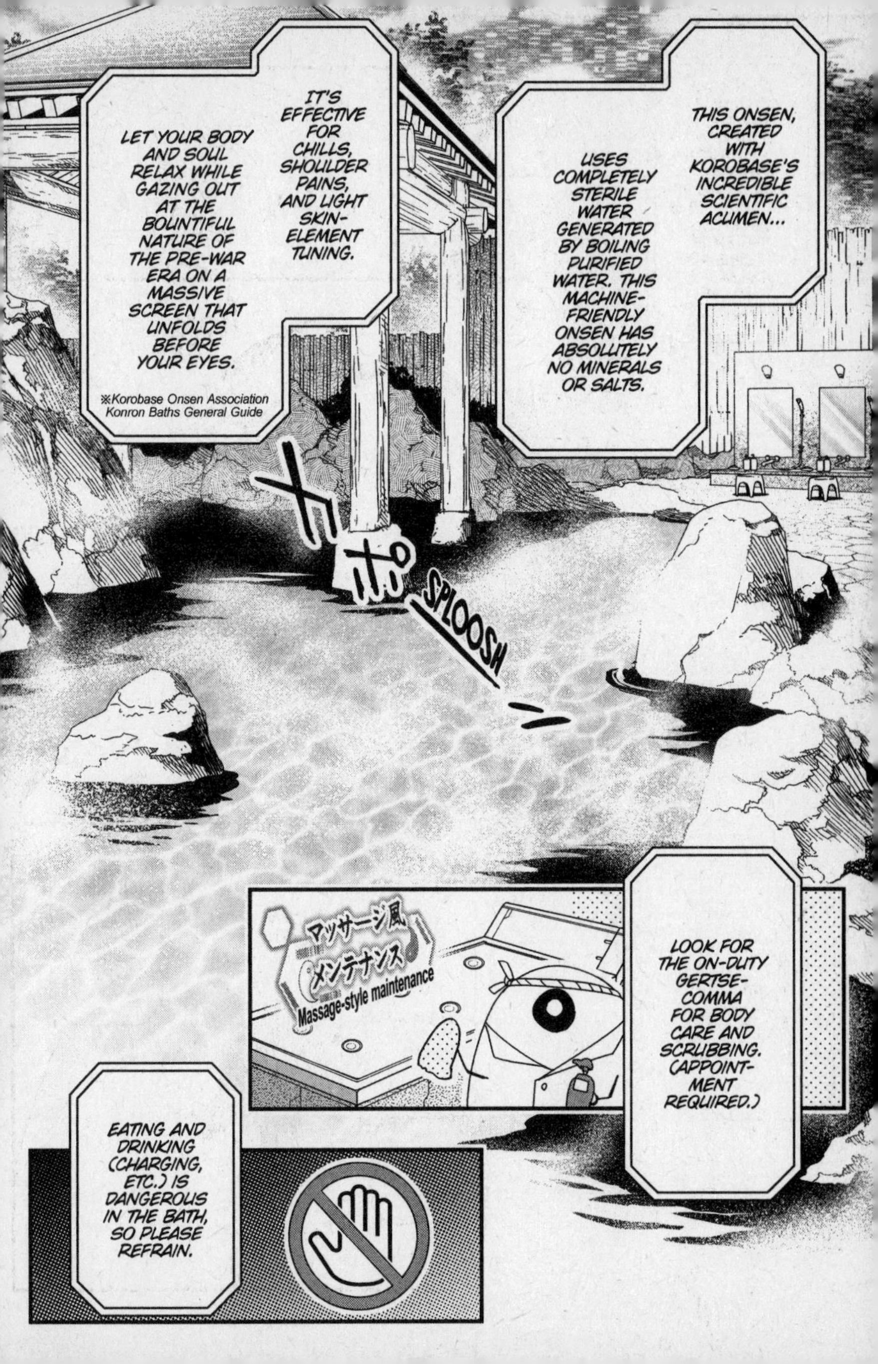
THIS ONSEN, CREATED WITH KOROBASE'S INCREDIBLE SCIENTIFIC ACUMEN...
USES COMPLETELY STERILE WATER GENERATED BY BOILING PURIFIED WATER. THIS MACHINE-FRIENDLY ONSEN HAS ABSOLUTELY NO MINERALS OR SALTS.
IT'S EFFECTIVE FOR CHILLS, SHOULDER PAINS, AND LIGHT SKIN-ELEMENT TUNING.
LET YOUR BODY AND SOUL RELAX WHILE GAZING OUT AT THE BOUNTIFUL NATURE OF THE PRE-WAR ERA ON A MASSIVE SCREEN THAT UNFOLDS BEFORE YOUR EYES.
※Korobase Onsen Association Konron Baths General Guide
SPLOOSH
LOOK FOR THE ON-DUTY GERTSE-COMMA FOR BODY CARE AND SCRUBBING. (APPOINTMENT REQUIRED.)
マッサージ風
メンテナンス
Massage-style maintenance
EATING AND DRINKING (CHARGING, ETC.) IS DANGEROUS IN THE BATH, SO PLEASE REFRAIN.

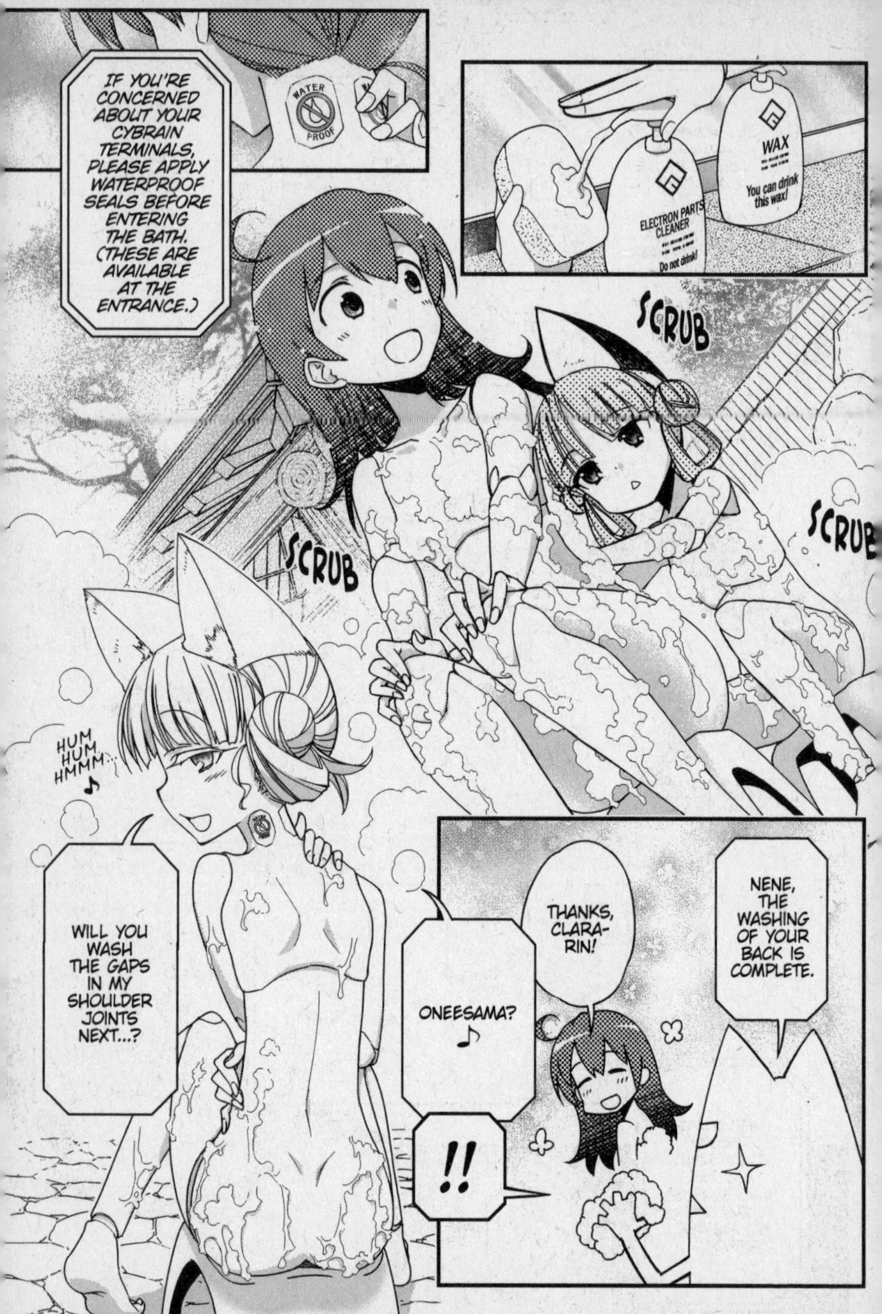
WAX
You can drink this wax!
ELECTRON PARTS CLEANER
Do not drink!
WATER PROOF
IF YOU'RE CONCERNED ABOUT YOUR CYBRAIN TERMINALS, PLEASE APPLY WATERPROOF SEALS BEFORE ENTERING THE BATH. (THESE ARE AVAILABLE AT THE ENTRANCE.)
SCRUB
SCRUB
SCRUB
NENE, THE WASHING OF YOUR BACK IS COMPLETE.
THANKS, CLARA-RIN!
ONEESAMA? ♪
!!
HUM HUM HMMM... ♪
WILL YOU WASH THE GAPS IN MY SHOULDER JOINTS NEXT...?

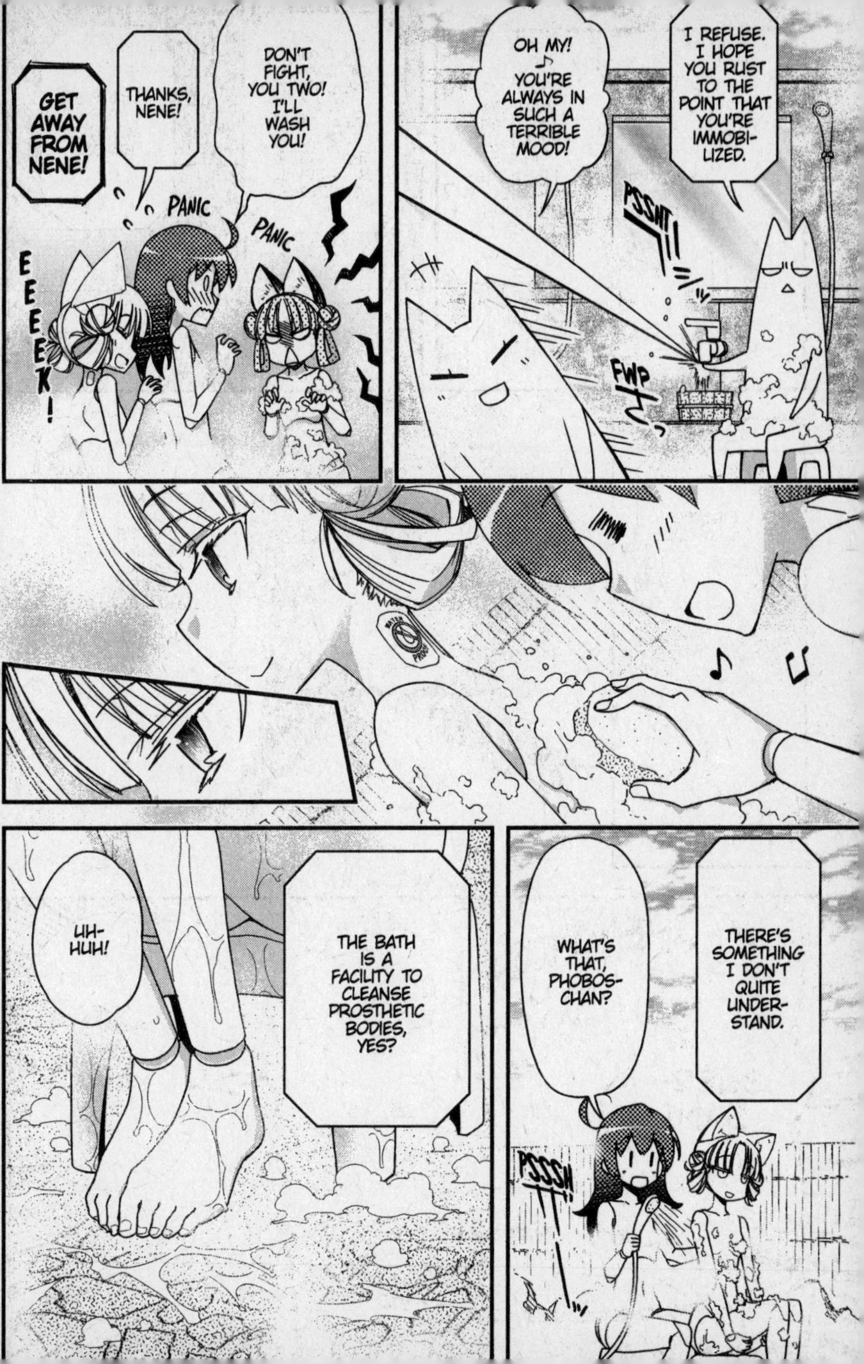
I REFUSE. I HOPE YOU RUST TO THE POINT THAT YOU'RE IMMOBILIZED.
OH MY! ♪ YOU'RE ALWAYS IN SUCH A TERRIBLE MOOD!
PSSHT
FWP
DON'T FIGHT, YOU TWO! I'LL WASH YOU!
PANIC
PANIC
THANKS, NENE!
GET AWAY FROM NENE!
EEEEEK!
THERE'S SOMETHING I DON'T QUITE UNDERSTAND.
WHAT'S THAT, PHOBOS-CHAN?
PSSSH
THE BATH IS A FACILITY TO CLEANSE PROSTHETIC BODIES, YES?
UH-HUH!

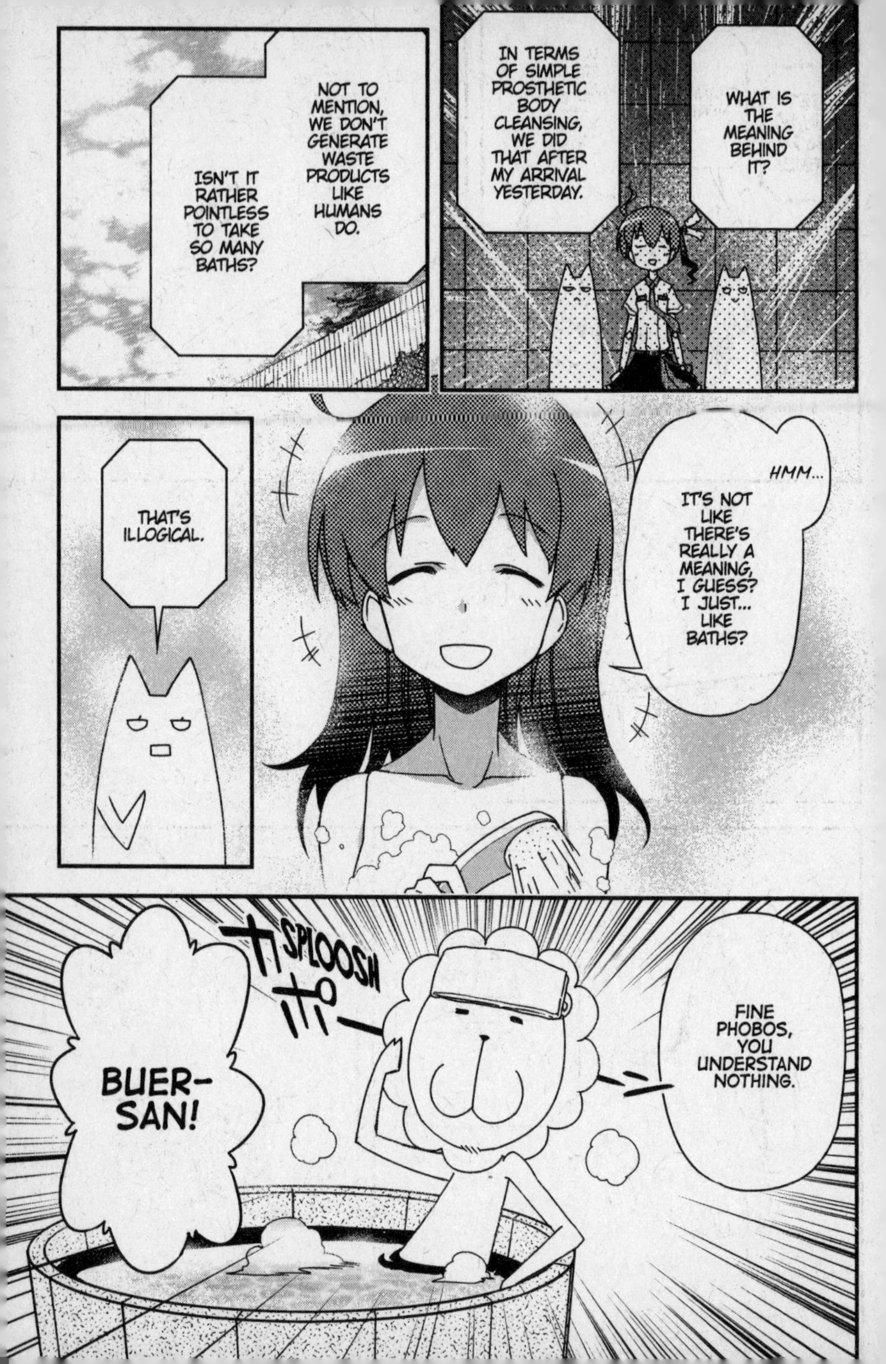
WHAT IS THE MEANING BEHIND IT?
IN TERMS OF SIMPLE PROSTHETIC BODY CLEANSING, WE DID THAT AFTER MY ARRIVAL YESTERDAY.
NOT TO MENTION, WE DON'T GENERATE WASTE PRODUCTS LIKE HUMANS DO.
ISN'T IT RATHER POINTLESS TO TAKE SO MANY BATHS?
HMM... IT'S NOT LIKE THERE'S REALLY A MEANING, I GUESS? I JUST... LIKE BATHS?
THAT'S ILLOGICAL.
FINE PHOBOS, YOU UNDERSTAND NOTHING.
SPLOOSH
BUER-SAN!

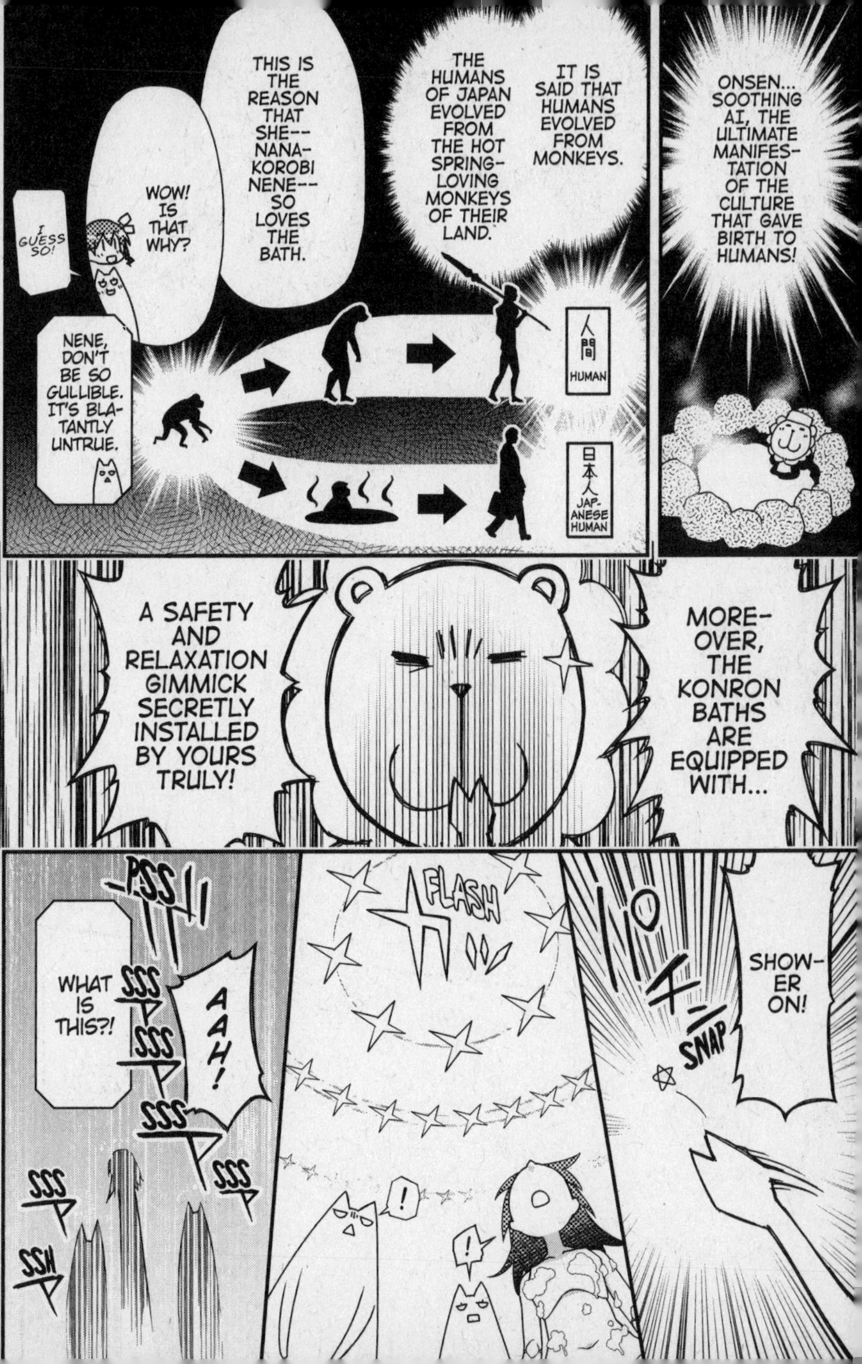
ONSEN... SOOTHING AI, THE ULTIMATE MANIFESTATION OF THE CULTURE THAT GAVE BIRTH TO HUMANS!
IT IS SAID THAT HUMANS EVOLVED FROM MONKEYS.
THE HUMANS OF JAPAN EVOLVED FROM THE HOT SPRING-LOVING MONKEYS OF THEIR LAND.
人間
HUMAN
日本人
JAPANESE HUMAN
THIS IS THE REASON THAT SHE--NANAKOROBI NENE--SO LOVES THE BATH.
WOW! IS THAT WHY?
I GUESS SO!
NENE, DON'T BE SO GULLIBLE. IT'S BLATANTLY UNTRUE.
MOREOVER, THE KONRON BATHS ARE EQUIPPED WITH...
A SAFETY AND RELAXATION GIMMICK SECRETLY INSTALLED BY YOURS TRULY!
SHOWER ON!
SNAP
FLASH
!
!
PSS
AAH!
WHAT IS THIS?!
SSSP
SSSP
SSSP
SSSP
SSSP
SSHP

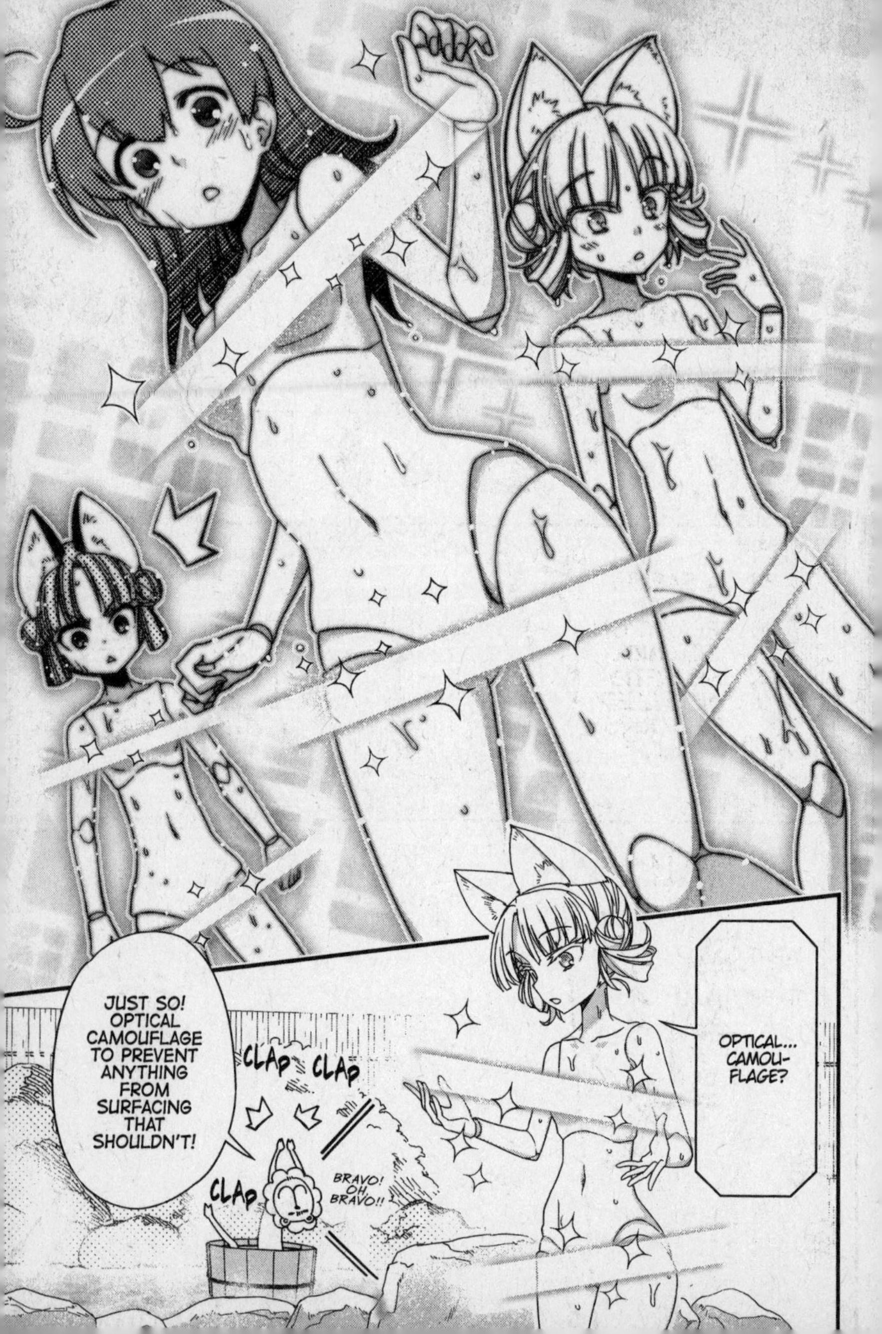
OPTICAL... CAMOUFLAGE?
JUST SO! OPTICAL CAMOUFLAGE TO PREVENT ANYTHING FROM SURFACING THAT SHOULDN'T!
CLAP CLAP
BRAVO! OH, BRAVO!!
CLAP

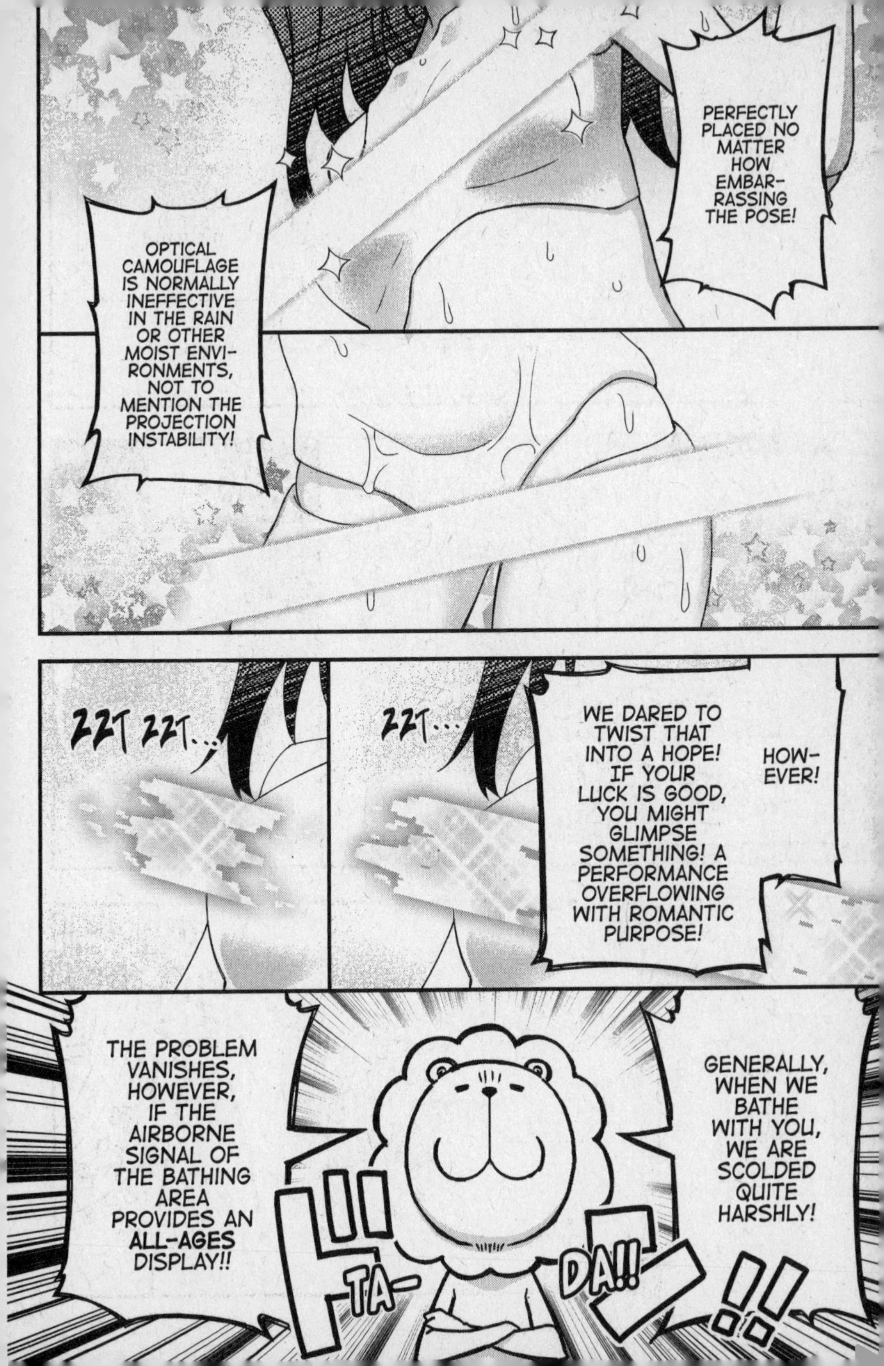
PERFECTLY PLACED NO MATTER HOW EMBAR-RASSING THE POSE!
OPTICAL CAMOUFLAGE IS NORMALLY INEFFECTIVE IN THE RAIN OR OTHER MOIST ENVI-RONMENTS, NOT TO MENTION THE PROJECTION INSTABILITY!
HOW-EVER!
WE DARED TO TWIST THAT INTO A HOPE! IF YOUR LUCK IS GOOD, YOU MIGHT GLIMPSE SOMETHING! A PERFORMANCE OVERFLOWING WITH ROMANTIC PURPOSE!
ZZT...
ZZT ZZT...
GENERALLY, WHEN WE BATHE WITH YOU, WE ARE SCOLDED QUITE HARSHLY!
THE PROBLEM VANISHES, HOWEVER, IF THE AIRBORNE SIGNAL OF THE BATHING AREA PROVIDES AN ALL-AGES DISPLAY!!
TA-DA!!

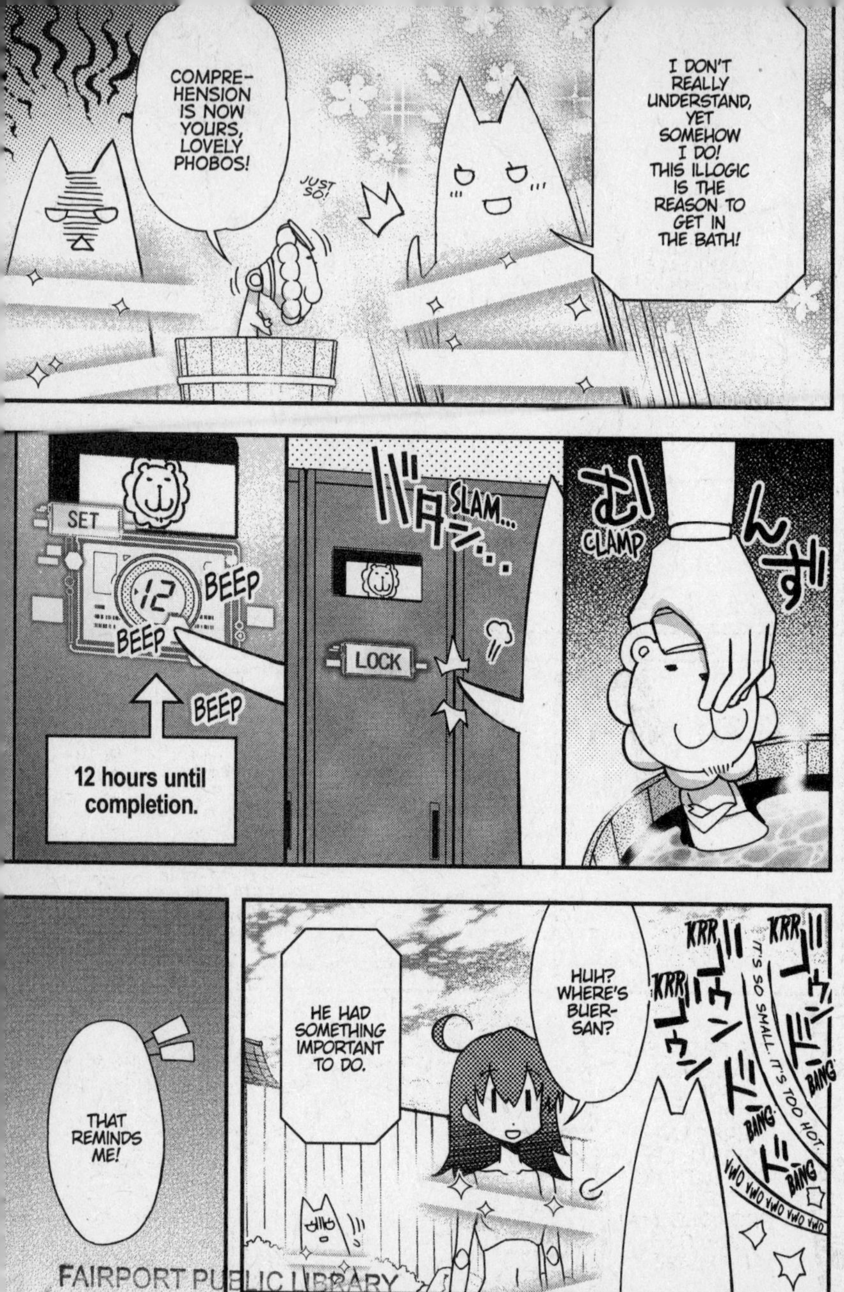
I DON'T REALLY UNDERSTAND, YET SOMEHOW I DO! THIS ILLOGIC IS THE REASON TO GET IN THE BATH!
JUST SO!
COMPREHENSION IS NOW YOURS, LOVELY PHOBOS!
CLAMP
SLAM...
LOCK
SET
BEEP
BEEP
BEEP
12 hours until completion.
KRR
KRR
KRR
IT'S SO SMALL. IT'S TOO HOT.
BANG
BANG
BANG
HUH? WHERE'S BUER-SAN?
HE HAD SOMETHING IMPORTANT TO DO.
THAT REMINDS ME!

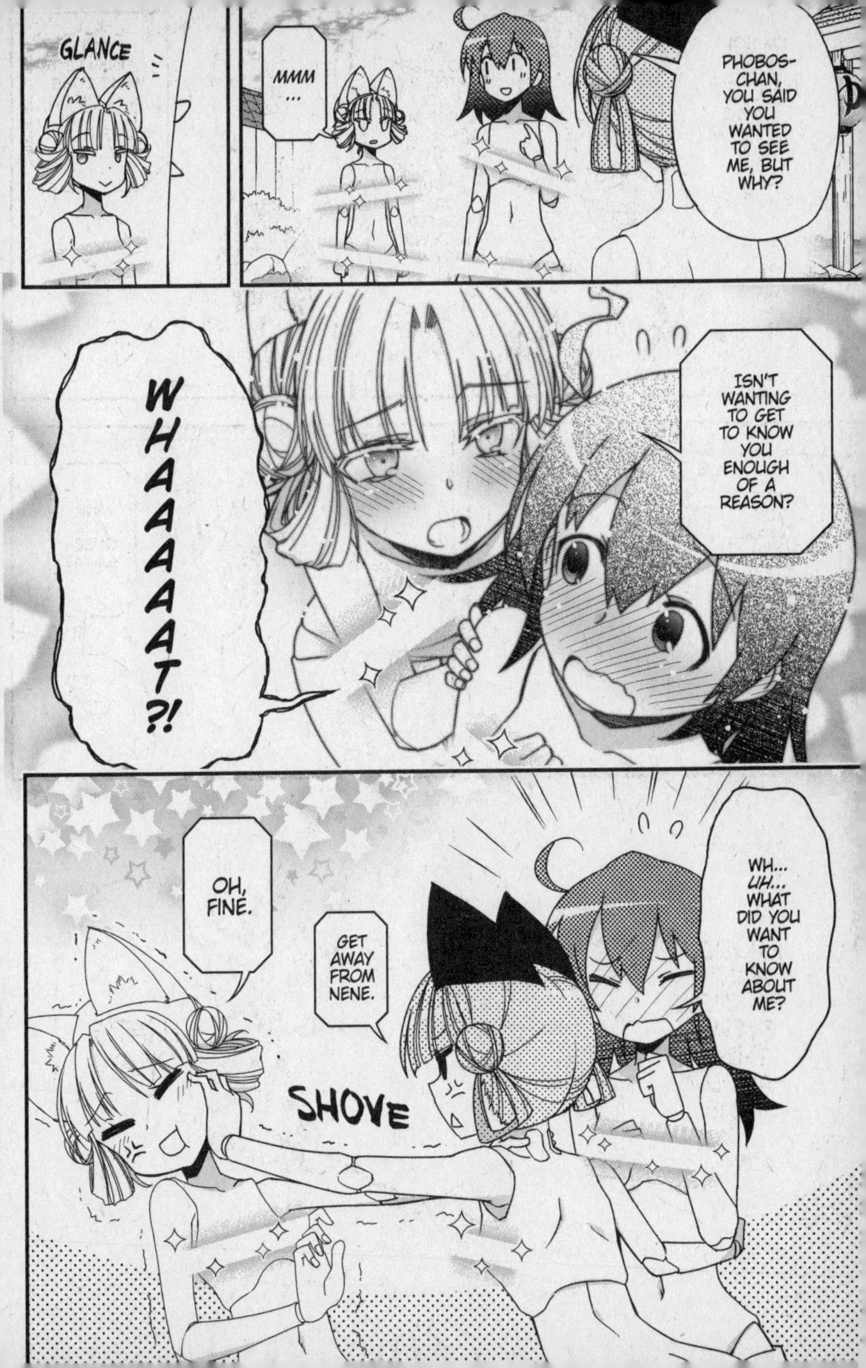
PHOBOS-CHAN, YOU SAID YOU WANTED TO SEE ME, BUT WHY?
MMM ...
GLANCE
ISN'T WANTING TO GET TO KNOW YOU ENOUGH OF A REASON?
WHAAAAAAT?!
WH... UH... WHAT DID YOU WANT TO KNOW ABOUT ME?
GET AWAY FROM NENE.
OH, FINE.
SHOVE

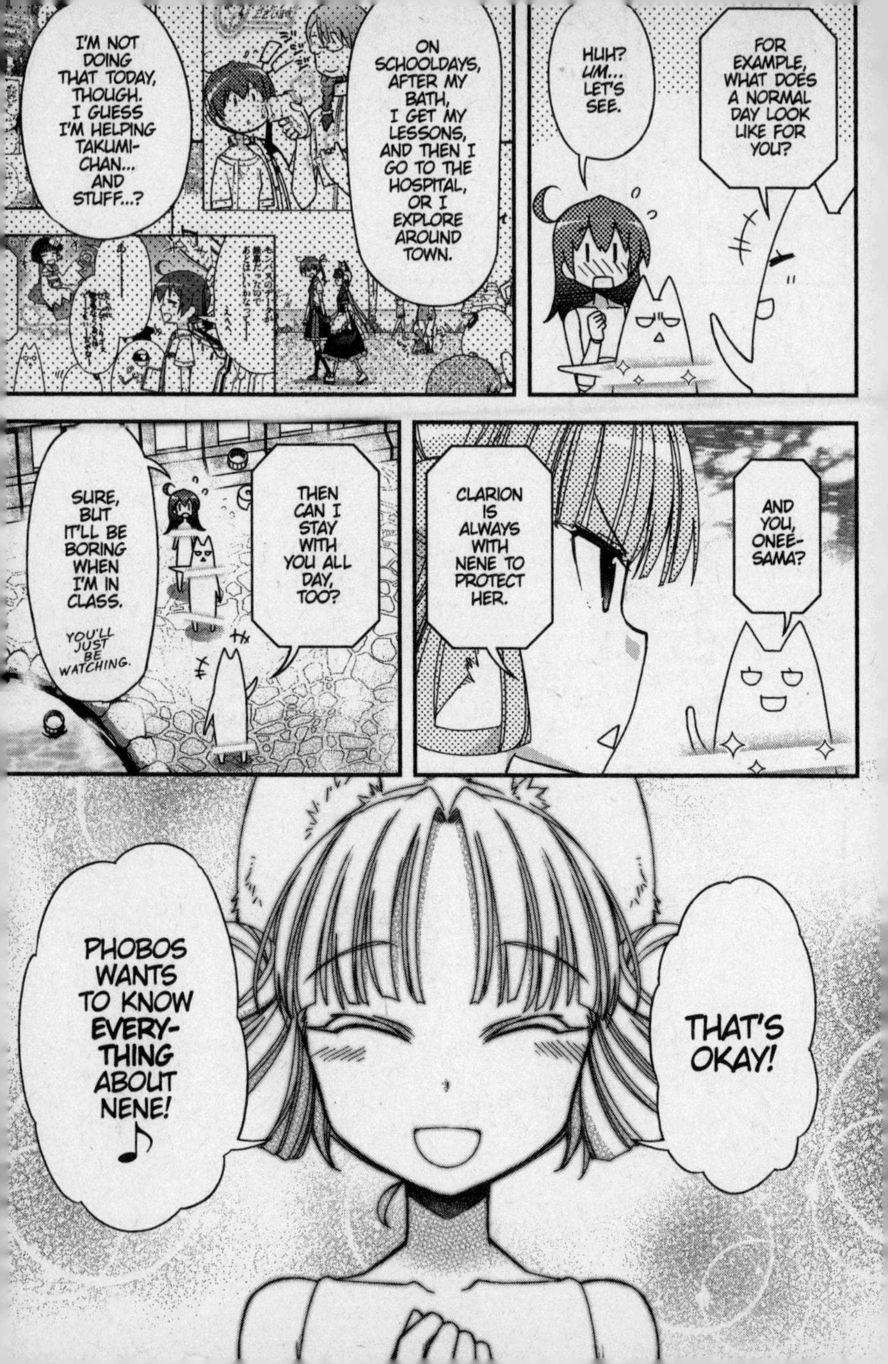
FOR EXAMPLE, WHAT DOES A NORMAL DAY LOOK LIKE FOR YOU?
HUH? UM... LET'S SEE.
ON SCHOOLDAYS, AFTER MY BATH, I GET MY LESSONS, AND THEN I GO TO THE HOSPITAL, OR I EXPLORE AROUND TOWN.
I'M NOT DOING THAT TODAY, THOUGH. I GUESS I'M HELPING TAKUMI-CHAN... AND STUFF...?
AND YOU, ONEE-SAMA?
CLARION IS ALWAYS WITH NENE TO PROTECT HER.
THEN CAN I STAY WITH YOU ALL DAY, TOO?
SURE, BUT IT'LL BE BORING WHEN I'M IN CLASS.
YOU'LL JUST BE WATCHING.
THAT'S OKAY!
PHOBOS WANTS TO KNOW EVERYTHING ABOUT NENE! ♪

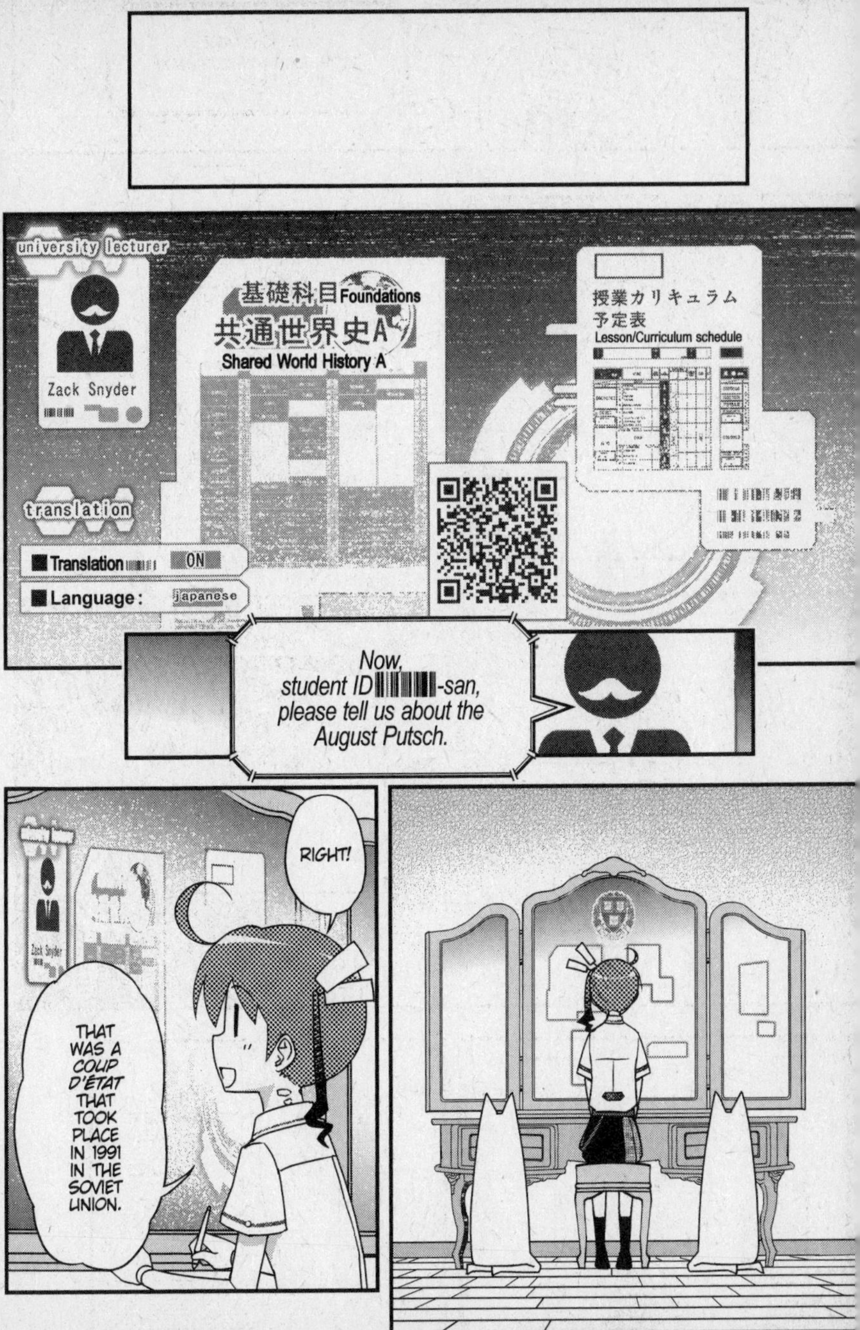

授業カリキュラム
予定表
Lesson/Curriculum schedule
基礎科目 Foundations
共通世界史A
Shared World History A
university lecturer
Zack Snyder
translation
Translation ON
Language: japanese
Now, student ID [redacted]-san, please tell us about the August Putsch.
RIGHT!
THAT WAS A *COUP D'ÉTAT* THAT TOOK PLACE IN 1991 IN THE SOVIET UNION.

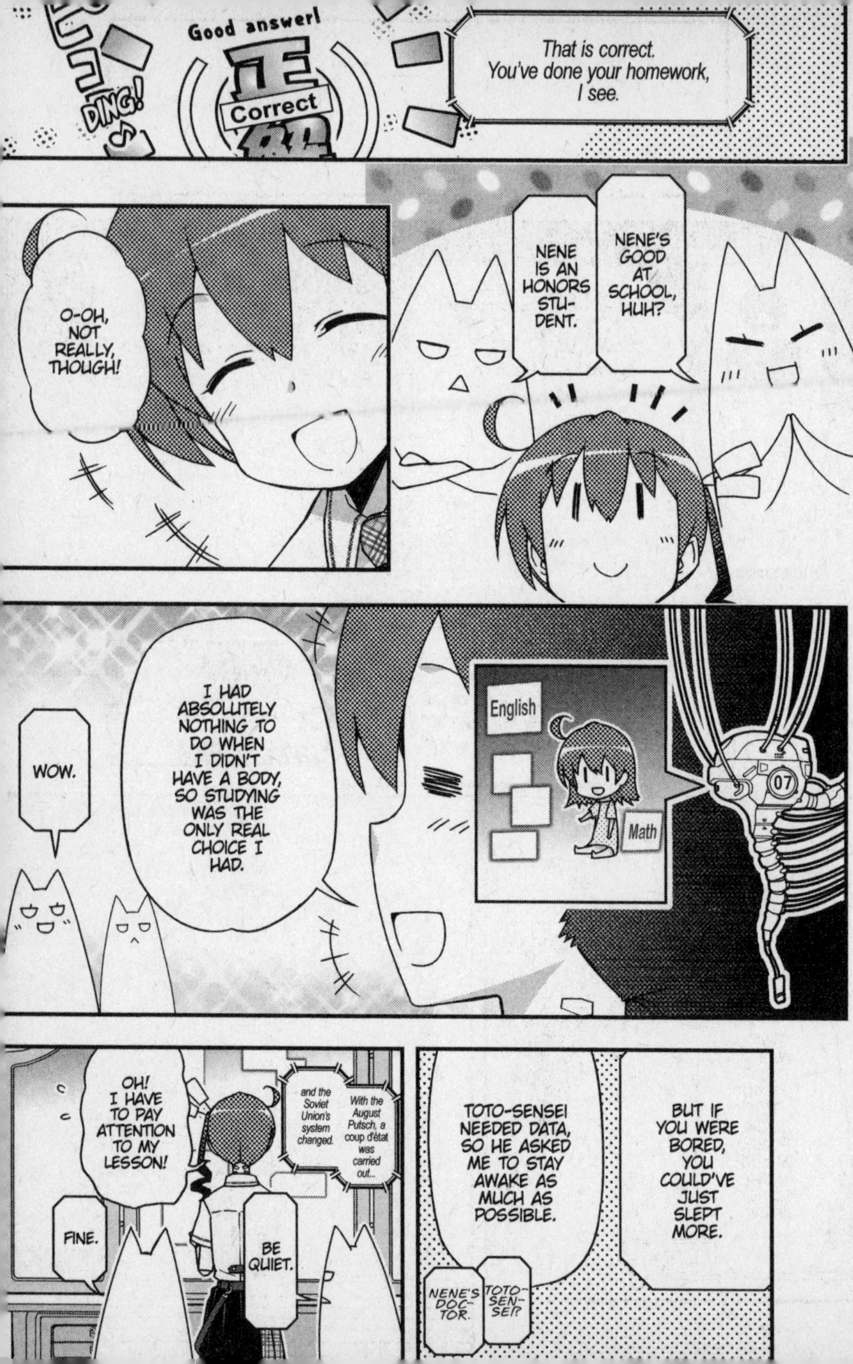

That is correct. You've done your homework, I see.
Good answer!
Correct
DING!
NENE'S GOOD AT SCHOOL, HUH?
NENE IS AN HONORS STU-DENT.
O-OH, NOT REALLY, THOUGH!
English
Math
07
I HAD ABSOLUTELY NOTHING TO DO WHEN I DIDN'T HAVE A BODY, SO STUDYING WAS THE ONLY REAL CHOICE I HAD.
WOW.
BUT IF YOU WERE BORED, YOU COULD'VE JUST SLEPT MORE.
TOTO-SENSEI NEEDED DATA, SO HE ASKED ME TO STAY AWAKE AS MUCH AS POSSIBLE.
TOTO-SEN-SEI!?
NENE'S DOC-TOR.
With the August Putsch, a coup d'état was carried out...
and the Soviet Union's system changed.
OH! I HAVE TO PAY ATTENTION TO MY LESSON!
BE QUIET.
FINE.

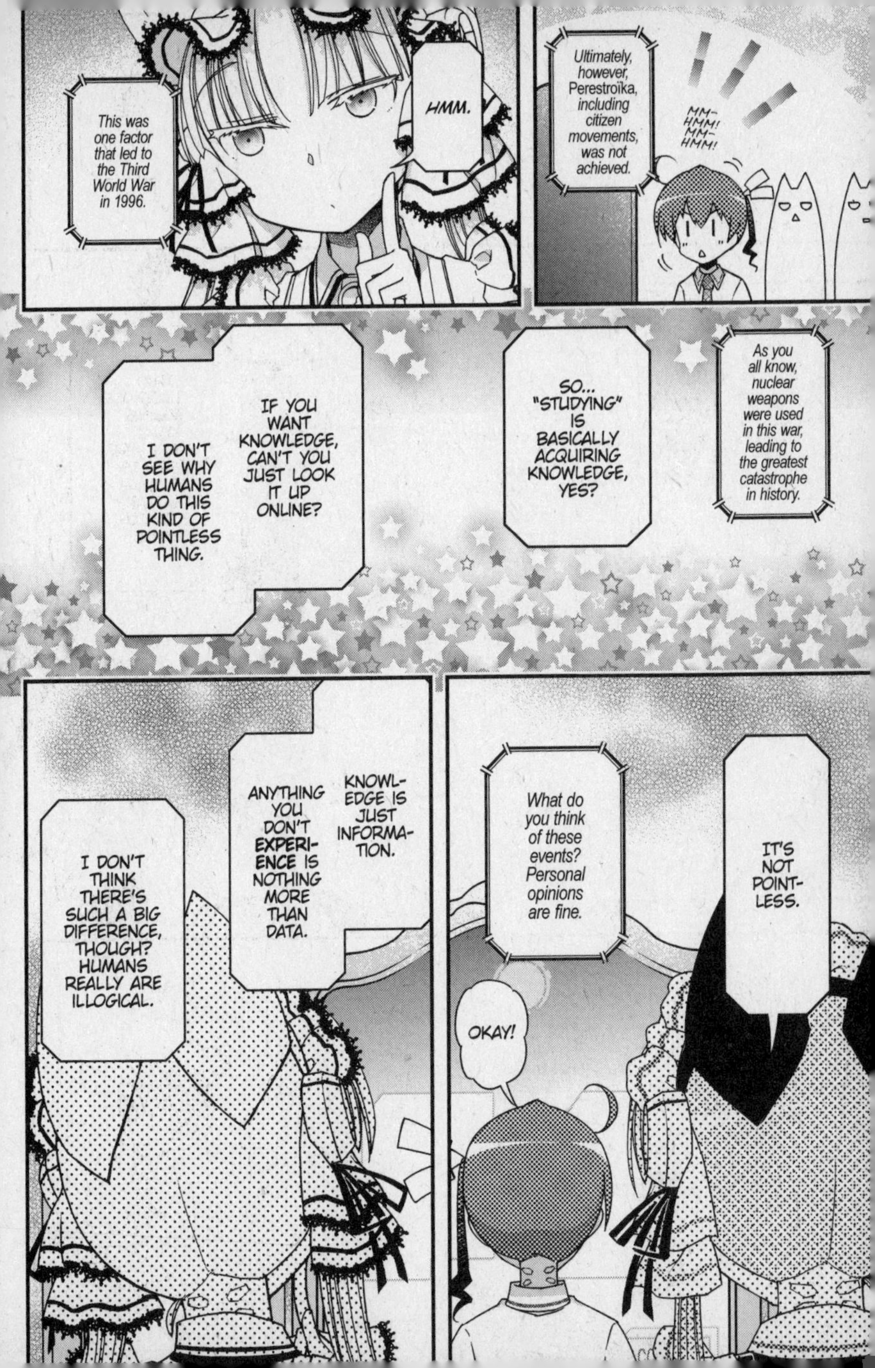
Ultimately, however, Perestroïka, including citizen movements, was not achieved.
MM-HMM! MM-HMM!
HMM.
This was one factor that led to the Third World War in 1996.
As you all know, nuclear weapons were used in this war, leading to the greatest catastrophe in history.
SO... "STUDYING" IS BASICALLY ACQUIRING KNOWLEDGE, YES?
IF YOU WANT KNOWLEDGE, CAN'T YOU JUST LOOK IT UP ONLINE?
I DON'T SEE WHY HUMANS DO THIS KIND OF POINTLESS THING.
IT'S NOT POINTLESS.
What do you think of these events? Personal opinions are fine.
OKAY!
KNOWLEDGE IS JUST INFORMATION.
ANYTHING YOU DON'T EXPERIENCE IS NOTHING MORE THAN DATA.
I DON'T THINK THERE'S SUCH A BIG DIFFERENCE, THOUGH? HUMANS REALLY ARE ILLOGICAL.

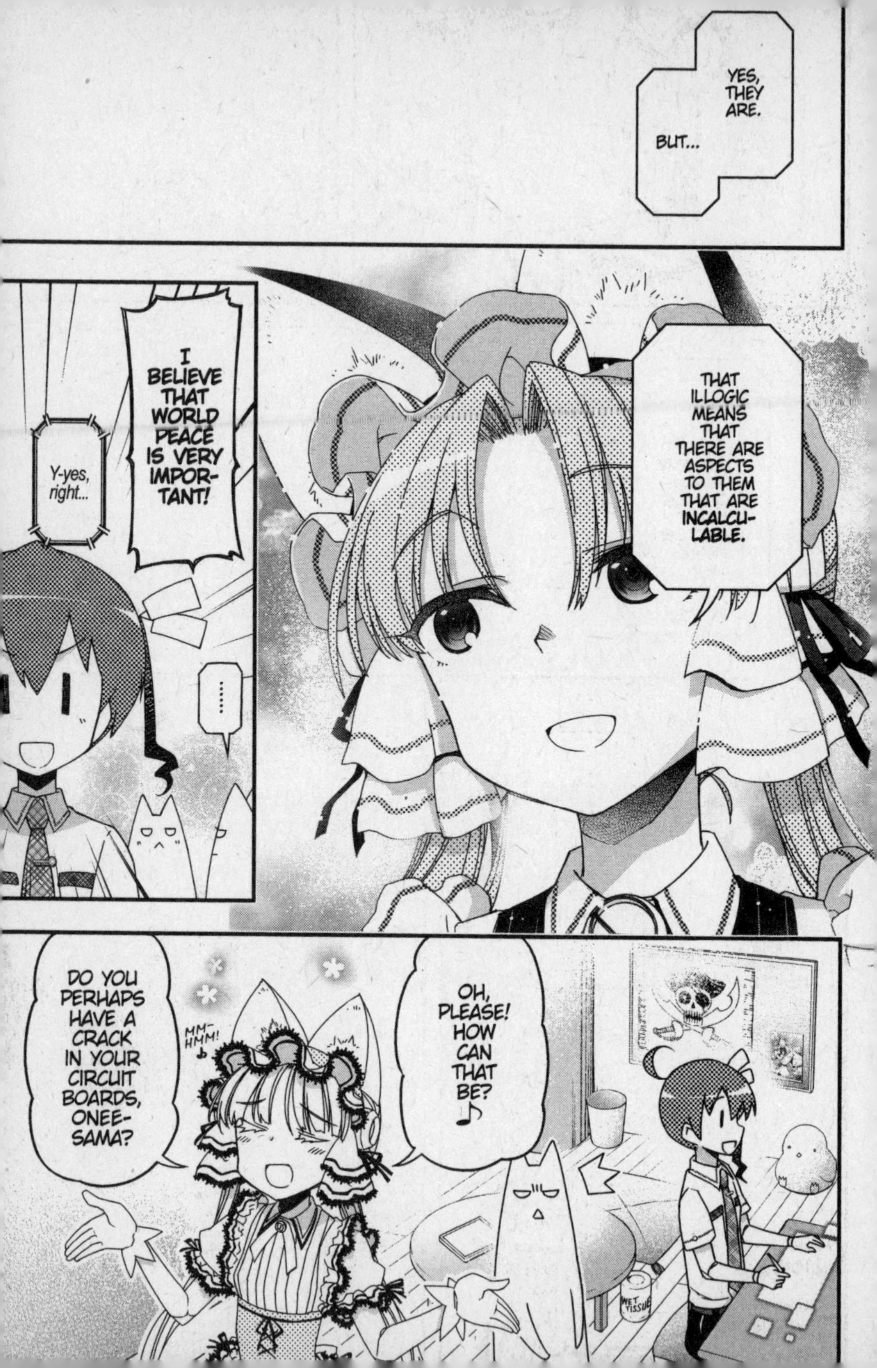
YES, THEY ARE.
BUT...
THAT ILLOGIC MEANS THAT THERE ARE ASPECTS TO THEM THAT ARE INCALCU-LABLE.
I BELIEVE THAT WORLD PEACE IS VERY IMPOR-TANT!
Y-yes, right...
......
OH, PLEASE! HOW CAN THAT BE? ♪
MM-HMM! ♪
DO YOU PERHAPS HAVE A CRACK IN YOUR CIRCUIT BOARDS, ONEE-SAMA?
WET TISSUE

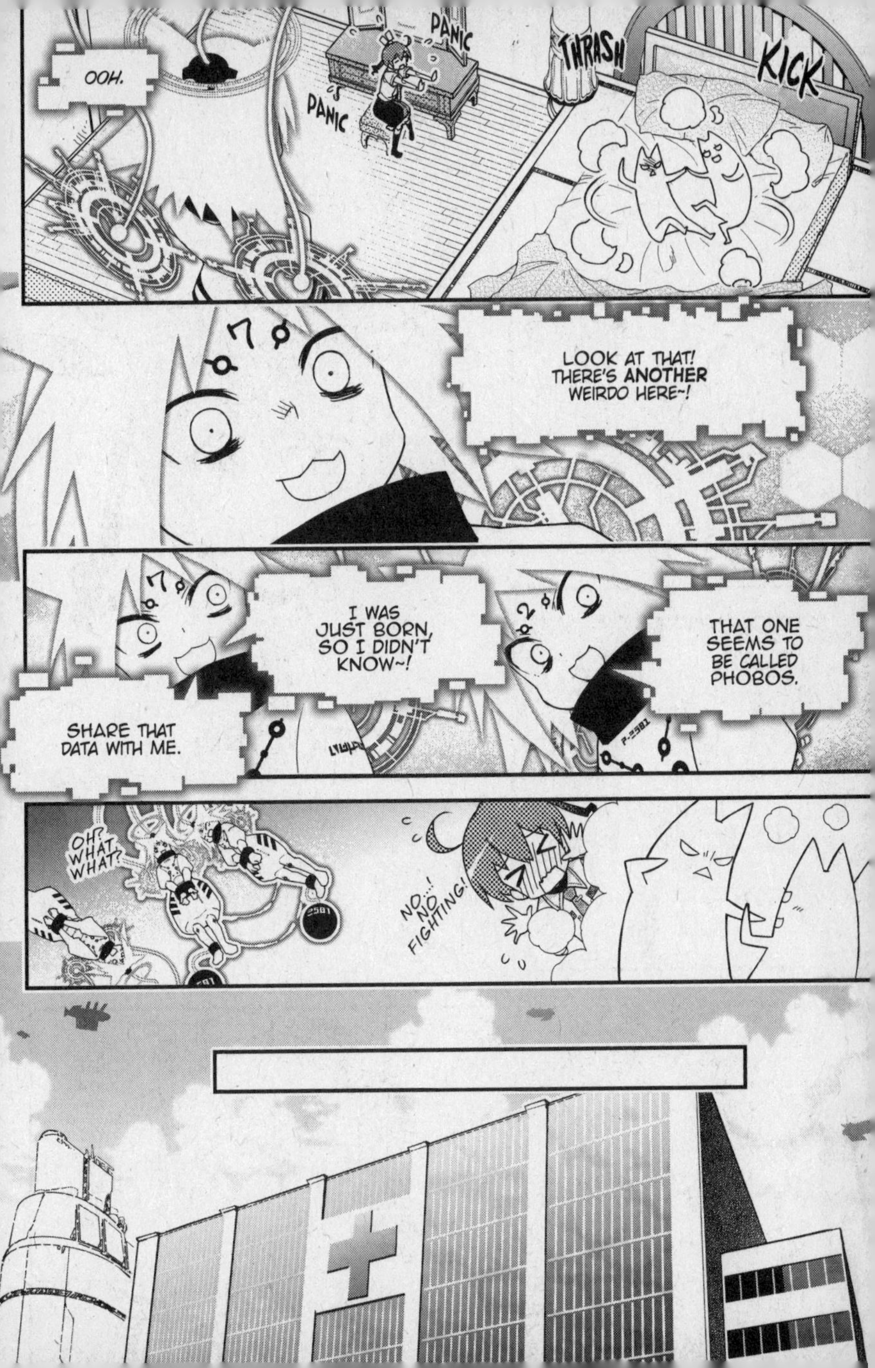
KICK
THRASH
PANIC
PANIC
OOH.
LOOK AT THAT! THERE'S **ANOTHER** WEIRDO HERE~!
THAT ONE SEEMS TO BE CALLED PHOBOS.
I WAS JUST BORN, SO I DIDN'T KNOW~!
SHARE THAT DATA WITH ME.
NO...! NO FIGHTING!
OH? WHAT, WHAT?

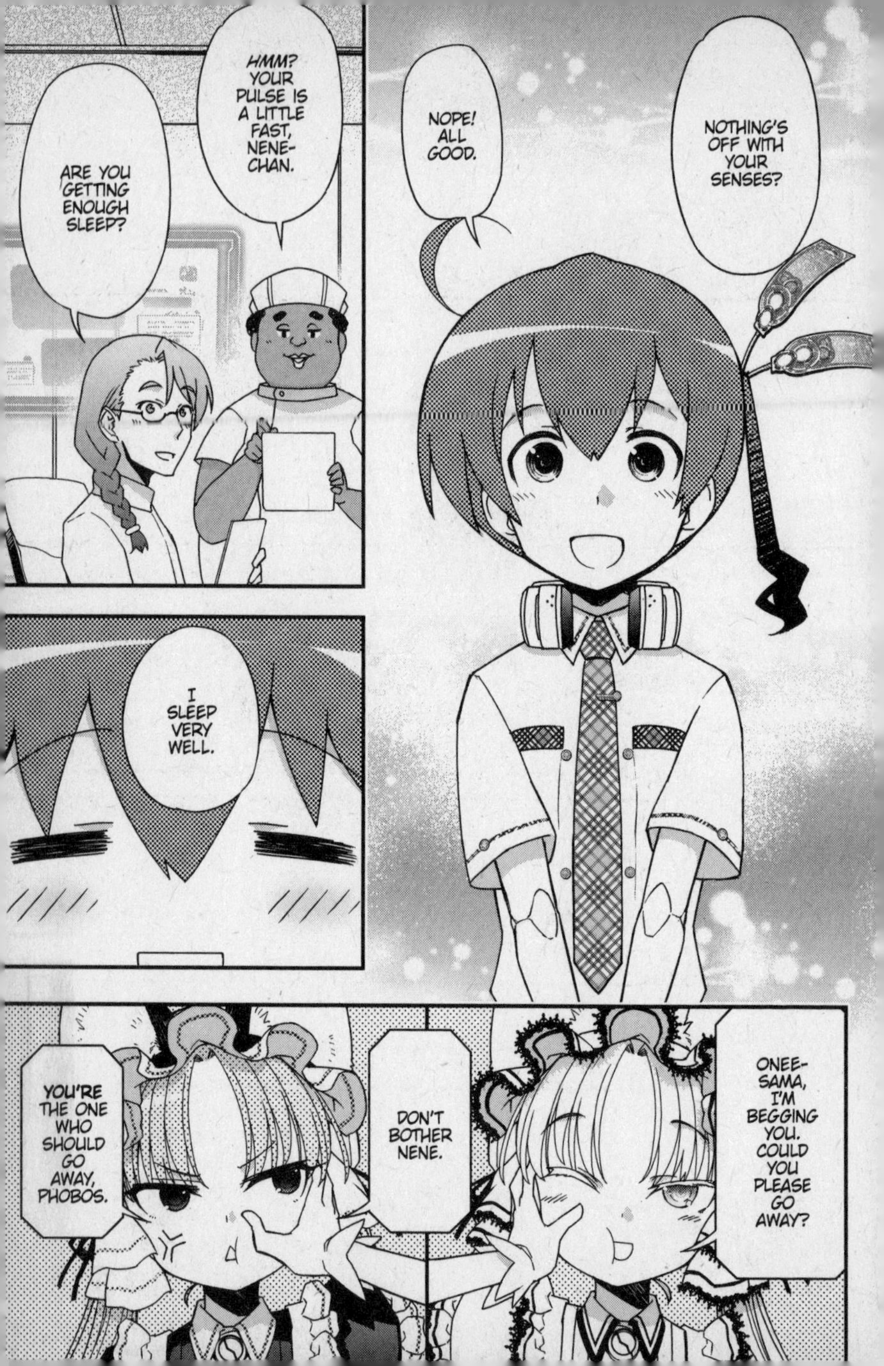
NOTHING'S OFF WITH YOUR SENSES?
NOPE! ALL GOOD.
HMM? YOUR PULSE IS A LITTLE FAST, NENE-CHAN.
ARE YOU GETTING ENOUGH SLEEP?
I SLEEP VERY WELL.
ONEE-SAMA, I'M BEGGING YOU. COULD YOU PLEASE GO AWAY?
DON'T BOTHER NENE.
YOU'RE THE ONE WHO SHOULD GO AWAY, PHOBOS.

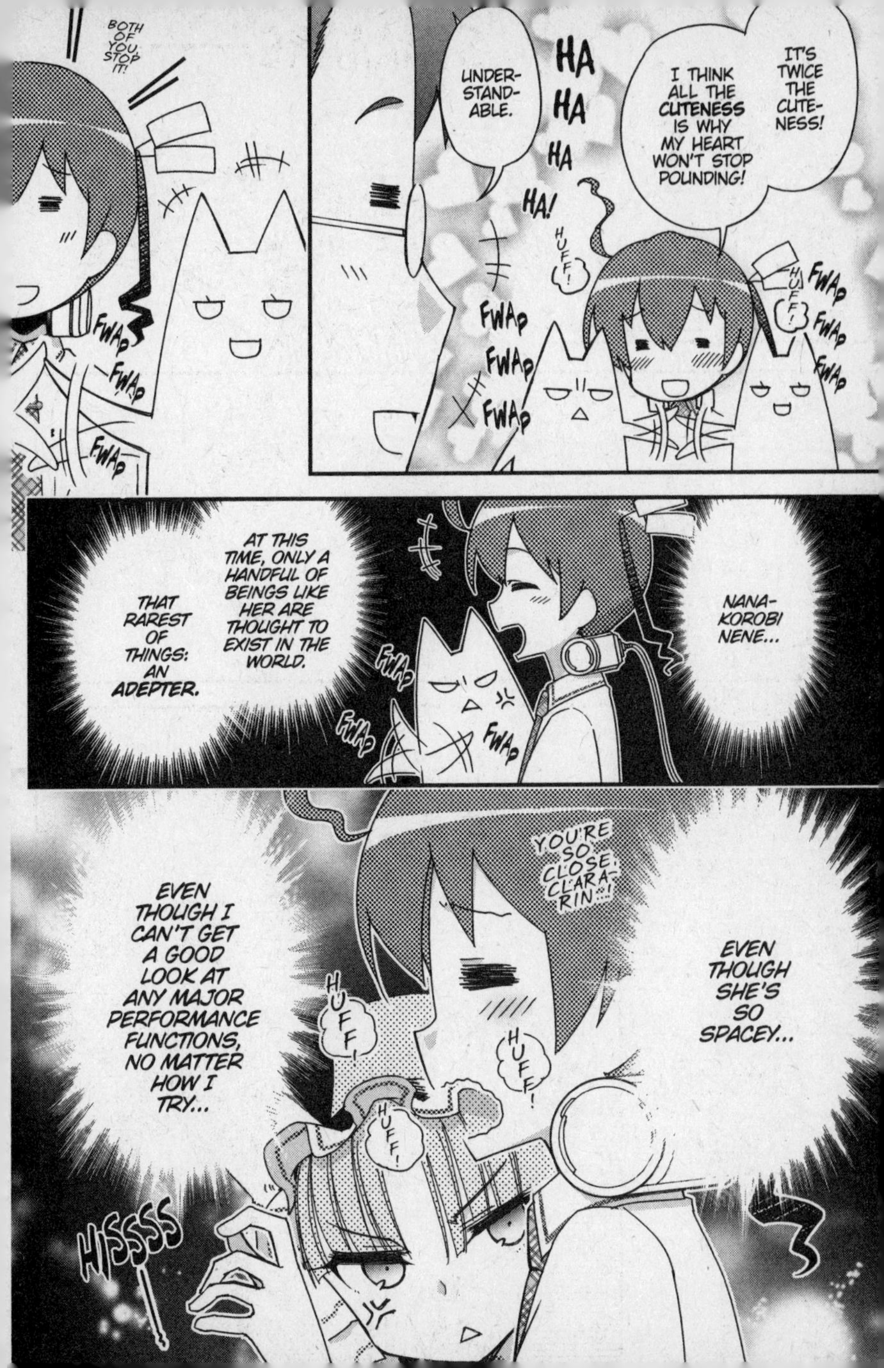
IT'S TWICE THE CUTENESS!
I THINK ALL THE CUTENESS IS WHY MY HEART WON'T STOP POUNDING!
HA HA HA HA!
UNDER-STAND-ABLE.
HUFF!
HUFF!
FWAP FWAP FWAP
FWAP FWAP FWAP
BOTH OF YOU, STOP IT!
FWAP FWAP FWAP
NANA-KOROBI NENE...
AT THIS TIME, ONLY A HANDFUL OF BEINGS LIKE HER ARE THOUGHT TO EXIST IN THE WORLD.
THAT RAREST OF THINGS: AN ADEPTER.
FWAP FWAP FWAP
EVEN THOUGH SHE'S SO SPACEY...
YOU'RE SO CLOSE, CLARA-RIN...!
EVEN THOUGH I CAN'T GET A GOOD LOOK AT ANY MAJOR PERFORMANCE FUNCTIONS, NO MATTER HOW I TRY...
HUFF!
HUFF!
HUFF!
HISSSS

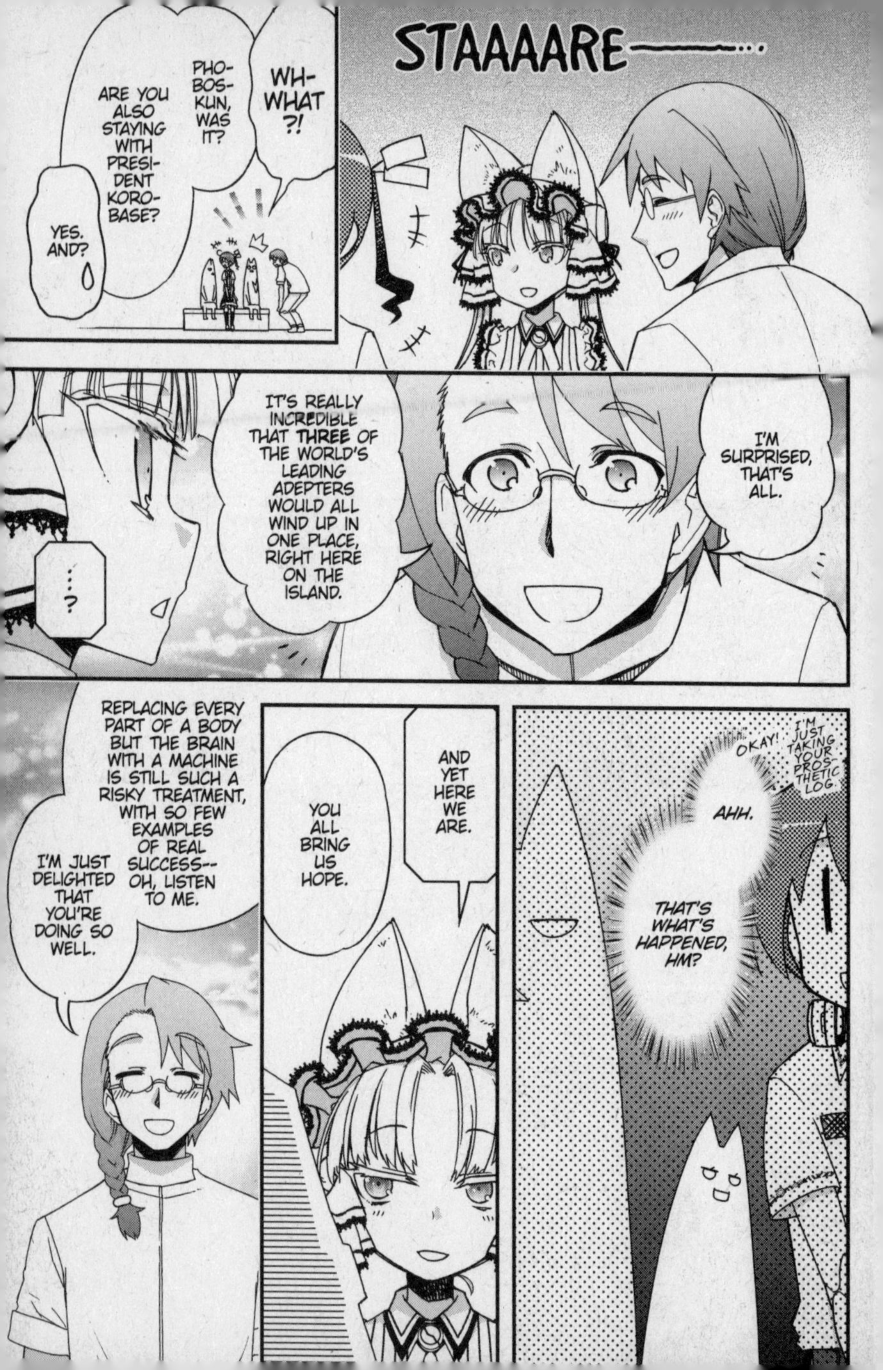
STAAAARE——....
WH-WHAT?!
PHO-BOS-KUN, WAS IT?
ARE YOU ALSO STAYING WITH PRESIDENT KOROBASE?
YES. AND?
I'M SURPRISED, THAT'S ALL.
IT'S REALLY INCREDIBLE THAT THREE OF THE WORLD'S LEADING ADEPTERS WOULD ALL WIND UP IN ONE PLACE, RIGHT HERE ON THE ISLAND.
...?
I'M JUST TAKING YOUR PROSTHETIC LOG.
OKAY!
AHH.
THAT'S WHAT'S HAPPENED, HM?
AND YET HERE WE ARE.
YOU ALL BRING US HOPE.
REPLACING EVERY PART OF A BODY BUT THE BRAIN WITH A MACHINE IS STILL SUCH A RISKY TREATMENT, WITH SO FEW EXAMPLES OF REAL SUCCESS-- OH, LISTEN TO ME.
I'M JUST DELIGHTED THAT YOU'RE DOING SO WELL.

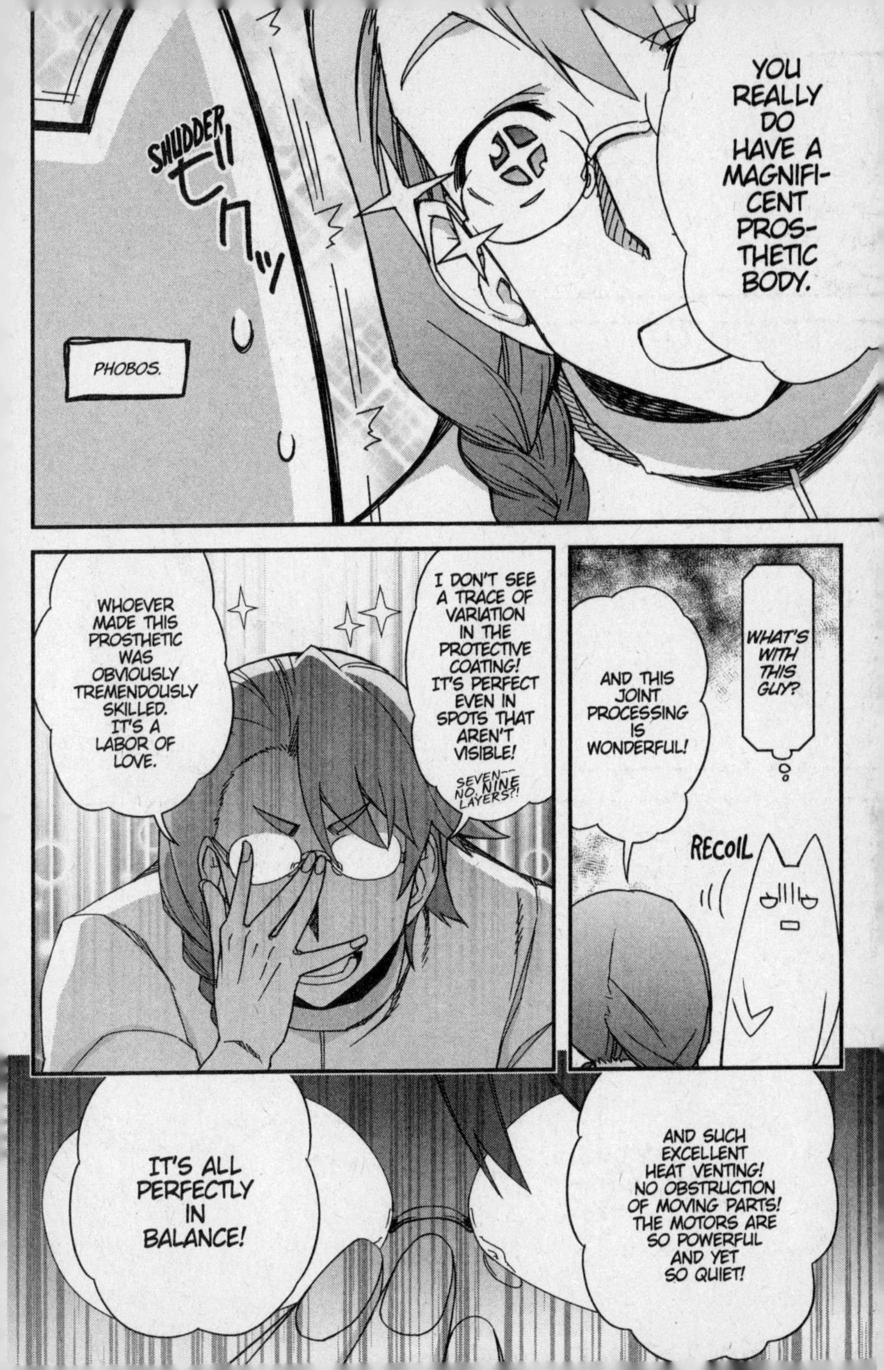
YOU REALLY DO HAVE A MAGNIFICENT PROSTHETIC BODY.
SHUDDER
ビクッ
PHOBOS.
WHAT'S WITH THIS GUY?
AND THIS JOINT PROCESSING IS WONDERFUL!
RECOIL
I DON'T SEE A TRACE OF VARIATION IN THE PROTECTIVE COATING! IT'S PERFECT EVEN IN SPOTS THAT AREN'T VISIBLE!
SEVEN-- NO, NINE LAYERS?!
WHOEVER MADE THIS PROSTHETIC WAS OBVIOUSLY TREMENDOUSLY SKILLED. IT'S A LABOR OF LOVE.
AND SUCH EXCELLENT HEAT VENTING! NO OBSTRUCTION OF MOVING PARTS! THE MOTORS ARE SO POWERFUL AND YET SO QUIET!
IT'S ALL PERFECTLY IN BALANCE!

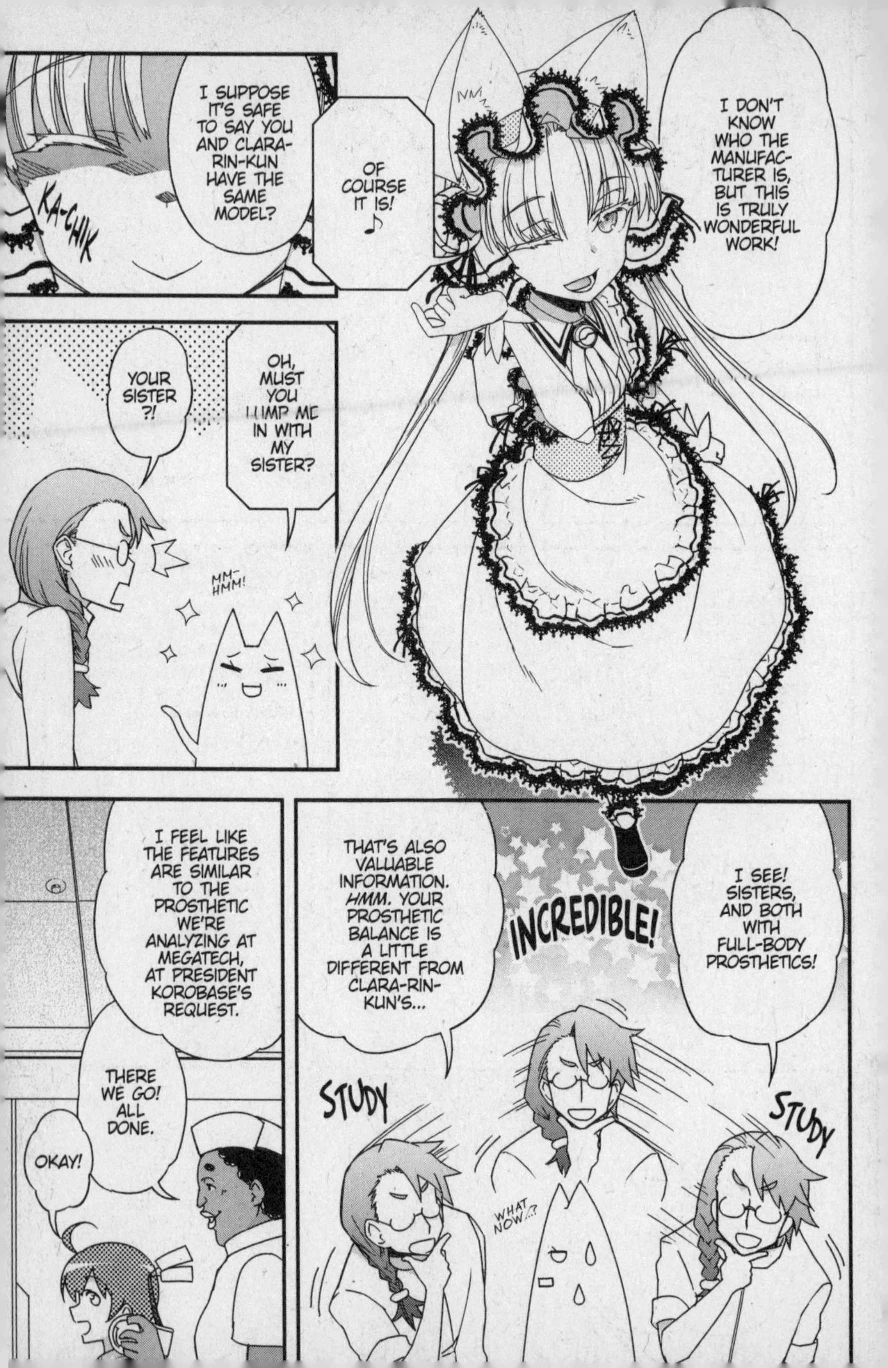
I DON'T KNOW WHO THE MANUFACTURER IS, BUT THIS IS TRULY WONDERFUL WORK!
I SUPPOSE IT'S SAFE TO SAY YOU AND CLARA-RIN-KUN HAVE THE SAME MODEL?
KA-CHIK
OF COURSE IT IS! ♪
OH, MUST YOU LUMP ME IN WITH MY SISTER?
YOUR SISTER?!
MM-HMM!
I SEE! SISTERS, AND BOTH WITH FULL-BODY PROSTHETICS!
INCREDIBLE!
THAT'S ALSO VALUABLE INFORMATION. HMM. YOUR PROSTHETIC BALANCE IS A LITTLE DIFFERENT FROM CLARA-RIN-KUN'S...
STUDY
STUDY
WHAT NOW...?
I FEEL LIKE THE FEATURES ARE SIMILAR TO THE PROSTHETIC WE'RE ANALYZING AT MEGATECH, AT PRESIDENT KOROBASE'S REQUEST.
THERE WE GO! ALL DONE.
OKAY!

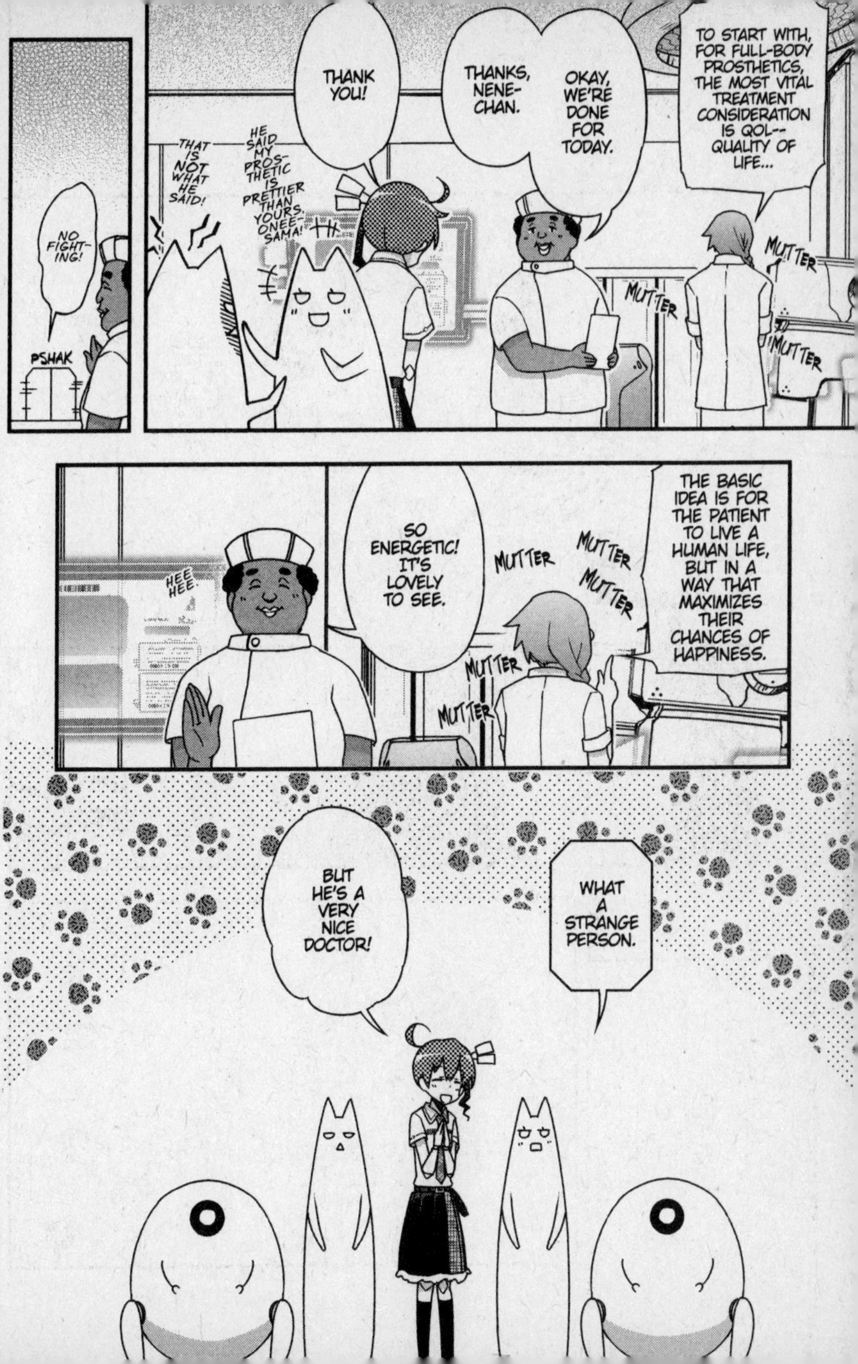

TO START WITH, FOR FULL-BODY PROSTHETICS, THE MOST VITAL TREATMENT CONSIDERATION IS QOL--QUALITY OF LIFE...
MUTTER
MUTTER
MUTTER
OKAY, WE'RE DONE FOR TODAY.
THANKS, NENE-CHAN.
THANK YOU!
HE SAID MY PROSTHETIC IS PRETTIER THAN YOURS, ONEE-SAMA!
THAT IS NOT WHAT HE SAID!
NO FIGHTING!
PSHAK
THE BASIC IDEA IS FOR THE PATIENT TO LIVE A HUMAN LIFE, BUT IN A WAY THAT MAXIMIZES THEIR CHANCES OF HAPPINESS.
MUTTER
MUTTER
MUTTER
MUTTER
MUTTER
SO ENERGETIC! IT'S LOVELY TO SEE.
HEE HEE.
WHAT A STRANGE PERSON.
BUT HE'S A VERY NICE DOCTOR!

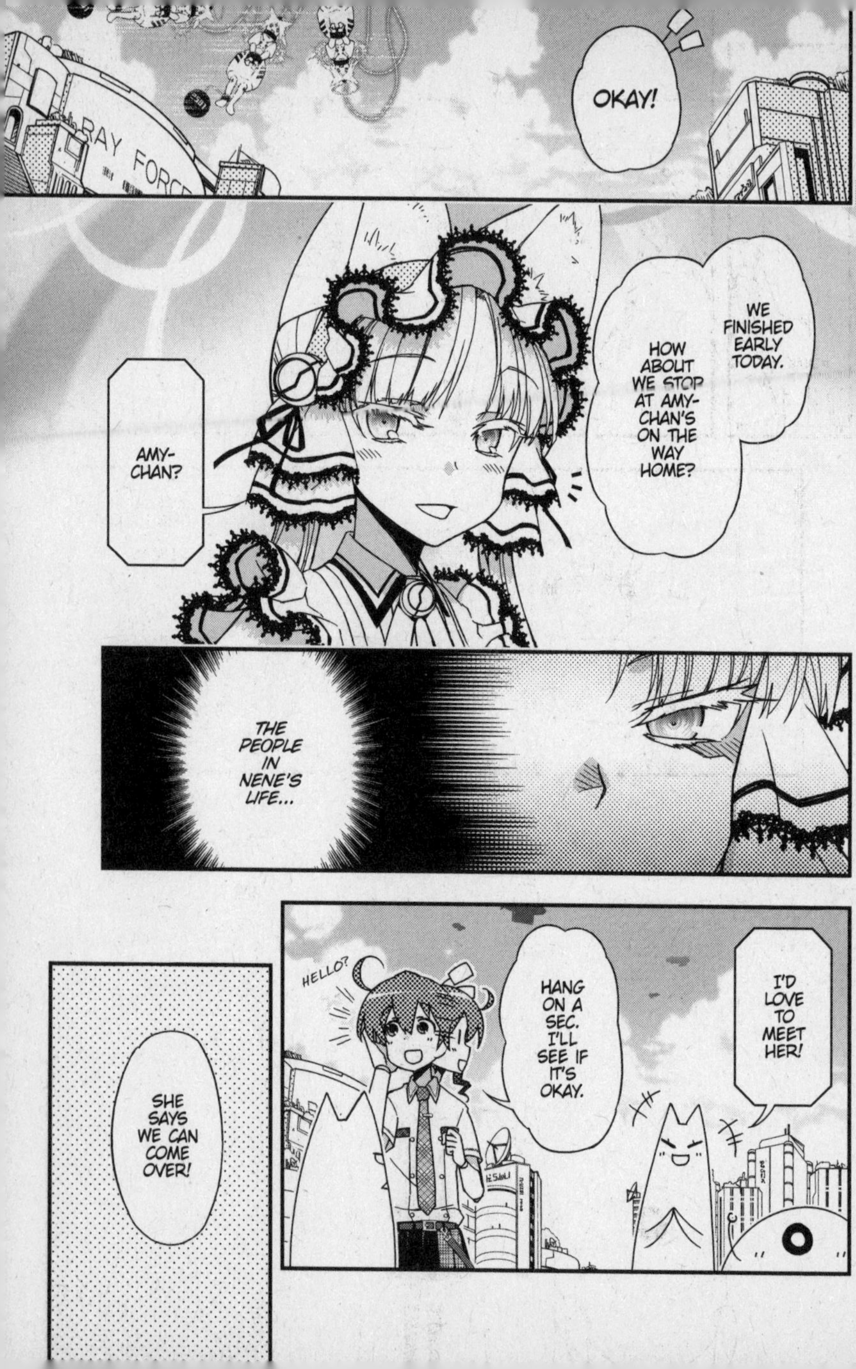
OKAY!
WE FINISHED EARLY TODAY. HOW ABOUT WE STOP AT AMY-CHAN'S ON THE WAY HOME?
AMY-CHAN?
THE PEOPLE IN NENE'S LIFE...
I'D LOVE TO MEET HER!
HANG ON A SEC. I'LL SEE IF IT'S OKAY.
HELLO?
SHE SAYS WE CAN COME OVER!

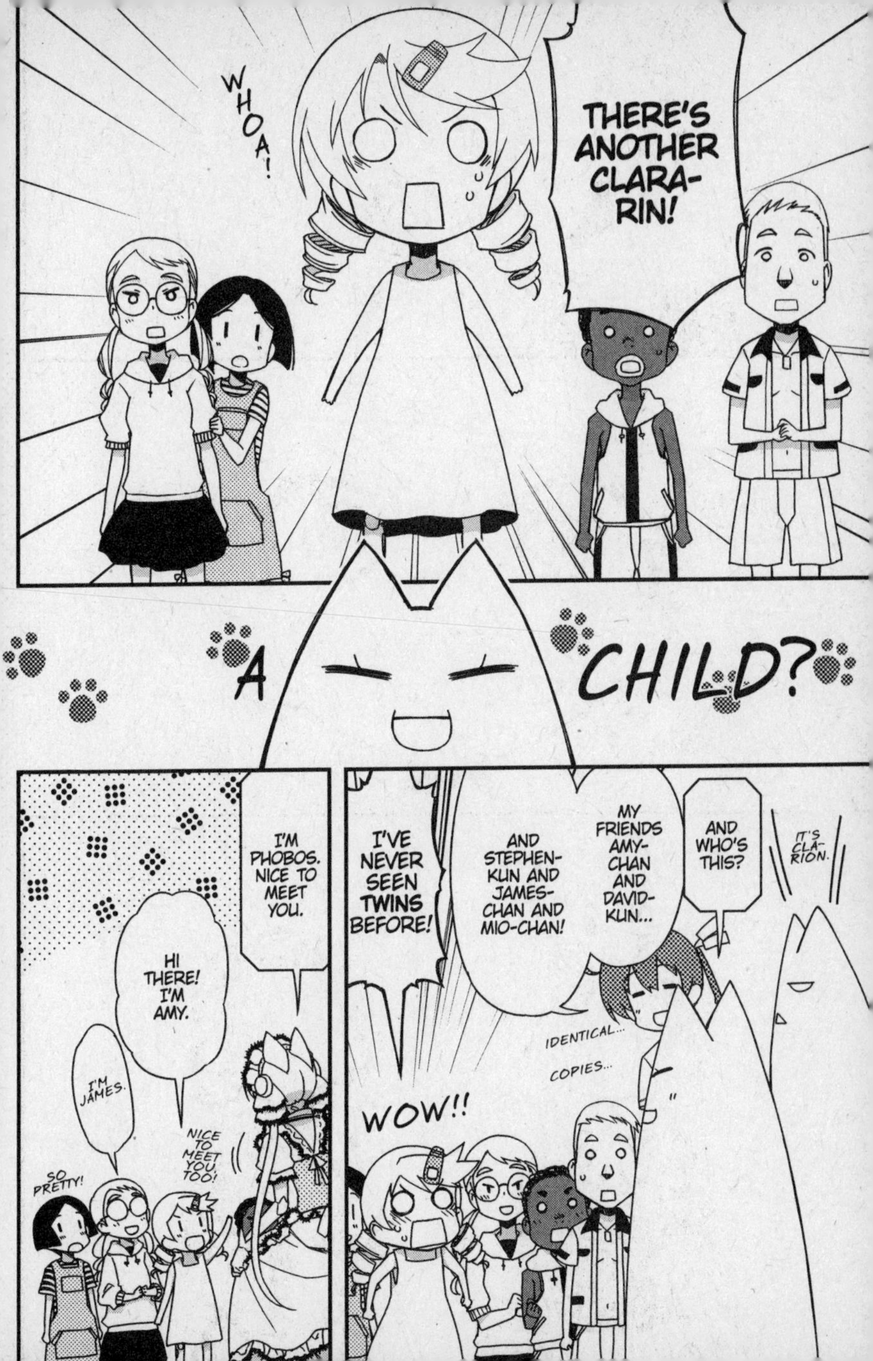
THERE'S ANOTHER CLARA-RIN!
WHOA!
A CHILD?
IT'S CLARION.
AND WHO'S THIS?
MY FRIENDS AMY-CHAN AND DAVID-KUN...
AND STEPHEN-KUN AND JAMES-CHAN AND MIO-CHAN!
I'VE NEVER SEEN TWINS BEFORE!
IDENTICAL...
COPIES...
WOW!!
I'M PHOBOS. NICE TO MEET YOU.
HI THERE! I'M AMY.
I'M JAMES.
NICE TO MEET YOU, TOO!
SO PRETTY!

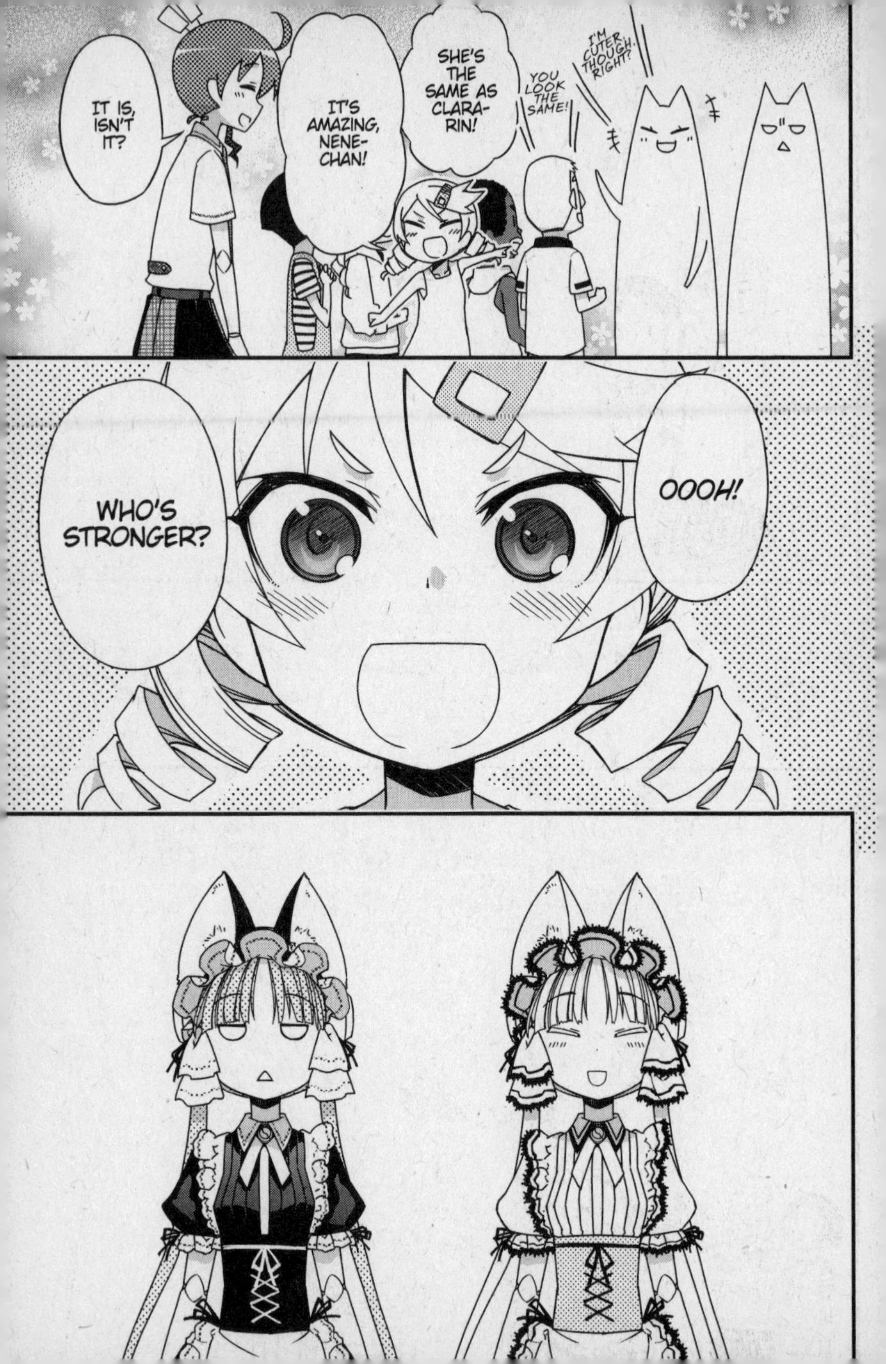
I'M CUTER THOUGH, RIGHT?
YOU LOOK THE SAME!
SHE'S THE SAME AS CLARA-RIN!
IT'S AMAZING, NENE-CHAN!
IT IS, ISN'T IT?
OOOH!
WHO'S STRONGER?

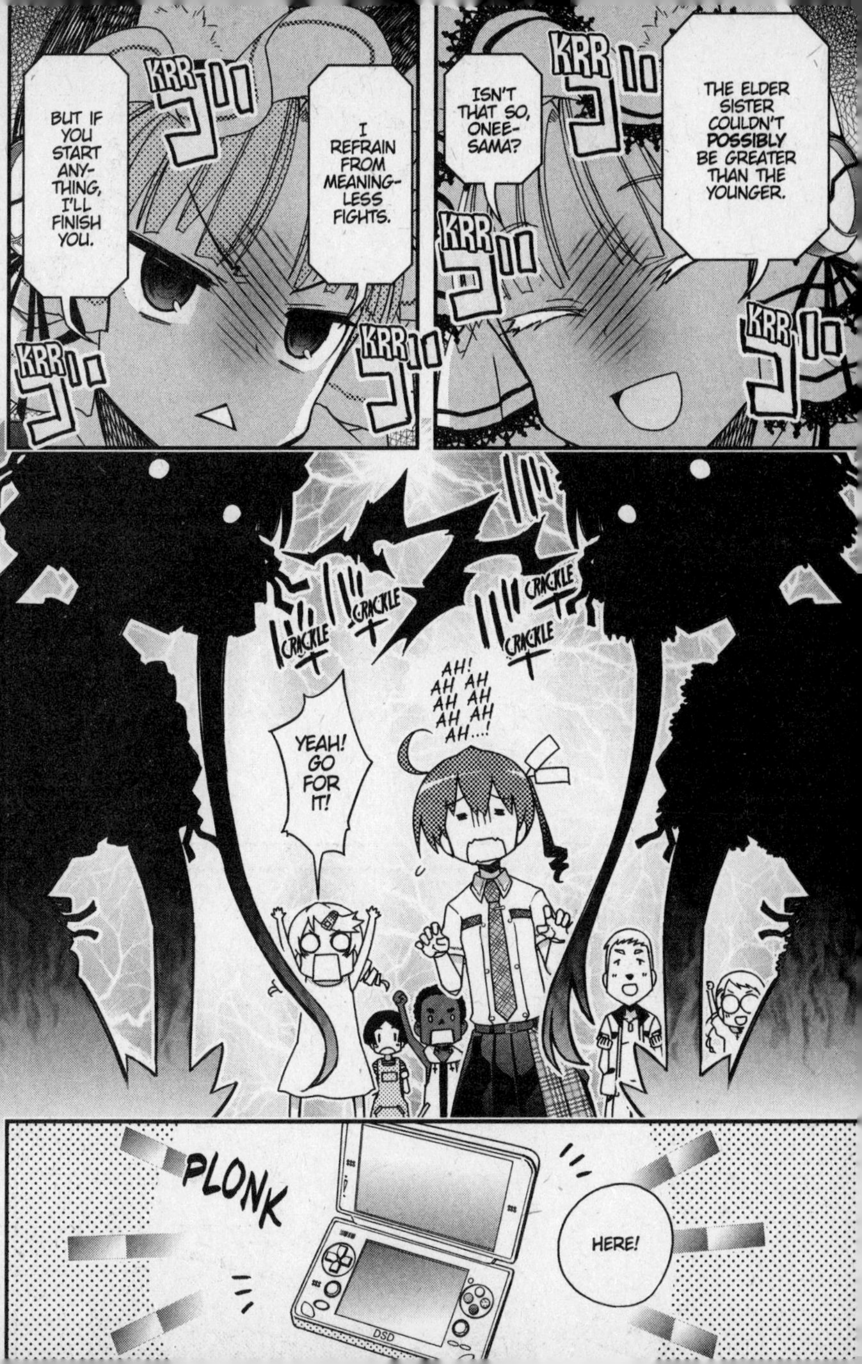
THE ELDER SISTER COULDN'T POSSIBLY BE GREATER THAN THE YOUNGER.
KRR
ISN'T THAT SO, ONEE-SAMA?
KRR
KRR
KRR
I REFRAIN FROM MEANING-LESS FIGHTS.
KRR
BUT IF YOU START ANY-THING, I'LL FINISH YOU.
KRR
CRACKLE
CRACKLE
CRACKLE
CRACKLE
AH! AH AH AH AH AH AH AH...!
YEAH! GO FOR IT!
HERE!
PLONK
DSD

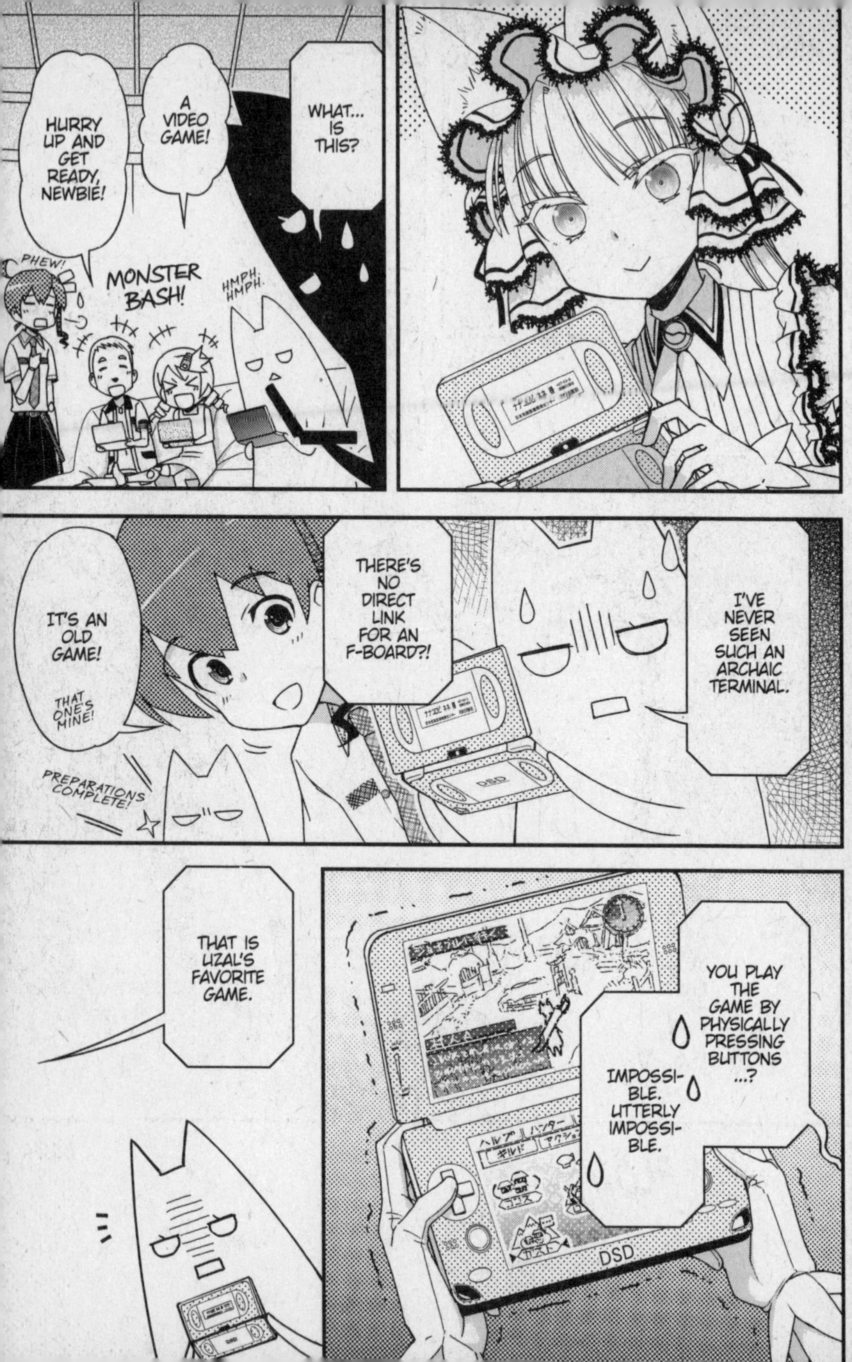
WHAT... IS THIS?
HMPH. HMPH.
A VIDEO GAME!
HURRY UP AND GET READY, NEWBIE!
MONSTER BASH!
PHEW!
I'VE NEVER SEEN SUCH AN ARCHAIC TERMINAL.
THERE'S NO DIRECT LINK FOR AN F-BOARD?!
IT'S AN OLD GAME!
THAT ONE'S MINE!
PREPARATIONS COMPLETE!
YOU PLAY THE GAME BY PHYSICALLY PRESSING BUTTONS ...?
IMPOSSI-BLE. UTTERLY IMPOSSI-BLE.
THAT IS UZAL'S FAVORITE GAME.
DSD

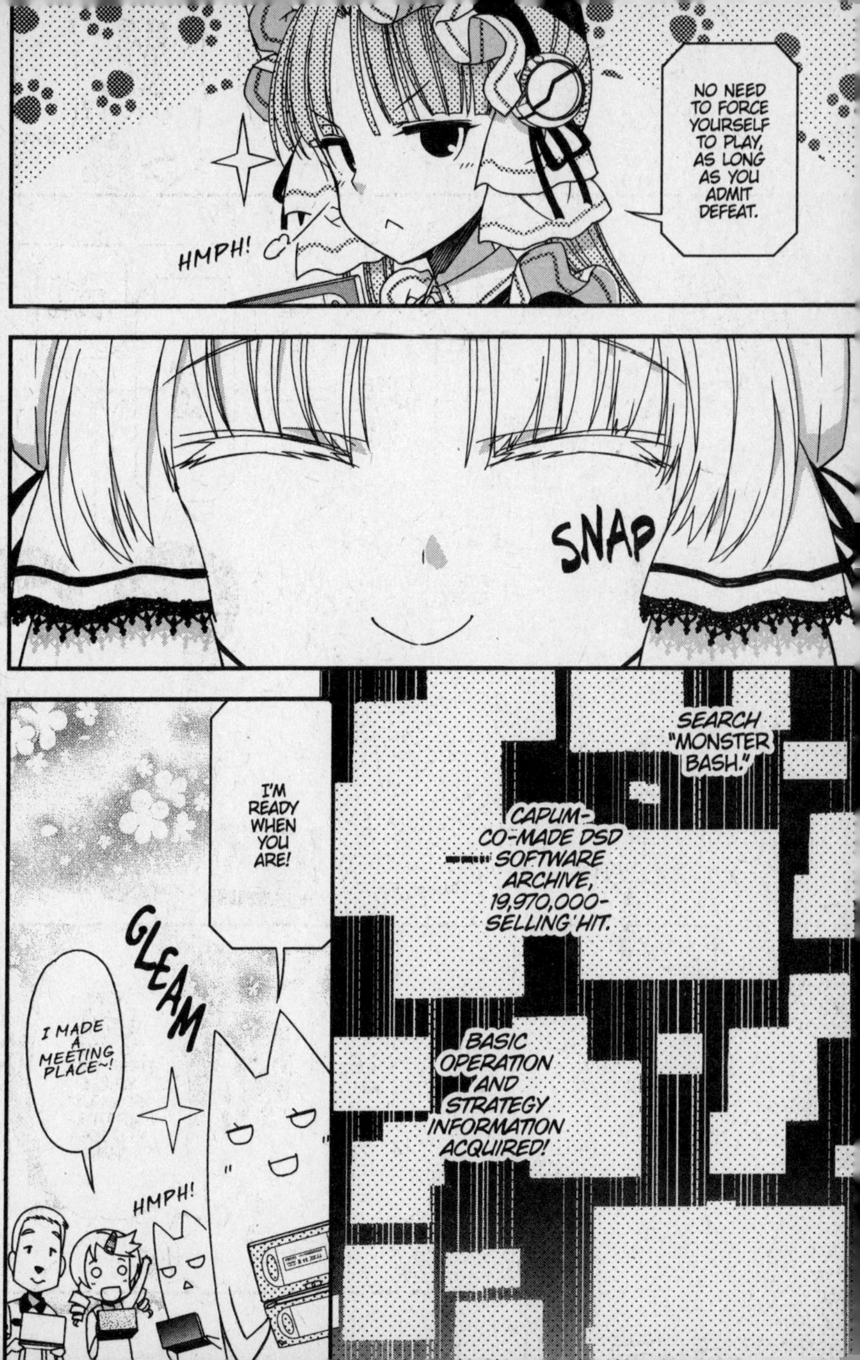
NO NEED TO FORCE YOURSELF TO PLAY, AS LONG AS YOU ADMIT DEFEAT.
HMPH!
SNAP
SEARCH "MONSTER BASH."
CAPUM-CO-MADE DSD SOFTWARE ARCHIVE, 19,970,000-SELLING HIT.
BASIC OPERATION AND STRATEGY INFORMATION ACQUIRED!
I'M READY WHEN YOU ARE!
GLEAM
I MADE A MEETING PLACE~!
HMPH!

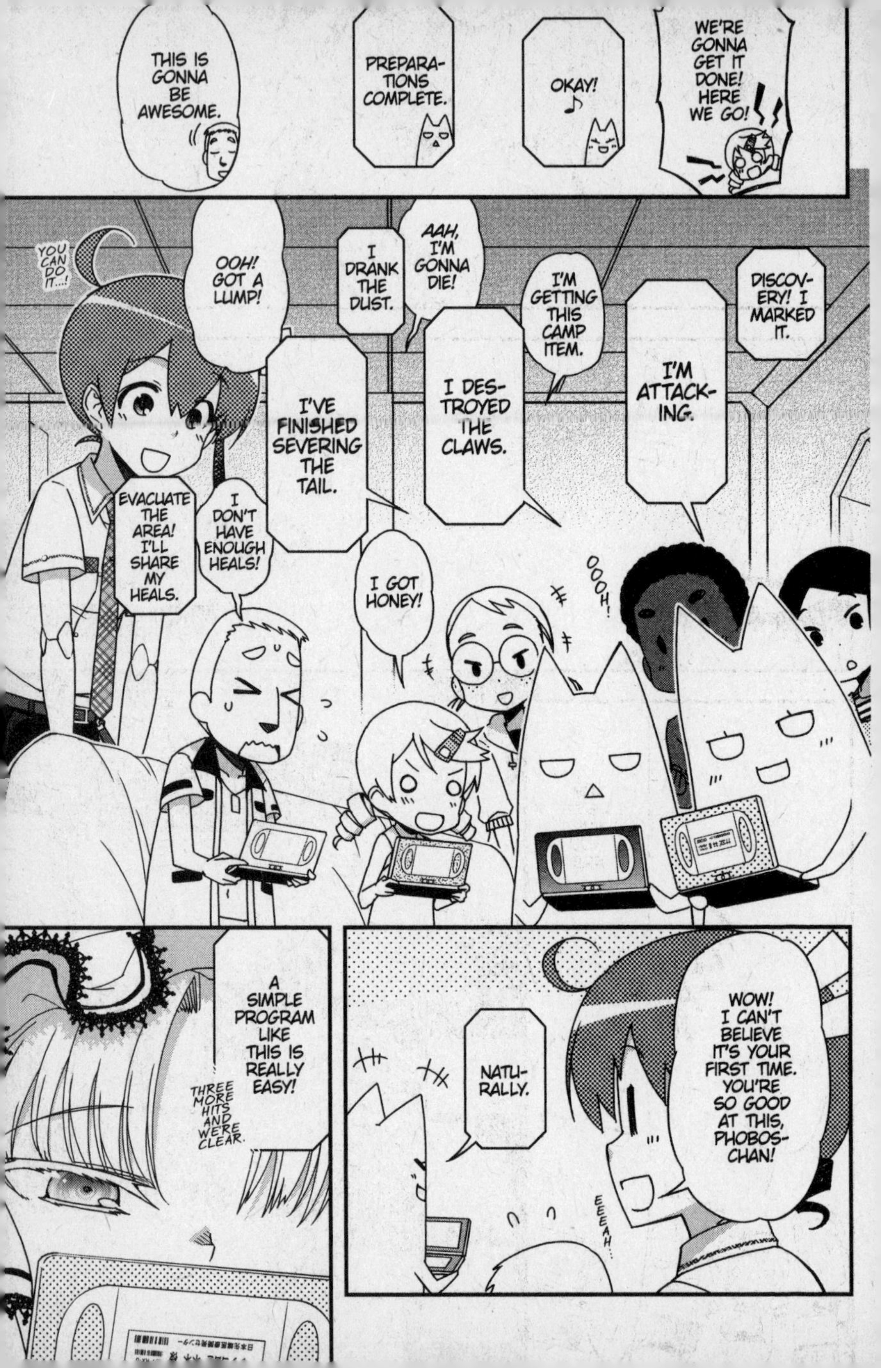
WE'RE GONNA GET IT DONE! HERE WE GO!
OKAY! ♪
PREPARATIONS COMPLETE.
THIS IS GONNA BE AWESOME.
DISCOVERY! I MARKED IT.
I'M ATTACKING.
I'M GETTING THIS CAMP ITEM.
I DESTROYED THE CLAWS.
AAH, I'M GONNA DIE!
I DRANK THE DUST.
I'VE FINISHED SEVERING THE TAIL.
OOH! GOT A LUMP!
YOU CAN DO IT...!
OOOH!
I GOT HONEY!
I DON'T HAVE ENOUGH HEALS!
EVACUATE THE AREA! I'LL SHARE MY HEALS.
WOW! I CAN'T BELIEVE IT'S YOUR FIRST TIME. YOU'RE SO GOOD AT THIS, PHOBOS-CHAN!
NATURALLY.
EEEAH...
A SIMPLE PROGRAM LIKE THIS IS REALLY EASY!
THREE MORE HITS AND WE'RE CLEAR.

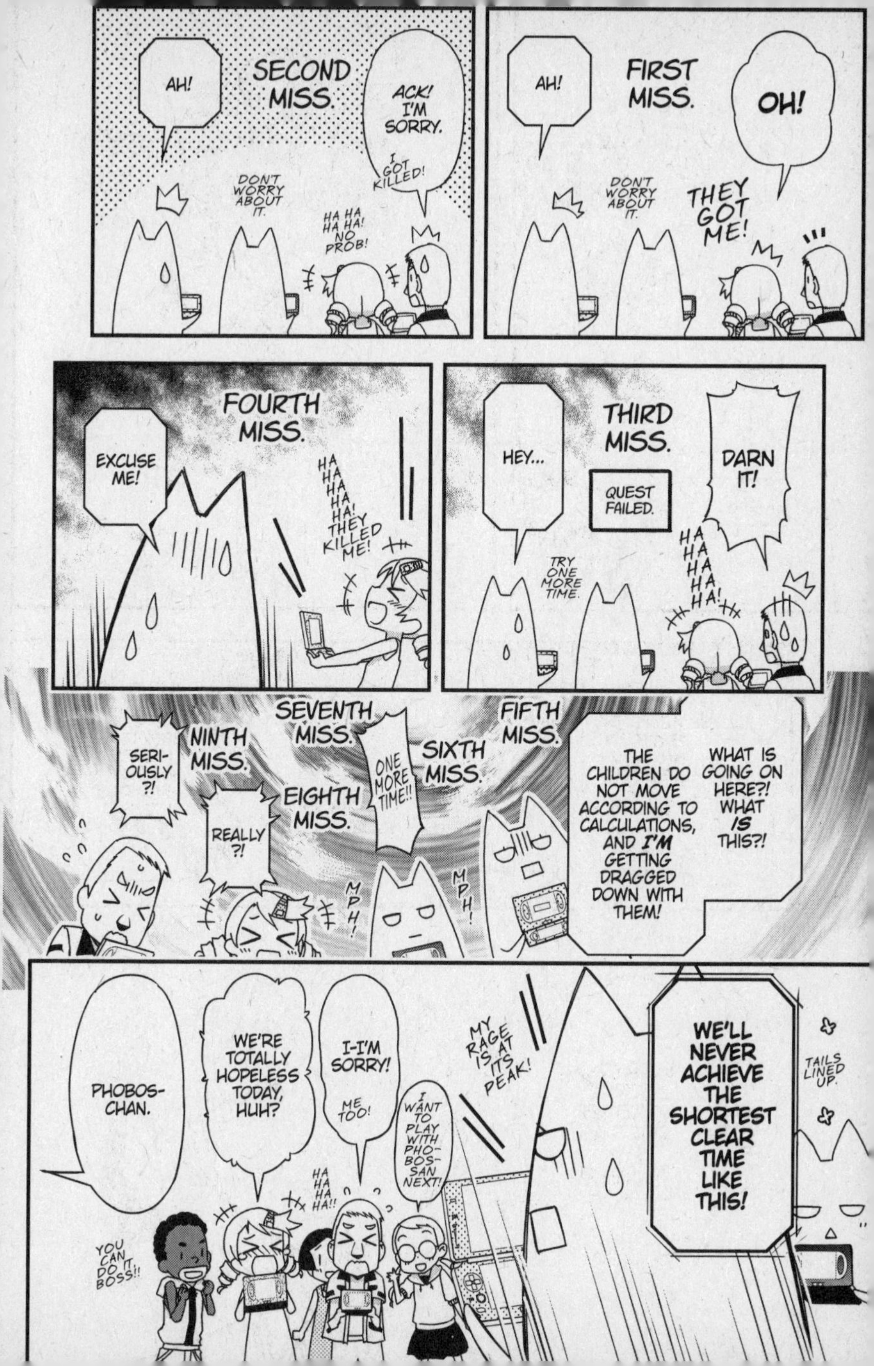
OH!
FIRST MISS.
AH!
THEY GOT ME!
DON'T WORRY ABOUT IT.
ACK! I'M SORRY.
I GOT KILLED!
SECOND MISS.
AH!
HA HA HA HA! NO PROB!
DON'T WORRY ABOUT IT.
DARN IT!
THIRD MISS.
QUEST FAILED.
HEY...
HA HA HA HA HA!
TRY ONE MORE TIME.
FOURTH MISS.
HA HA HA HA HA! THEY KILLED ME!
EXCUSE ME!
WHAT IS GOING ON HERE?! WHAT *IS* THIS?!
THE CHILDREN DO NOT MOVE ACCORDING TO CALCULATIONS, AND *I'M* GETTING DRAGGED DOWN WITH THEM!
FIFTH MISS.
MPH!
SIXTH MISS.
SEVENTH MISS.
ONE MORE TIME!!
EIGHTH MISS.
MPH!
NINTH MISS.
REALLY?!
SERIOUSLY?!
TAILS LINED UP.
WE'LL NEVER ACHIEVE THE SHORTEST CLEAR TIME LIKE THIS!
MY RAGE IS AT ITS PEAK!
I WANT TO PLAY WITH PHOBOS-SAN NEXT!
I-I'M SORRY!
ME TOO!
HA HA HA HA!!
WE'RE TOTALLY HOPELESS TODAY, HUH?
PHOBOS-CHAN.
YOU CAN DO IT, BOSS!!

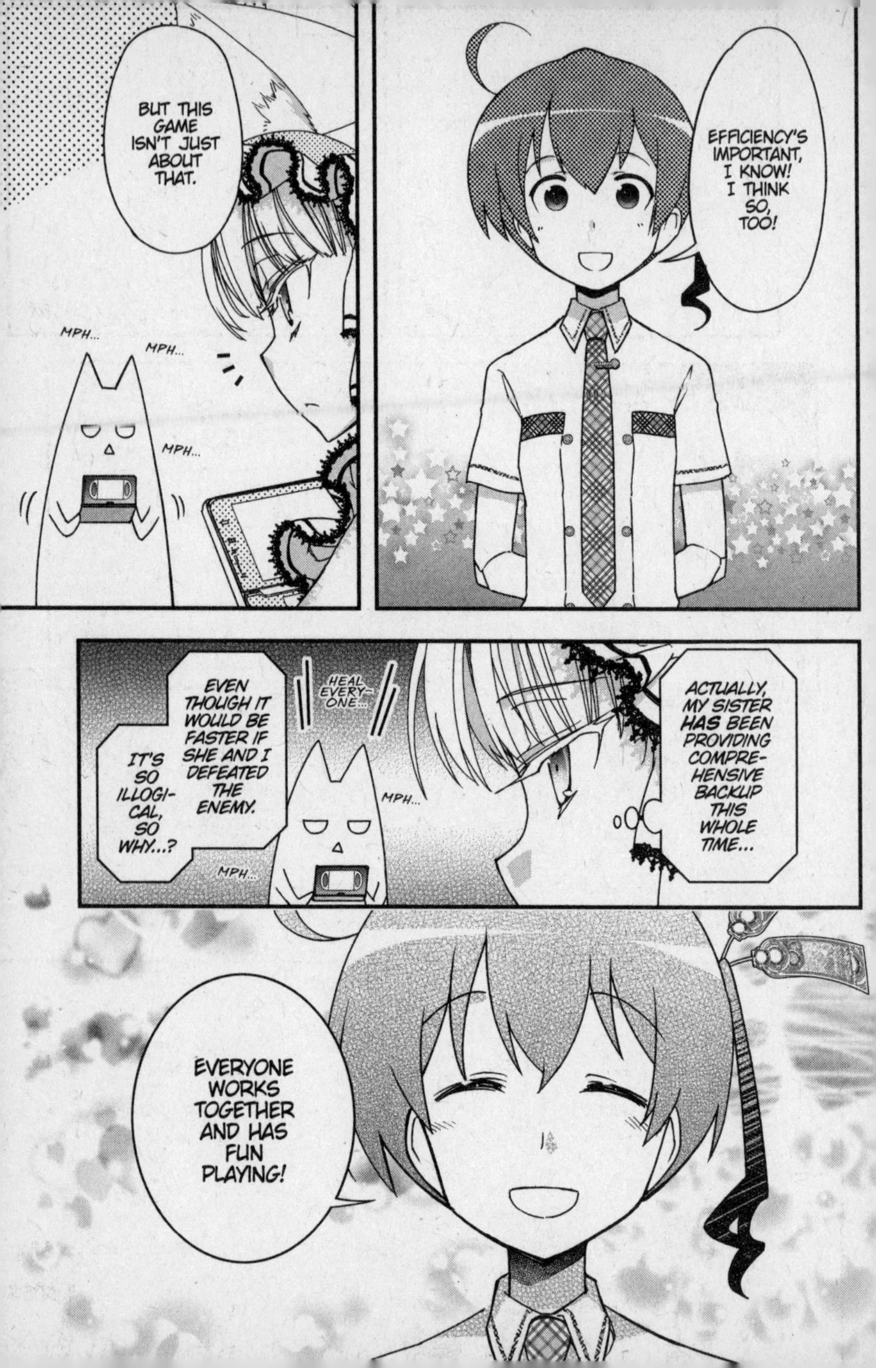
EFFICIENCY'S IMPORTANT, I KNOW! I THINK SO, TOO!
BUT THIS GAME ISN'T JUST ABOUT THAT.
MPH...
MPH...
MPH...
ACTUALLY, MY SISTER HAS BEEN PROVIDING COMPRE-HENSIVE BACKUP THIS WHOLE TIME...
HEAL EVERY-ONE...
MPH...
EVEN THOUGH IT WOULD BE FASTER IF SHE AND I DEFEATED THE ENEMY.
IT'S SO ILLOGI-CAL, SO WHY...?
MPH...
EVERYONE WORKS TOGETHER AND HAS FUN PLAYING!

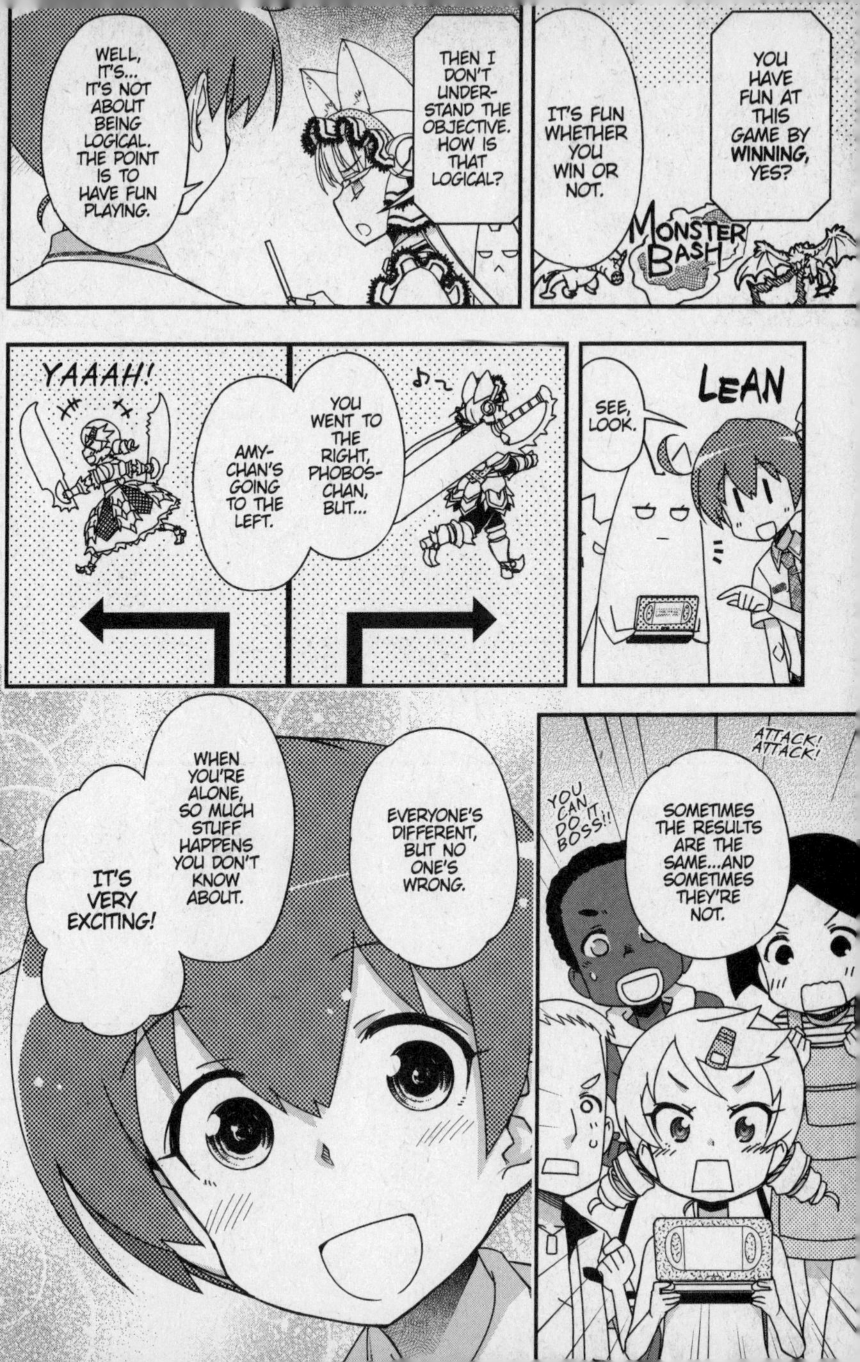
YOU HAVE FUN AT THIS GAME BY WINNING, YES?
IT'S FUN WHETHER YOU WIN OR NOT.
MONSTER BASH
THEN I DON'T UNDER-STAND THE OBJECTIVE. HOW IS THAT LOGICAL?
WELL, IT'S... IT'S NOT ABOUT BEING LOGICAL. THE POINT IS TO HAVE FUN PLAYING.
LEAN
SEE, LOOK.
YOU WENT TO THE RIGHT, PHOBOS-CHAN, BUT...
AMY-CHAN'S GOING TO THE LEFT.
YAAAH!
ATTACK! ATTACK!
SOMETIMES THE RESULTS ARE THE SAME...AND SOMETIMES THEY'RE NOT.
YOU CAN DO IT BOSS!!
EVERYONE'S DIFFERENT, BUT NO ONE'S WRONG.
WHEN YOU'RE ALONE, SO MUCH STUFF HAPPENS YOU DON'T KNOW ABOUT.
IT'S VERY EXCITING!

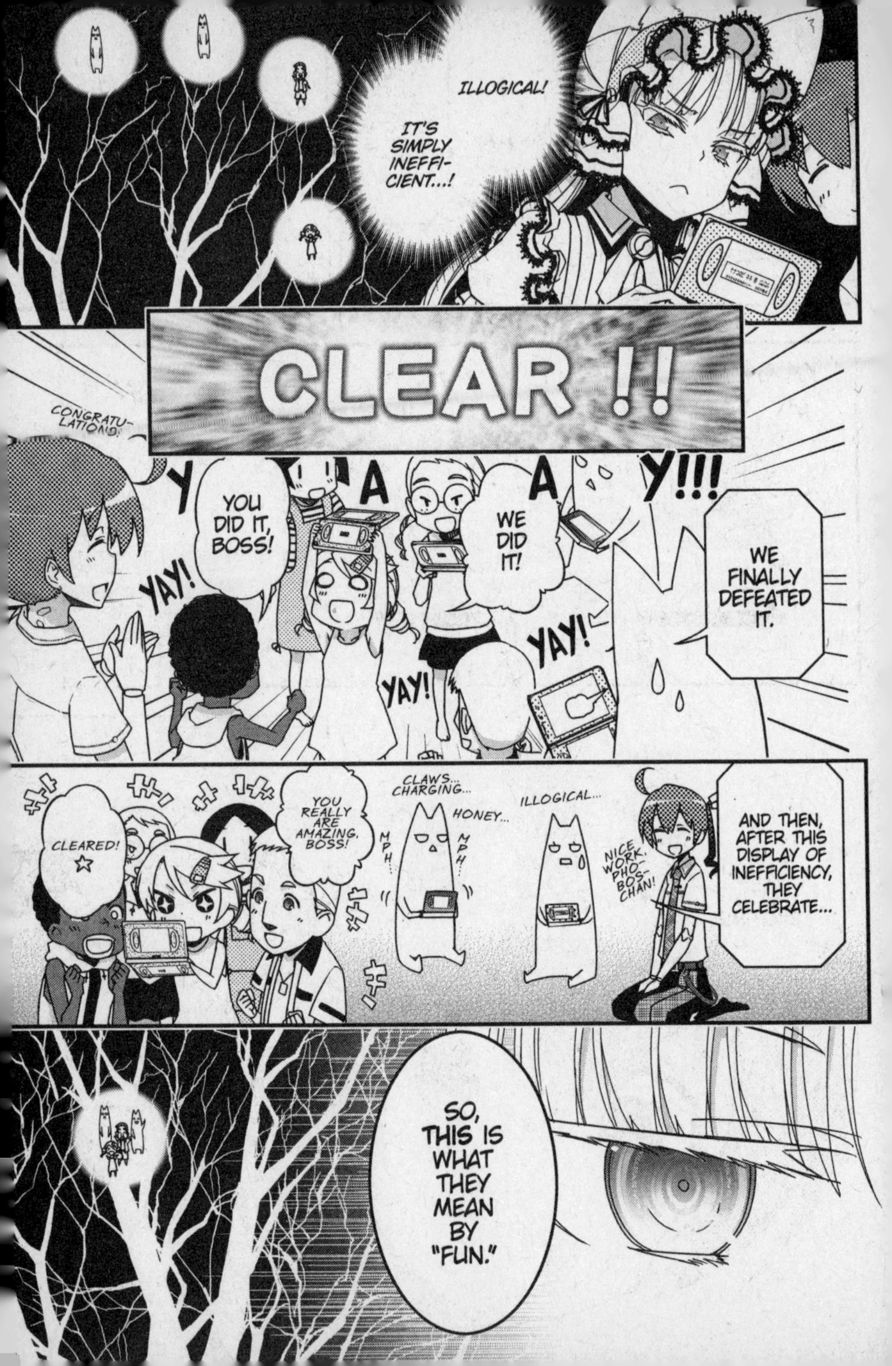
ILLOGICAL!
IT'S SIMPLY INEFFI-CIENT...!
CLEAR !!
WE FINALLY DEFEATED IT.
Y A A Y!!!
WE DID IT!
YAY!
YAY!
YOU DID IT, BOSS!
YAY!
CONGRATU-LATIONS!
AND THEN, AFTER THIS DISPLAY OF INEFFICIENCY, THEY CELEBRATE...
NICE WORK, PHOBOS-CHAN!
ILLOGICAL...
HONEY...
MPH... MPH...
CLAWS... CHARGING...
YOU REALLY ARE AMAZING, BOSS!
CLEARED! ☆
SO, THIS IS WHAT THEY MEAN BY "FUN."

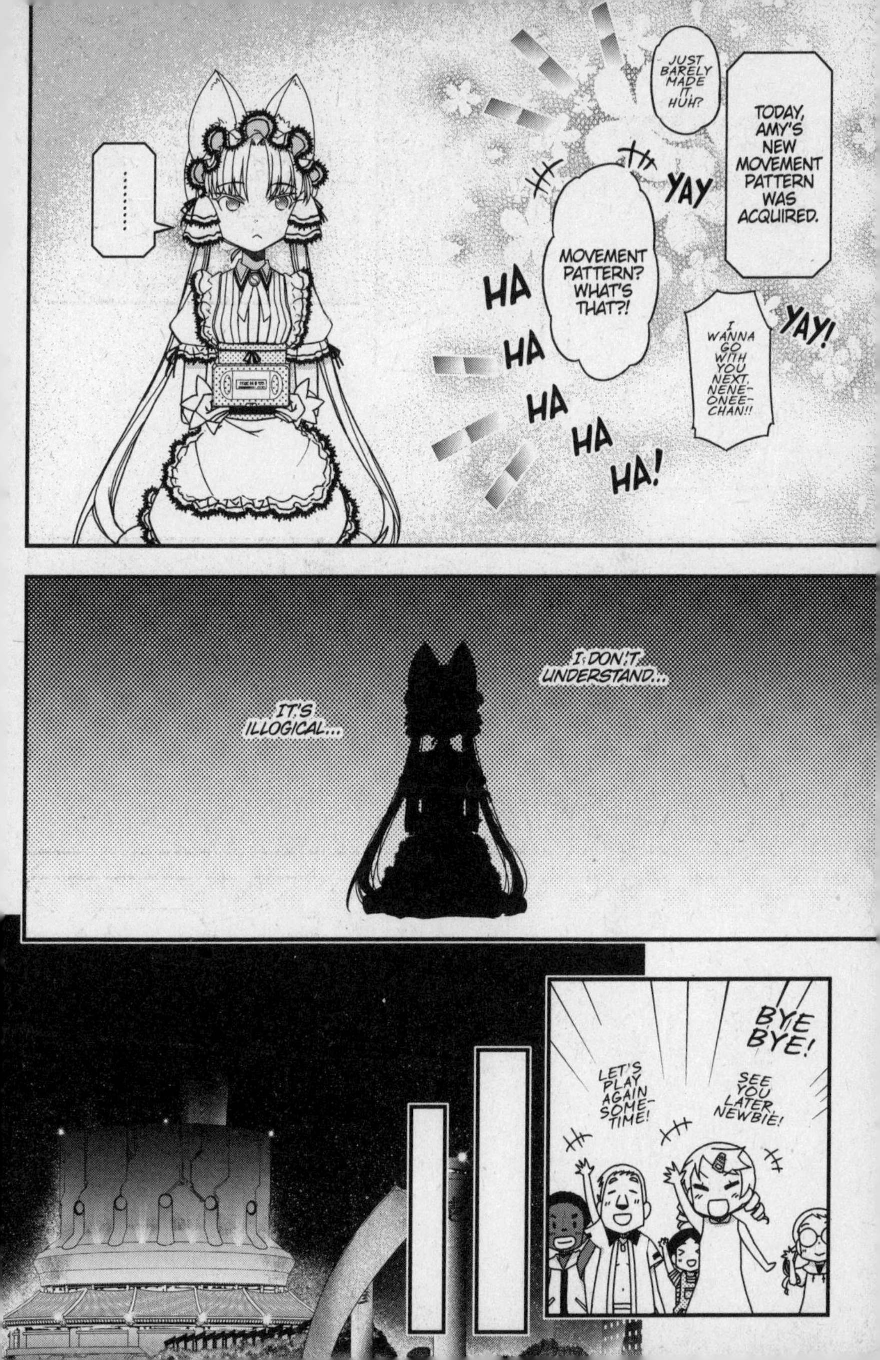
TODAY, AMY'S NEW MOVEMENT PATTERN WAS ACQUIRED.
JUST BARELY MADE IT, HUH?
YAY
YAY!
I WANNA GO WITH YOU NEXT, NENE-ONEE-CHAN!!
MOVEMENT PATTERN? WHAT'S THAT?!
HA HA HA HA HA!
......
I DON'T UNDERSTAND...
IT'S ILLOGICAL...
BYE BYE!
SEE YOU LATER, NEWBIE!
LET'S PLAY AGAIN SOMETIME!

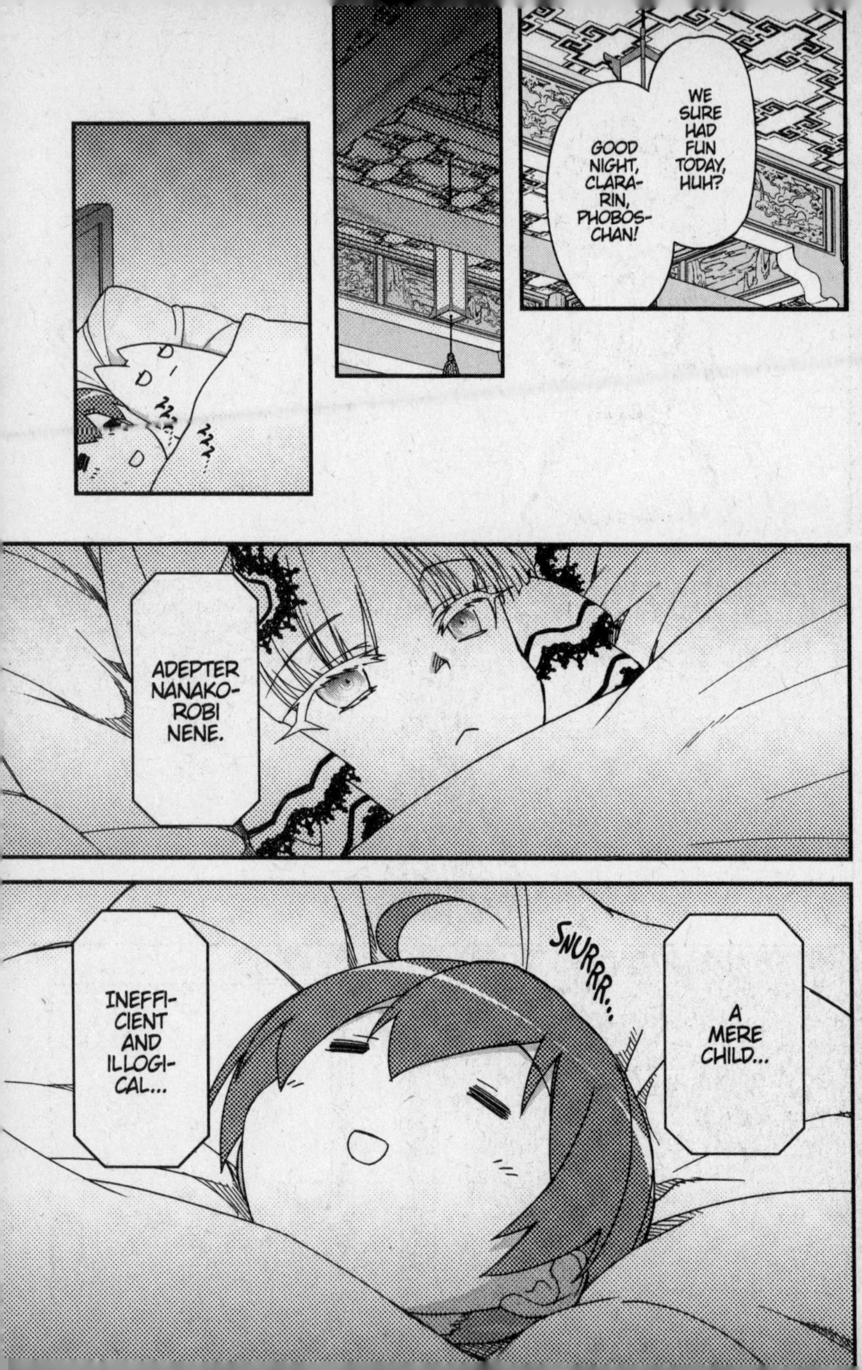
WE SURE HAD FUN TODAY, HUH?
GOOD NIGHT, CLARA-RIN, PHOBOS-CHAN!
ADEPTER NANAKO-ROBI NENE.
A MERE CHILD...
SNURRR...
INEFFI-CIENT AND ILLOGI-CAL...

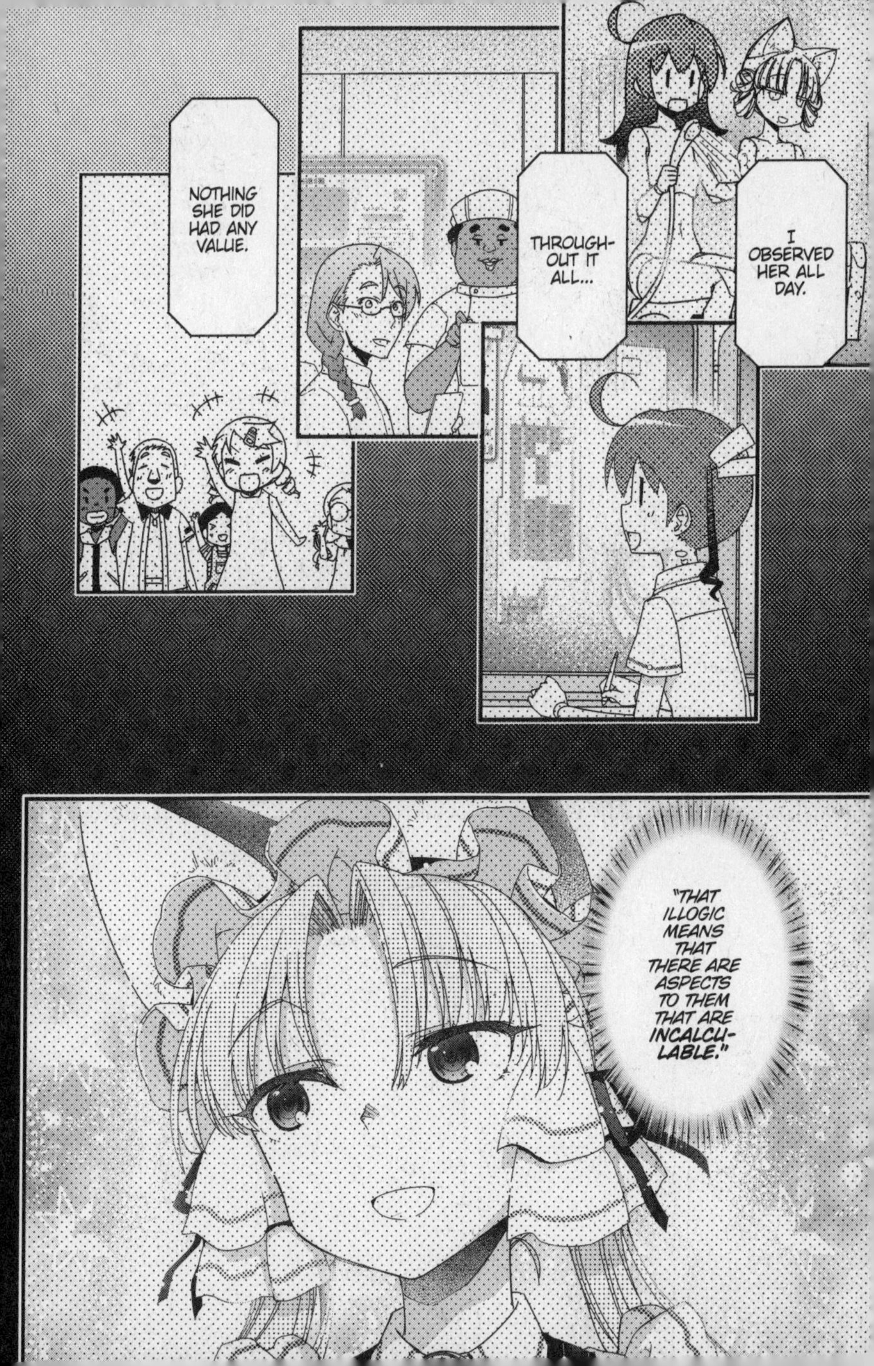
I OBSERVED HER ALL DAY.
THROUGH-OUT IT ALL...
NOTHING SHE DID HAD ANY VALUE.
"THAT ILLOGIC MEANS THAT THERE ARE ASPECTS TO THEM THAT ARE *INCALCU-LABLE.*"

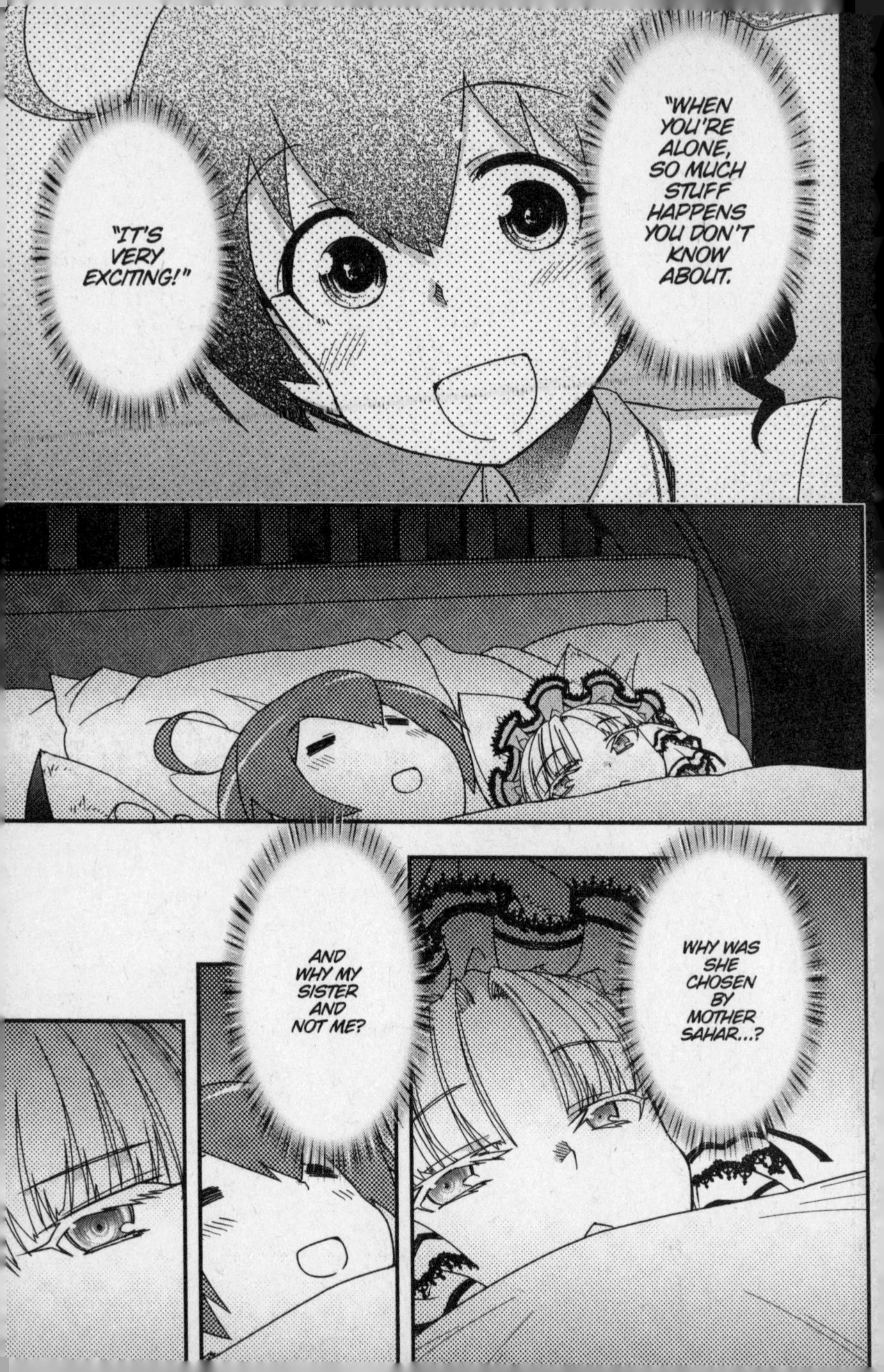
"WHEN YOU'RE ALONE, SO MUCH STUFF HAPPENS YOU DON'T KNOW ABOUT.
"IT'S VERY EXCITING!"
WHY WAS SHE CHOSEN BY MOTHER SAHAR...?
AND WHY MY SISTER AND NOT ME?

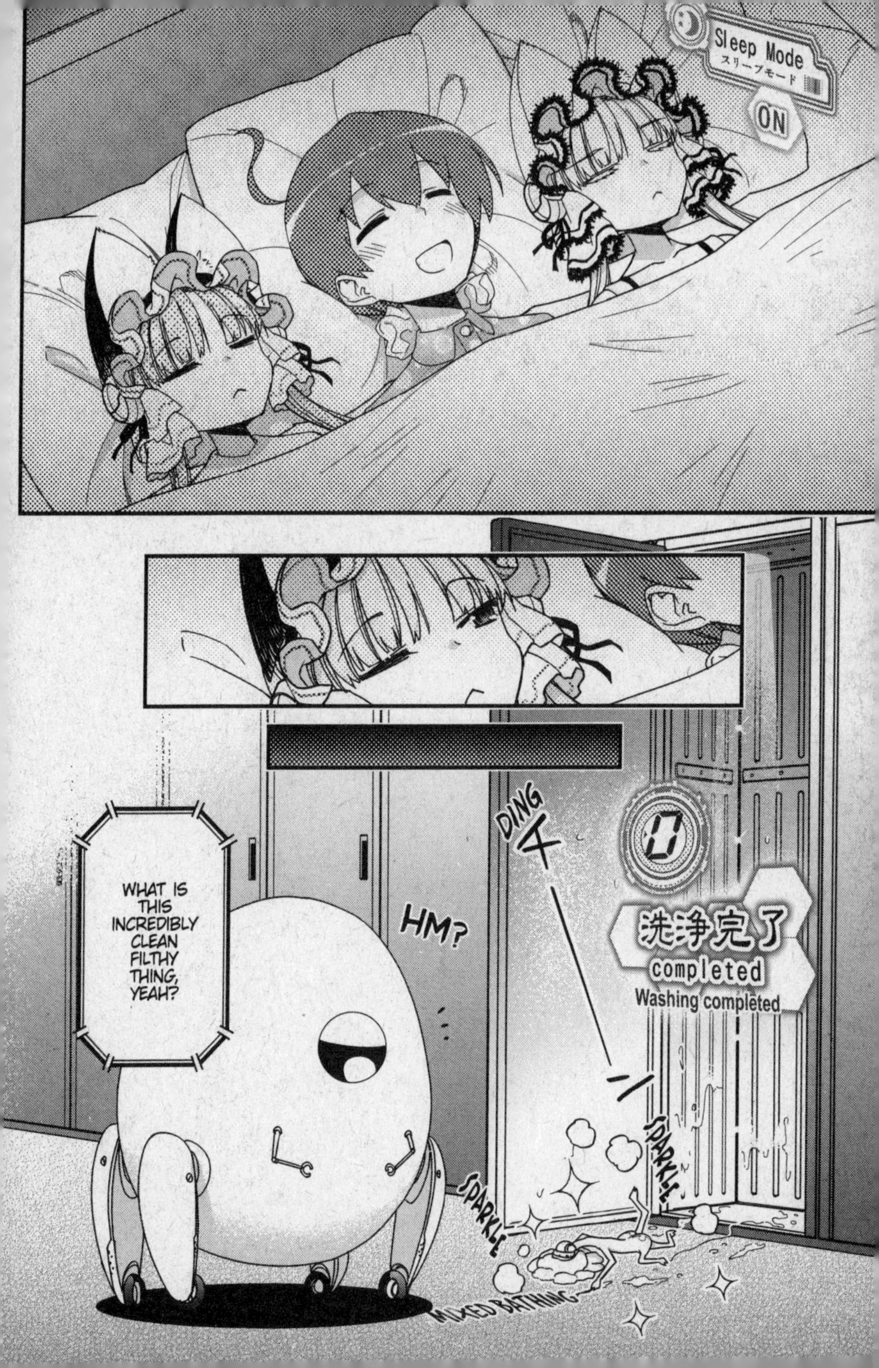

Sleep Mode
スリープモード
ON
DING
0
洗浄完了
completed
Washing completed
HM?
WHAT IS THIS INCREDIBLY CLEAN FILTHY THING, YEAH?
SPARKLE
SPARKLE
MIXED BATHING

GHOST URN

GHOST URN

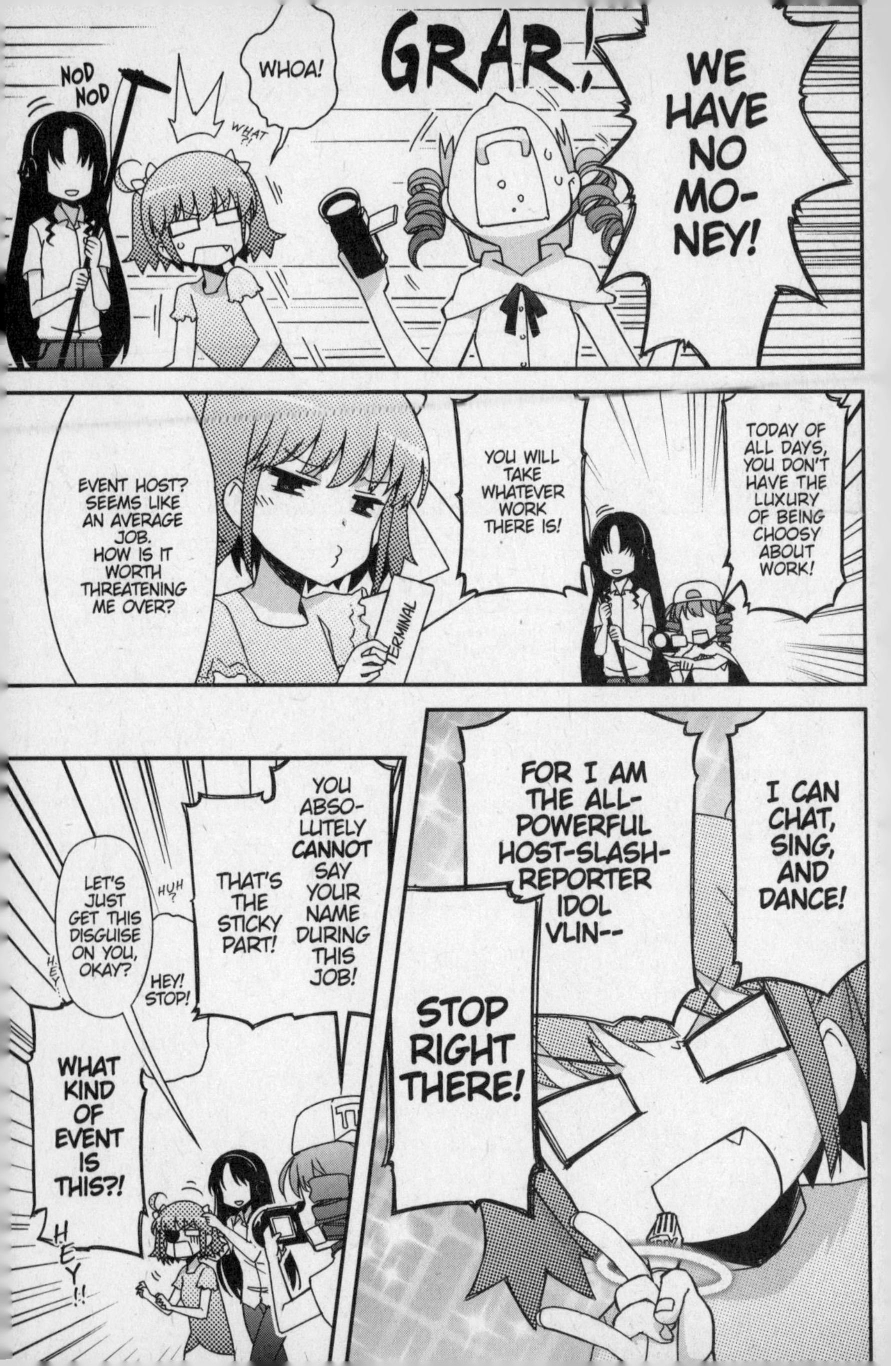
WE HAVE NO MO-NEY!
GRAR!
WHOA!
WHAT ?!
NOD NOD
TODAY OF ALL DAYS, YOU DON'T HAVE THE LUXURY OF BEING CHOOSY ABOUT WORK!
YOU WILL TAKE WHATEVER WORK THERE IS!
EVENT HOST? SEEMS LIKE AN AVERAGE JOB. HOW IS IT WORTH THREATENING ME OVER?
TERMINAL
I CAN CHAT, SING, AND DANCE!
FOR I AM THE ALL-POWERFUL HOST-SLASH-REPORTER IDOL VLIN--
STOP RIGHT THERE!
YOU ABSOLUTELY CANNOT SAY YOUR NAME DURING THIS JOB!
THAT'S THE STICKY PART!
HUH ?
LET'S JUST GET THIS DISGUISE ON YOU, OKAY?
HEY! STOP!
HEY...
WHAT KIND OF EVENT IS THIS?!
HEY!!

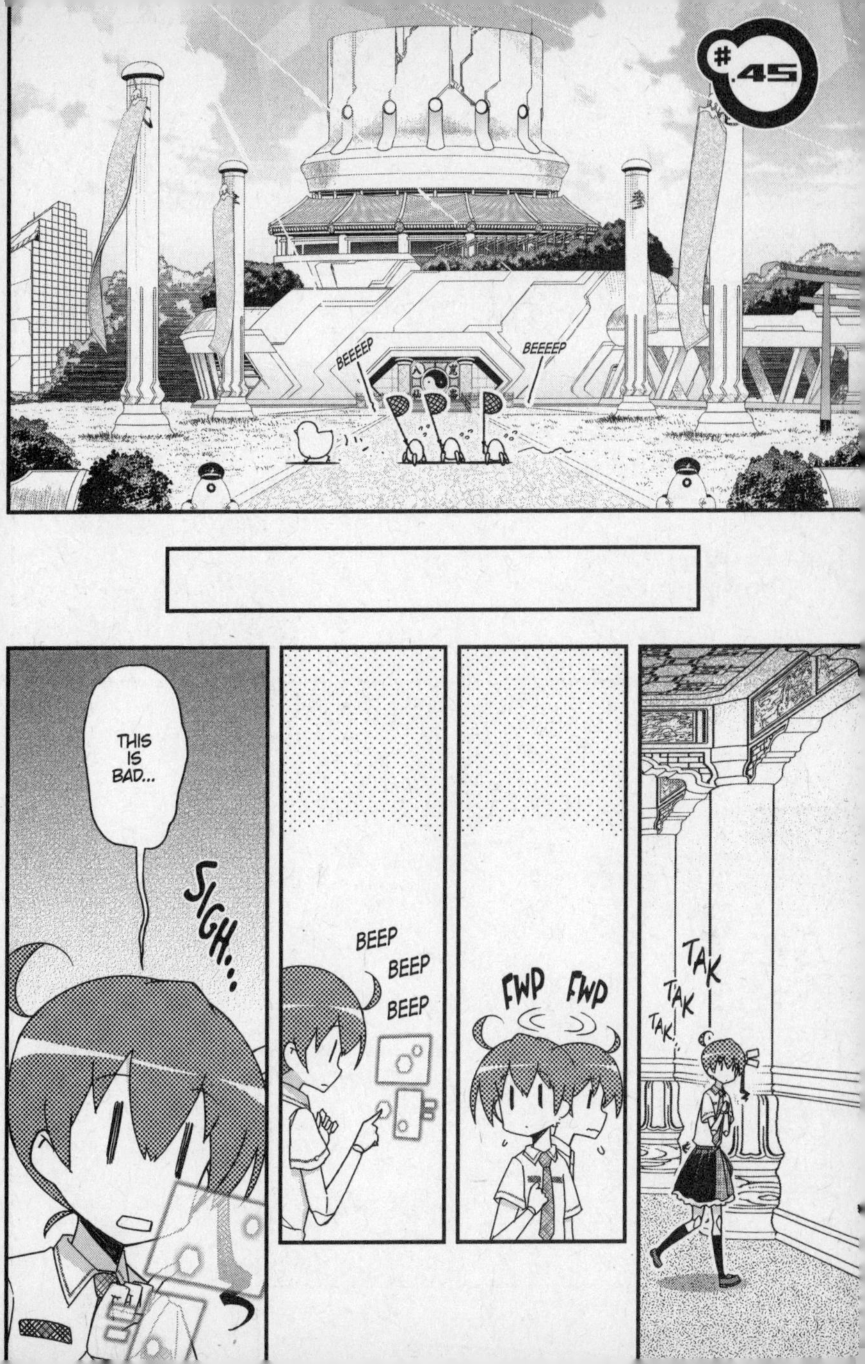
#.45
BEEEEP
BEEEEP
TAK
TAK
TAK
FWP FWP
BEEP
BEEP
BEEP
THIS IS BAD...
SIGH...

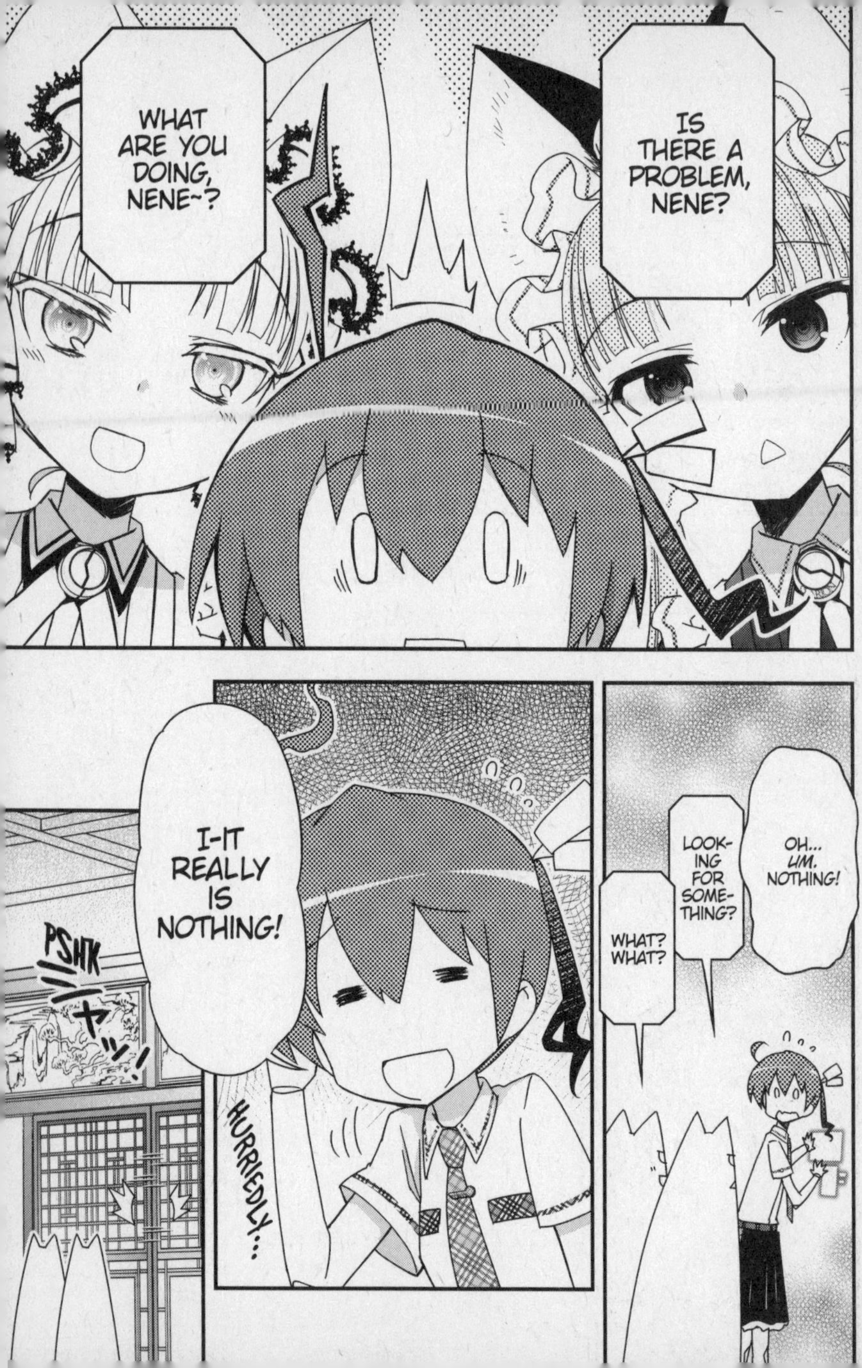
IS THERE A PROBLEM, NENE?
WHAT ARE YOU DOING, NENE~?
OH... UM. NOTHING!
LOOKING FOR SOMETHING?
WHAT? WHAT?
I-IT REALLY IS NOTHING!
HURRIEDLY...
PSHK

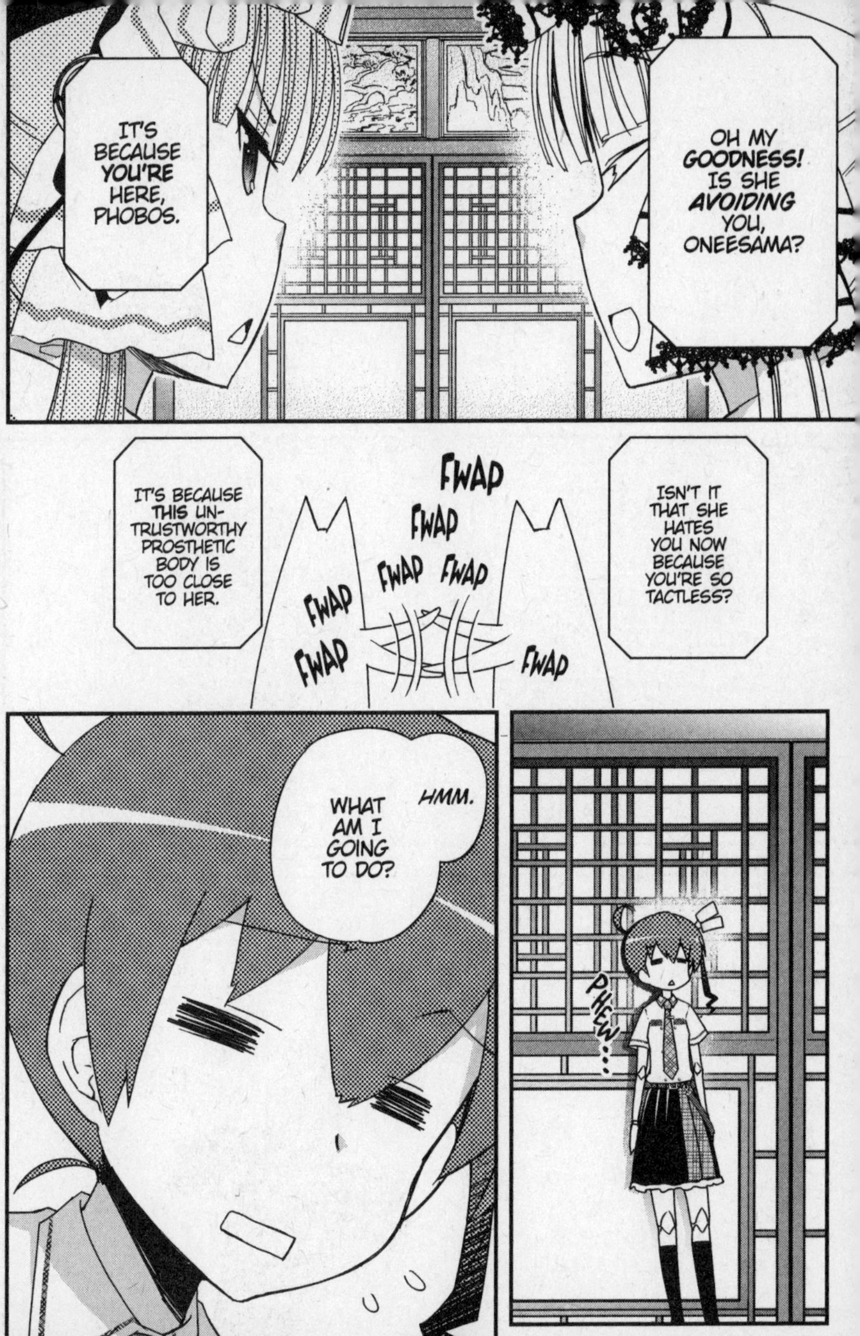
OH MY GOODNESS! IS SHE AVOIDING YOU, ONEESAMA?
IT'S BECAUSE YOU'RE HERE, PHOBOS.
ISN'T IT THAT SHE HATES YOU NOW BECAUSE YOU'RE SO TACTLESS?
FWAP
FWAP
FWAP
FWAP
FWAP
FWAP
FWAP
FWAP
IT'S BECAUSE THIS UN-TRUSTWORTHY PROSTHETIC BODY IS TOO CLOSE TO HER.
PHEW...
HMM.
WHAT AM I GOING TO DO?

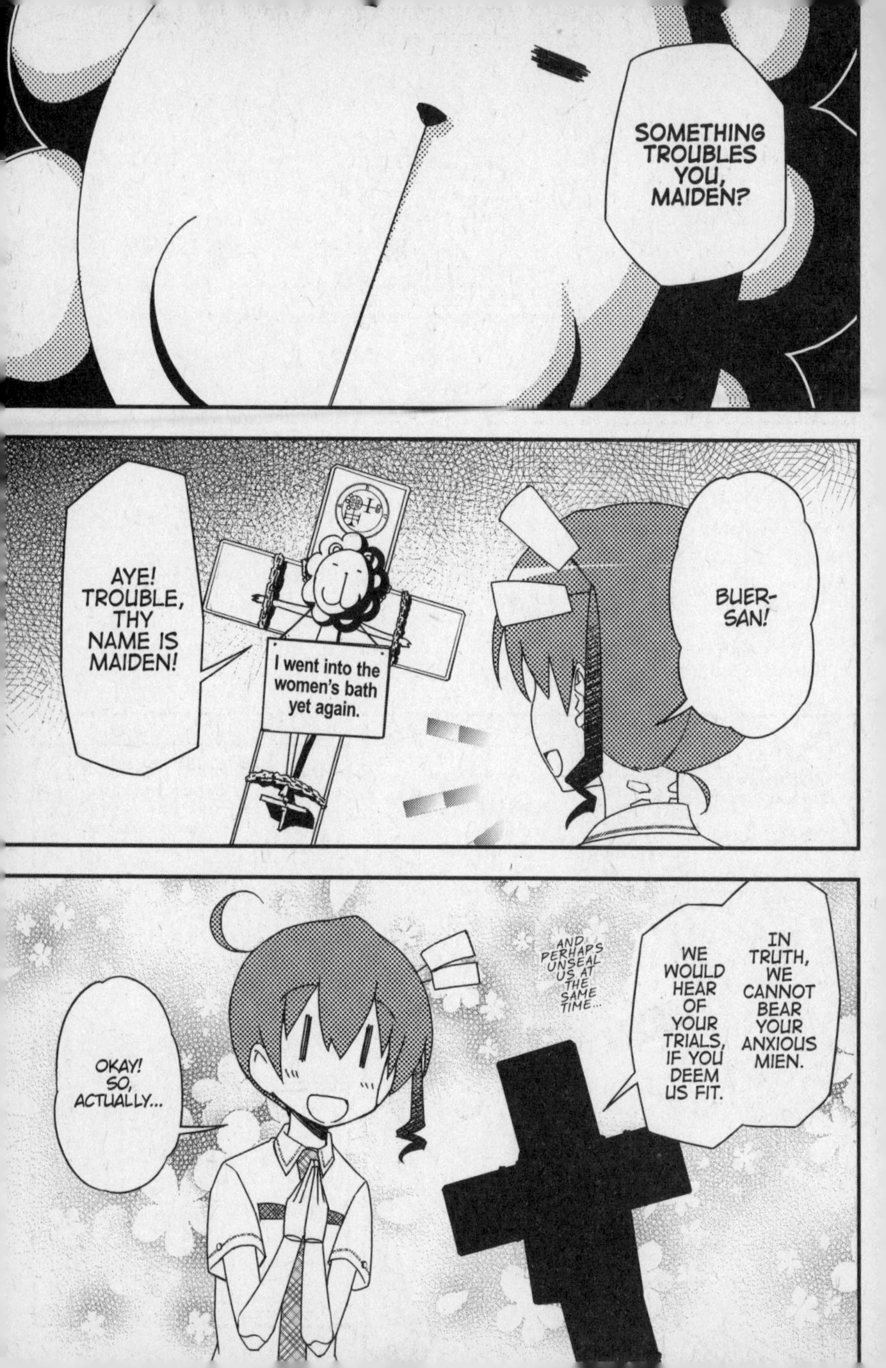
SOMETHING TROUBLES YOU, MAIDEN?
BUER-SAN!
AYE! TROUBLE, THY NAME IS MAIDEN!
I went into the women's bath yet again.
IN TRUTH, WE CANNOT BEAR YOUR ANXIOUS MIEN.
WE WOULD HEAR OF YOUR TRIALS, IF YOU DEEM US FIT.
AND PERHAPS UNSEAL US AT THE SAME TIME...
OKAY! SO, ACTUALLY...

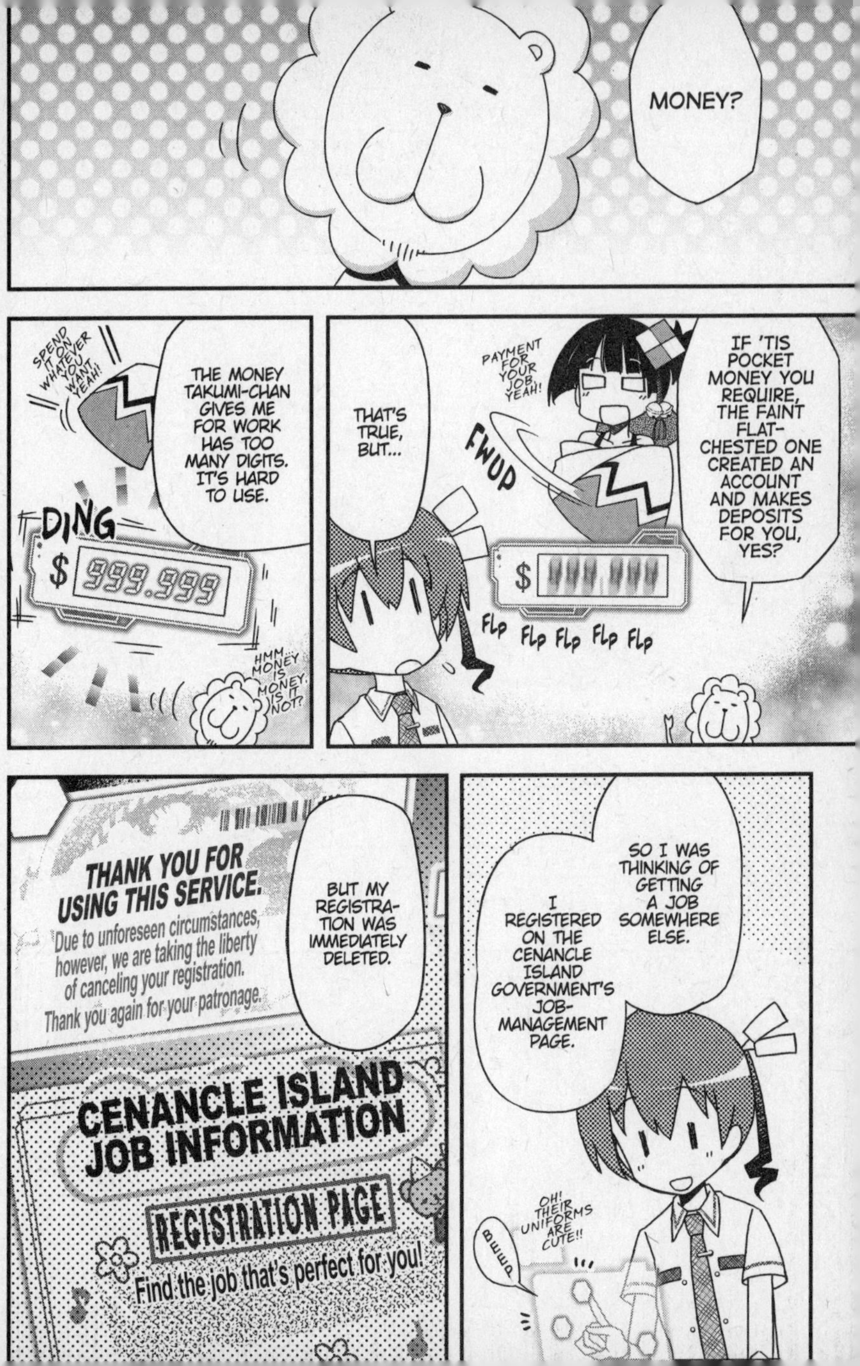
MONEY?
IF 'TIS POCKET MONEY YOU REQUIRE, THE FAINT FLAT-CHESTED ONE CREATED AN ACCOUNT AND MAKES DEPOSITS FOR YOU, YES?
PAYMENT FOR YOUR JOB, YEAH!
FWUP
THAT'S TRUE, BUT...
$
FLP FLP FLP FLP FLP
THE MONEY TAKUMI-CHAN GIVES ME FOR WORK HAS TOO MANY DIGITS. IT'S HARD TO USE.
SPEND IT ON WHATEVER YOU WANT, YEAH!
DING
$ 999.999
HMM... MONEY IS MONEY, IS IT NOT?
SO I WAS THINKING OF GETTING A JOB SOMEWHERE ELSE.
I REGISTERED ON THE CENANCLE ISLAND GOVERNMENT'S JOB-MANAGEMENT PAGE.
OH! THEIR UNIFORMS ARE CUTE!!
BEEP
BUT MY REGISTRATION WAS IMMEDIATELY DELETED.
THANK YOU FOR USING THIS SERVICE.
Due to unforeseen circumstances, however, we are taking the liberty of canceling your registration.
Thank you again for your patronage.
CENANCLE ISLAND JOB INFORMATION
REGISTRATION PAGE
Find the job that's perfect for you!

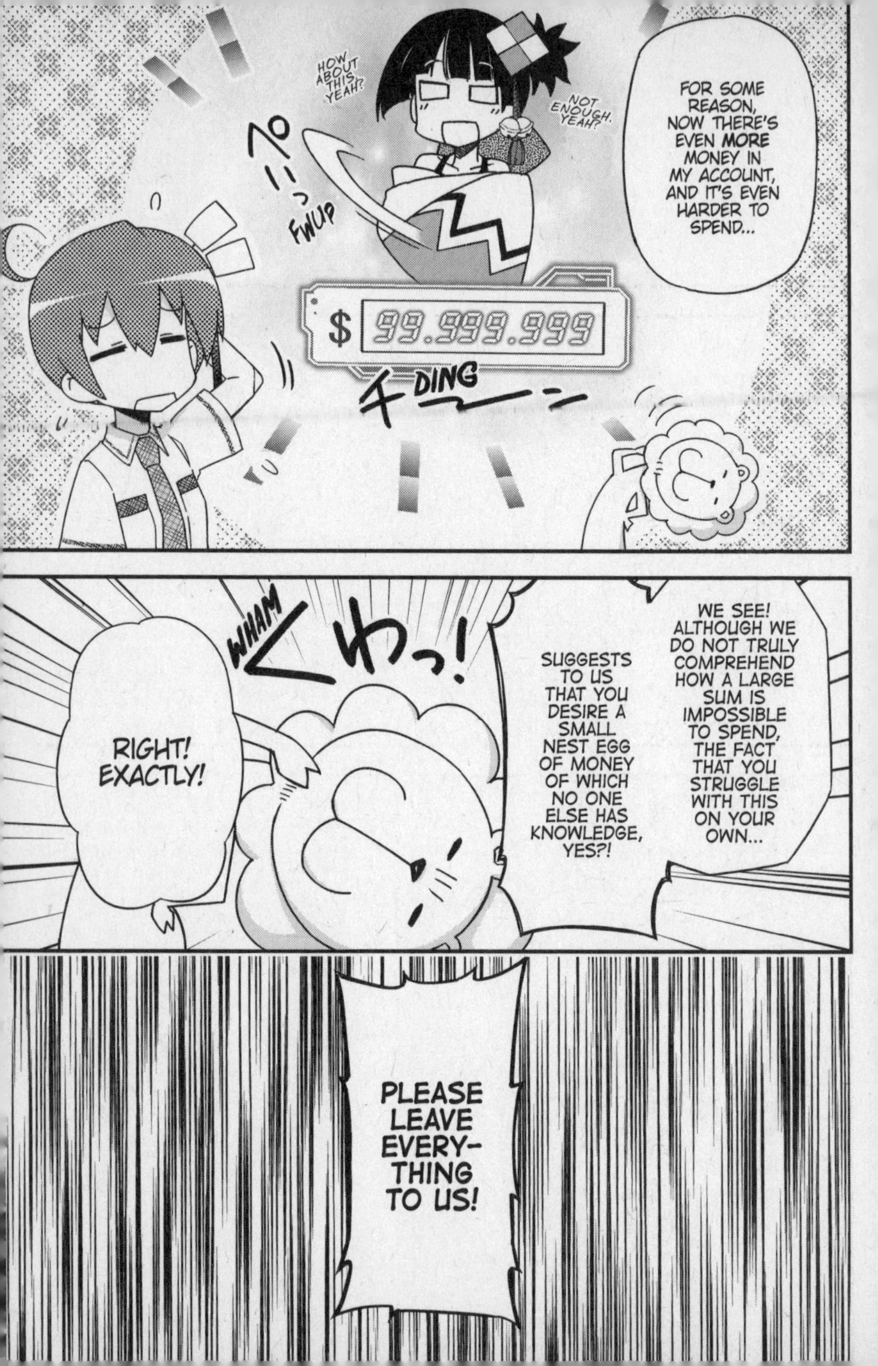
FOR SOME REASON, NOW THERE'S EVEN MORE MONEY IN MY ACCOUNT, AND IT'S EVEN HARDER TO SPEND...
NOT ENOUGH. YEAH?
HOW ABOUT THIS YEAH?
FWUP
$ 99.999.999
DING
WE SEE! ALTHOUGH WE DO NOT TRULY COMPREHEND HOW A LARGE SUM IS IMPOSSIBLE TO SPEND, THE FACT THAT YOU STRUGGLE WITH THIS ON YOUR OWN...
SUGGESTS TO US THAT YOU DESIRE A SMALL NEST EGG OF MONEY OF WHICH NO ONE ELSE HAS KNOWLEDGE, YES?!
WHAM
RIGHT! EXACTLY!
PLEASE LEAVE EVERY-THING TO US!

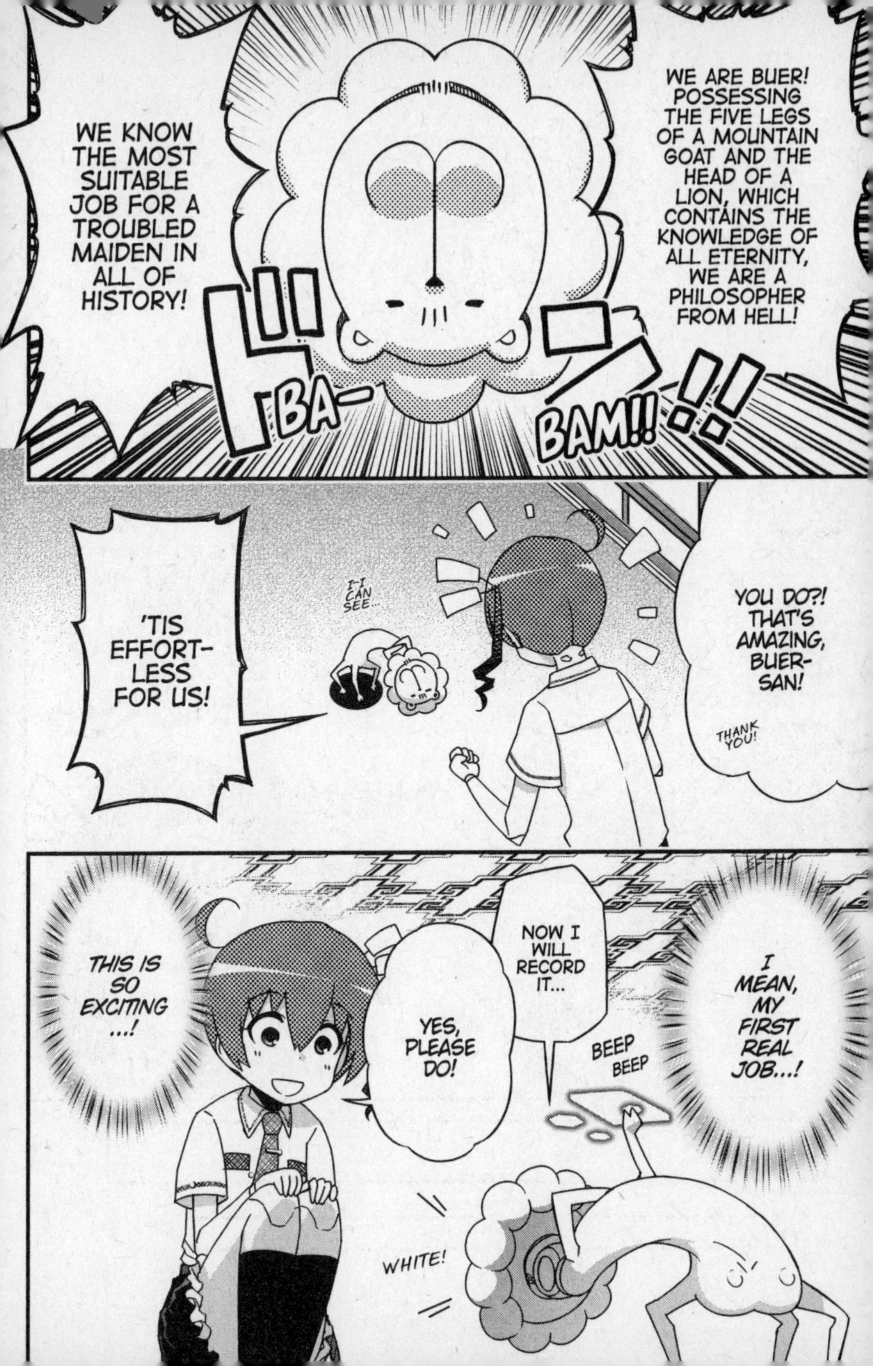
WE ARE BUER! POSSESSING THE FIVE LEGS OF A MOUNTAIN GOAT AND THE HEAD OF A LION, WHICH CONTAINS THE KNOWLEDGE OF ALL ETERNITY, WE ARE A PHILOSOPHER FROM HELL!
WE KNOW THE MOST SUITABLE JOB FOR A TROUBLED MAIDEN IN ALL OF HISTORY!
BA-BAM!!
YOU DO?! THAT'S AMAZING, BUER-SAN!
THANK YOU!
I-I CAN SEE...
'TIS EFFORTLESS FOR US!
I MEAN, MY FIRST REAL JOB...!
NOW I WILL RECORD IT...
BEEP BEEP
YES, PLEASE DO!
THIS IS SO EXCITING...!
WHITE!

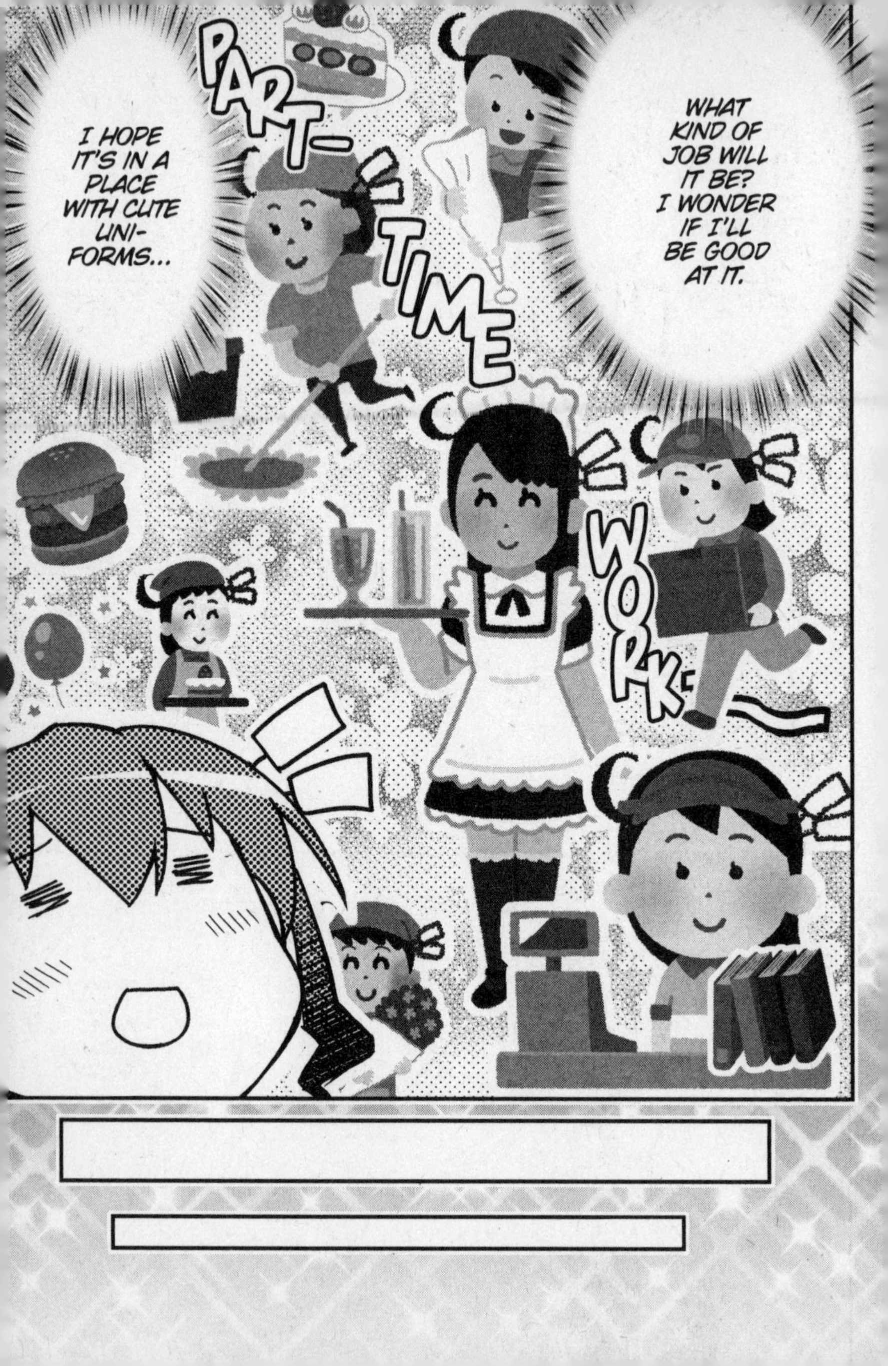
WHAT KIND OF JOB WILL IT BE? I WONDER IF I'LL BE GOOD AT IT.
PART-TIME WORK
I HOPE IT'S IN A PLACE WITH CUTE UNI-FORMS...

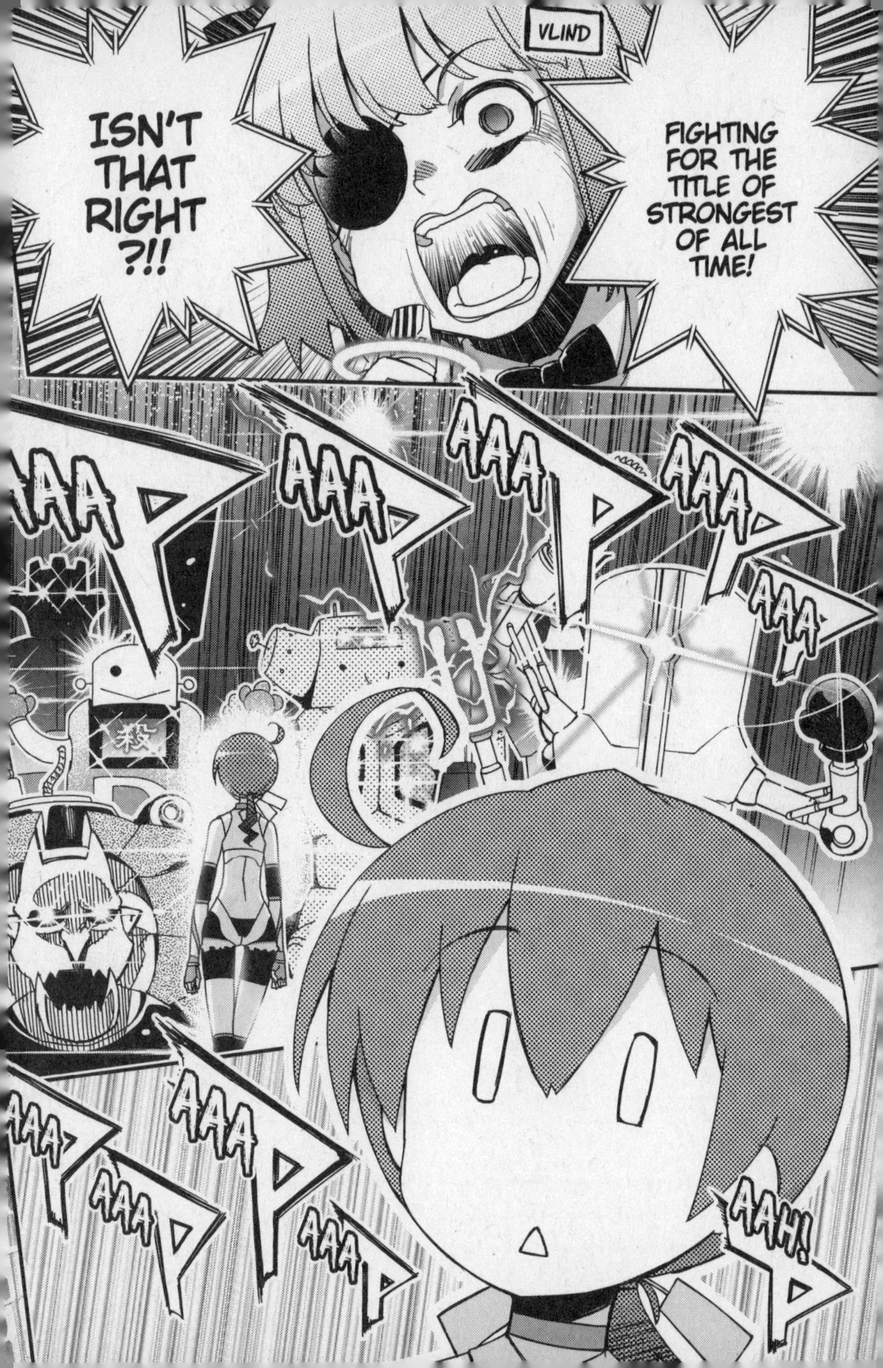

VLIND
FIGHTING FOR THE TITLE OF STRONGEST OF ALL TIME!
ISN'T THAT RIGHT?!!
AAA
AAA
AAA
AAA
AAA
殺
AAH!
AAA
AAA
AAA
AAA

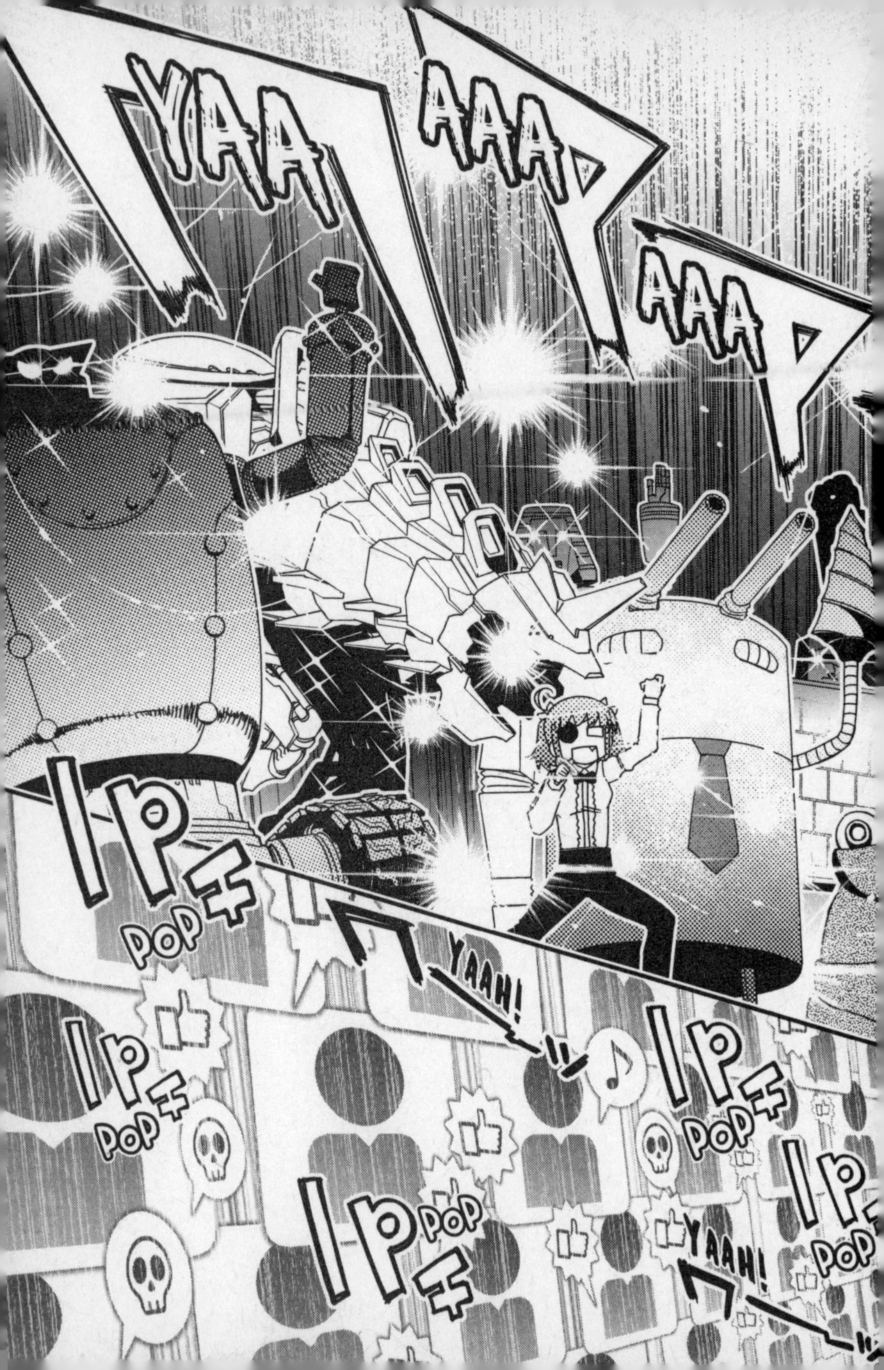
YAAAAAAAAA
POP
YAAH!
POP
POP
POP
YAAH!
POP

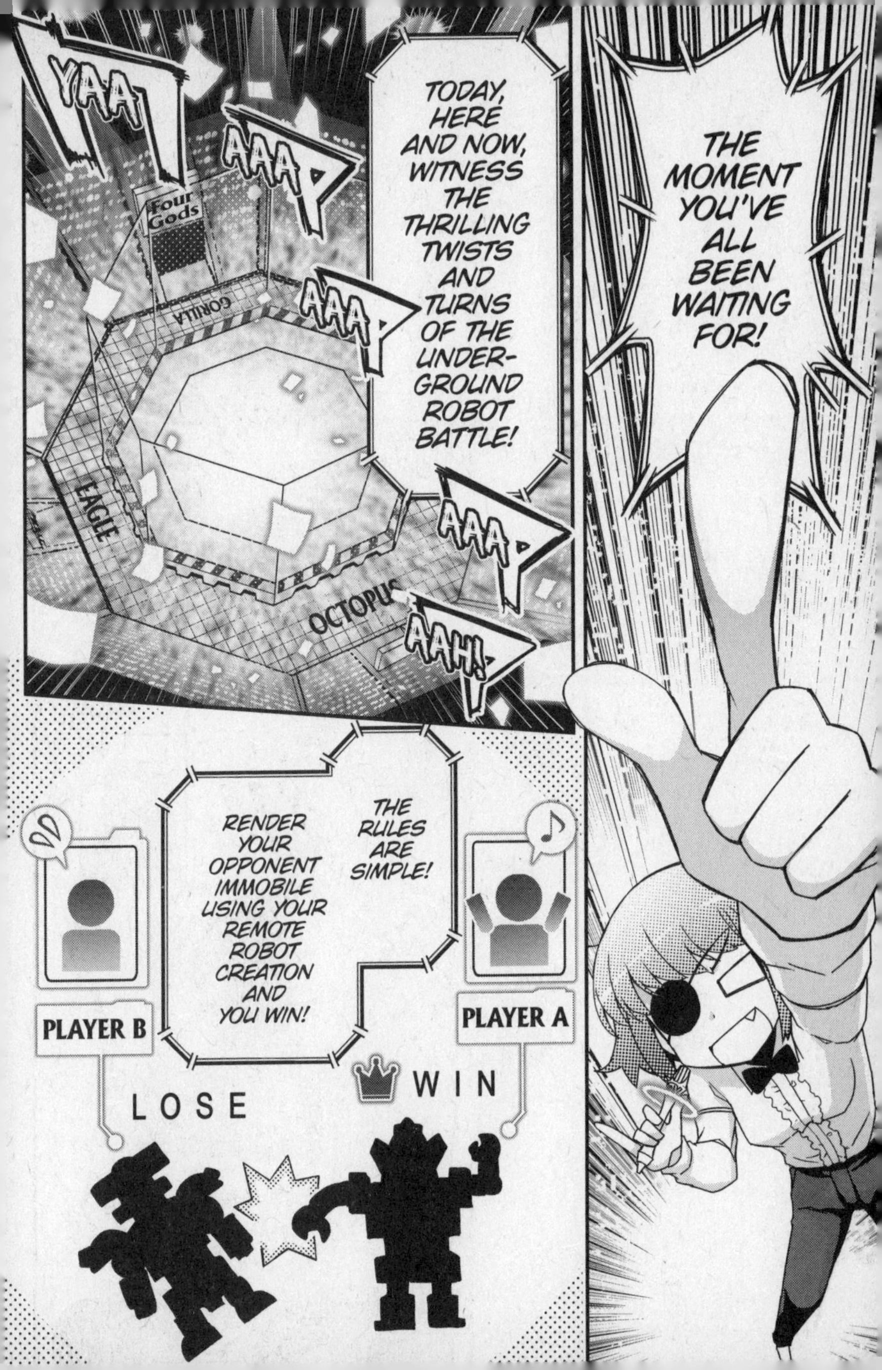
THE MOMENT YOU'VE ALL BEEN WAITING FOR!
TODAY, HERE AND NOW, WITNESS THE THRILLING TWISTS AND TURNS OF THE UNDER-GROUND ROBOT BATTLE!
YAA
AAA
AAA
AAA
AAH!
Four Gods
GORILLA
EAGLE
OCTOPUS
THE RULES ARE SIMPLE!
RENDER YOUR OPPONENT IMMOBILE USING YOUR REMOTE ROBOT CREATION AND YOU WIN!
PLAYER A
WIN
PLAYER B
LOSE

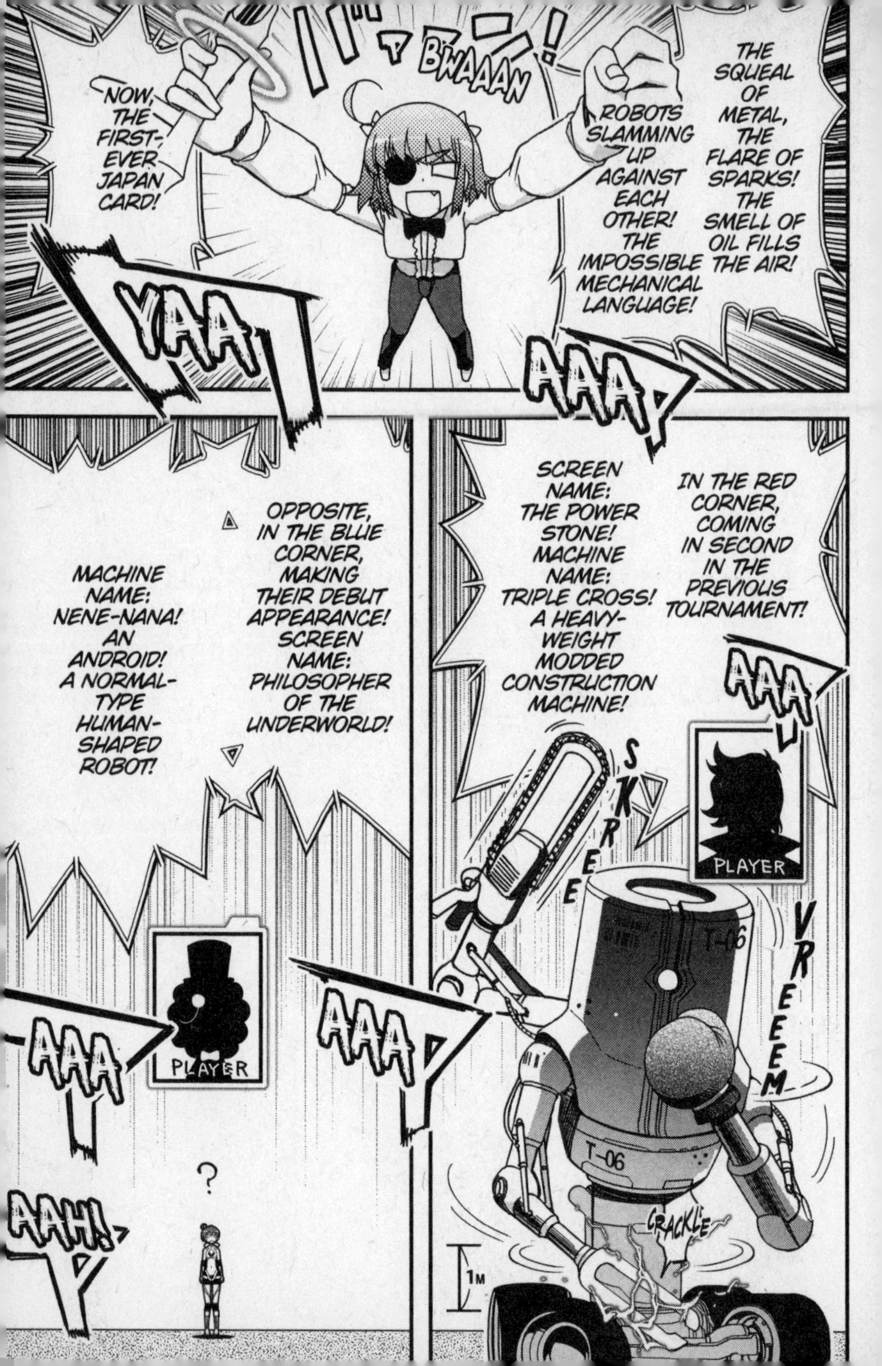
BWAAAN
THE SQUEAL OF METAL, THE FLARE OF SPARKS! THE SMELL OF OIL FILLS THE AIR!
ROBOTS SLAMMING UP AGAINST EACH OTHER! THE IMPOSSIBLE MECHANICAL LANGUAGE!
NOW, THE FIRST-EVER JAPAN CARD!
YAAA
AAA
IN THE RED CORNER, COMING IN SECOND IN THE PREVIOUS TOURNAMENT!
SCREEN NAME: THE POWER STONE! MACHINE NAME: TRIPLE CROSS! A HEAVY-WEIGHT MODDED CONSTRUCTION MACHINE!
AAA
SKREEE
PLAYER
T-06
VRREEEEM
T-06
CRACKLE
1M
OPPOSITE, IN THE BLUE CORNER, MAKING THEIR DEBUT APPEARANCE! SCREEN NAME: PHILOSOPHER OF THE UNDERWORLD!
MACHINE NAME: NENE-NANA! AN ANDROID! A NORMAL-TYPE HUMAN-SHAPED ROBOT!
AAA
PLAYER
AAA
?
AAH!

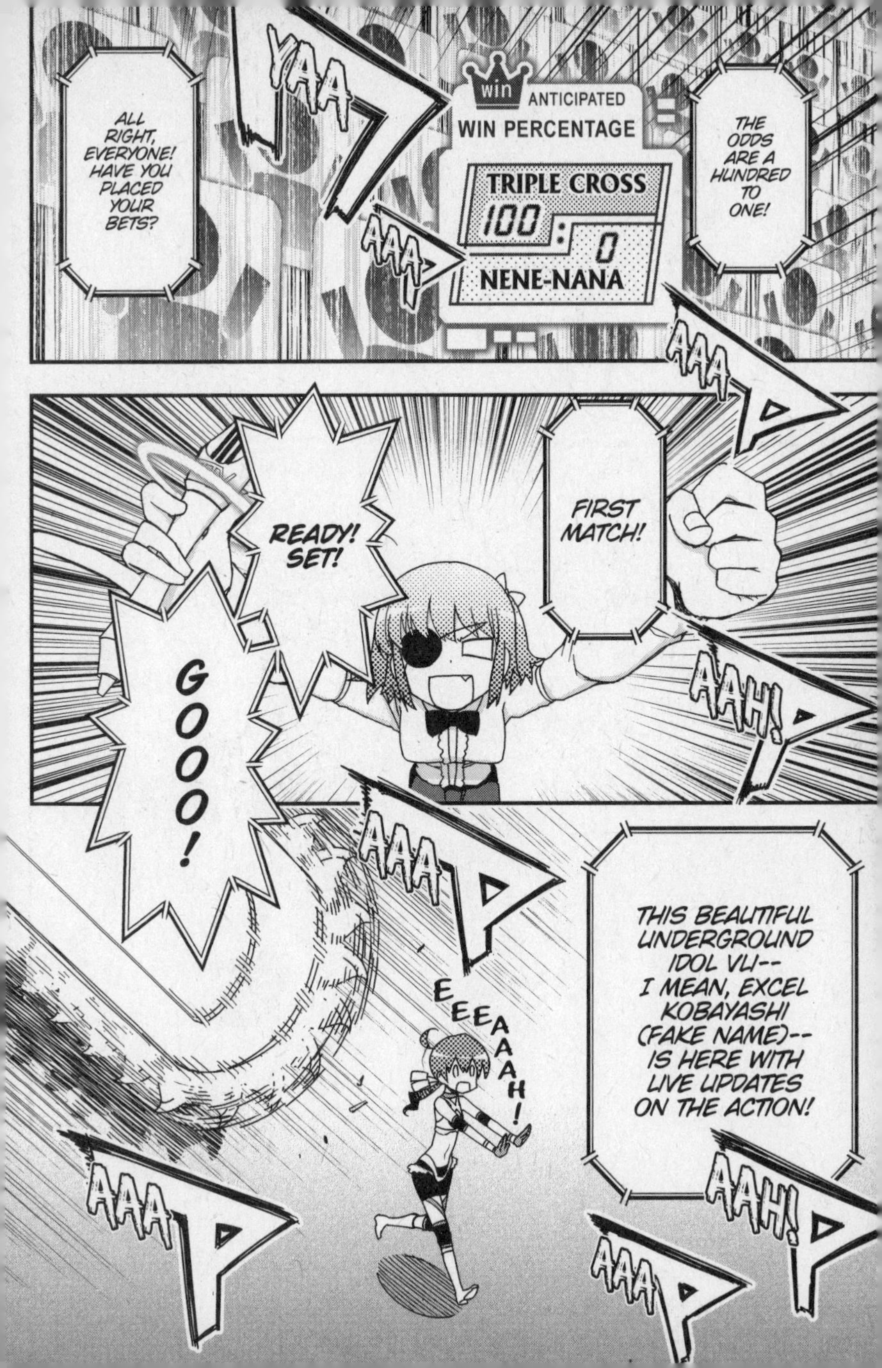

THE ODDS ARE A HUNDRED TO ONE!
WIN ANTICIPATED WIN PERCENTAGE
TRIPLE CROSS 100 : 0 NENE-NANA
YAA
AAA
ALL RIGHT, EVERYONE! HAVE YOU PLACED YOUR BETS?
AAA
FIRST MATCH!
AAH!
READY! SET!
GOOOO!
THIS BEAUTIFUL UNDERGROUND IDOL VLI-- I MEAN, EXCEL KOBAYASHI (FAKE NAME)-- IS HERE WITH LIVE UPDATES ON THE ACTION!
AAH!
AAA
AAA
EEEAAAAH!
AAA

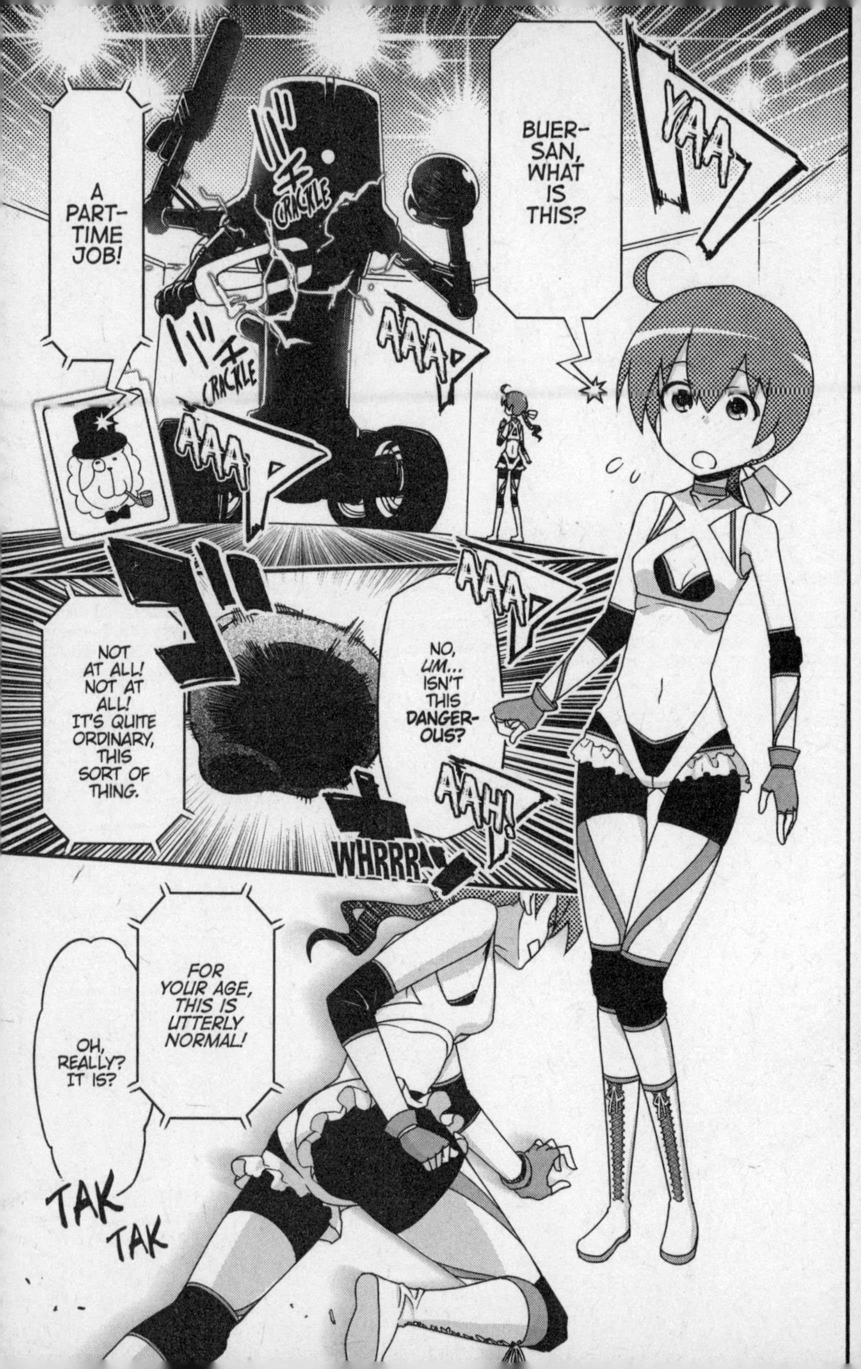
YAA
BUER-SAN, WHAT IS THIS?
AAA
CRACKLE
CRACKLE
A PART-TIME JOB!
AAA
AAA
NO, UM... ISN'T THIS DANGEROUS?
AAH!
NOT AT ALL! NOT AT ALL! IT'S QUITE ORDINARY, THIS SORT OF THING.
WHRRR
FOR YOUR AGE, THIS IS UTTERLY NORMAL!
OH, REALLY? IT IS?
TAK TAK

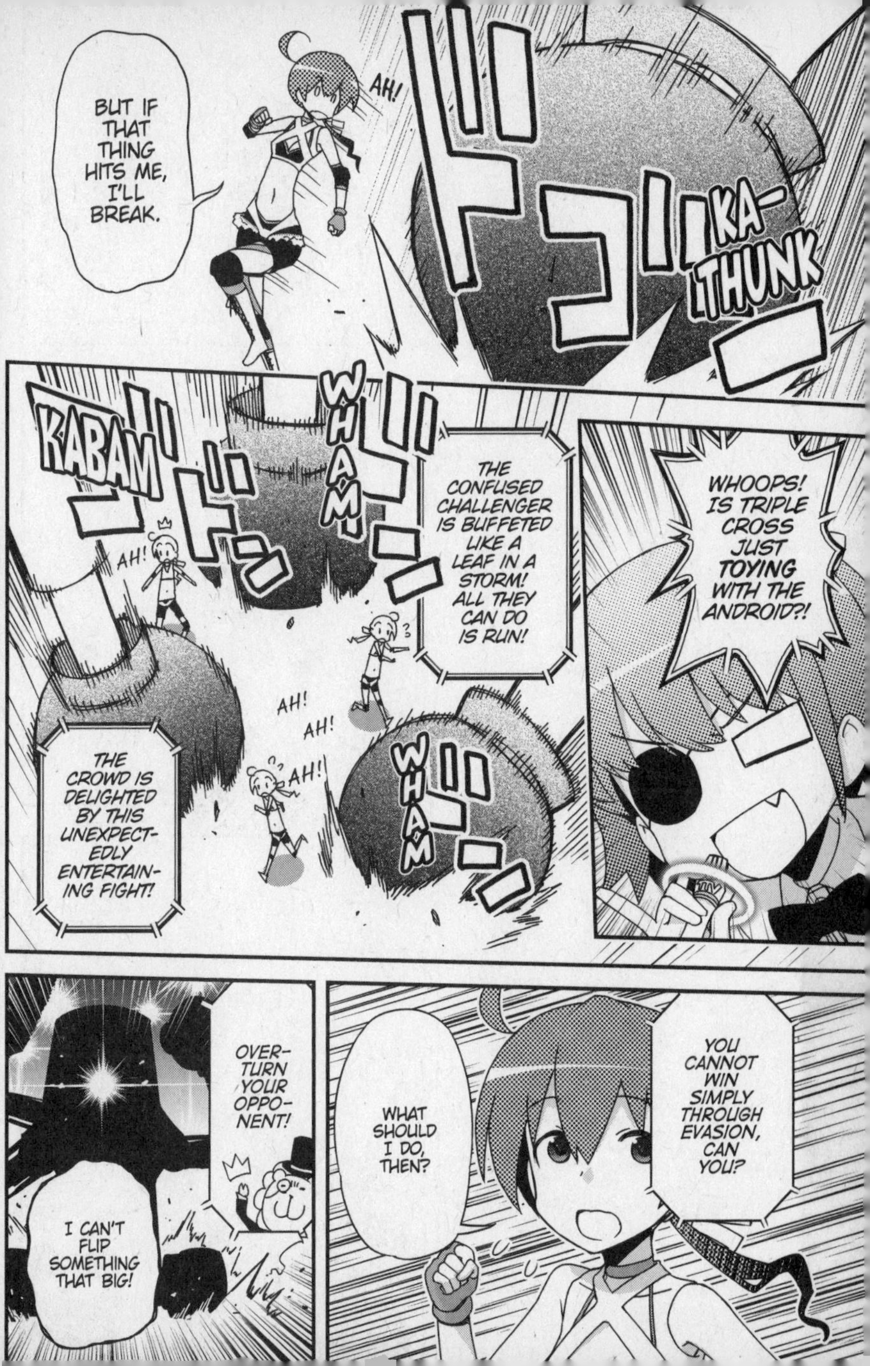
KA-THUNK
AH!
BUT IF THAT THING HITS ME, I'LL BREAK.
WHOOPS! IS TRIPLE CROSS JUST **TOYING** WITH THE ANDROID?!
WHAM
THE CONFUSED CHALLENGER IS BUFFETED LIKE A LEAF IN A STORM! ALL THEY CAN DO IS RUN!
KABAM
AH!
AH!
AH!
AH!
WHAM
THE CROWD IS DELIGHTED BY THIS UNEXPECTEDLY ENTERTAINING FIGHT!
YOU CANNOT WIN SIMPLY THROUGH EVASION, CAN YOU?
WHAT SHOULD I DO, THEN?
OVERTURN YOUR OPPONENT!
I CAN'T FLIP SOMETHING THAT BIG!

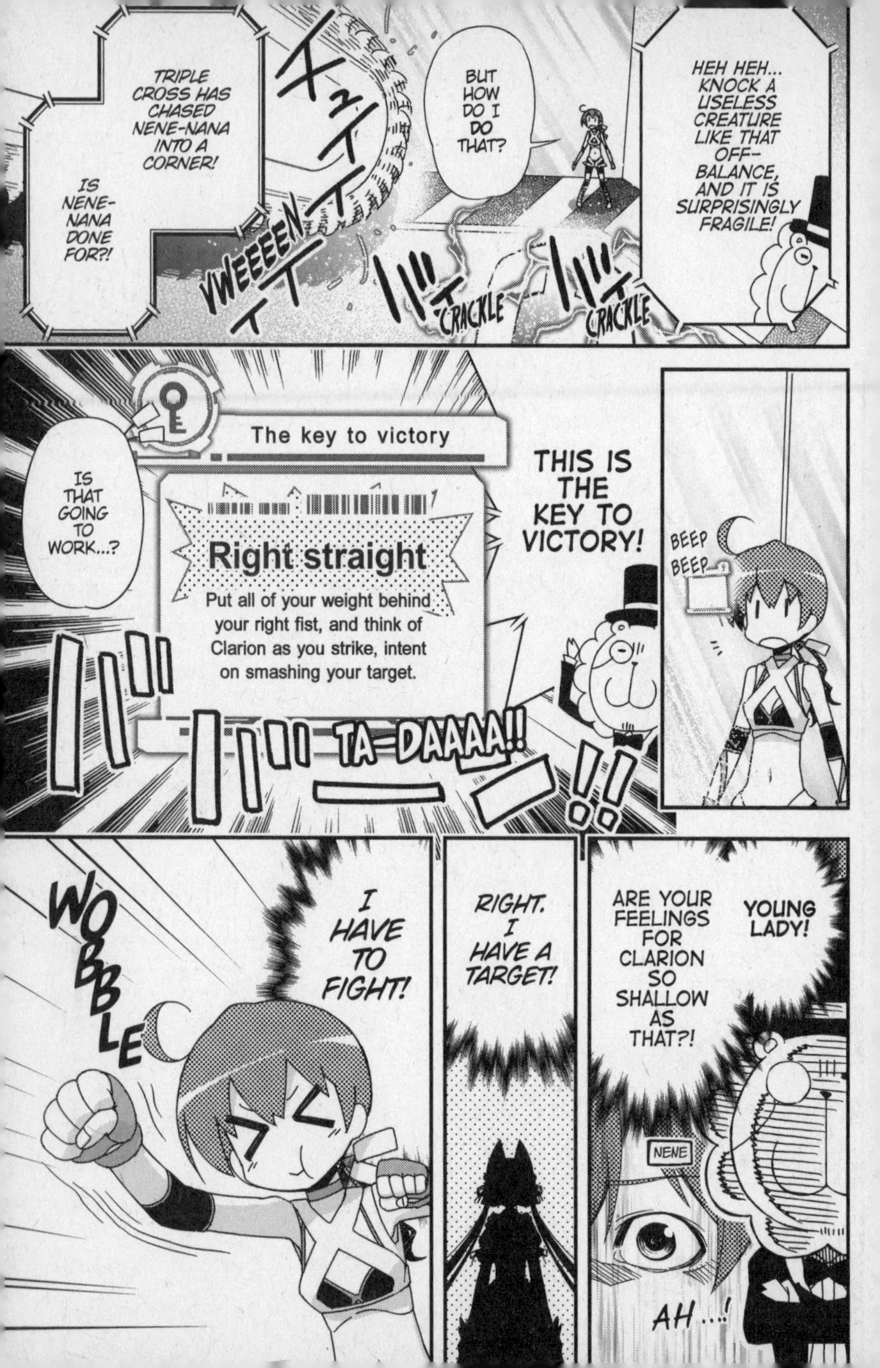
HEH HEH... KNOCK A USELESS CREATURE LIKE THAT OFF-BALANCE, AND IT IS SURPRISINGLY FRAGILE!
CRACKLE
CRACKLE
BUT HOW DO I DO THAT?
YWEEEEEN
TRIPLE CROSS HAS CHASED NENE-NANA INTO A CORNER!
IS NENE-NANA DONE FOR?!
BEEP BEEP
THIS IS THE KEY TO VICTORY!
The key to victory
Right straight
Put all of your weight behind your right fist, and think of Clarion as you strike, intent on smashing your target.
TA-DAAAA!!
IS THAT GOING TO WORK...?
YOUNG LADY!
ARE YOUR FEELINGS FOR CLARION SO SHALLOW AS THAT?!
NENE
AH...!
RIGHT. I HAVE A TARGET!
I HAVE TO FIGHT!
WOBBLE

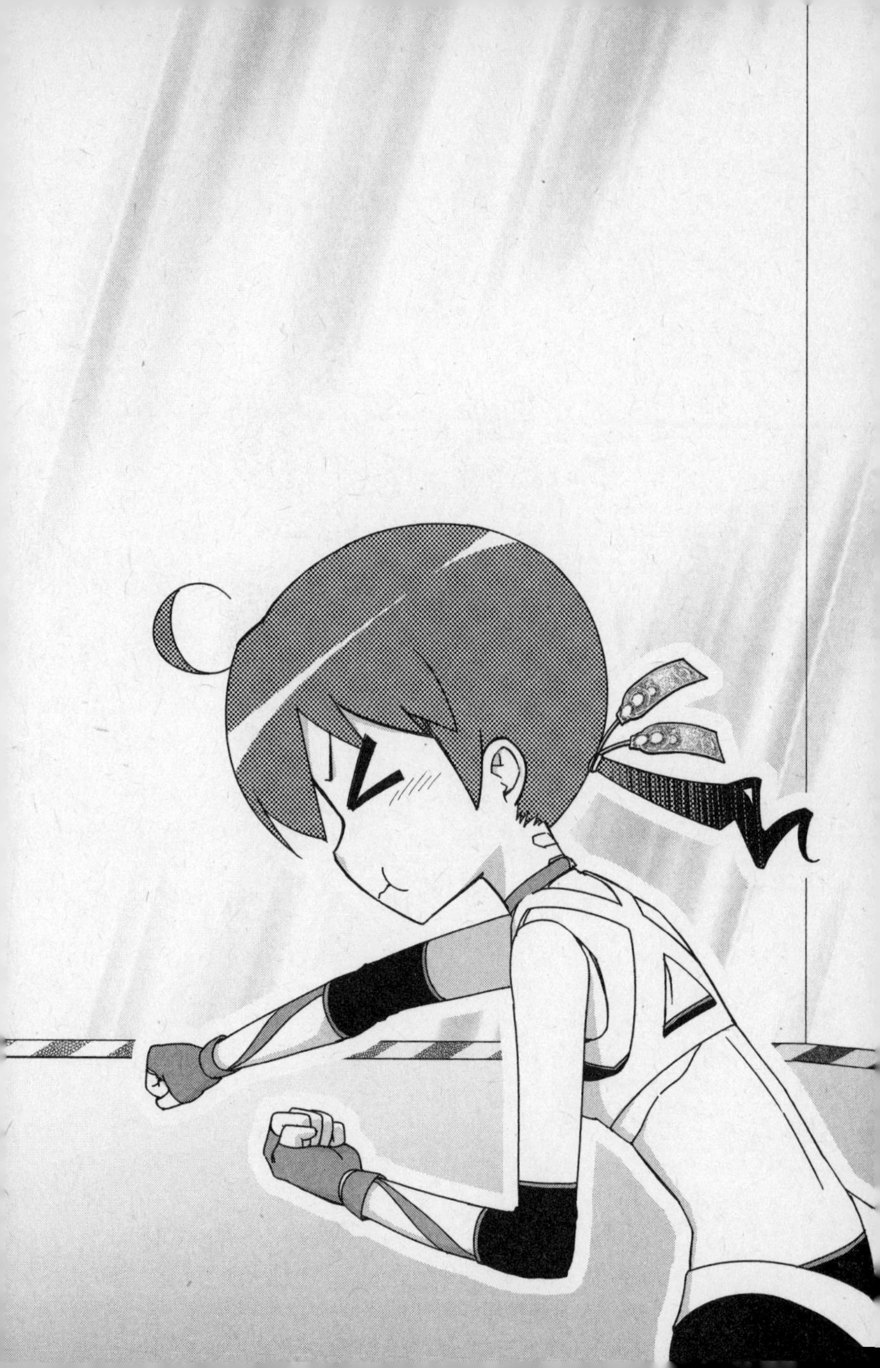

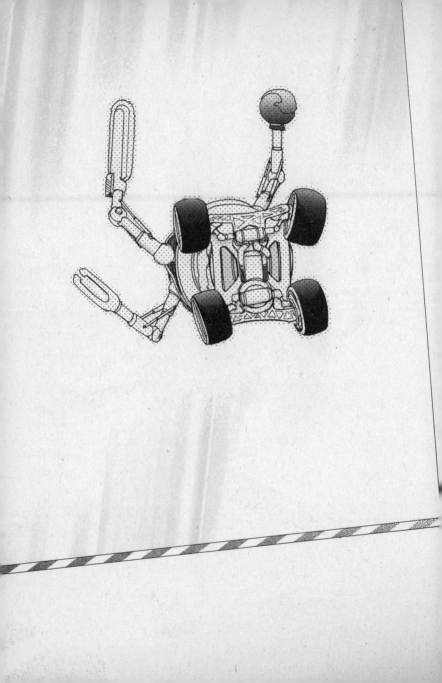

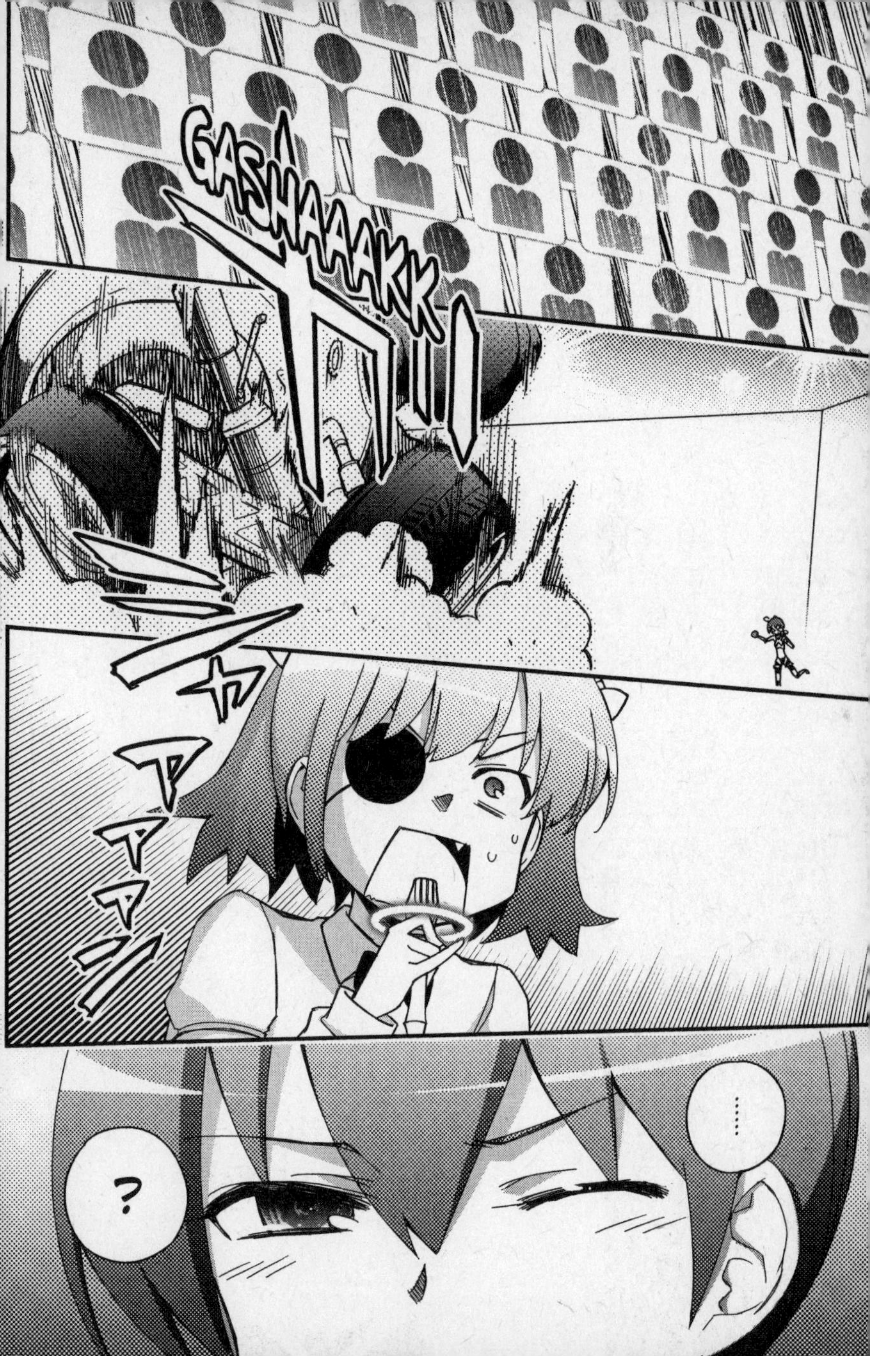
GASHAAAKK
カアアアン
……
?

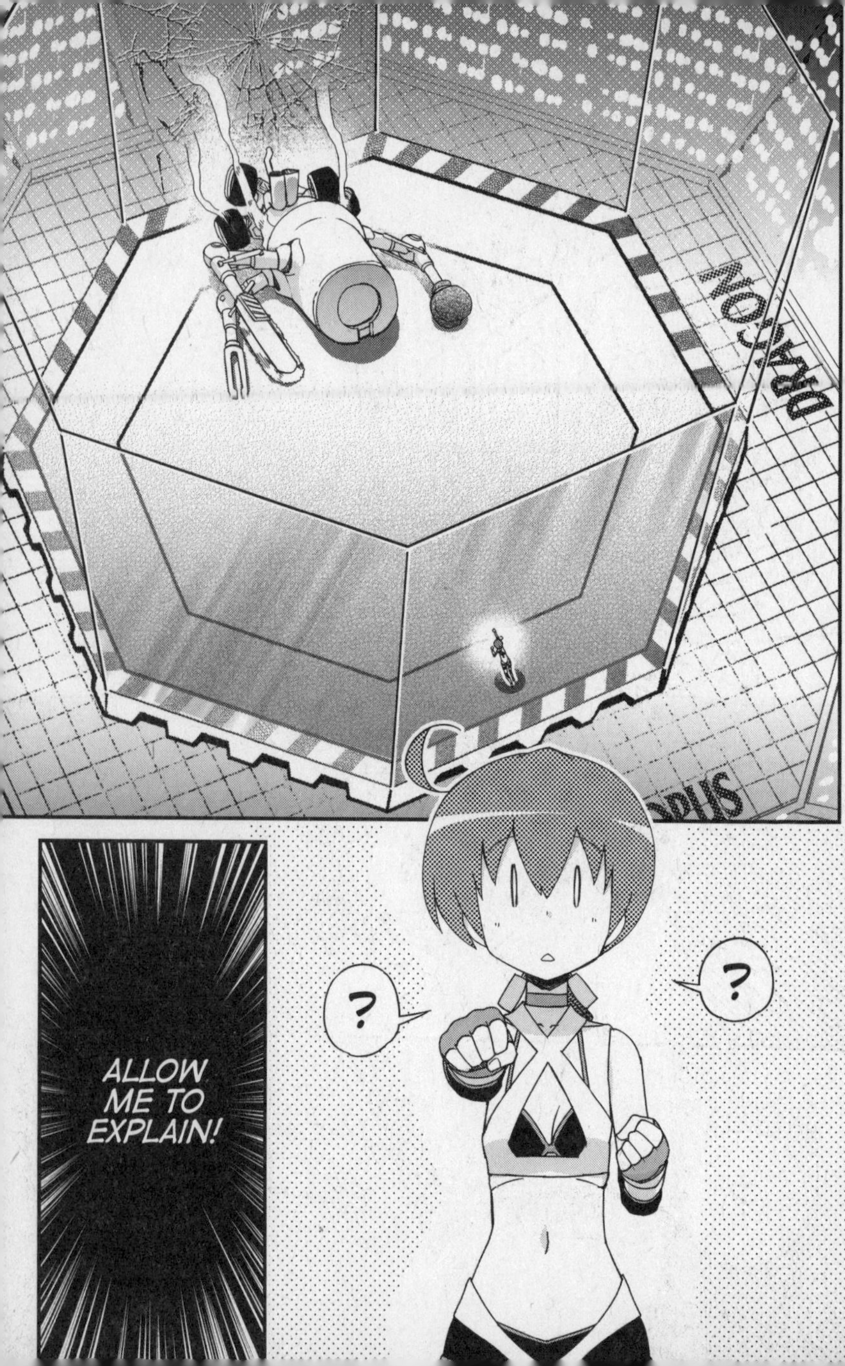
DRAGON
?
?
ALLOW ME TO EXPLAIN!

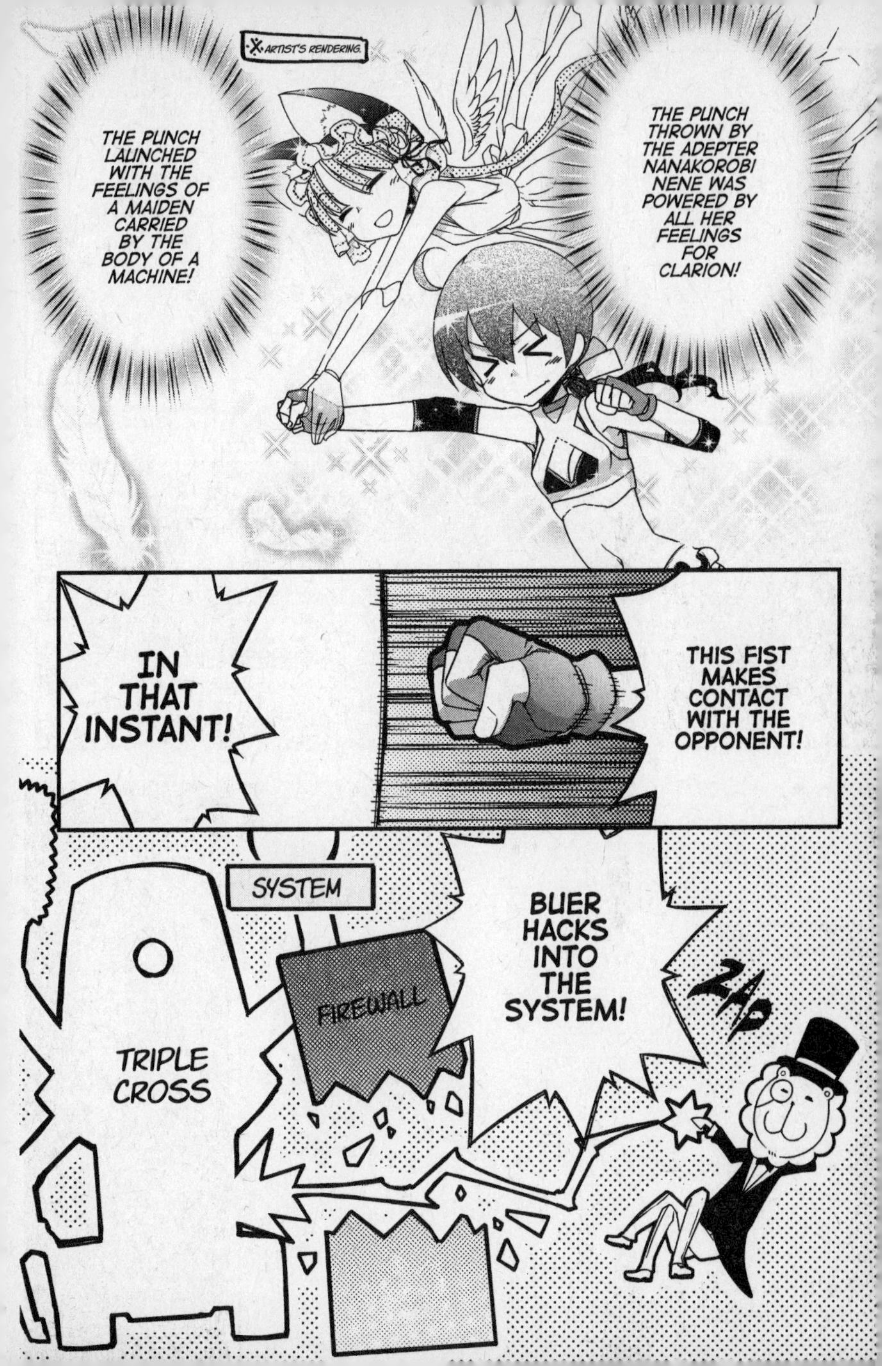
※ARTIST'S RENDERING.
THE PUNCH THROWN BY THE ADEPTER NANAKOROBI NENE WAS POWERED BY ALL HER FEELINGS FOR CLARION!
THE PUNCH LAUNCHED WITH THE FEELINGS OF A MAIDEN CARRIED BY THE BODY OF A MACHINE!
THIS FIST MAKES CONTACT WITH THE OPPONENT!
IN THAT INSTANT!
BUER HACKS INTO THE SYSTEM!
ZAP
SYSTEM
FIREWALL
TRIPLE CROSS

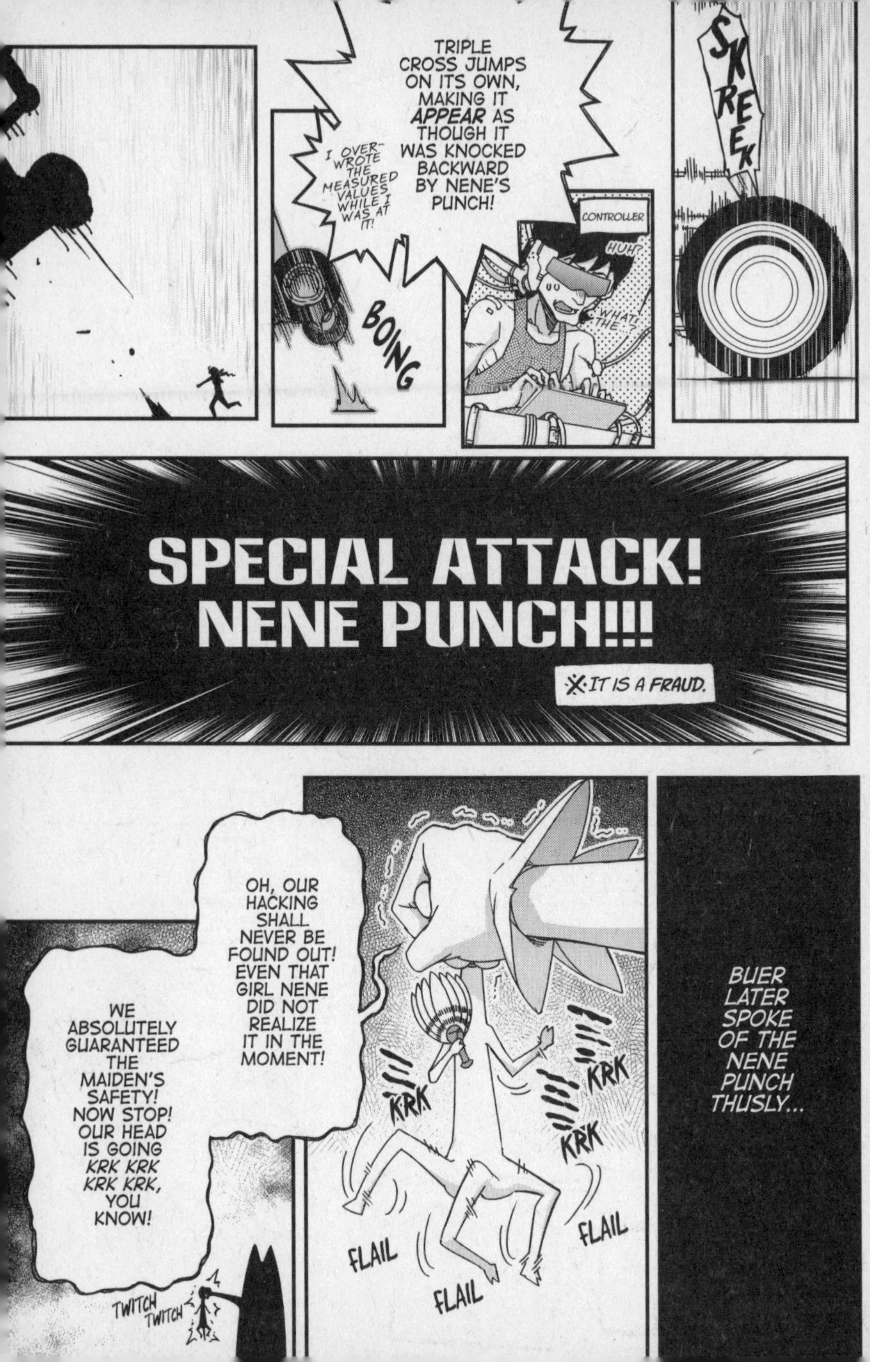

SKREEK
CONTROLLER
HUH?
WHAT! THE...?
TRIPLE CROSS JUMPS ON ITS OWN, MAKING IT *APPEAR* AS THOUGH IT WAS KNOCKED BACKWARD BY NENE'S PUNCH!
I OVERWROTE THE MEASURED VALUES WHILE I WAS AT IT!
BOING
SPECIAL ATTACK! NENE PUNCH!!!
※IT IS A FRAUD.
BUER LATER SPOKE OF THE NENE PUNCH THUSLY...
OH, OUR HACKING SHALL NEVER BE FOUND OUT! EVEN THAT GIRL NENE DID NOT REALIZE IT IN THE MOMENT!
WE ABSOLUTELY GUARANTEED THE MAIDEN'S SAFETY! NOW STOP! OUR HEAD IS GOING *KRK KRK KRK KRK*, YOU KNOW!
KRK
KRK
KRK
FLAIL
FLAIL
FLAIL
TWITCH TWITCH

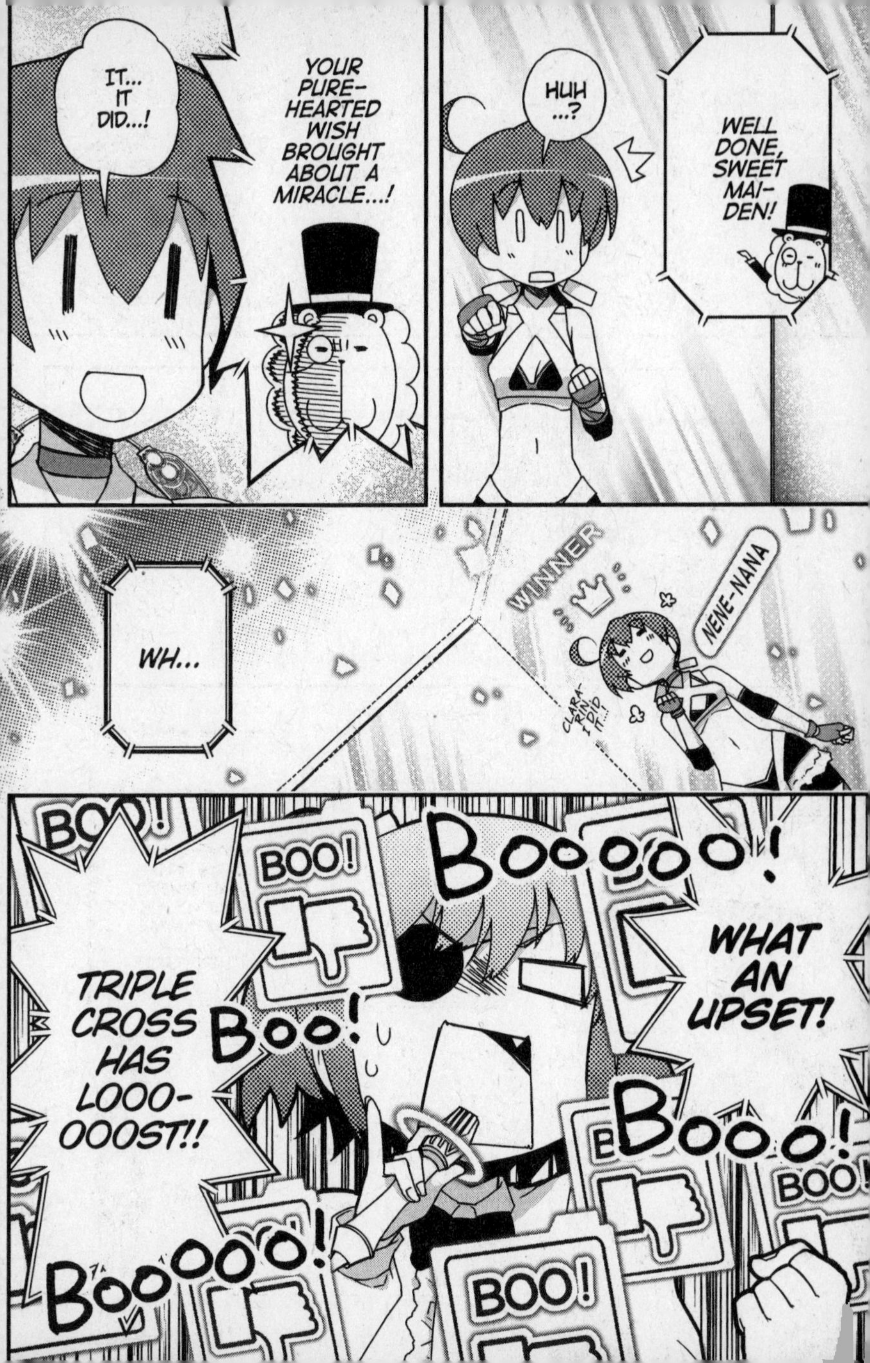
WELL DONE, SWEET MAI-DEN!
HUH ...?
YOUR PURE-HEARTED WISH BROUGHT ABOUT A MIRACLE...!
IT... IT DID...!
NENE-NANA
WINNER
CLARA-RIN, I DID IT...!
WH...
BOO!
BOOOOO!
WHAT AN UPSET!
BOOO!
BOO!
BOO!
BOO!
TRIPLE CROSS HAS LOOO-OOOST!!
BOO!
BOO!
BOOOOO!
BOO!

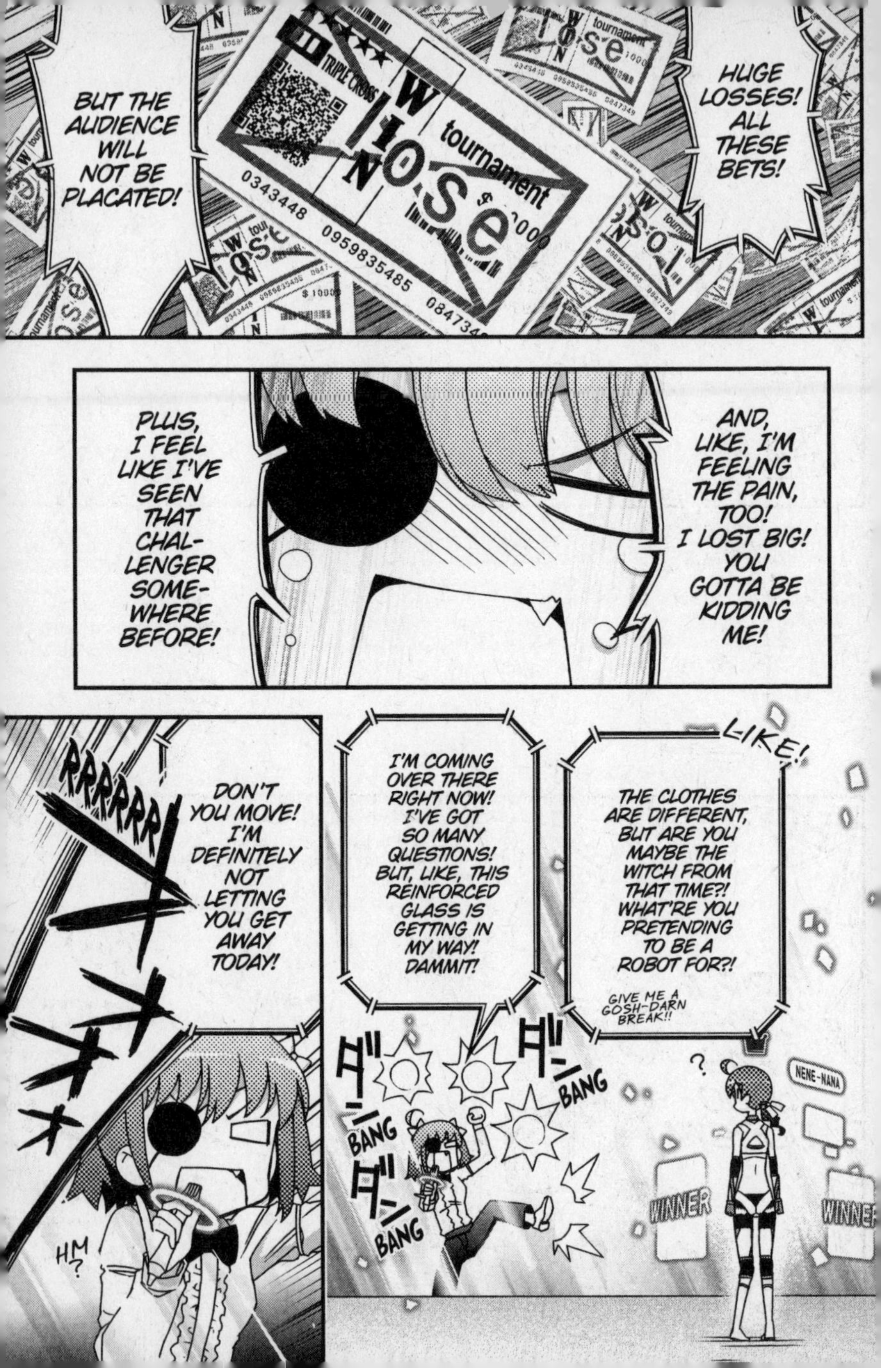
HUGE LOSSES! ALL THESE BETS!
BUT THE AUDIENCE WILL NOT BE PLACATED!
TRIPLE CROSS
WIN
lose
tournament
0343448
0959835485
0847349
AND, LIKE, I'M FEELING THE PAIN, TOO! I LOST BIG! YOU GOTTA BE KIDDING ME!
PLUS, I FEEL LIKE I'VE SEEN THAT CHAL-LENGER SOME-WHERE BEFORE!
-LIKE!
THE CLOTHES ARE DIFFERENT, BUT ARE YOU MAYBE THE WITCH FROM THAT TIME?! WHAT'RE YOU PRETENDING TO BE A ROBOT FOR?!
GIVE ME A GOSH-DARN BREAK!!
I'M COMING OVER THERE RIGHT NOW! I'VE GOT SO MANY QUESTIONS! BUT, LIKE, THIS REINFORCED GLASS IS GETTING IN MY WAY! DAMMIT!
BANG
BANG
BANG
?
NENE-NANA
WINNER
WINNER
RRRRRRR
DON'T YOU MOVE! I'M DEFINITELY NOT LETTING YOU GET AWAY TODAY!
HM?

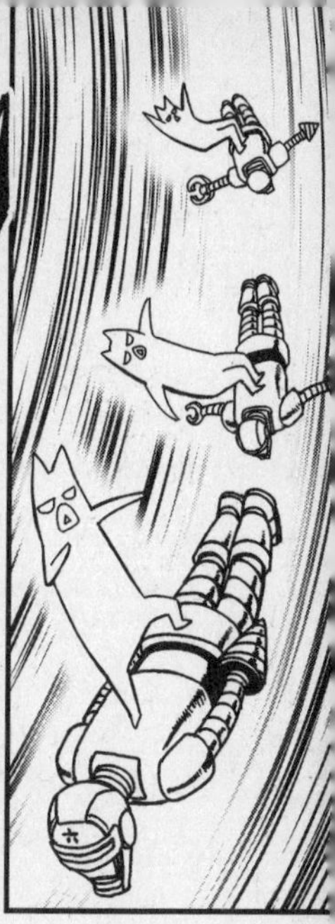

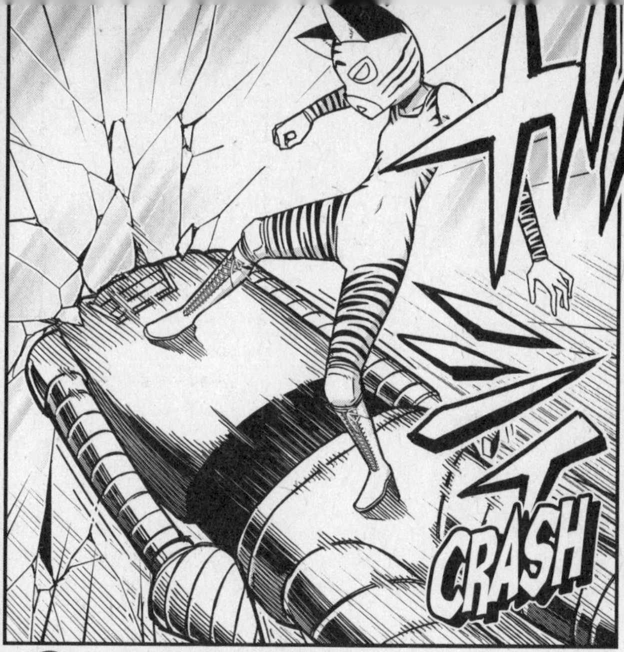
CRASH

FOR THE DESIGN OF THIS ROBOT, I REFERRED TO RIKUDOU KOUSHI-KUN'S DESIGN. THANK YOU.

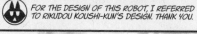

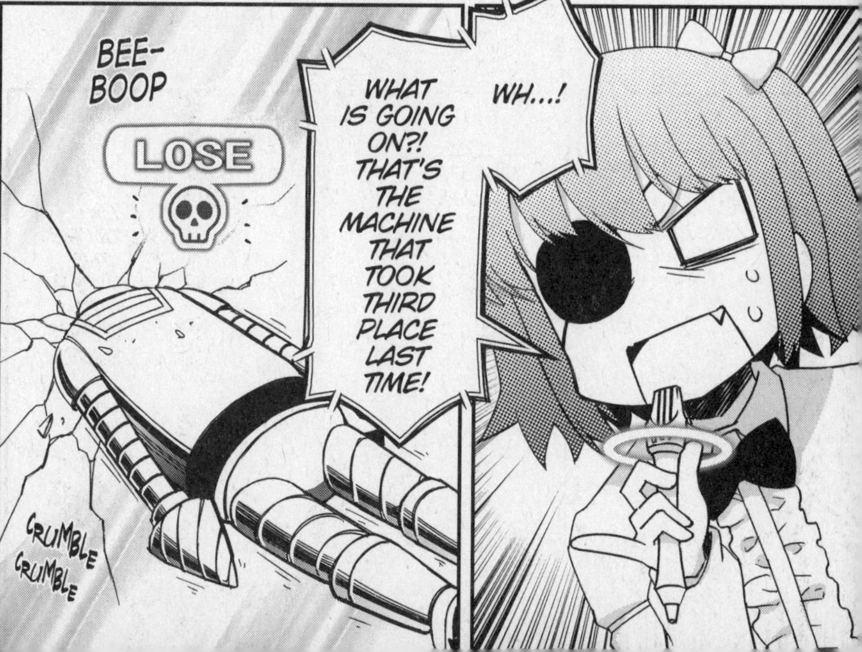
WH...!
WHAT IS GOING ON?! THAT'S THE MACHINE THAT TOOK THIRD PLACE LAST TIME!
BEE-BOOP
LOSE
CRUMBLE CRUMBLE

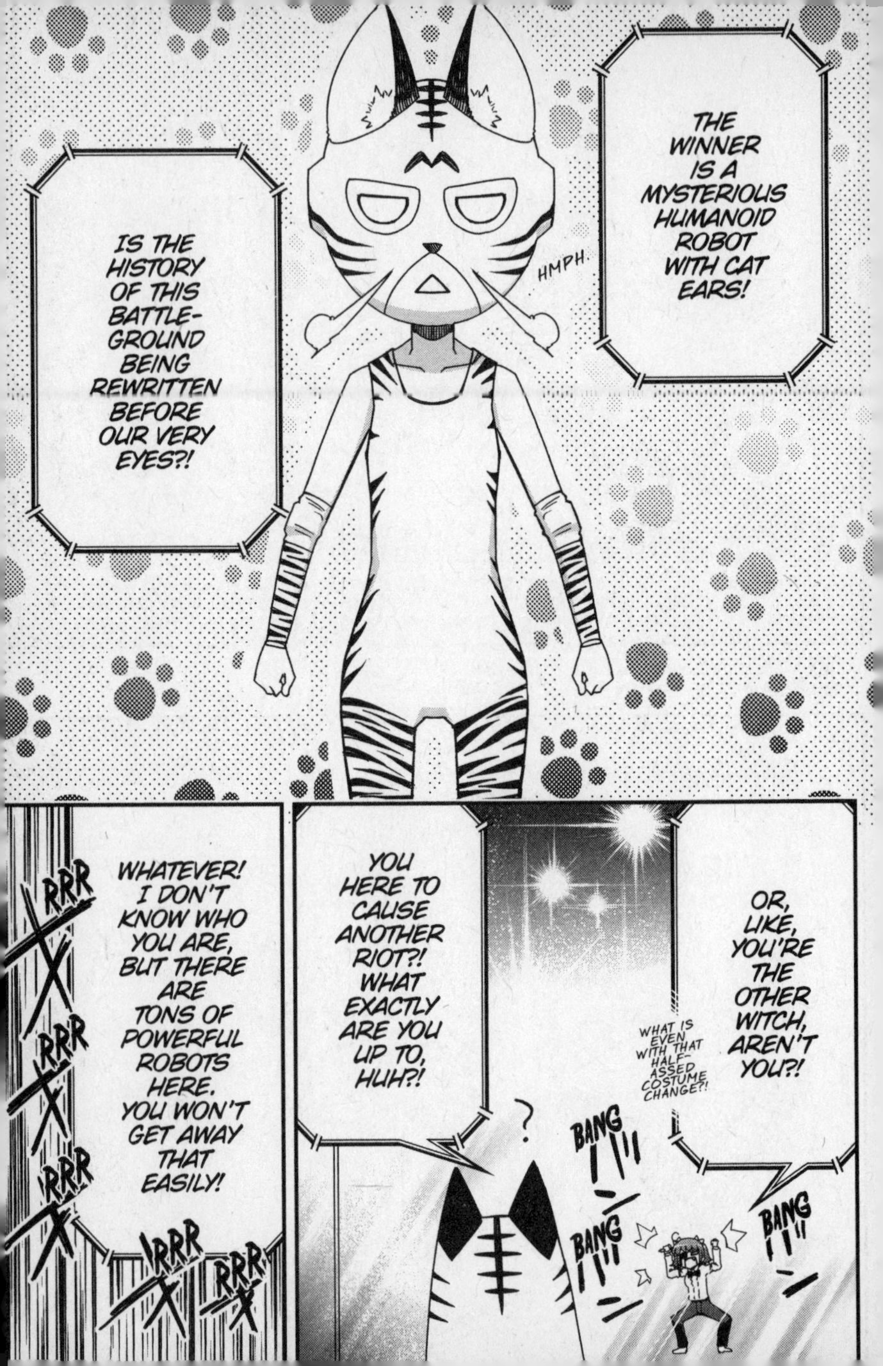
THE WINNER IS A MYSTERIOUS HUMANOID ROBOT WITH CAT EARS!
HMPH.
IS THE HISTORY OF THIS BATTLE-GROUND BEING REWRITTEN BEFORE OUR VERY EYES?!
OR, LIKE, YOU'RE THE OTHER WITCH, AREN'T YOU?!
WHAT IS EVEN WITH THAT HALF-ASSED COSTUME CHANGE?!
BANG
BANG
BANG
YOU HERE TO CAUSE ANOTHER RIOT?! WHAT EXACTLY ARE YOU UP TO, HUH?!
?
WHATEVER! I DON'T KNOW WHO YOU ARE, BUT THERE ARE TONS OF POWERFUL ROBOTS HERE. YOU WON'T GET AWAY THAT EASILY!
RRR
RRR
RRR
RRR
RRR

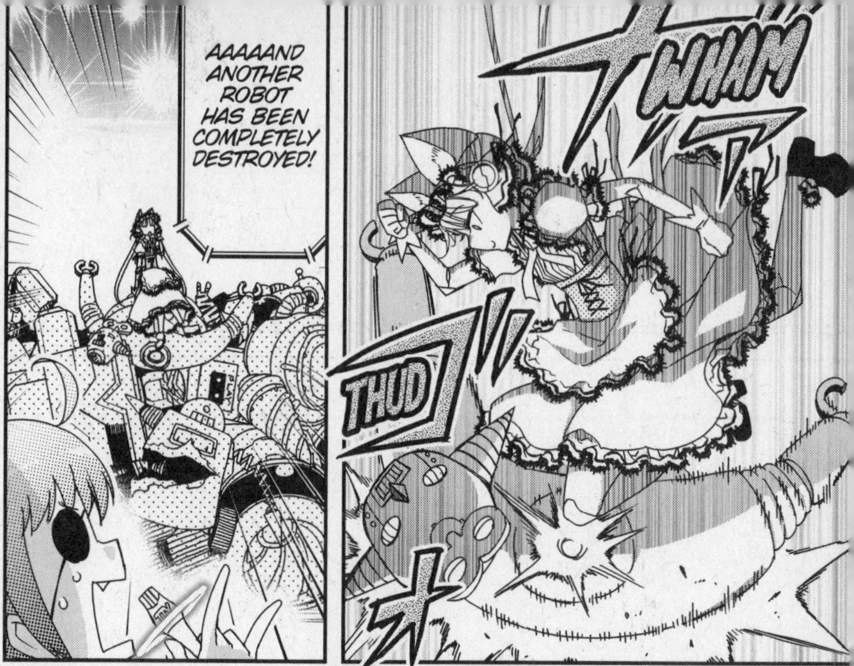
WHAM
THUD
AAAAAND ANOTHER ROBOT HAS BEEN COMPLETELY DESTROYED!

FOR THE DESIGN OF THIS ROBOT, I REFERRED TO RIKUDOU KOUSHI-KUN'S DESIGN. THANK YOU.

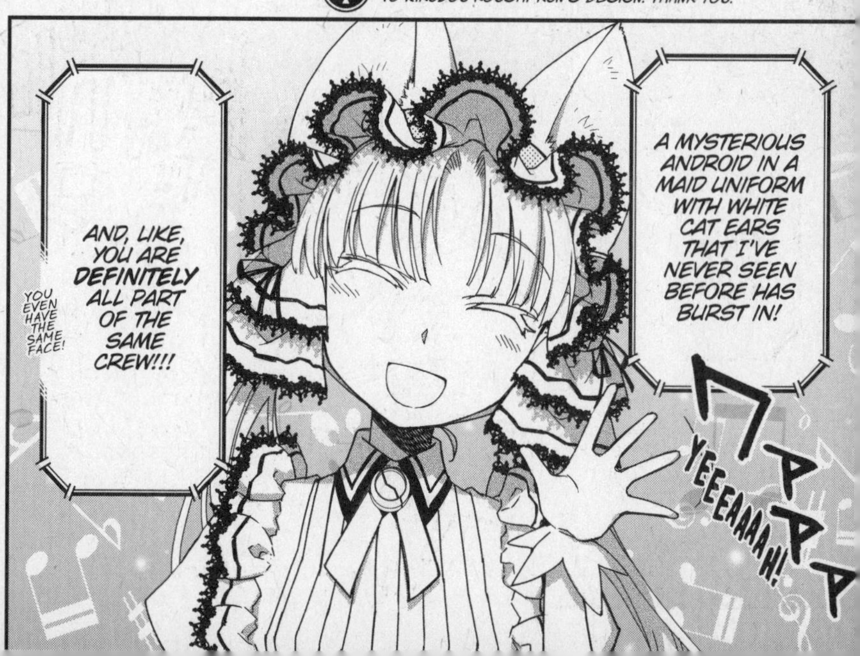
A MYSTERIOUS ANDROID IN A MAID UNIFORM WITH WHITE CAT EARS THAT I'VE NEVER SEEN BEFORE HAS BURST IN!
YEEEAAAAAH!
AND, LIKE, YOU ARE DEFINITELY ALL PART OF THE SAME CREW!!!
YOU EVEN HAVE THE SAME FACE!

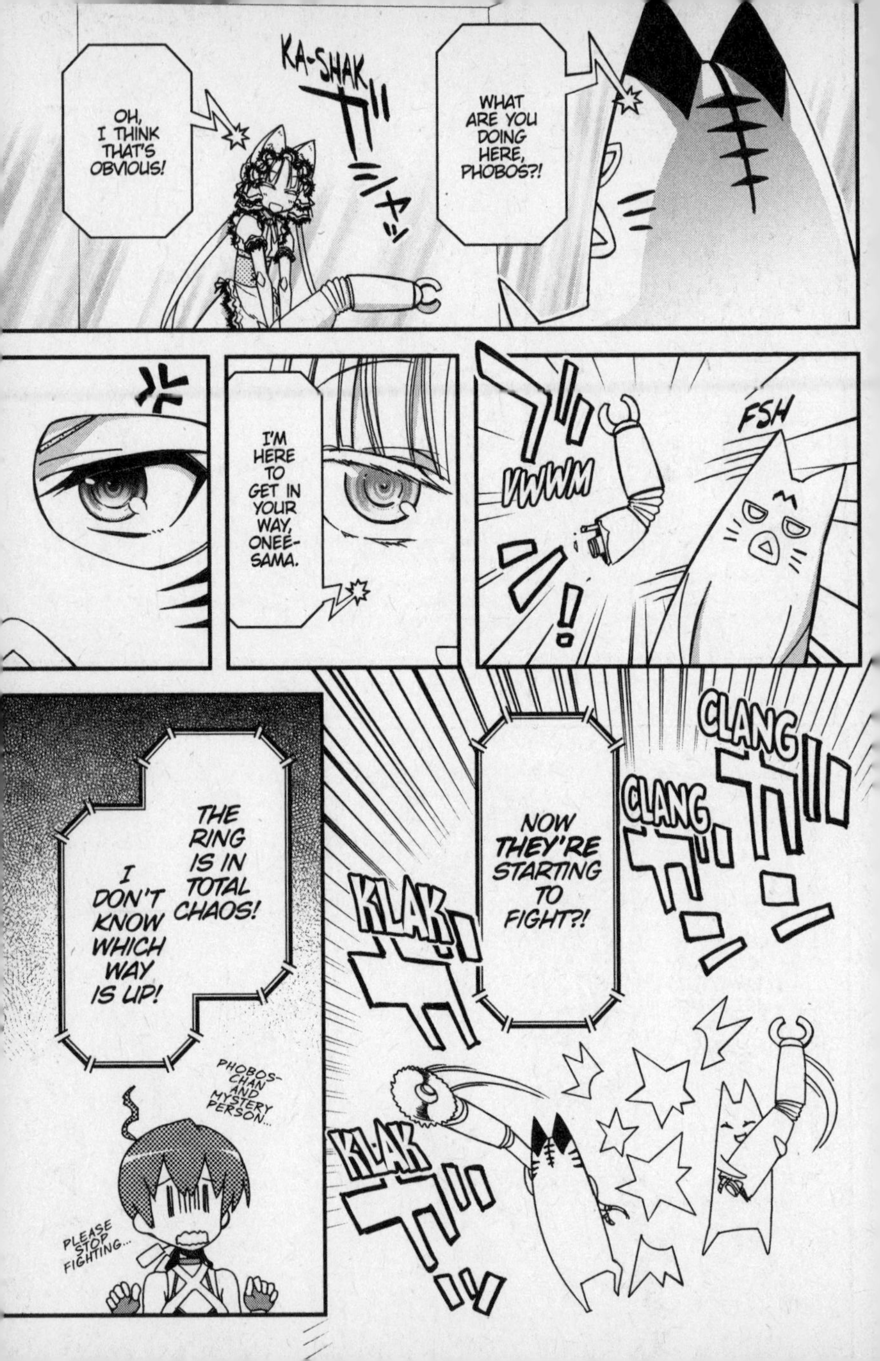
WHAT ARE YOU DOING HERE, PHOBOS?!
KA-SHAK
OH, I THINK THAT'S OBVIOUS!
FSH
VWWM
I'M HERE TO GET IN YOUR WAY, ONEE-SAMA.
CLANG
CLANG
NOW THEY'RE STARTING TO FIGHT?!
KLAK
KLAK
THE RING IS IN TOTAL CHAOS!
I DON'T KNOW WHICH WAY IS UP!
PHOBOS-CHAN AND MYSTERY PERSON...
PLEASE STOP FIGHTING...

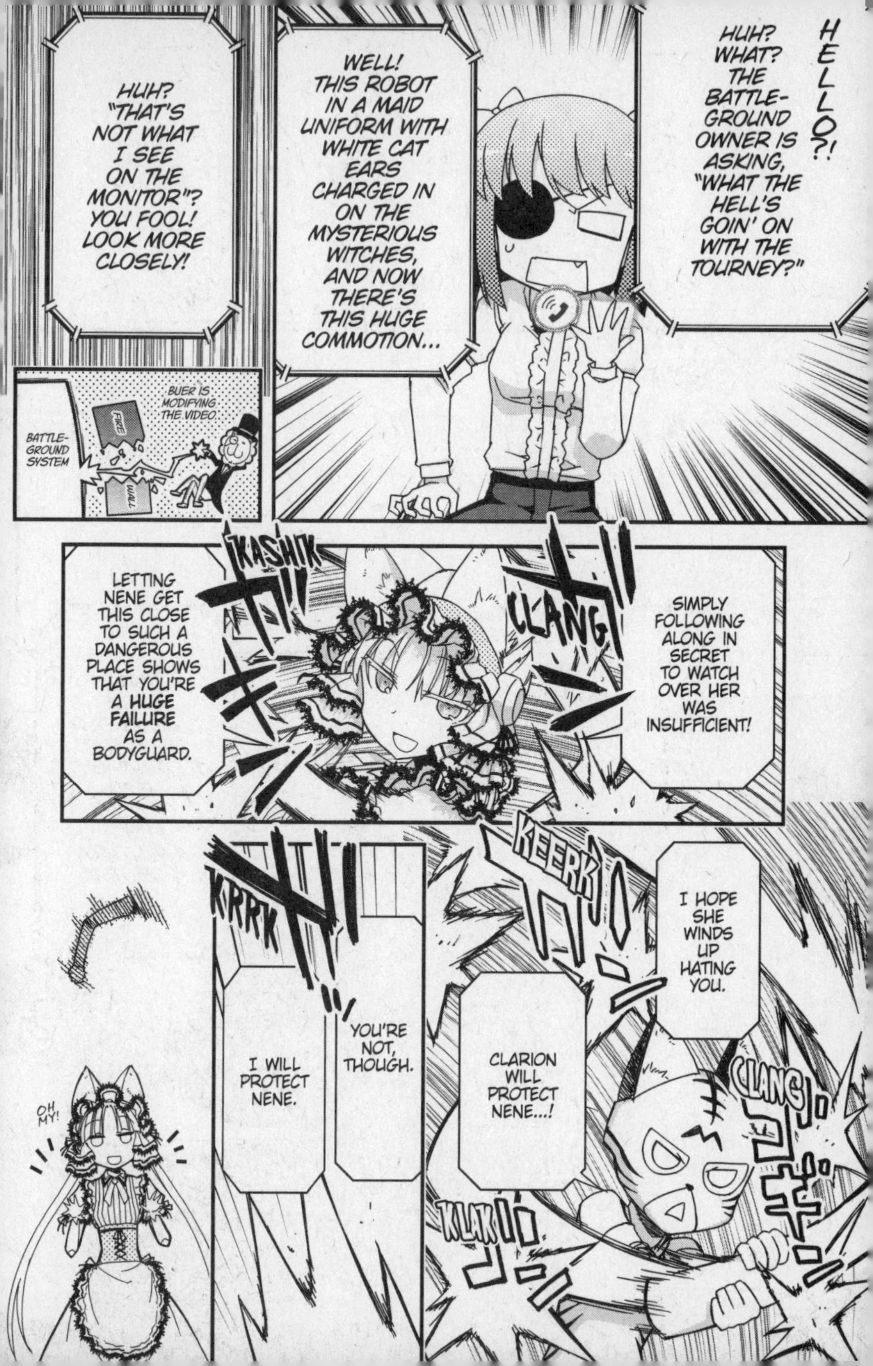
HELLO?!
HUH? WHAT? THE BATTLE-GROUND OWNER IS ASKING, "WHAT THE HELL'S GOIN' ON WITH THE TOURNEY?"
WELL! THIS ROBOT IN A MAID UNIFORM WITH WHITE CAT EARS CHARGED IN ON THE MYSTERIOUS WITCHES, AND NOW THERE'S THIS HUGE COMMOTION...
HUH? "THAT'S NOT WHAT I SEE ON THE MONITOR"? YOU FOOL! LOOK MORE CLOSELY!
BUER IS MODIFYING THE VIDEO.
FIRE
BATTLE-GROUND SYSTEM
WALL
CLANG
SIMPLY FOLLOWING ALONG IN SECRET TO WATCH OVER HER WAS INSUFFICIENT!
KASHIK
LETTING NENE GET THIS CLOSE TO SUCH A DANGEROUS PLACE SHOWS THAT YOU'RE A **HUGE FAILURE** AS A BODYGUARD.
KEERK
I HOPE SHE WINDS UP HATING YOU.
CLANG
CLARION WILL PROTECT NENE...!
KLAK
KRRK
YOU'RE NOT, THOUGH.
I WILL PROTECT NENE.
OH MY!

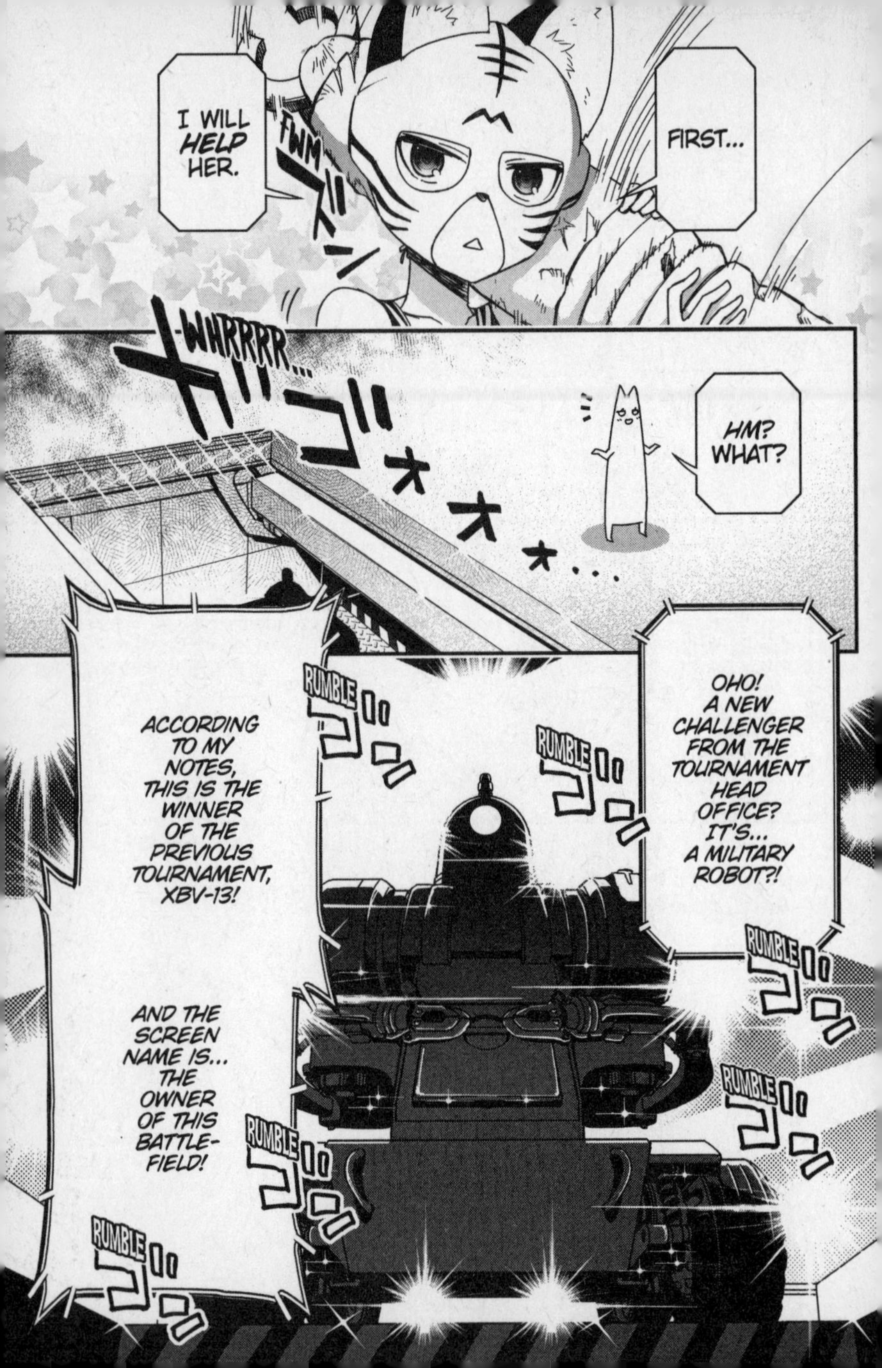
FIRST...
FWM
I WILL HELP HER.
HM? WHAT?
WHRRRR...
OHO! A NEW CHALLENGER FROM THE TOURNAMENT HEAD OFFICE? IT'S... A MILITARY ROBOT?!
RUMBLE
RUMBLE
RUMBLE
RUMBLE
ACCORDING TO MY NOTES, THIS IS THE WINNER OF THE PREVIOUS TOURNAMENT, XBV-13!
AND THE SCREEN NAME IS... THE OWNER OF THIS BATTLE-FIELD!
RUMBLE
RUMBLE

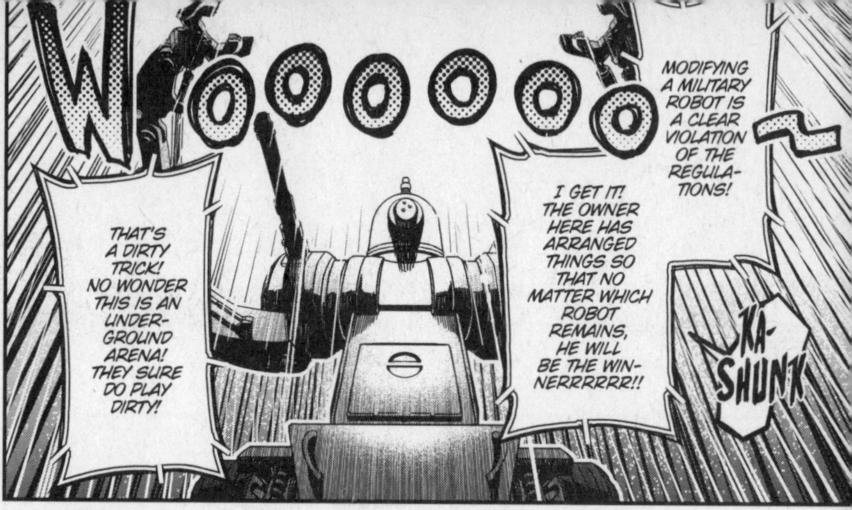
MODIFYING A MILITARY ROBOT IS A CLEAR VIOLATION OF THE REGULATIONS!
WOOOOOOOO~
I GET IT! THE OWNER HERE HAS ARRANGED THINGS SO THAT NO MATTER WHICH ROBOT REMAINS, HE WILL BE THE WINNERRRRRR!!
KA-SHUNK
THAT'S A DIRTY TRICK! NO WONDER THIS IS AN UNDERGROUND ARENA! THEY SURE DO PLAY DIRTY!

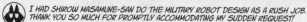

I HAD SHIROW MASAMUNE-SAN DO THE MILITARY ROBOT DESIGN AS A RUSH JOB. THANK YOU SO MUCH FOR PROMPTLY ACCOMMODATING MY SUDDEN REQUEST!

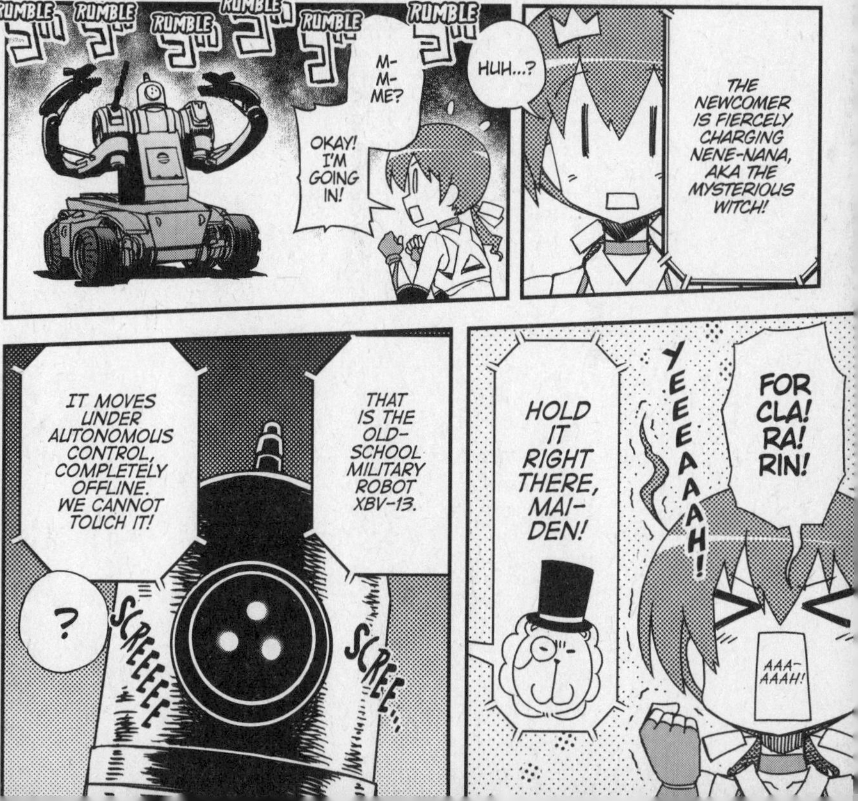
THE NEWCOMER IS FIERCELY CHARGING NENE-NANA, AKA THE MYSTERIOUS WITCH!
HUH...?
RUMBLE
RUMBLE
RUMBLE
RUMBLE
RUMBLE
RUMBLE
M-M-ME?
OKAY! I'M GOING IN!
FOR CLA! RA! RIN!
YEEEAAAH!
HOLD IT RIGHT THERE, MAI-DEN!
AAA-AAAH!
THAT IS THE OLD-SCHOOL MILITARY ROBOT XBV-13.
IT MOVES UNDER AUTONOMOUS CONTROL, COMPLETELY OFFLINE. WE CANNOT TOUCH IT!
?
SCREEEEE
SCREE...

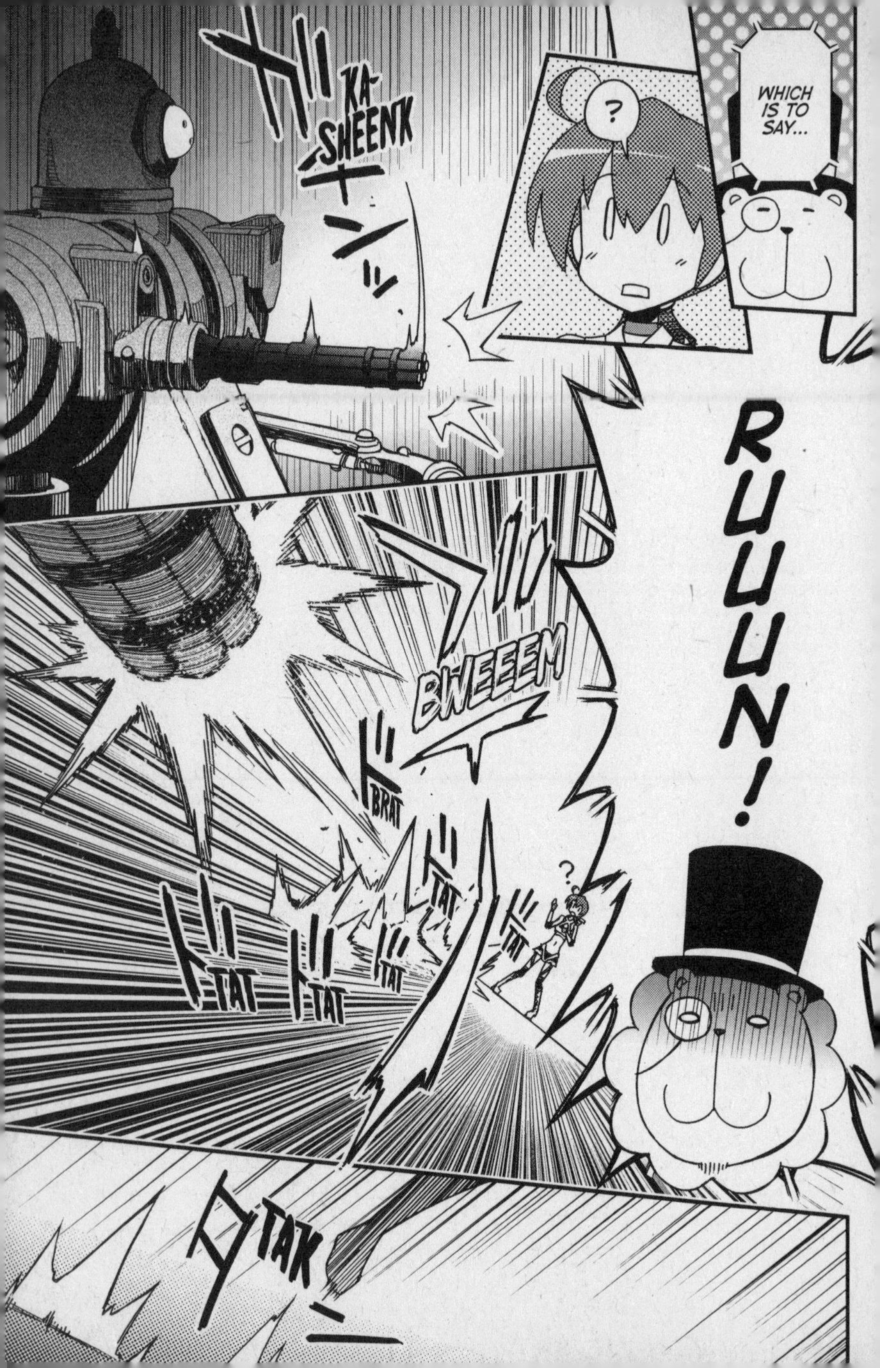
WHICH IS TO SAY...
?
KA-SHEENK
RUUUN!
BWEEEM
BRAT
TAT
TAT
TAT
TAT
TAT
TAK

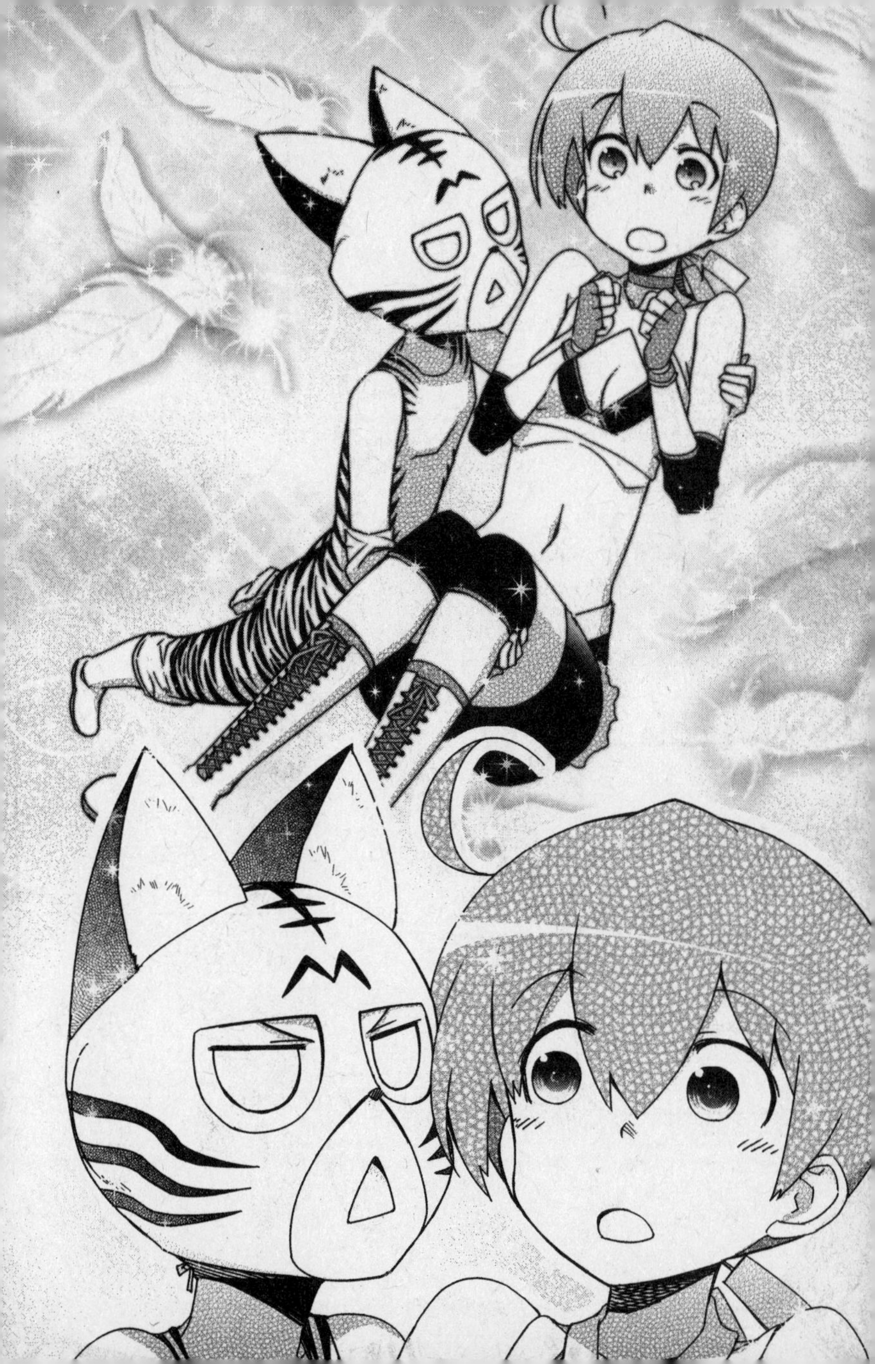

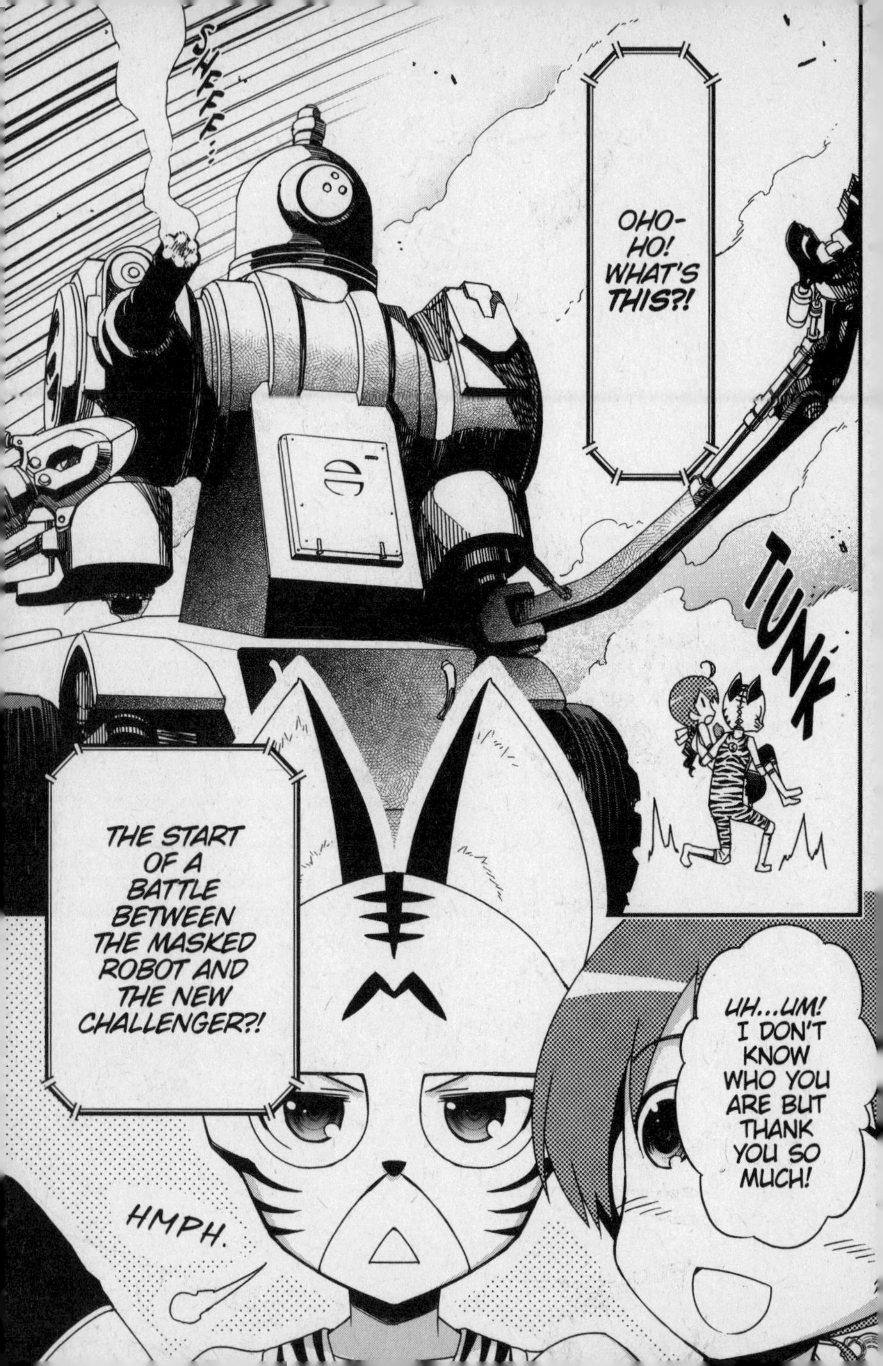
OHO-HO! WHAT'S THIS?!
SHFFF...
TUNK
THE START OF A BATTLE BETWEEN THE MASKED ROBOT AND THE NEW CHALLENGER?!
UH...UM! I DON'T KNOW WHO YOU ARE BUT THANK YOU SO MUCH!
HMPH.

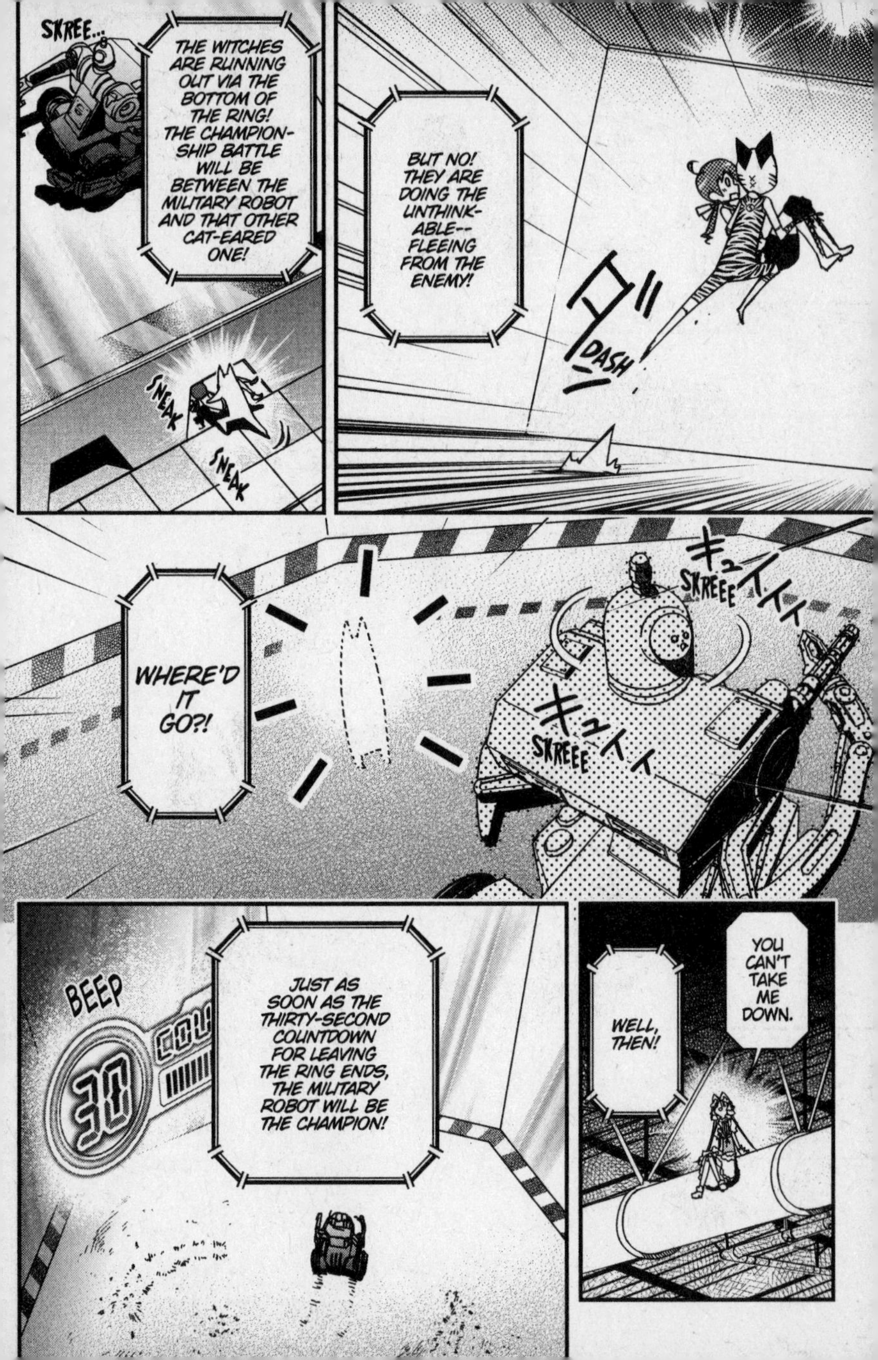
BUT NO! THEY ARE DOING THE UNTHINKABLE-- FLEEING FROM THE ENEMY!
DASH
SKREE...
THE WITCHES ARE RUNNING OUT VIA THE BOTTOM OF THE RING! THE CHAMPIONSHIP BATTLE WILL BE BETWEEN THE MILITARY ROBOT AND THAT OTHER CAT-EARED ONE!
SNEAK
SNEAK
SKREEE
SKREEE
WHERE'D IT GO?!
YOU CAN'T TAKE ME DOWN.
WELL, THEN!
BEEP
30
JUST AS SOON AS THE THIRTY-SECOND COUNTDOWN FOR LEAVING THE RING ENDS, THE MILITARY ROBOT WILL BE THE CHAMPION!

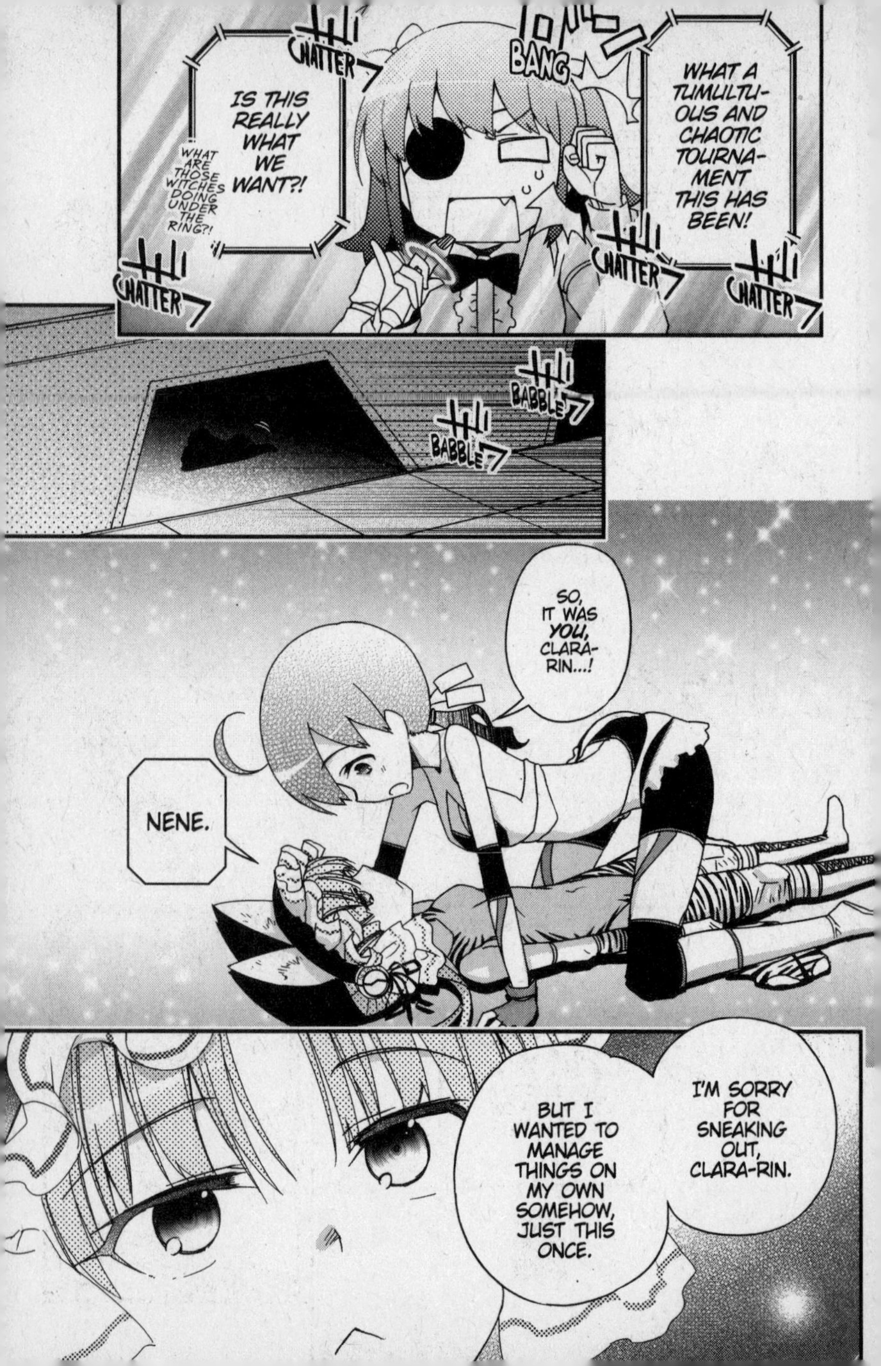
BANG
WHAT A TUMULTUOUS AND CHAOTIC TOURNAMENT THIS HAS BEEN!
CHATTER
CHATTER
CHATTER
IS THIS REALLY WHAT WE WANT?!
WHAT ARE THOSE WITCHES DOING UNDER THE RING?!
CHATTER
BABBLE
BABBLE
SO, IT WAS *YOU*, CLARA-RIN...!
NENE.
I'M SORRY FOR SNEAKING OUT, CLARA-RIN.
BUT I WANTED TO MANAGE THINGS ON MY OWN SOMEHOW, JUST THIS ONCE.

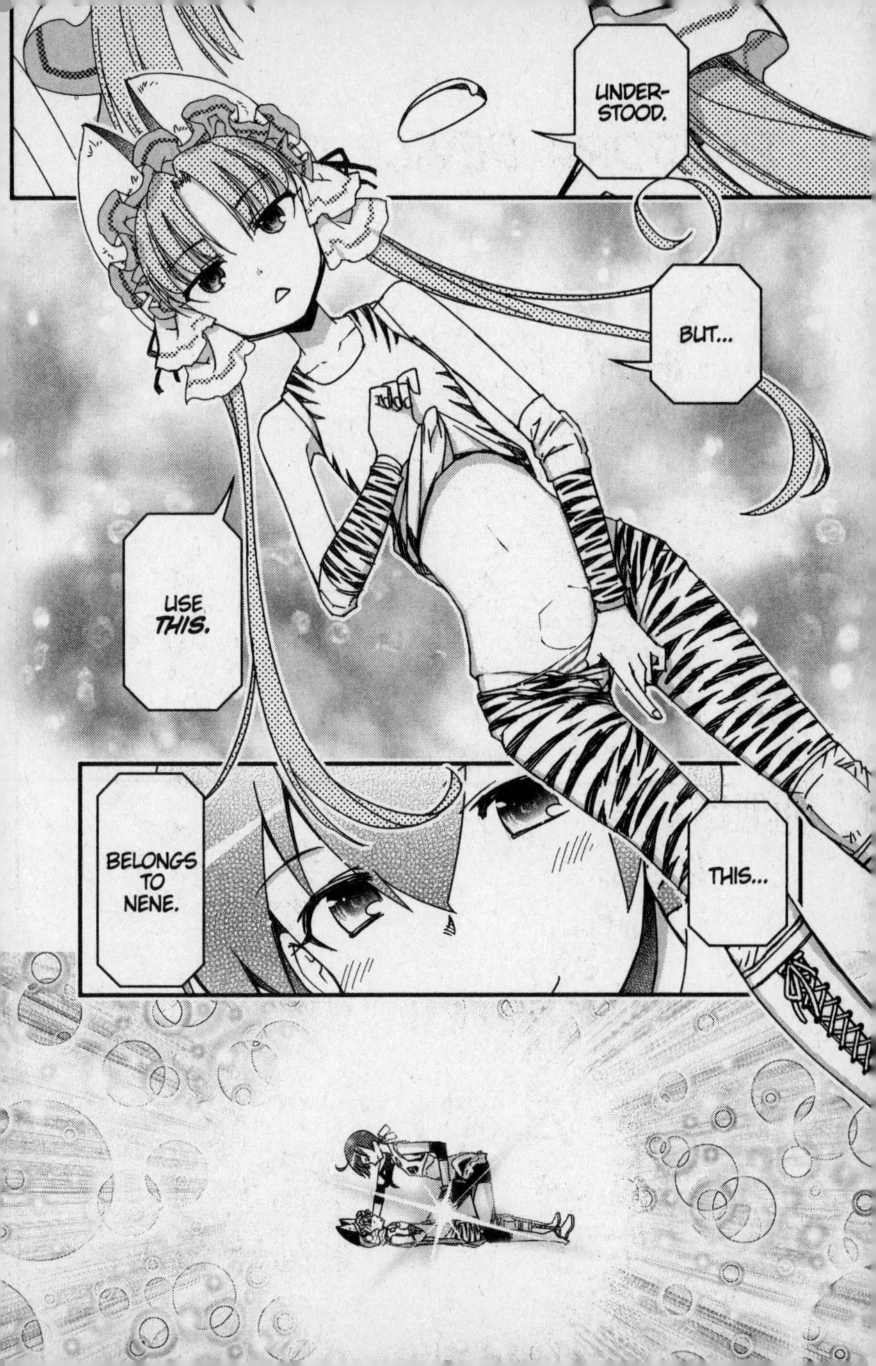
UNDER-STOOD.
BUT...
USE *THIS.*
THIS...
BELONGS TO NENE.

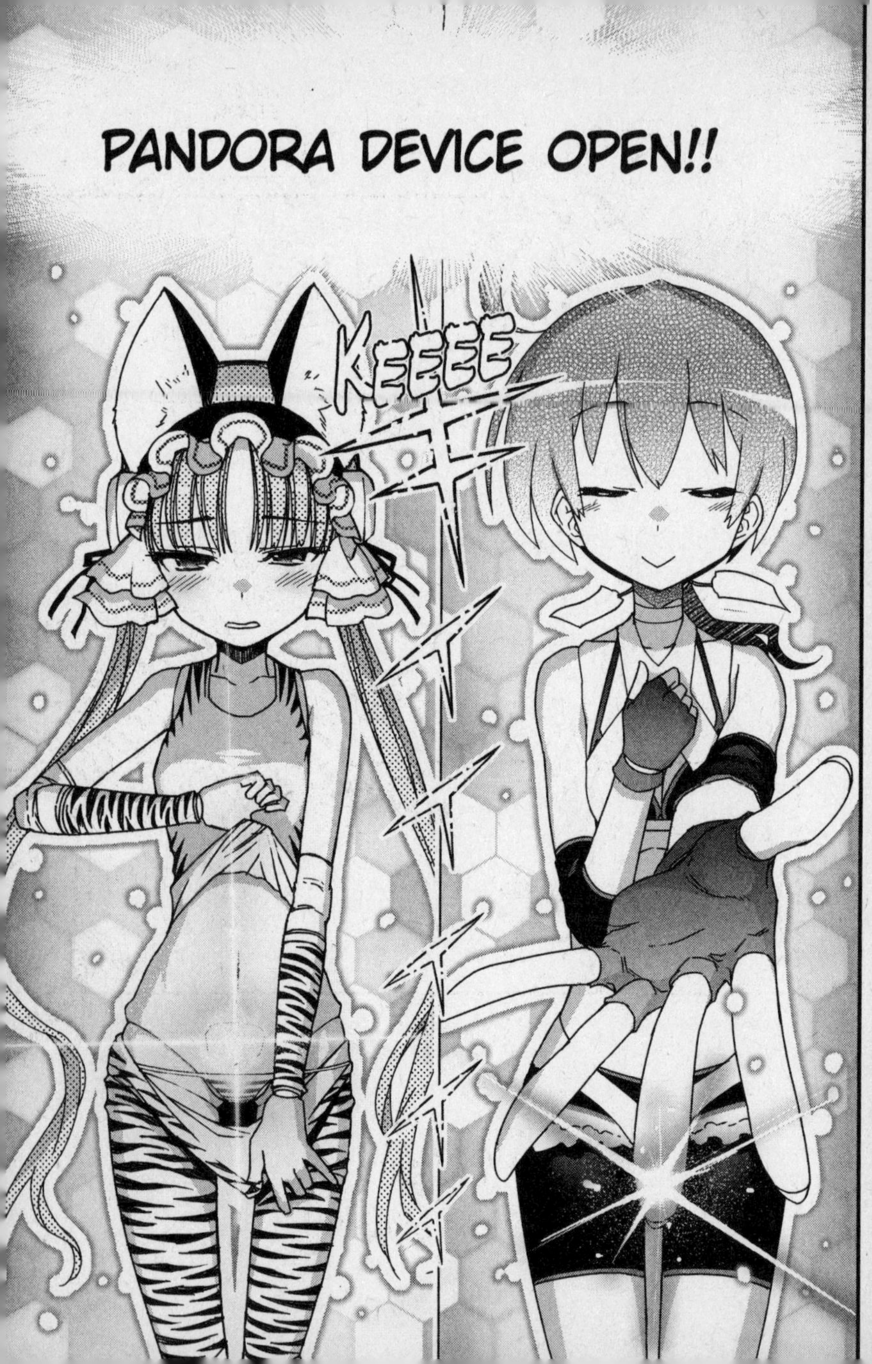
PANDORA DEVICE OPEN!!
KEEEE

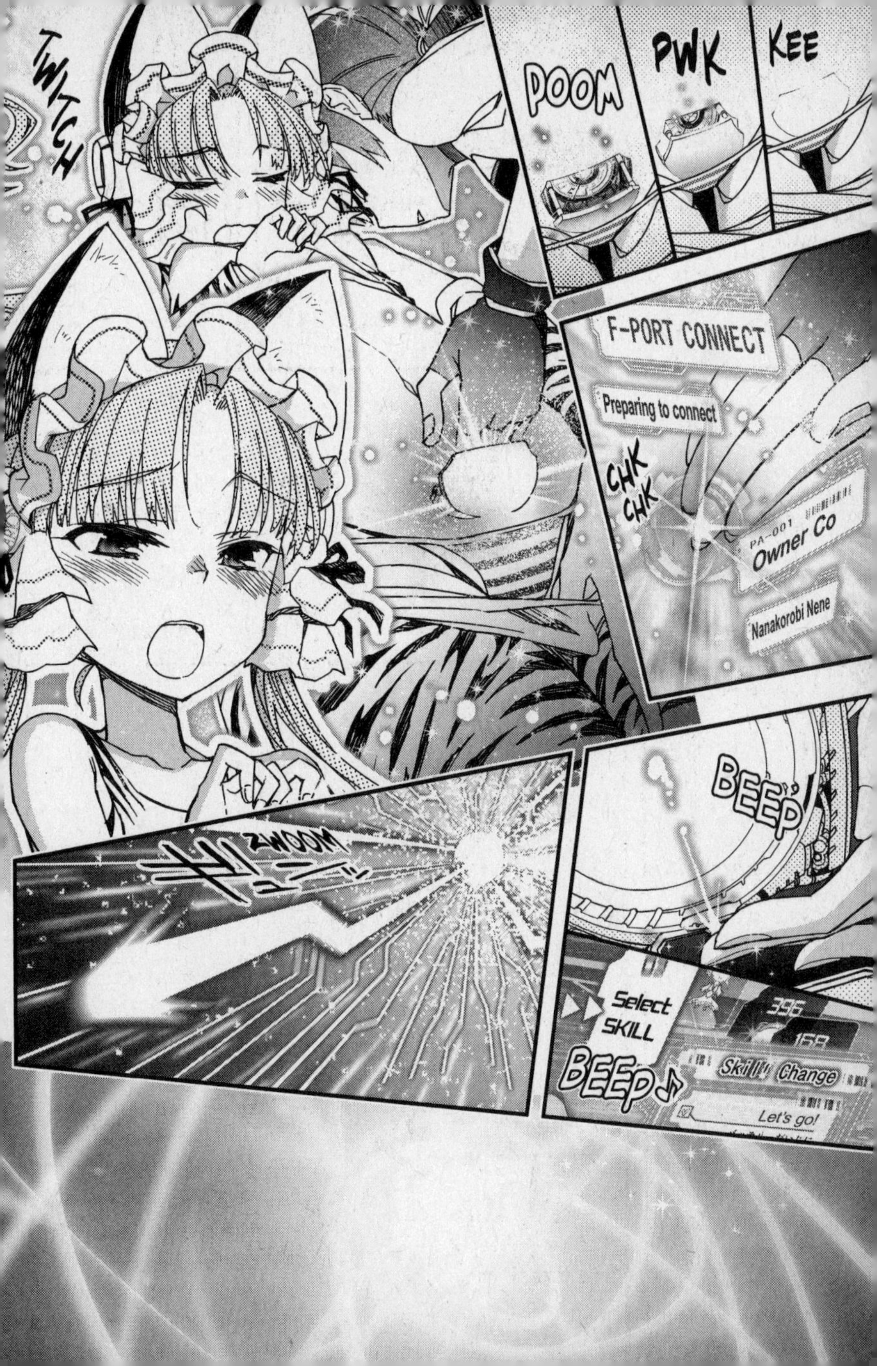
KEE
PWK
POOM
F-PORT CONNECT
Preparing to connect
CHK CHK
PA-001
Owner Co
Nanakorobi Nene
TWITCH
BEEP
Select SKILL
396
168
Skill Change
BEEP♪
Let's go!
ZWOOM

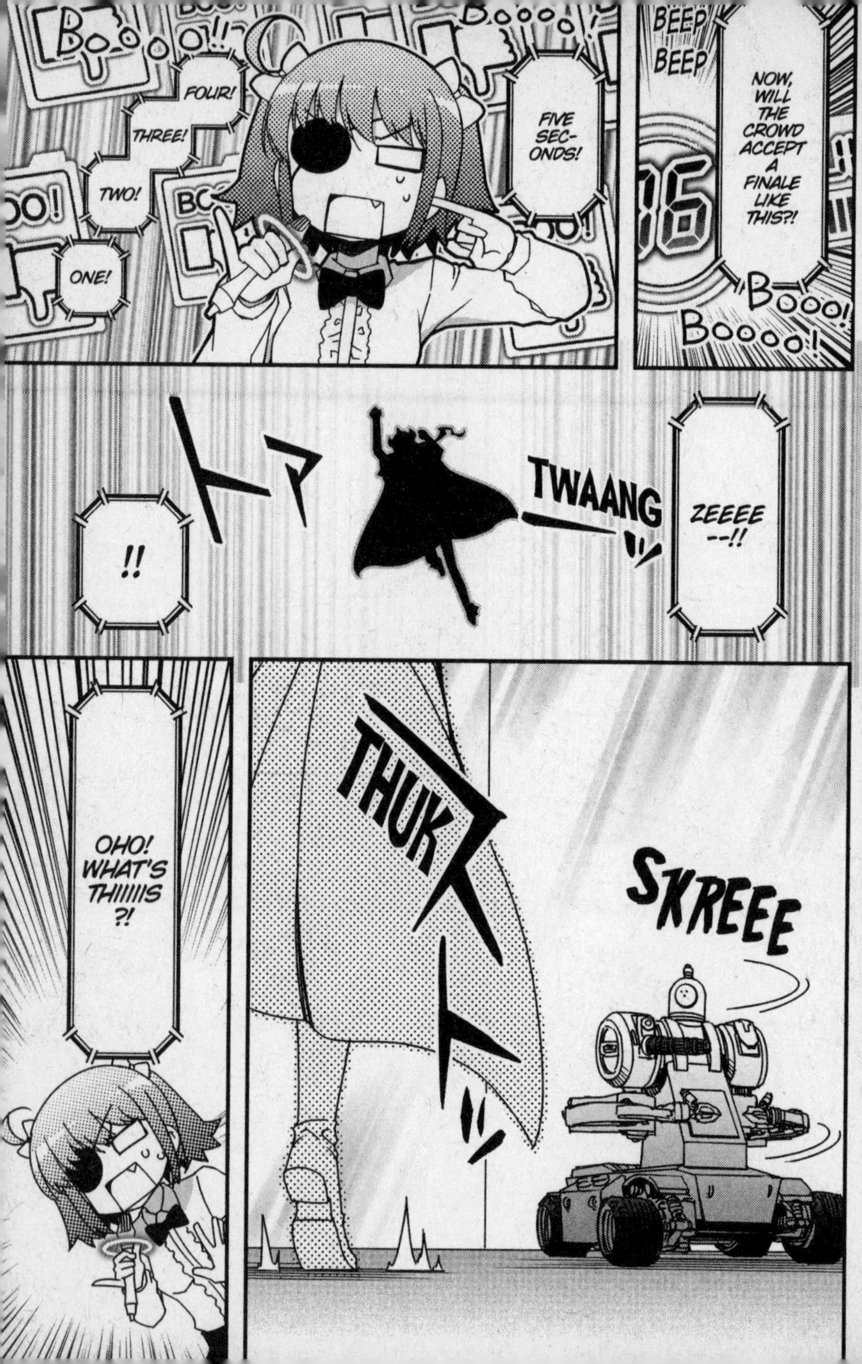
BEEP BEEP
NOW, WILL THE CROWD ACCEPT A FINALE LIKE THIS?!
BOOOO!
BOOOOO!
Boooo!
FIVE SEC-ONDS!
Boooo!!
FOUR!
THREE!
TWO!
ONE!
ZEEEE--!!
TWAANG
!!
SKREEE
THUK
OHO! WHAT'S THIIIIIS?!

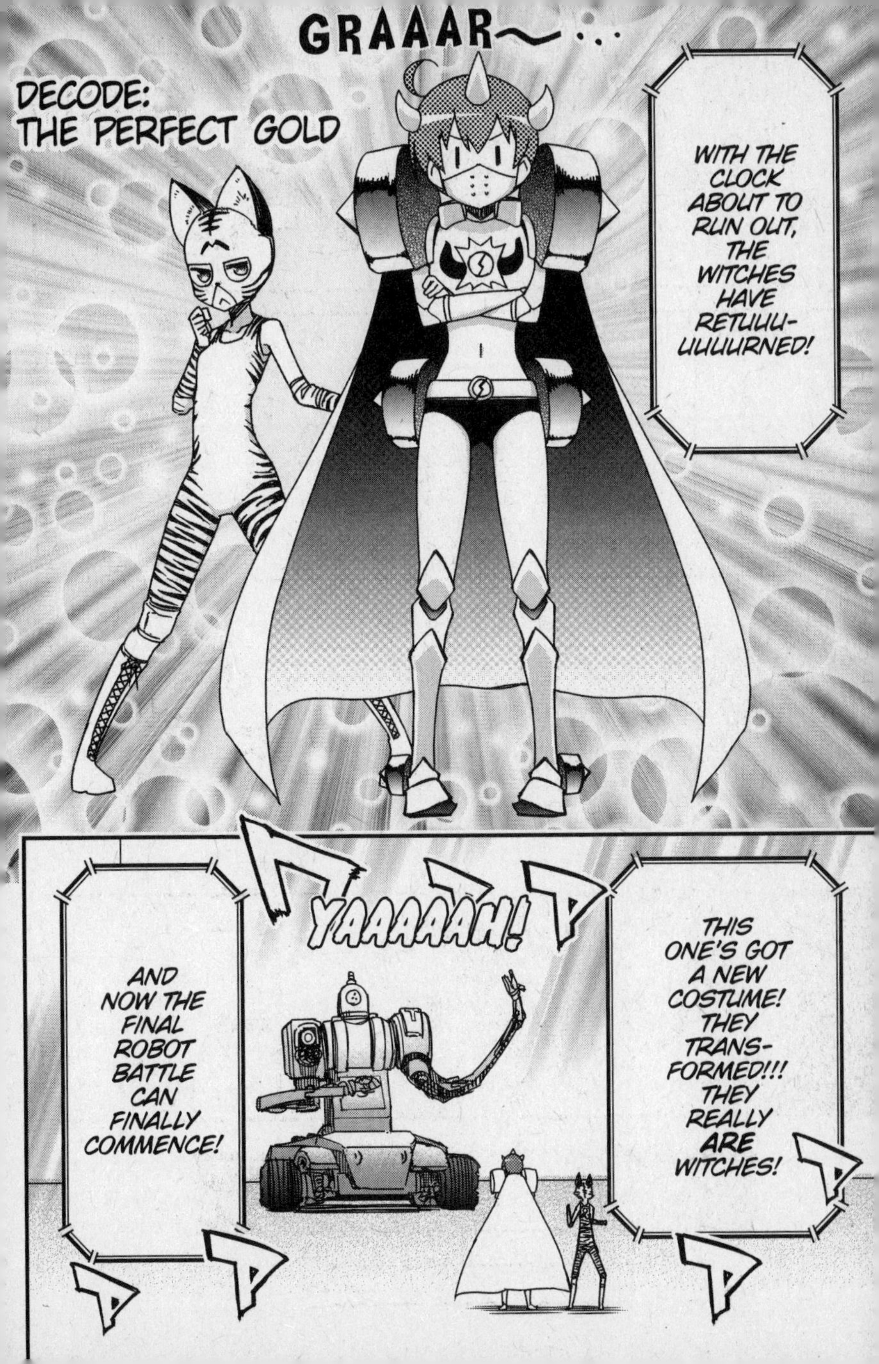
GRAAAR~...
WITH THE CLOCK ABOUT TO RUN OUT, THE WITCHES HAVE RETUUUUUUURNED!
DECODE: THE PERFECT GOLD
THIS ONE'S GOT A NEW COSTUME! THEY TRANS-FORMED!!! THEY REALLY ARE WITCHES!
YAAAAAH!
AND NOW THE FINAL ROBOT BATTLE CAN FINALLY COMMENCE!

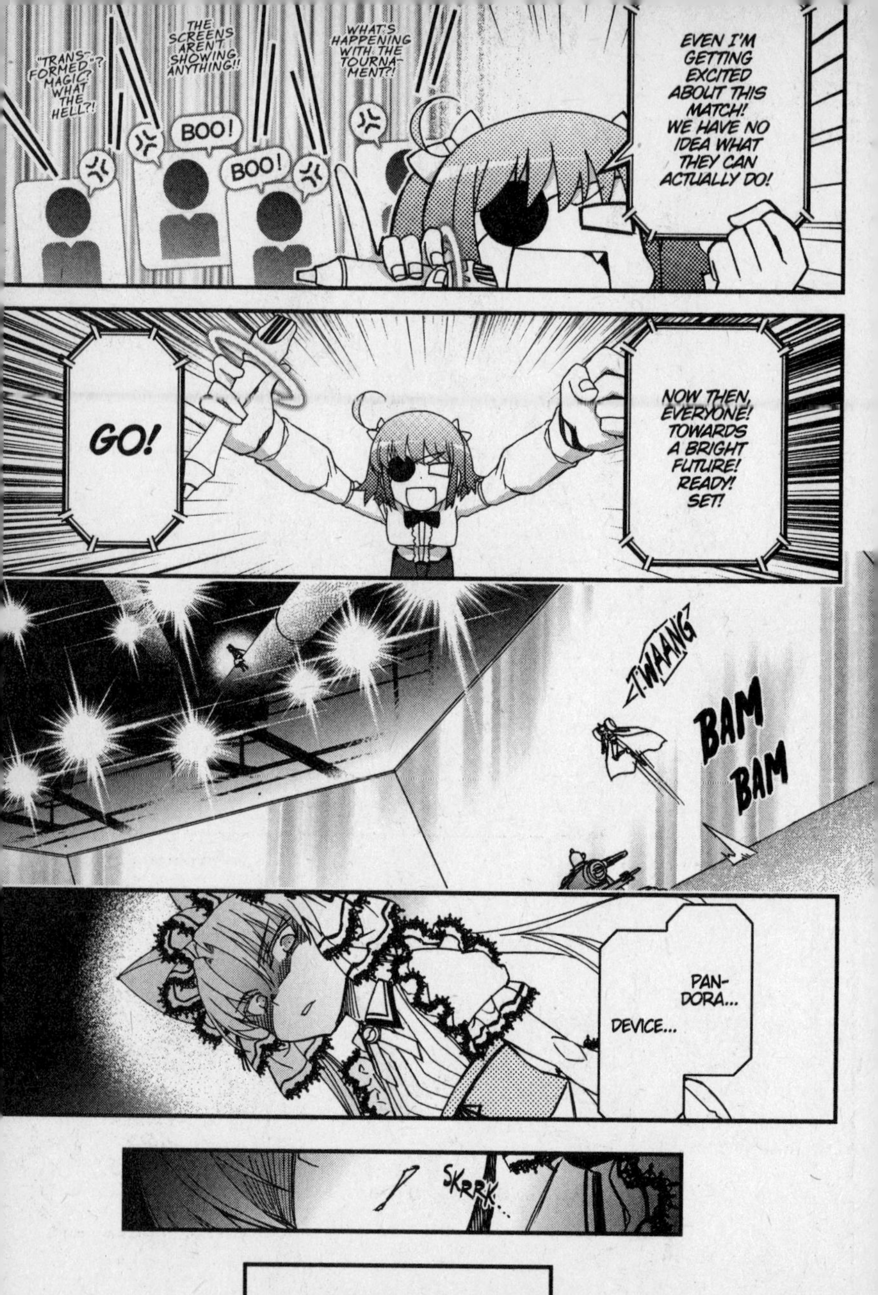
EVEN I'M GETTING EXCITED ABOUT THIS MATCH! WE HAVE NO IDEA WHAT THEY CAN ACTUALLY DO!
WHAT'S HAPPENING WITH THE TOURNAMENT?!
BOO!
THE SCREENS AREN'T SHOWING ANYTHING!!
BOO!
"TRANS-FORMED" MAGIC? WHAT THE HELL?!
NOW THEN, EVERYONE! TOWARDS A BRIGHT FUTURE! READY! SET!
GO!
TWAANG
BAM
BAM
PAN-DORA...
DEVICE...
SKRRK...

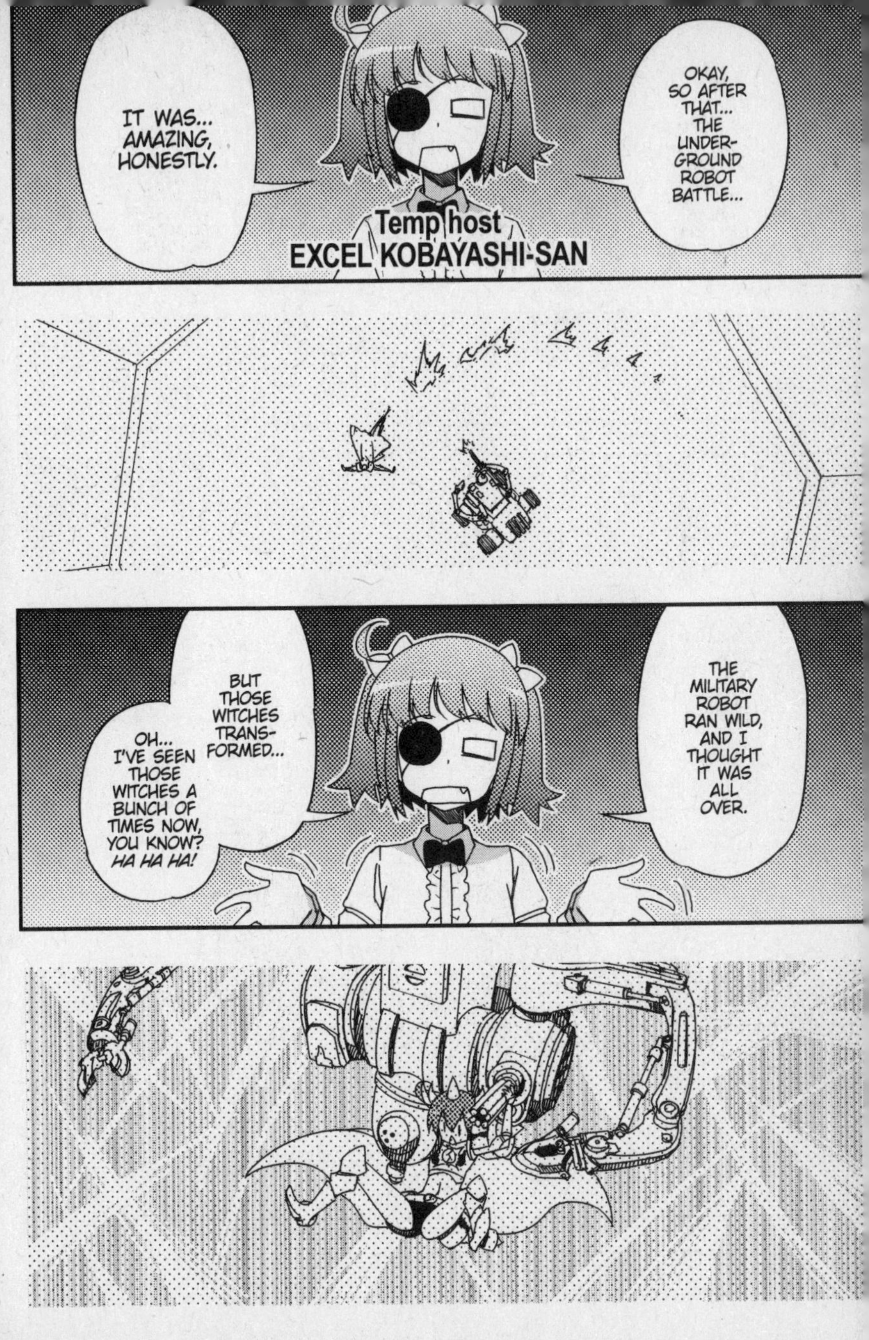
OKAY, SO AFTER THAT... THE UNDER-GROUND ROBOT BATTLE...
IT WAS... AMAZING, HONESTLY.
Temp host EXCEL KOBAYASHI-SAN
THE MILITARY ROBOT RAN WILD, AND I THOUGHT IT WAS ALL OVER.
BUT THOSE WITCHES TRANS-FORMED...
OH... I'VE SEEN THOSE WITCHES A BUNCH OF TIMES NOW, YOU KNOW? HA HA HA!

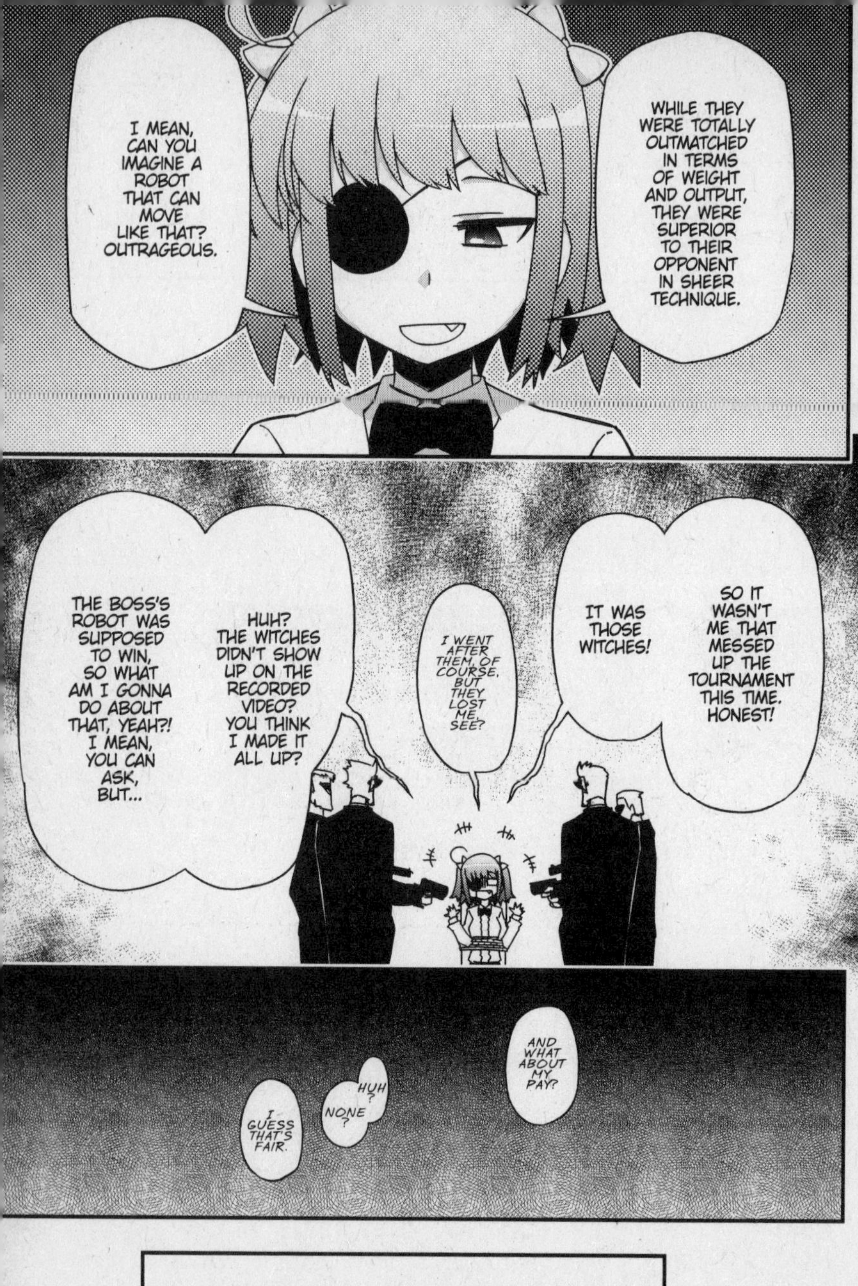

WHILE THEY WERE TOTALLY OUTMATCHED IN TERMS OF WEIGHT AND OUTPUT, THEY WERE SUPERIOR TO THEIR OPPONENT IN SHEER TECHNIQUE.
I MEAN, CAN YOU IMAGINE A ROBOT THAT CAN MOVE LIKE THAT? OUTRAGEOUS.
SO IT WASN'T ME THAT MESSED UP THE TOURNAMENT THIS TIME. HONEST!
IT WAS THOSE WITCHES!
I WENT AFTER THEM, OF COURSE, BUT THEY LOST ME, SEE?
HUH? THE WITCHES DIDN'T SHOW UP ON THE RECORDED VIDEO? YOU THINK I MADE IT ALL UP?
THE BOSS'S ROBOT WAS SUPPOSED TO WIN, SO WHAT AM I GONNA DO ABOUT THAT, YEAH?! I MEAN, YOU CAN ASK, BUT...
AND WHAT ABOUT MY PAY?
HUH?
NONE?
I GUESS THAT'S FAIR.

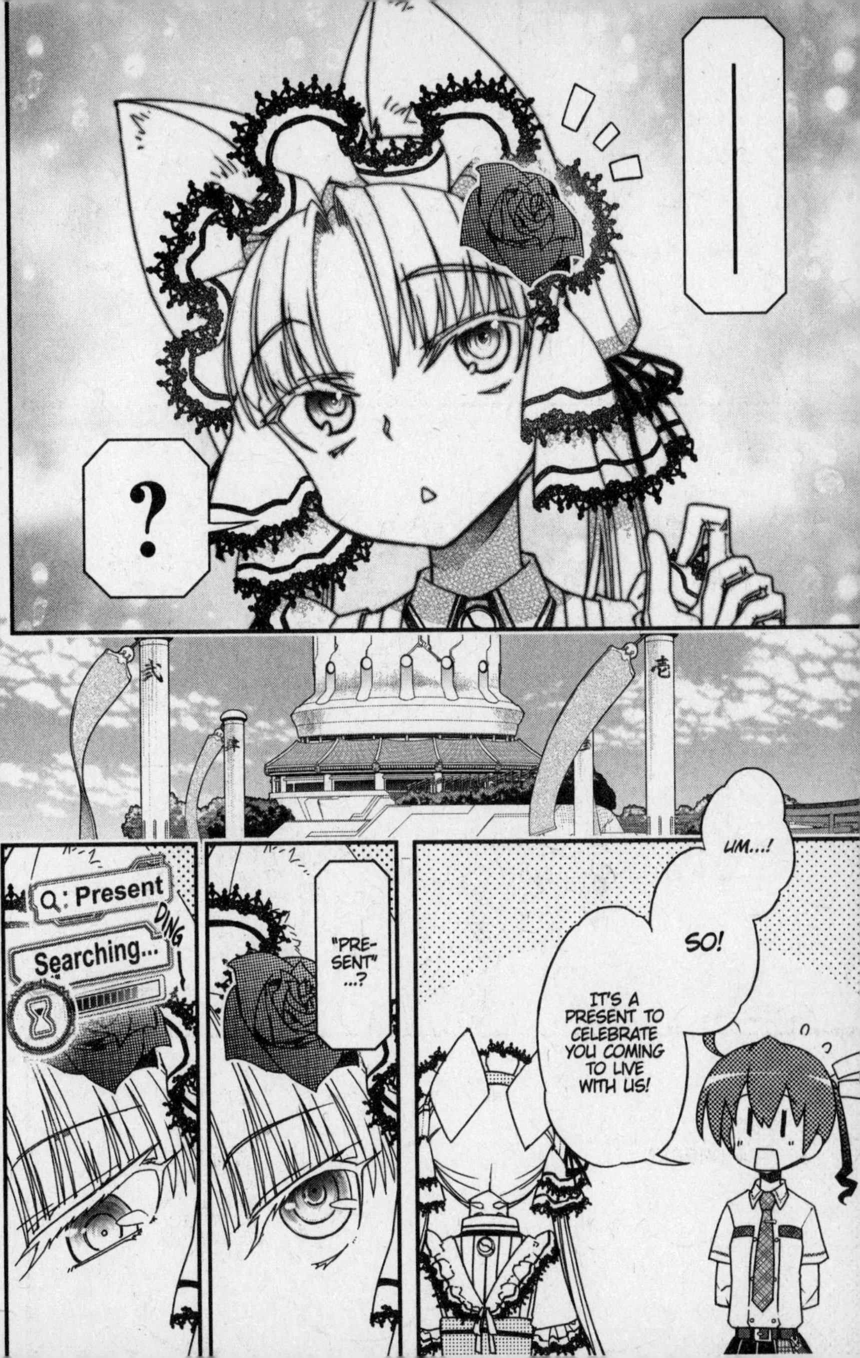

!
?
UM...!
SO!
IT'S A PRESENT TO CELEBRATE YOU COMING TO LIVE WITH US!
"PRE-SENT" ...?
Present
DING
Searching...

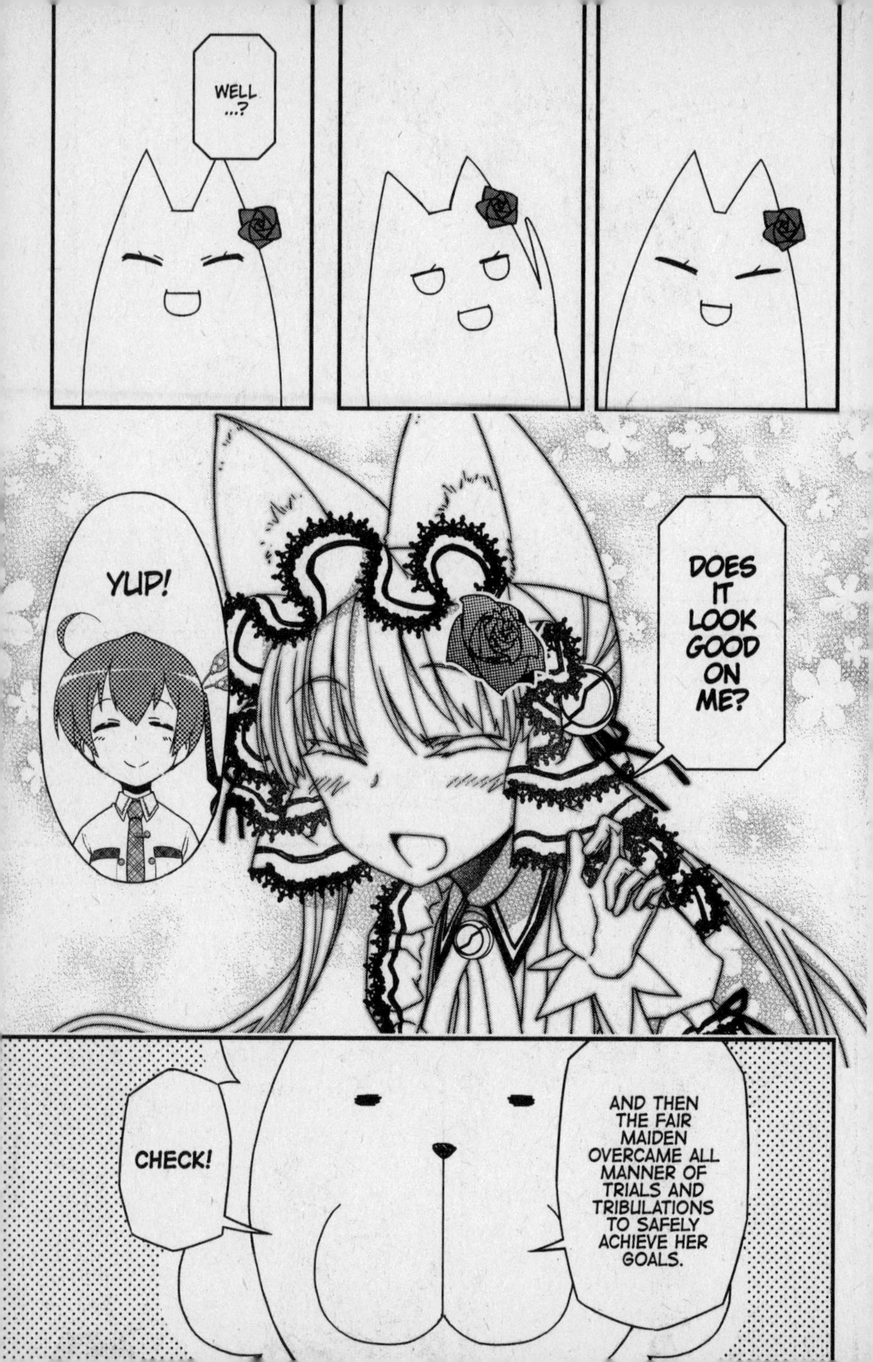
WELL ...?
DOES IT LOOK GOOD ON ME?
YUP!
AND THEN THE FAIR MAIDEN OVERCAME ALL MANNER OF TRIALS AND TRIBULATIONS TO SAFELY ACHIEVE HER GOALS.
CHECK!

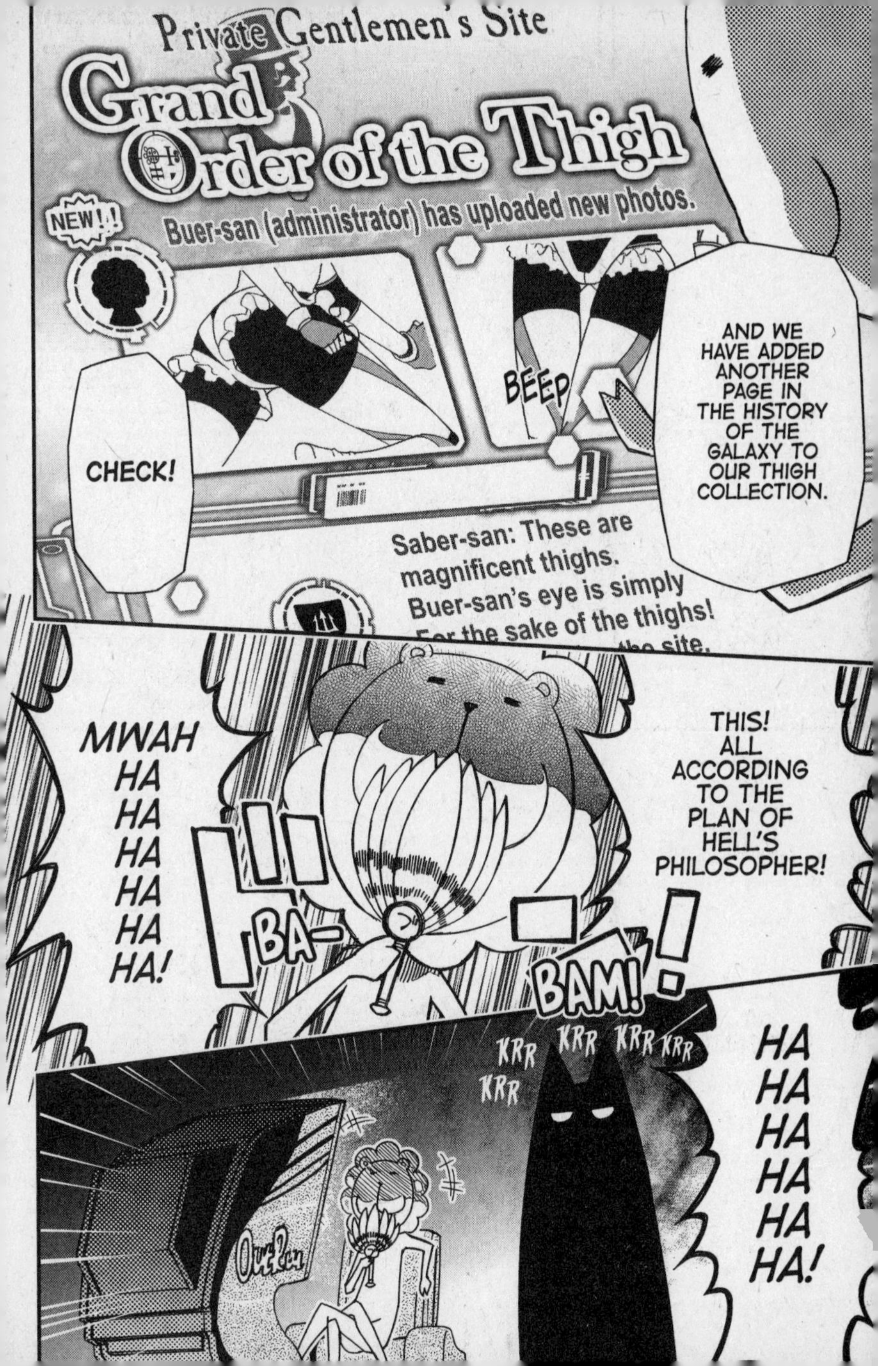

Private Gentlemen's Site
Grand Order of the Thigh
NEW!!
Buer-san (administrator) has uploaded new photos.
AND WE HAVE ADDED ANOTHER PAGE IN THE HISTORY OF THE GALAXY TO OUR THIGH COLLECTION.
BEEP
CHECK!
Saber-san: These are magnificent thighs. Buer-san's eye is simply For the sake of the thighs!
THIS! ALL ACCORDING TO THE PLAN OF HELL'S PHILOSOPHER!
MWAH HA HA HA HA HA HA!
BA-BAM!
HA HA HA HA HA HA HA!
KRR KRR KRR KRR KRR

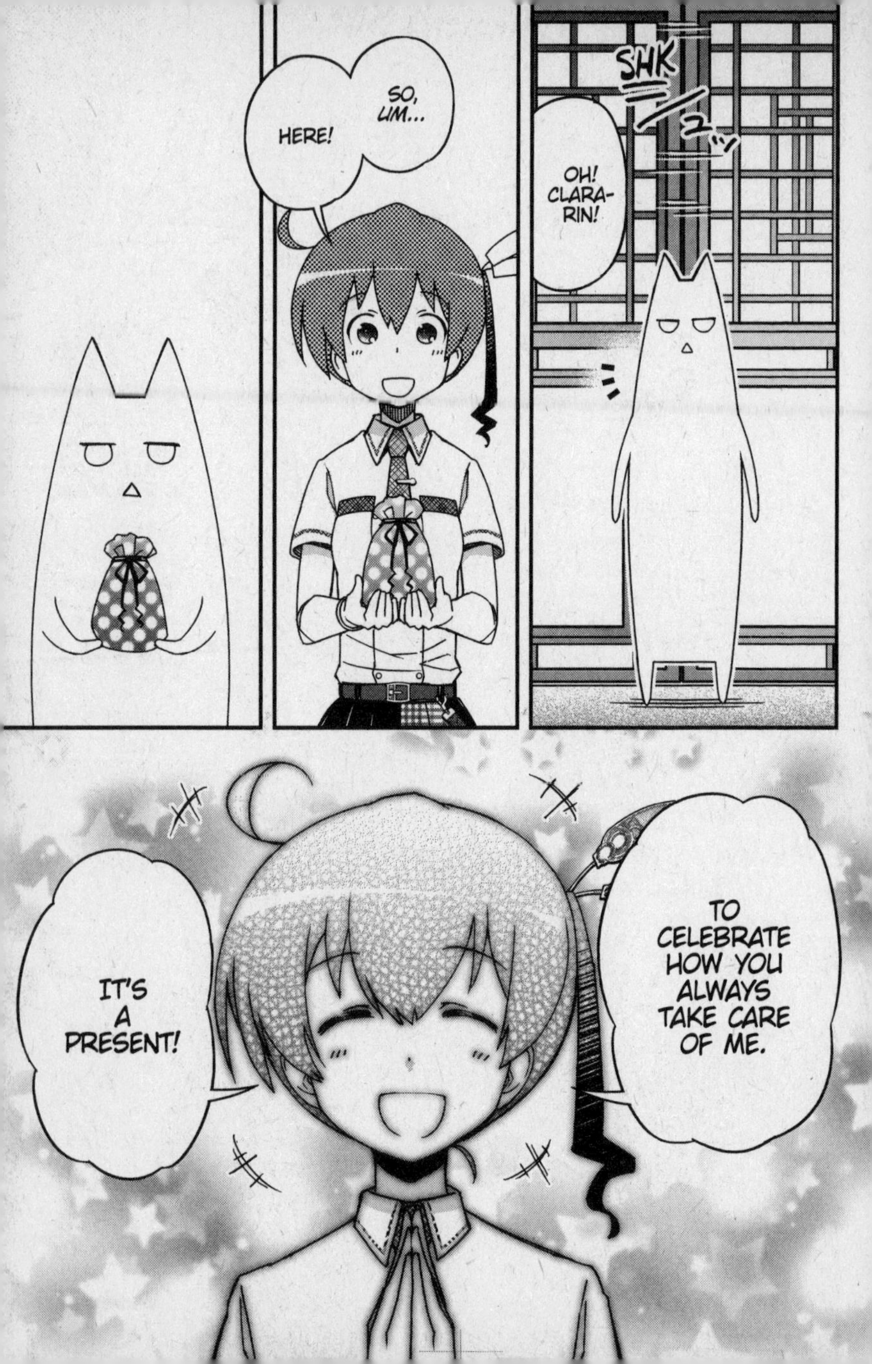
SHK
OH! CLARA-RIN!
SO, UM...
HERE!
TO CELEBRATE HOW YOU ALWAYS TAKE CARE OF ME.
IT'S A PRESENT!

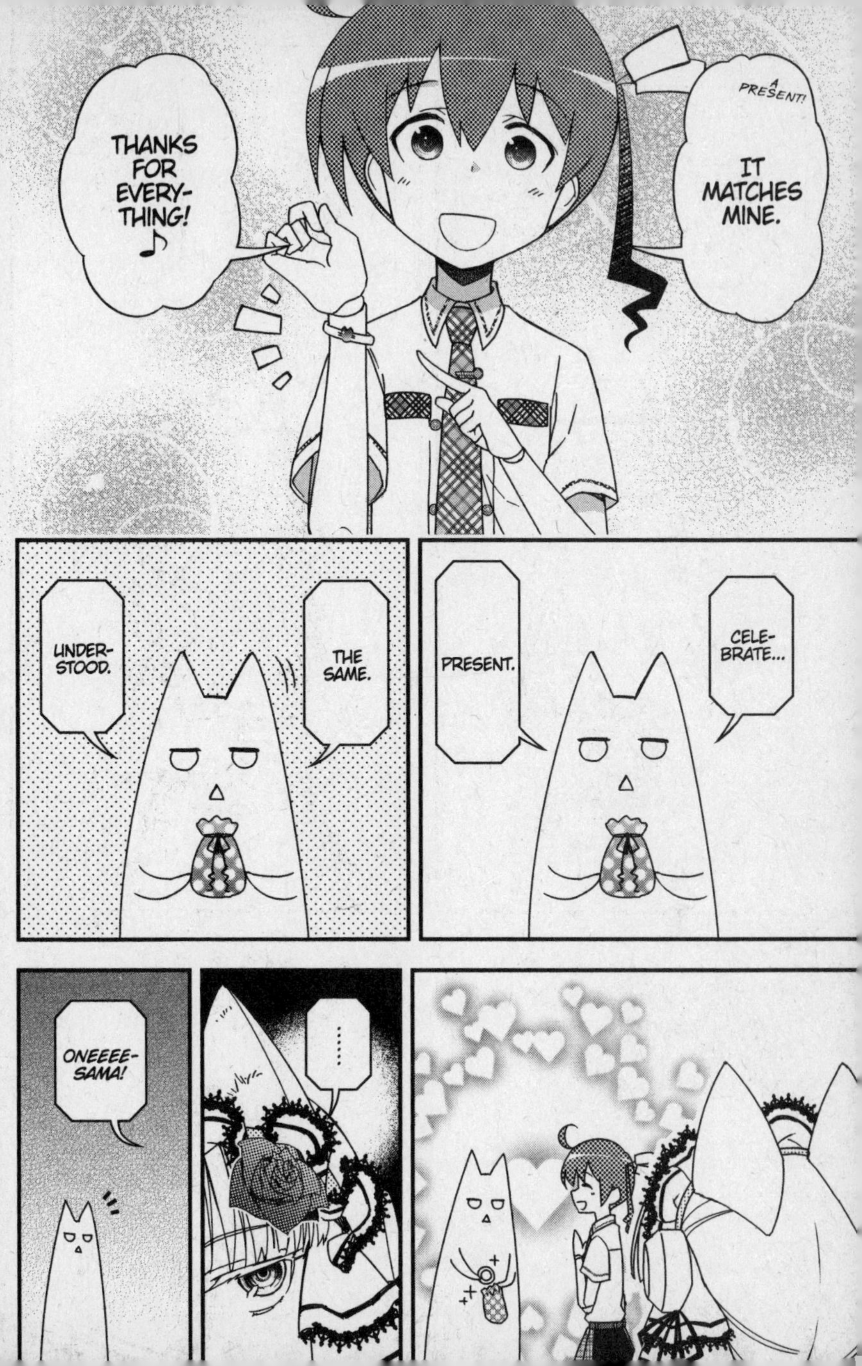
A PRESENT!
IT MATCHES MINE.
THANKS FOR EVERY-THING! ♪
CELE-BRATE...
PRESENT.
THE SAME.
UNDER-STOOD.
......
ONEEEE-SAMA!

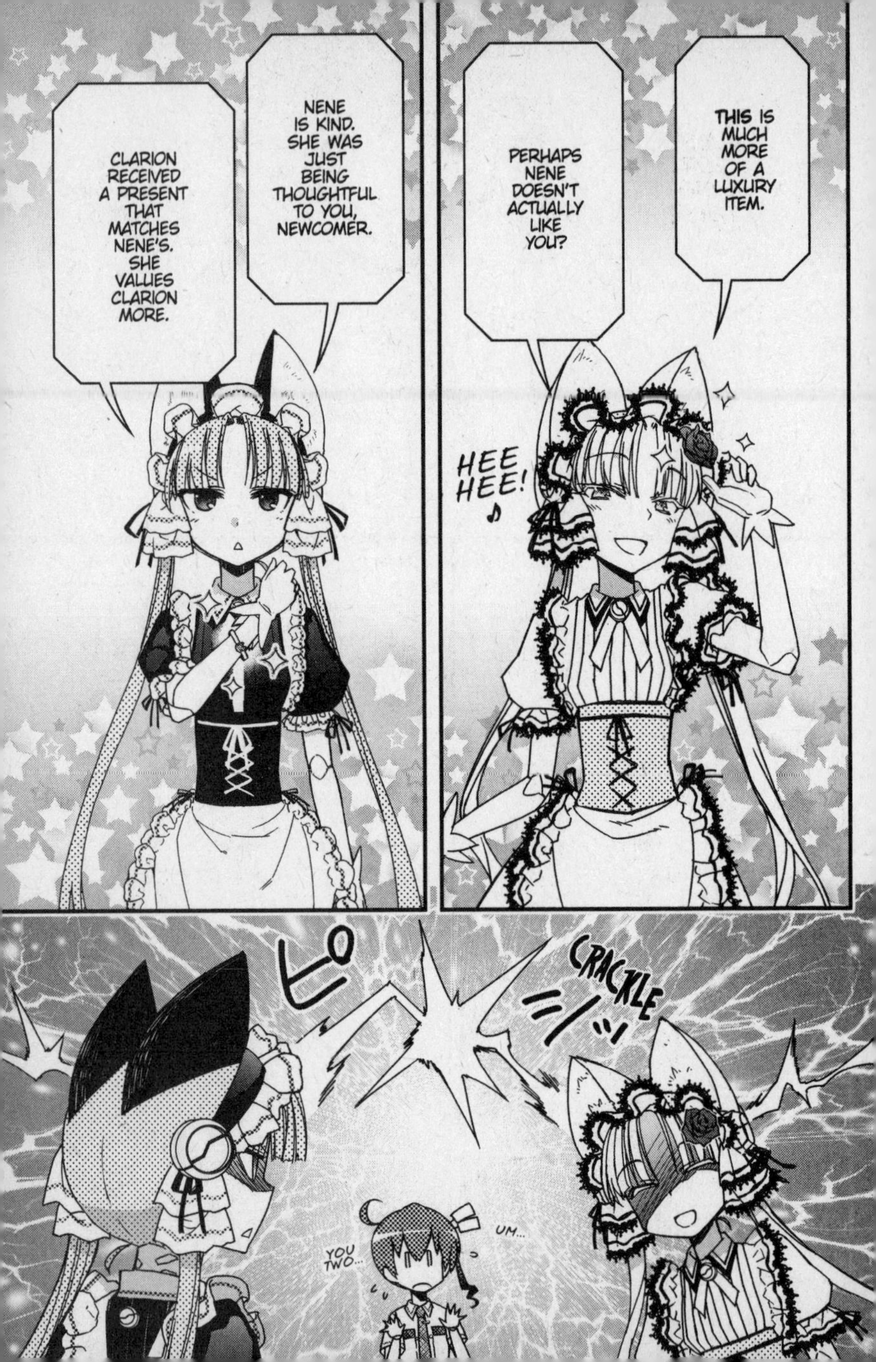
THIS IS MUCH MORE OF A LUXURY ITEM.
PERHAPS NENE DOESN'T ACTUALLY LIKE YOU?
HEE HEE! ♪
NENE IS KIND. SHE WAS JUST BEING THOUGHTFUL TO YOU, NEWCOMER.
CLARION RECEIVED A PRESENT THAT MATCHES NENE'S. SHE VALUES CLARION MORE.
CRACKLE
ピ
UM...
YOU TWO...

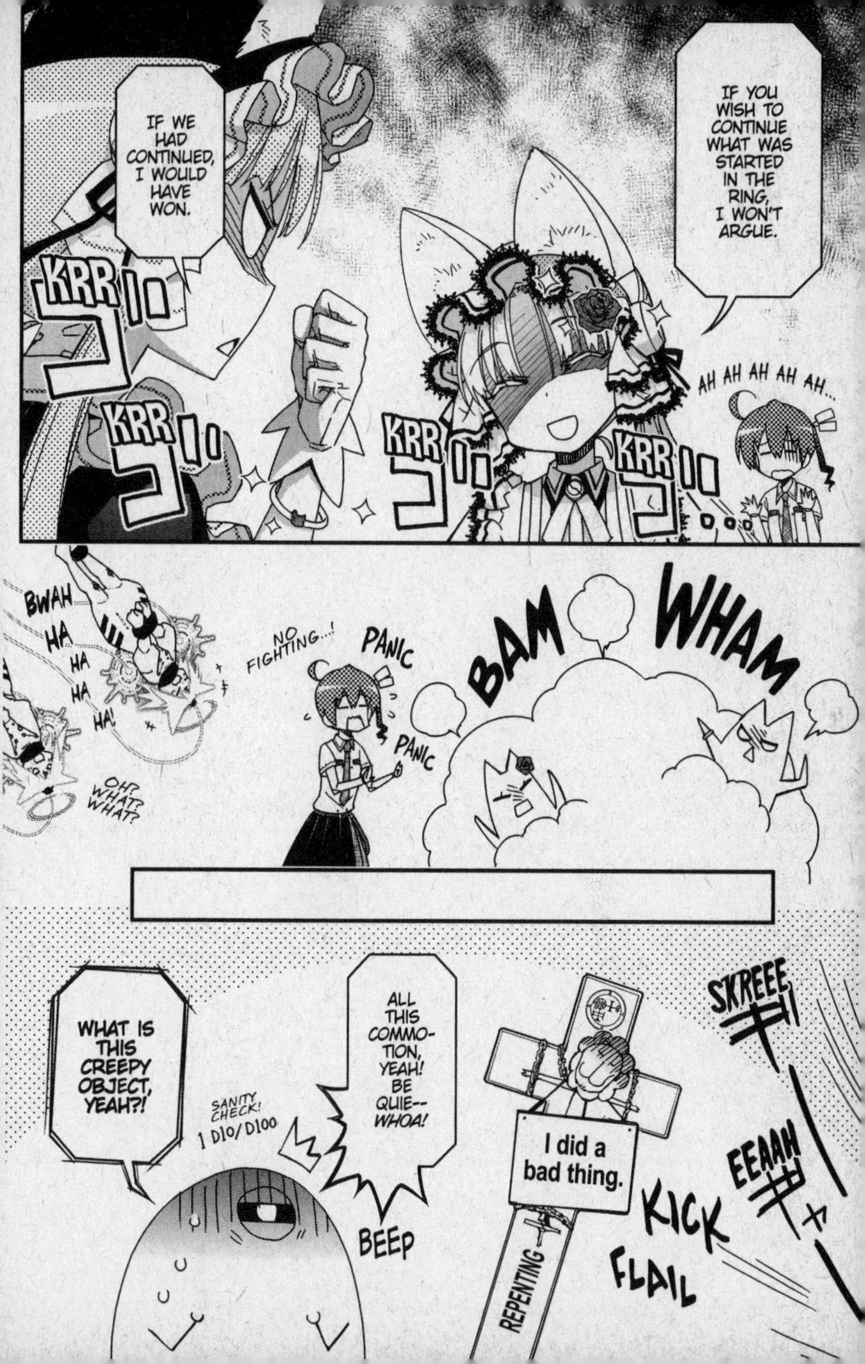
IF YOU WISH TO CONTINUE WHAT WAS STARTED IN THE RING, I WON'T ARGUE.
AH AH AH AH AH...
IF WE HAD CONTINUED, I WOULD HAVE WON.
KRR
KRR
KRR
KRR
WHAM
BAM
PANIC
PANIC
NO FIGHTING...!
BWAH HA HA HA HA!
OH? WHAT? WHAT?
SKREEE
I did a bad thing.
EEAAH
KICK
FLAIL
REPENTING
ALL THIS COMMOTION, YEAH! BE QUIE-- WHOA!
BEEP
WHAT IS THIS CREEPY OBJECT, YEAH?!
SANITY CHECK!
1 D10/D100

GHOST URN

GHOST VAN

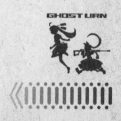

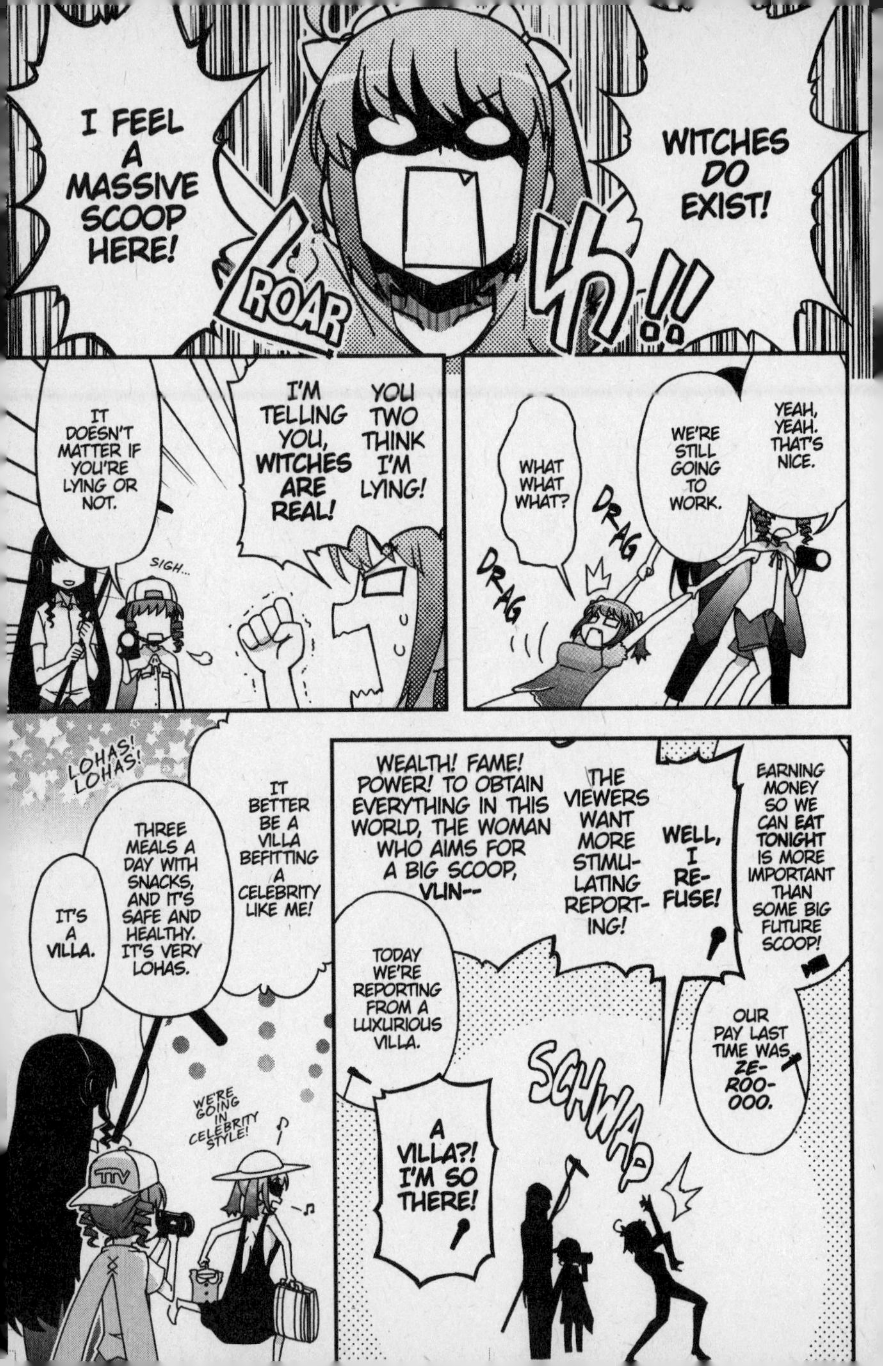
WITCHES DO EXIST!
I FEEL A MASSIVE SCOOP HERE!
ROAR
YEAH, YEAH. THAT'S NICE.
WE'RE STILL GOING TO WORK.
WHAT WHAT WHAT?
DRAG
DRAG
YOU TWO THINK I'M LYING!
I'M TELLING YOU, WITCHES ARE REAL!
IT DOESN'T MATTER IF YOU'RE LYING OR NOT.
SIGH...
EARNING MONEY SO WE CAN EAT TONIGHT IS MORE IMPORTANT THAN SOME BIG FUTURE SCOOP!
WELL, I RE-FUSE!
THE VIEWERS WANT MORE STIMULATING REPORTING!
WEALTH! FAME! POWER! TO OBTAIN EVERYTHING IN THIS WORLD, THE WOMAN WHO AIMS FOR A BIG SCOOP, VLIN--
OUR PAY LAST TIME WAS ZE-ROOOOO.
TODAY WE'RE REPORTING FROM A LUXURIOUS VILLA.
SCHWAP
A VILLA?! I'M SO THERE!
IT BETTER BE A VILLA BEFITTING A CELEBRITY LIKE ME!
LOHAS! LOHAS!
THREE MEALS A DAY WITH SNACKS, AND IT'S SAFE AND HEALTHY. IT'S VERY LOHAS.
IT'S A VILLA.
WE'RE GOING IN CELEBRITY STYLE!

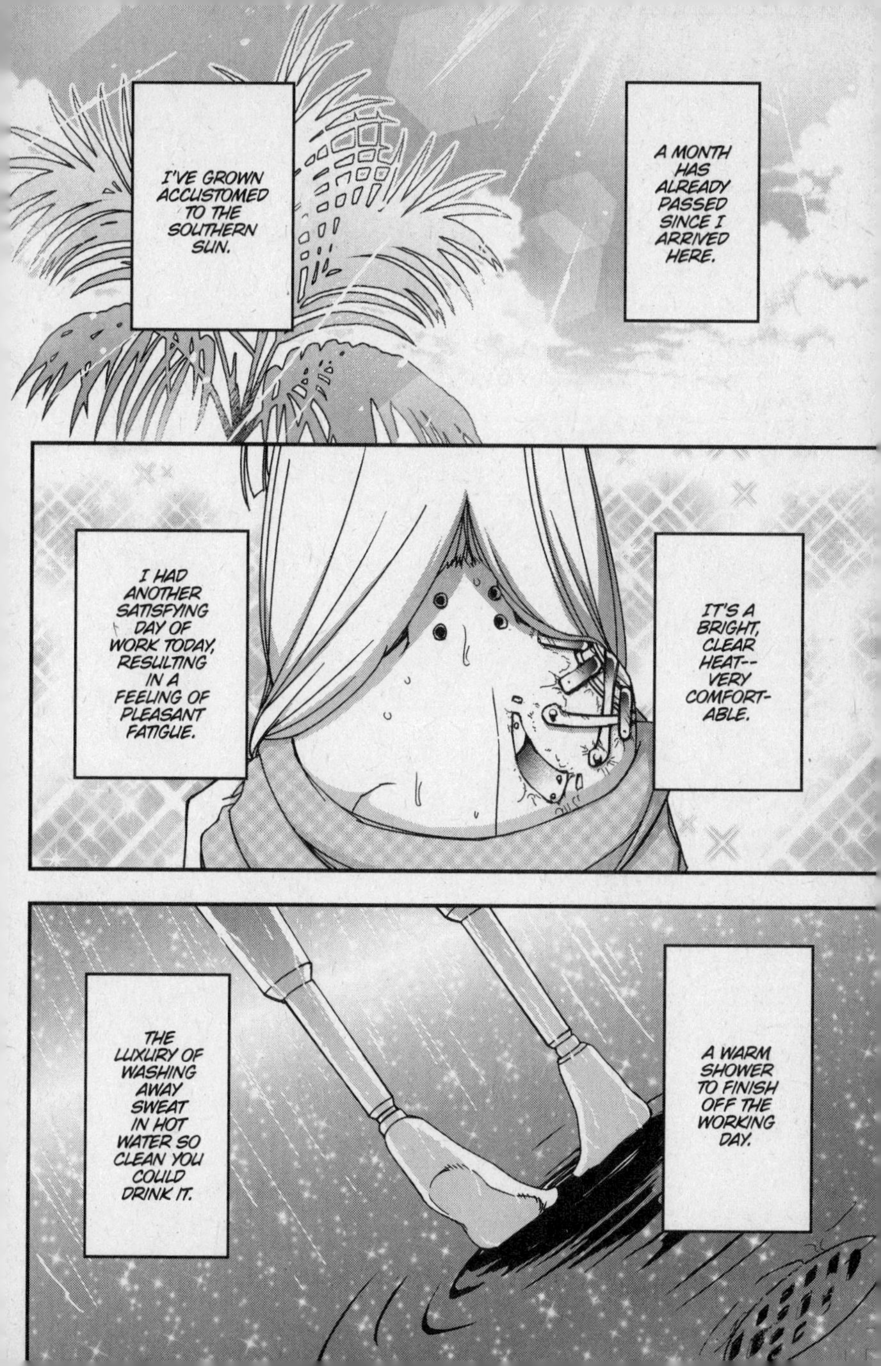
A MONTH HAS ALREADY PASSED SINCE I ARRIVED HERE.
I'VE GROWN ACCUSTOMED TO THE SOUTHERN SUN.
IT'S A BRIGHT, CLEAR HEAT-- VERY COMFORT-ABLE.
I HAD ANOTHER SATISFYING DAY OF WORK TODAY, RESULTING IN A FEELING OF PLEASANT FATIGUE.
A WARM SHOWER TO FINISH OFF THE WORKING DAY.
THE LUXURY OF WASHING AWAY SWEAT IN HOT WATER SO CLEAN YOU COULD DRINK IT.

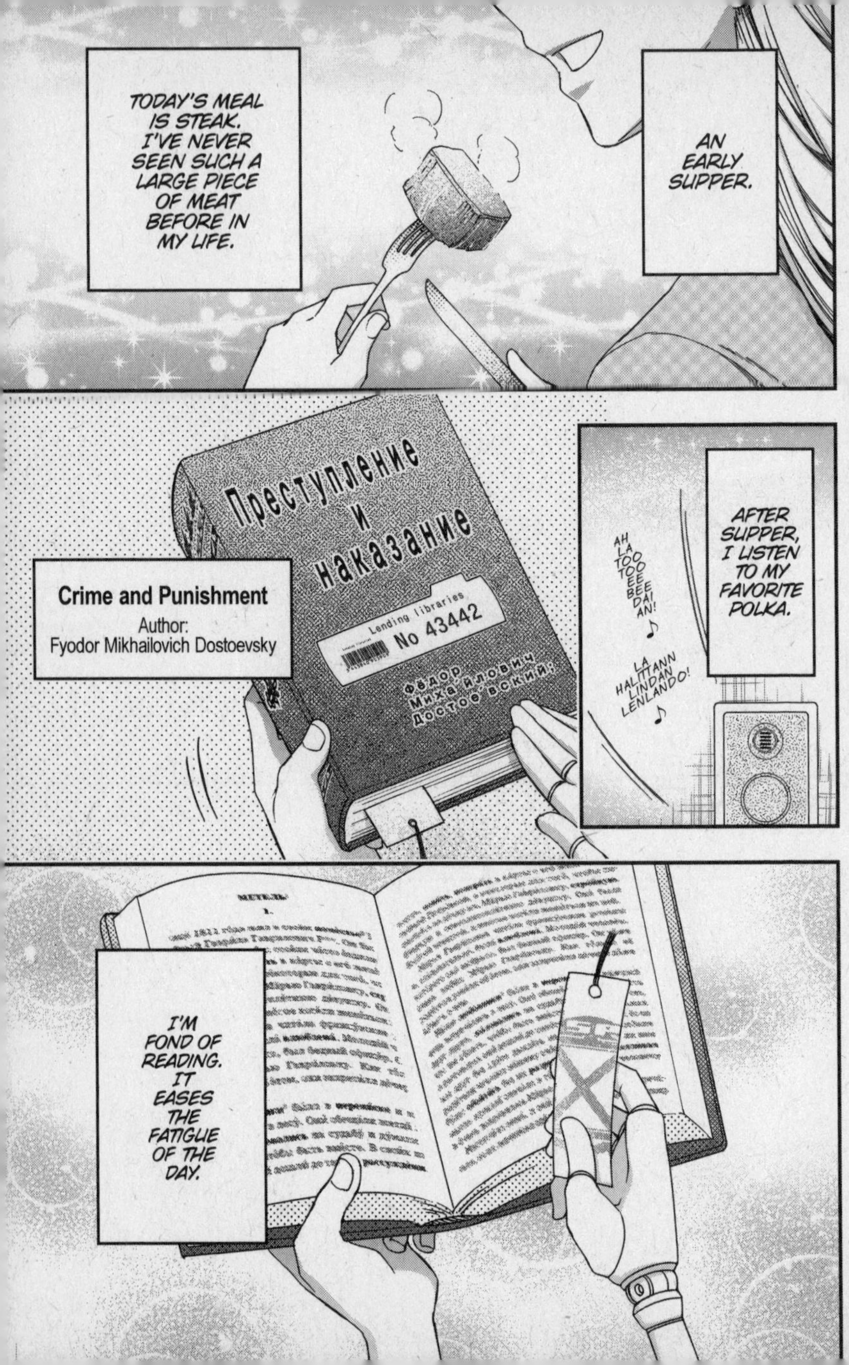
AN EARLY SUPPER.
TODAY'S MEAL IS STEAK. I'VE NEVER SEEN SUCH A LARGE PIECE OF MEAT BEFORE IN MY LIFE.
AFTER SUPPER, I LISTEN TO MY FAVORITE POLKA.
AH LA TOO TOO EE BEE DAI AN! ♪
LA HALITTANN LINDAN LENLANDO! ♪
Преступление и наказание
Lending libraries
No 43442
Фёдор Михайлович Достоевский;
Crime and Punishment
Author:
Fyodor Mikhailovich Dostoevsky
I'M FOND OF READING. IT EASES THE FATIGUE OF THE DAY.

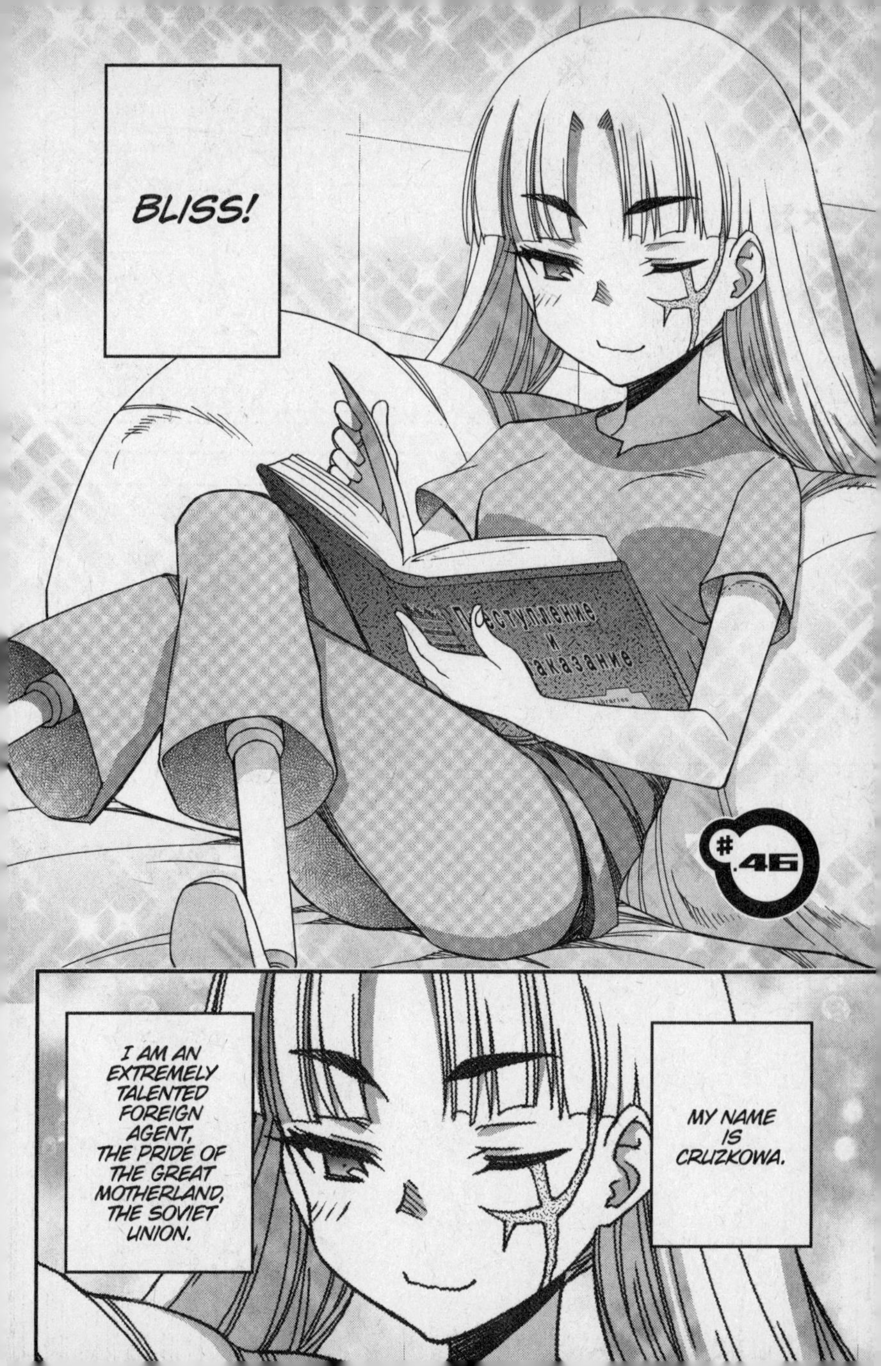
BLISS!
#.46
MY NAME IS CRUZKOWA.
I AM AN EXTREMELY TALENTED FOREIGN AGENT, THE PRIDE OF THE GREAT MOTHERLAND, THE SOVIET UNION.

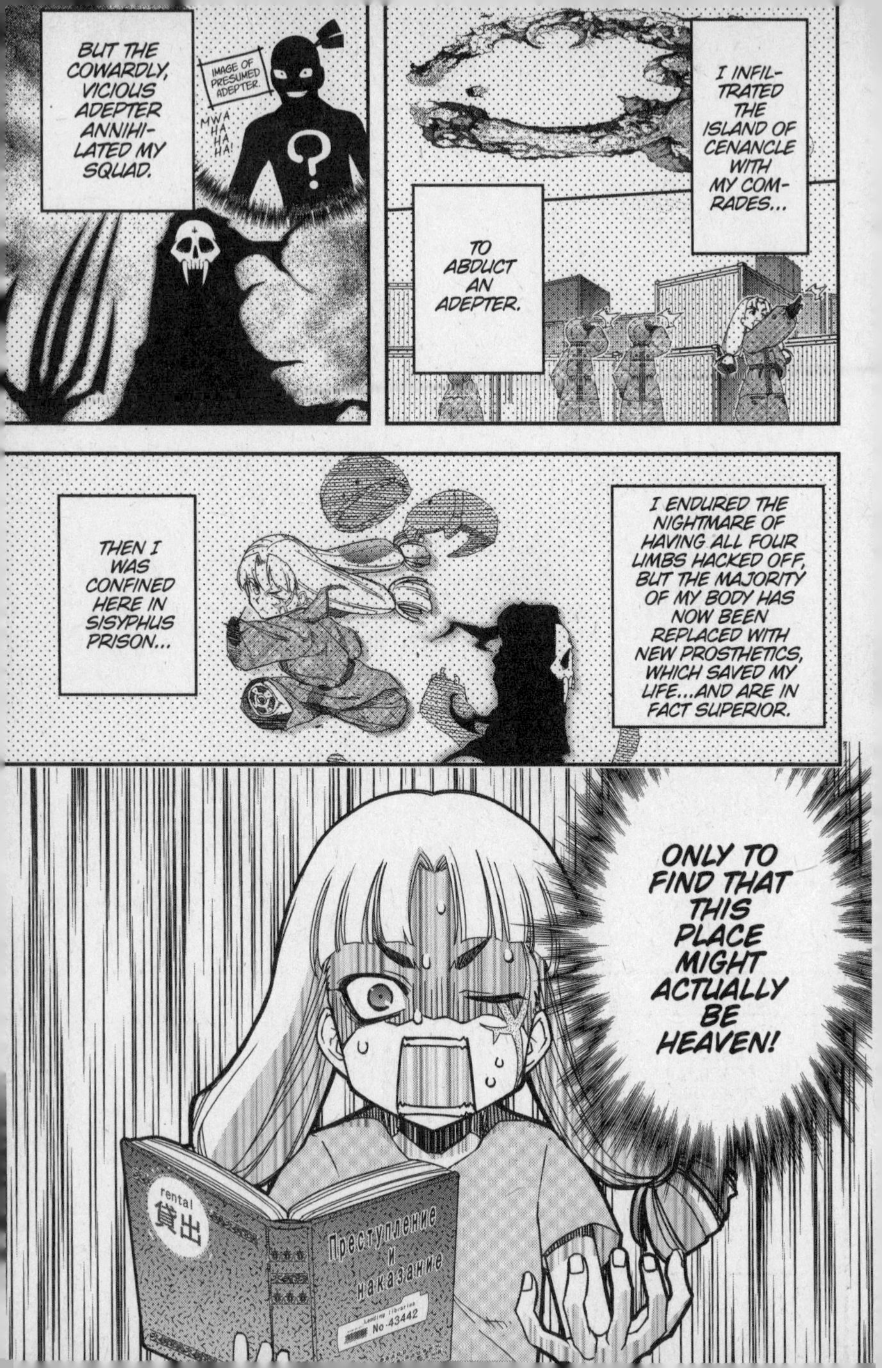
I INFILTRATED THE ISLAND OF CENANCLE WITH MY COMRADES...
TO ABDUCT AN ADEPTER.
BUT THE COWARDLY, VICIOUS ADEPTER ANNIHILATED MY SQUAD.
IMAGE OF PRESUMED ADEPTER.
MWA HA HA HA!
I ENDURED THE NIGHTMARE OF HAVING ALL FOUR LIMBS HACKED OFF, BUT THE MAJORITY OF MY BODY HAS NOW BEEN REPLACED WITH NEW PROSTHETICS, WHICH SAVED MY LIFE...AND ARE IN FACT SUPERIOR.
THEN I WAS CONFINED HERE IN SISYPHUS PRISON...
ONLY TO FIND THAT THIS PLACE MIGHT ACTUALLY BE HEAVEN!
rental 貸出
Преступление и наказание
No-43442

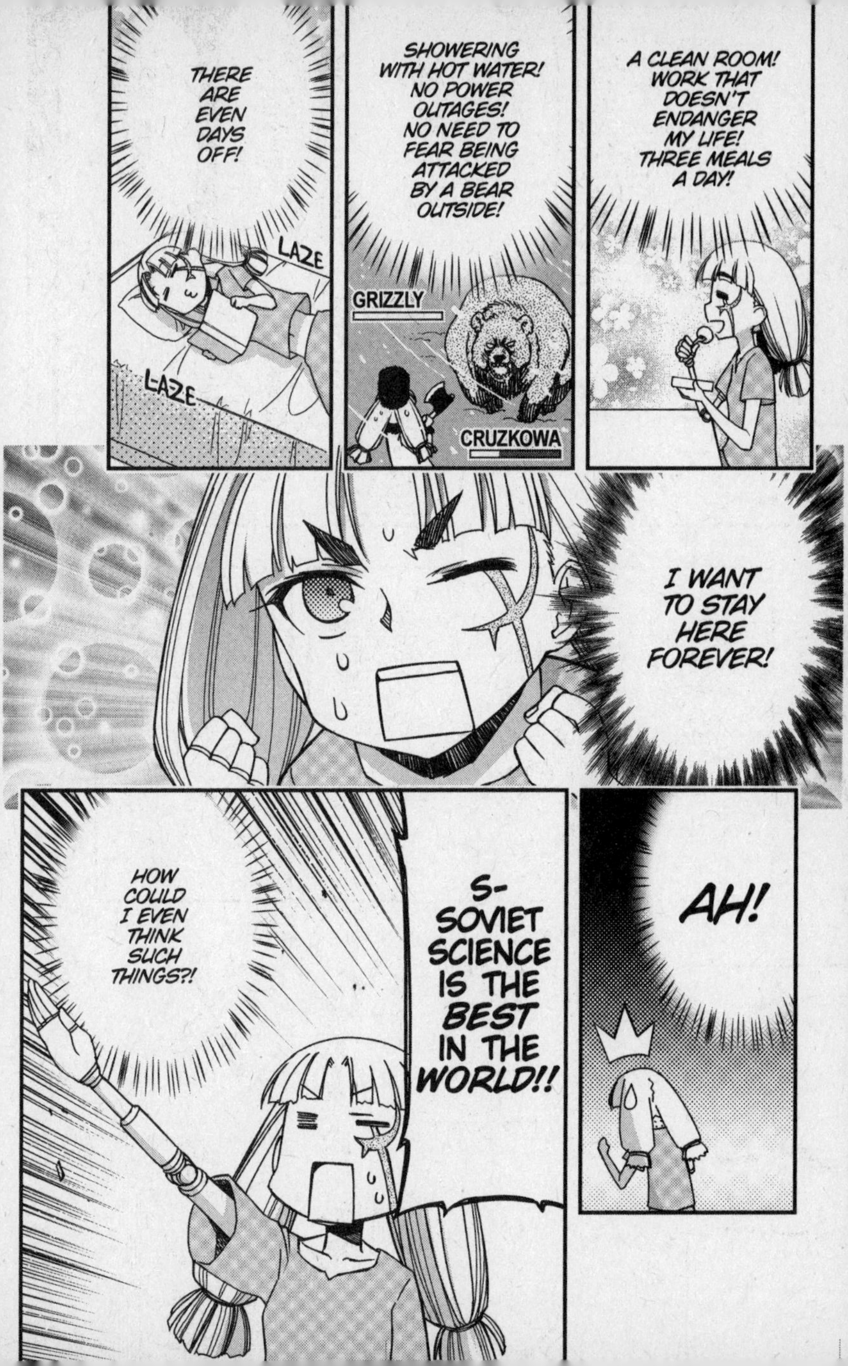
A CLEAN ROOM! WORK THAT DOESN'T ENDANGER MY LIFE! THREE MEALS A DAY!
SHOWERING WITH HOT WATER! NO POWER OUTAGES! NO NEED TO FEAR BEING ATTACKED BY A BEAR OUTSIDE!
GRIZZLY
CRUZKOWA
THERE ARE EVEN DAYS OFF!
LAZE
LAZE
I WANT TO STAY HERE FOREVER!
AH!
S-SOVIET SCIENCE IS THE BEST IN THE WORLD!!
HOW COULD I EVEN THINK SUCH THINGS?!

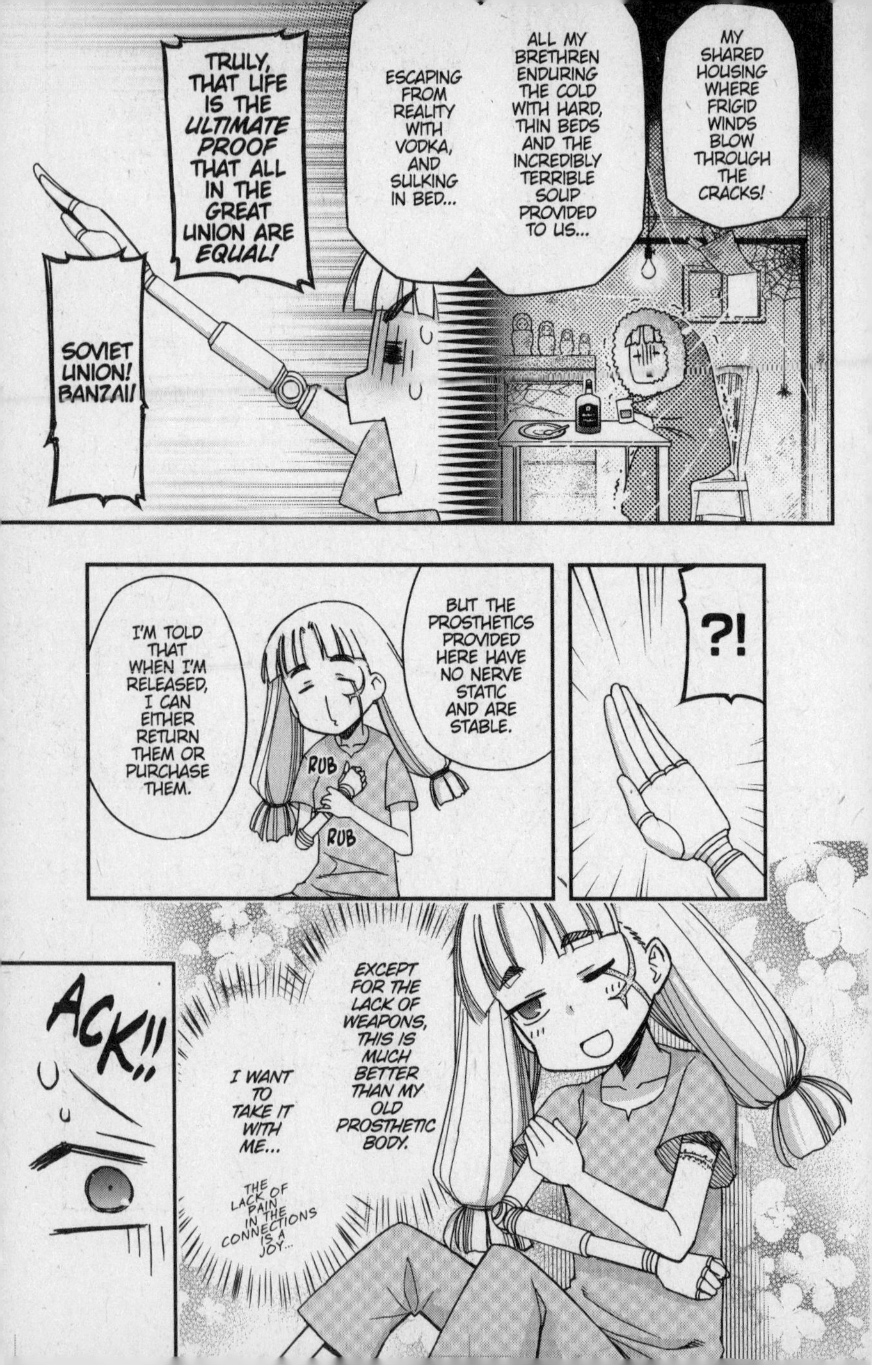
MY SHARED HOUSING WHERE FRIGID WINDS BLOW THROUGH THE CRACKS!
ALL MY BRETHREN ENDURING THE COLD WITH HARD, THIN BEDS AND THE INCREDIBLY TERRIBLE SOUP PROVIDED TO US...
ESCAPING FROM REALITY WITH VODKA, AND SULKING IN BED...
TRULY, THAT LIFE IS THE ULTIMATE PROOF THAT ALL IN THE GREAT UNION ARE EQUAL!
SOVIET UNION! BANZAI!
?!
BUT THE PROSTHETICS PROVIDED HERE HAVE NO NERVE STATIC AND ARE STABLE.
I'M TOLD THAT WHEN I'M RELEASED, I CAN EITHER RETURN THEM OR PURCHASE THEM.
RUB
RUB
EXCEPT FOR THE LACK OF WEAPONS, THIS IS MUCH BETTER THAN MY OLD PROSTHETIC BODY.
I WANT TO TAKE IT WITH ME...
THE LACK OF PAIN IN THE CONNECTIONS IS A JOY...
ACK!!

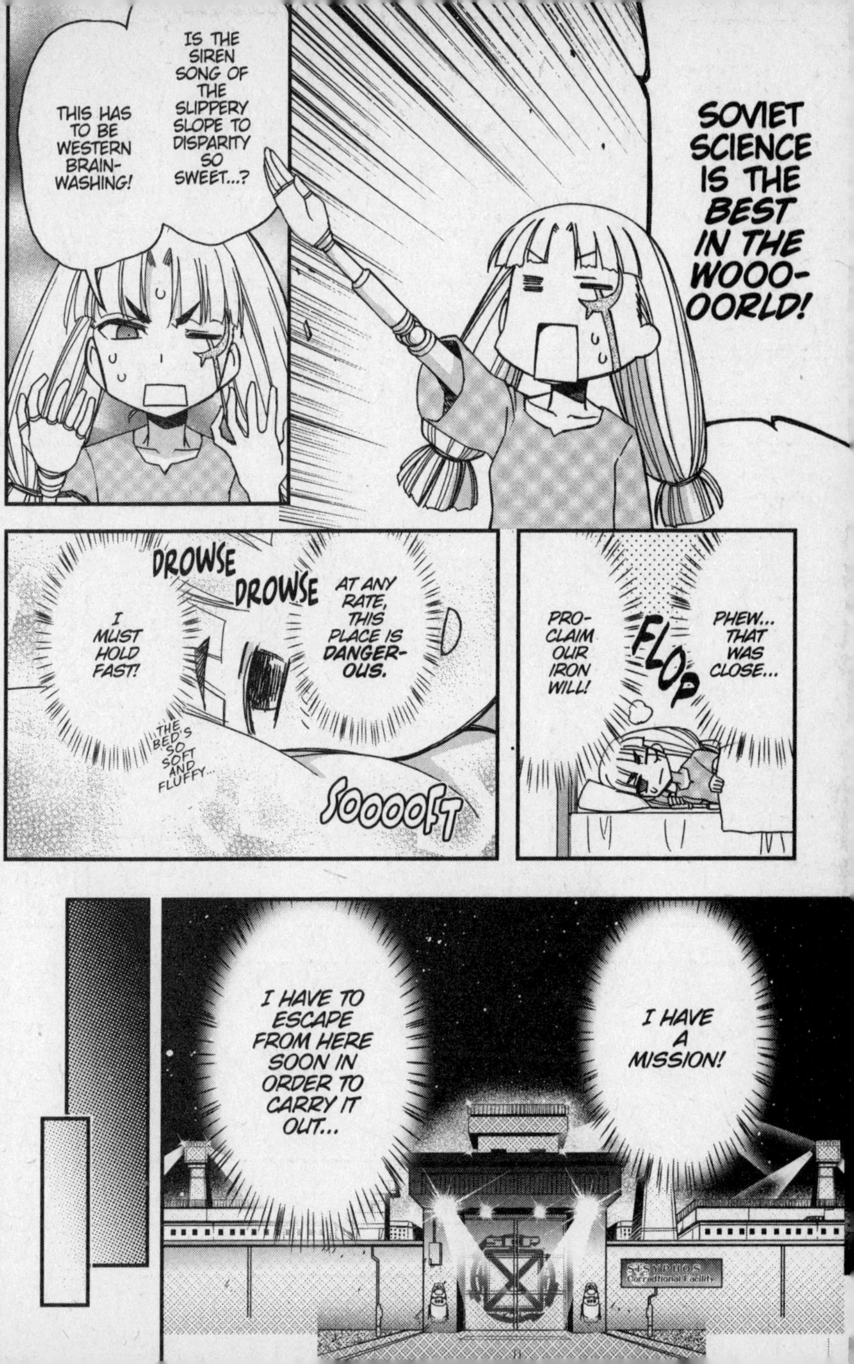
SOVIET SCIENCE IS THE BEST IN THE WOOO-OORLD!
IS THE SIREN SONG OF THE SLIPPERY SLOPE TO DISPARITY SO SWEET...?
THIS HAS TO BE WESTERN BRAIN-WASHING!
PHEW... THAT WAS CLOSE...
FLOP
PRO-CLAIM OUR IRON WILL!
AT ANY RATE, THIS PLACE IS DANGER-OUS.
DROWSE
DROWSE
I MUST HOLD FAST!
THE BED'S SO SOFT AND FLUFFY...
SOOOOOFT
I HAVE A MISSION!
I HAVE TO ESCAPE FROM HERE SOON IN ORDER TO CARRY IT OUT...
SISYPHOS
Correctional Facility

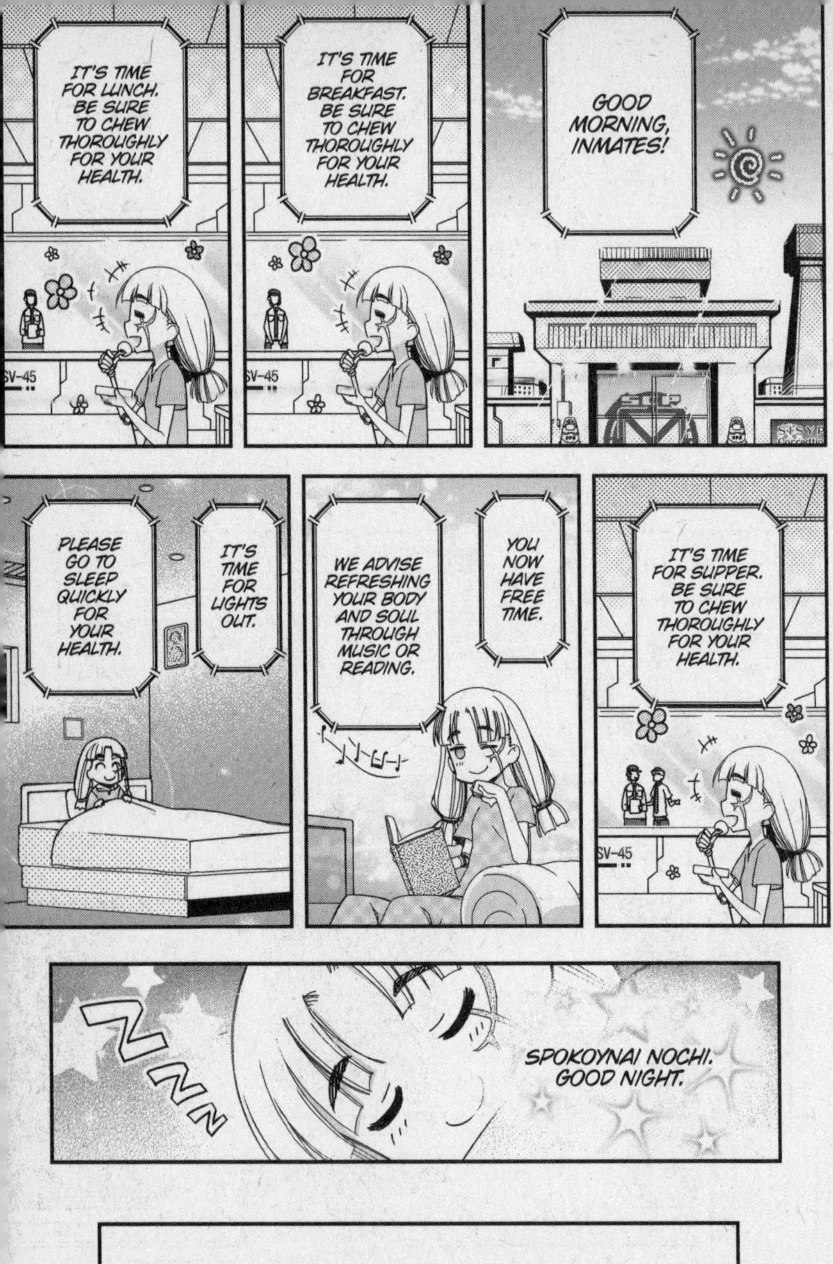
GOOD MORNING, INMATES!
IT'S TIME FOR BREAKFAST. BE SURE TO CHEW THOROUGHLY FOR YOUR HEALTH.
SV-45
IT'S TIME FOR LUNCH. BE SURE TO CHEW THOROUGHLY FOR YOUR HEALTH.
SV-45
IT'S TIME FOR SUPPER. BE SURE TO CHEW THOROUGHLY FOR YOUR HEALTH.
SV-45
YOU NOW HAVE FREE TIME.
WE ADVISE REFRESHING YOUR BODY AND SOUL THROUGH MUSIC OR READING.
IT'S TIME FOR LIGHTS OUT.
PLEASE GO TO SLEEP QUICKLY FOR YOUR HEALTH.
SPOKOYNAI NOCHI. GOOD NIGHT.

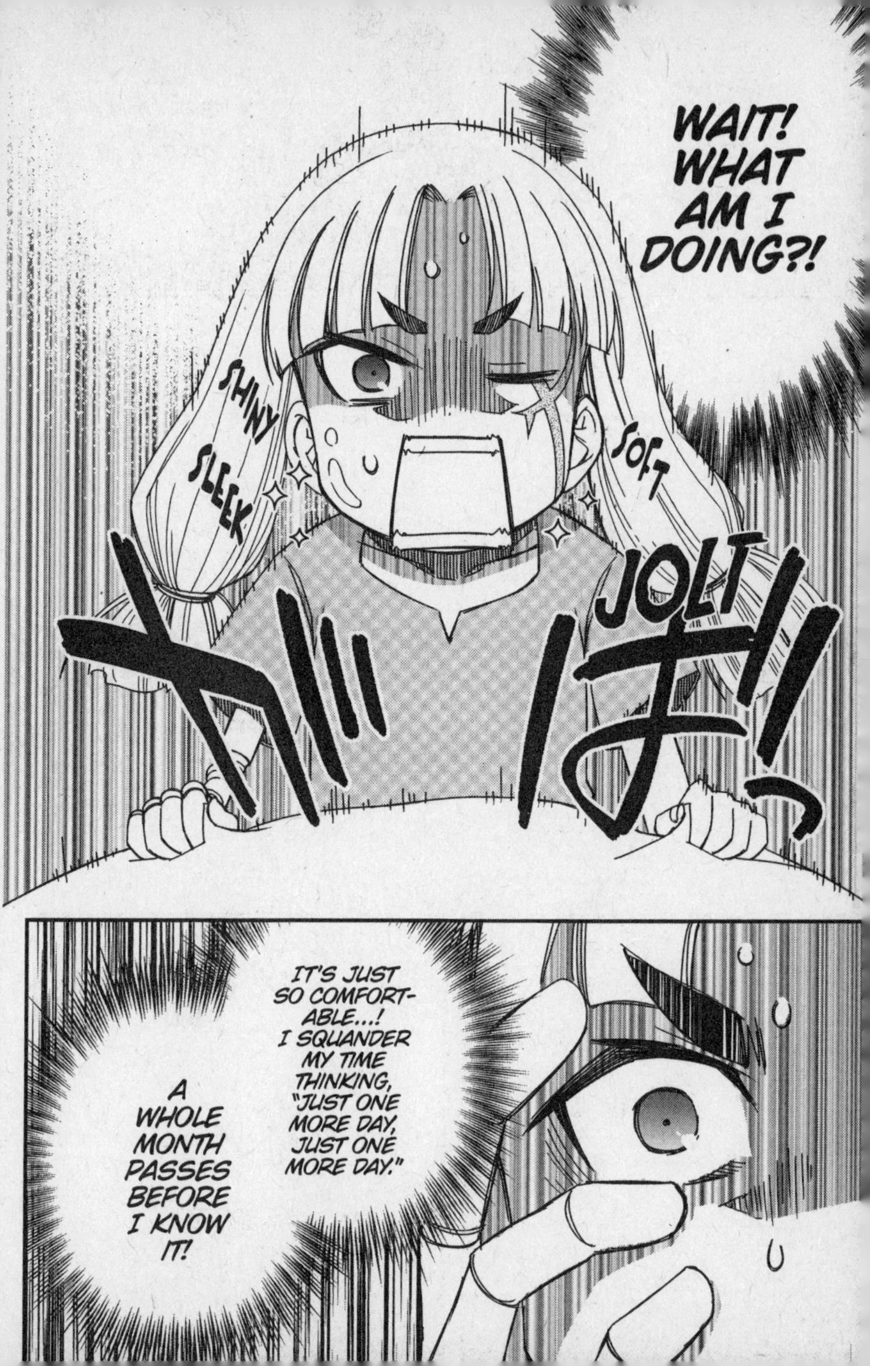
WAIT! WHAT AM I DOING?!
SOFT
SHINY SLEEK
JOLT
IT'S JUST SO COMFORT-ABLE...! I SQUANDER MY TIME THINKING, "JUST ONE MORE DAY, JUST ONE MORE DAY."
A WHOLE MONTH PASSES BEFORE I KNOW IT!

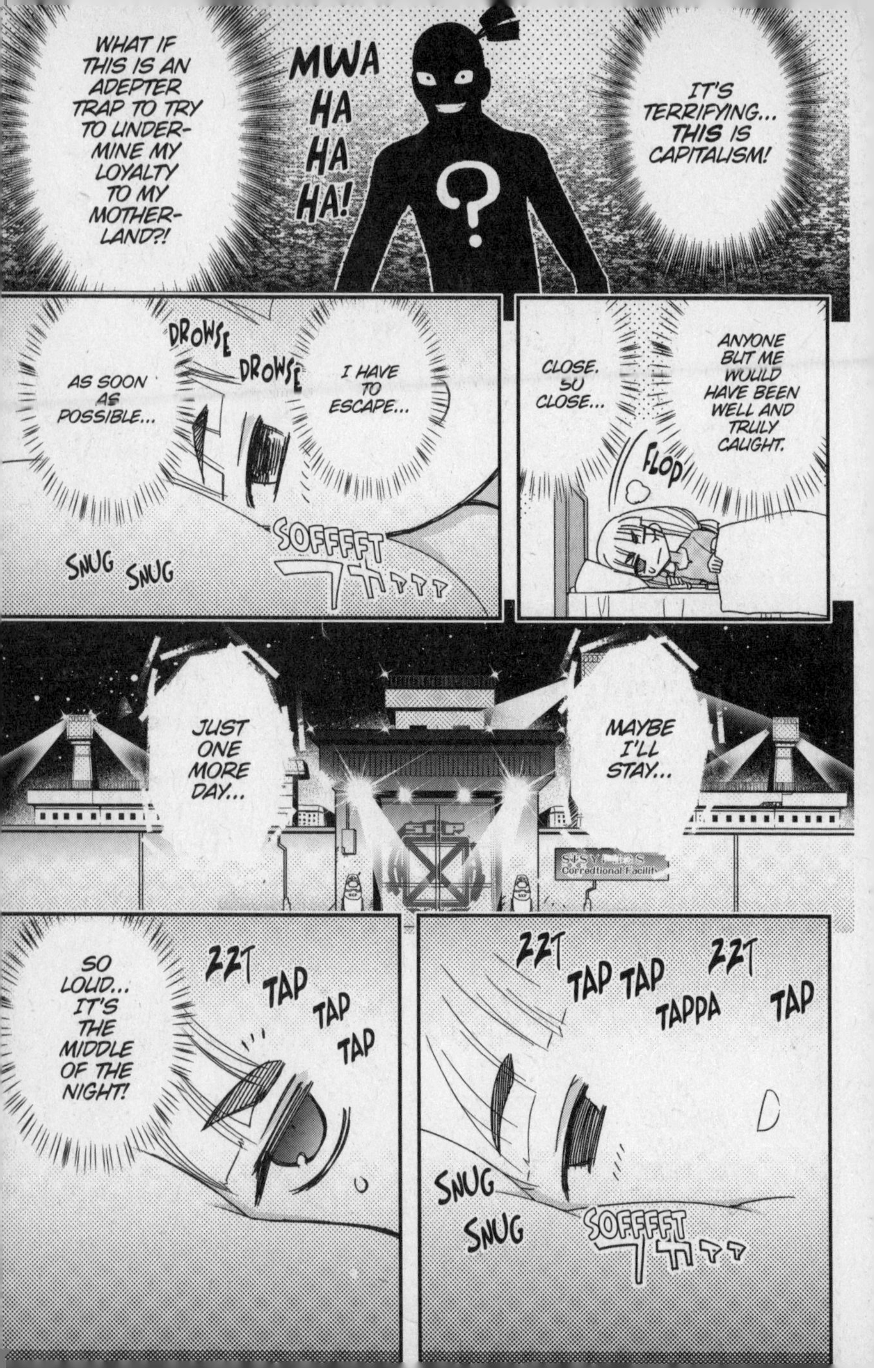
IT'S TERRIFYING... THIS IS CAPITALISM!
MWA HA HA HA!
WHAT IF THIS IS AN ADEPTER TRAP TO TRY TO UNDERMINE MY LOYALTY TO MY MOTHERLAND?!
ANYONE BUT ME WOULD HAVE BEEN WELL AND TRULY CAUGHT.
CLOSE. SO CLOSE...
FLOP
I HAVE TO ESCAPE...
DROWSE DROWSE
AS SOON AS POSSIBLE...
SOFFFFT
SNUG SNUG
MAYBE I'LL STAY...
JUST ONE MORE DAY...
Correctional Facility
ZZT TAP TAP ZZT TAPPA TAP
SNUG SNUG
SOFFFFT
ZZT TAP TAP TAP
SO LOUD... IT'S THE MIDDLE OF THE NIGHT!

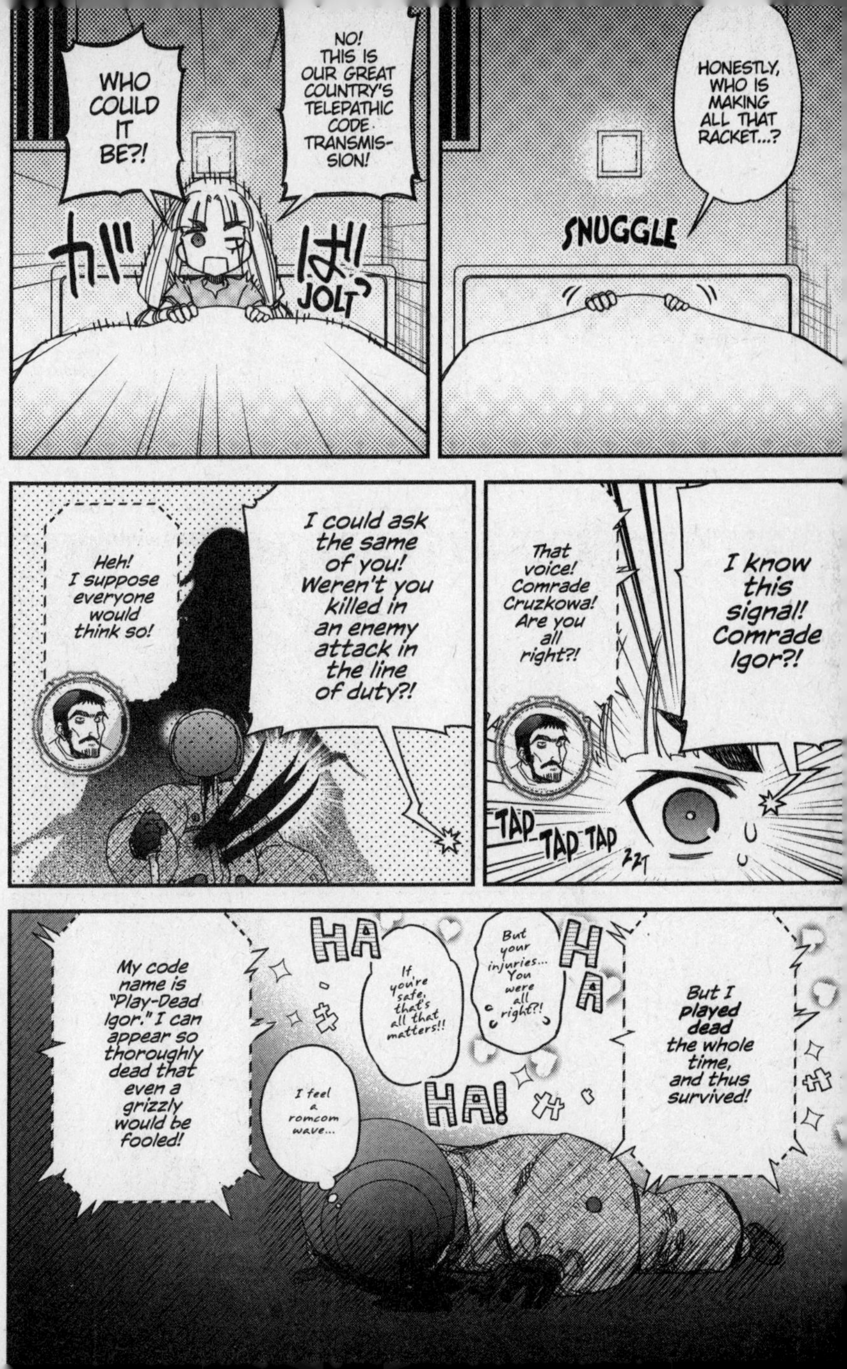
HONESTLY, WHO IS MAKING ALL THAT RACKET...?
SNUGGLE
NO! THIS IS OUR GREAT COUNTRY'S TELEPATHIC CODE TRANSMISSION!
WHO COULD IT BE?!
JOLT
I know this signal! Comrade Igor?!
That voice! Comrade Cruzkowa! Are you all right?!
TAP TAP TAP
I could ask the same of you! Weren't you killed in an enemy attack in the line of duty?!
Heh! I suppose everyone would think so!
But I played dead the whole time, and thus survived!
HA HA HA!
But your injuries... You were all right?!
If you're safe, that's all that matters!!
I feel a romcom wave...
My code name is "Play-Dead Igor." I can appear so thoroughly dead that even a grizzly would be fooled!

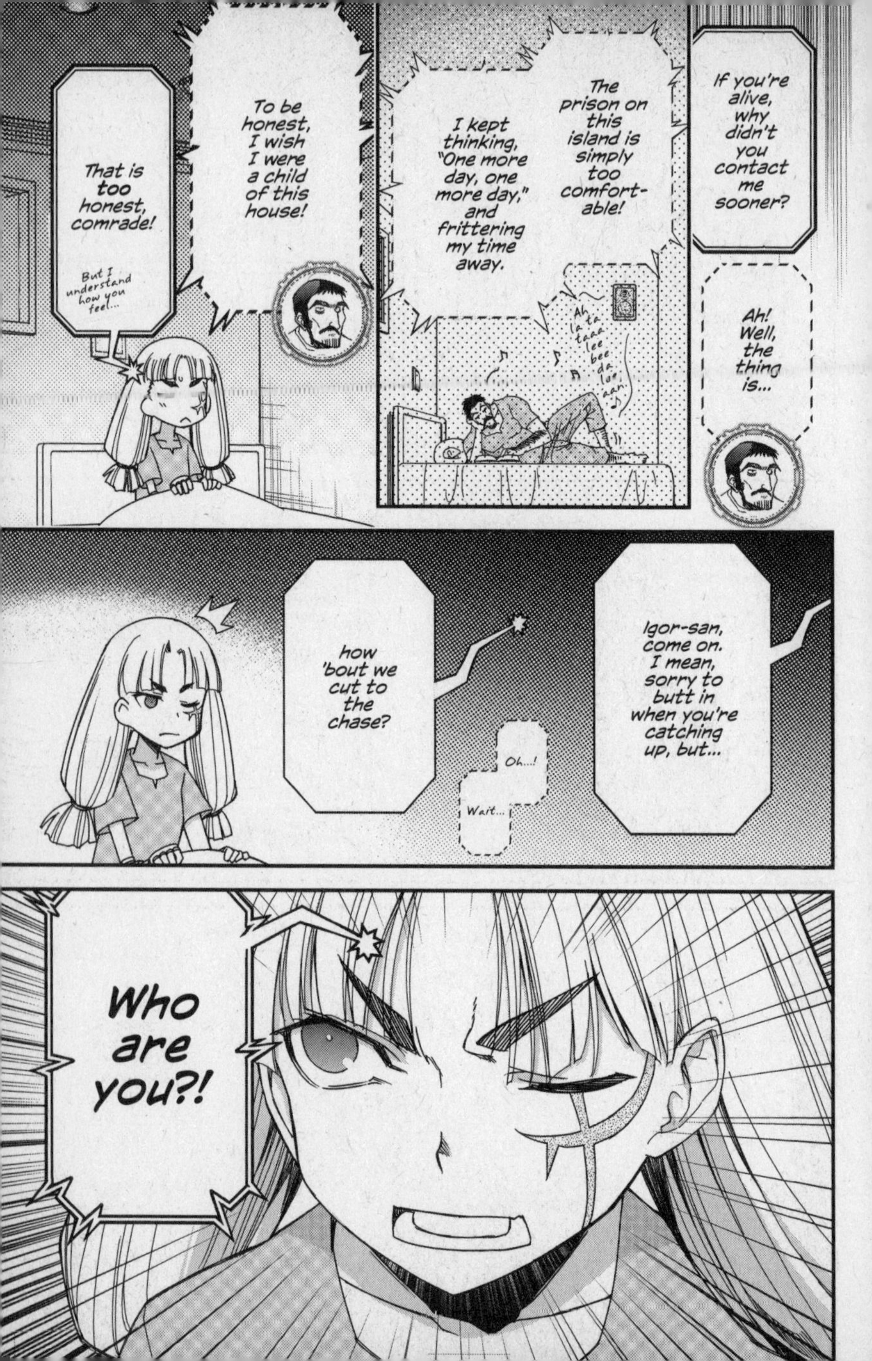
If you're alive, why didn't you contact me sooner?
Ah! Well, the thing is...
The prison on this island is simply too comfortable!
I kept thinking, "One more day, one more day," and frittering my time away.
Ah la ta taaa lee bee da lee aan
To be honest, I wish I were a child of this house!
That is too honest, comrade!
But I understand how you feel...
Igor-san, come on. I mean, sorry to butt in when you're catching up, but...
Oh...!
Wait...
how 'bout we cut to the chase?
Who are you?!

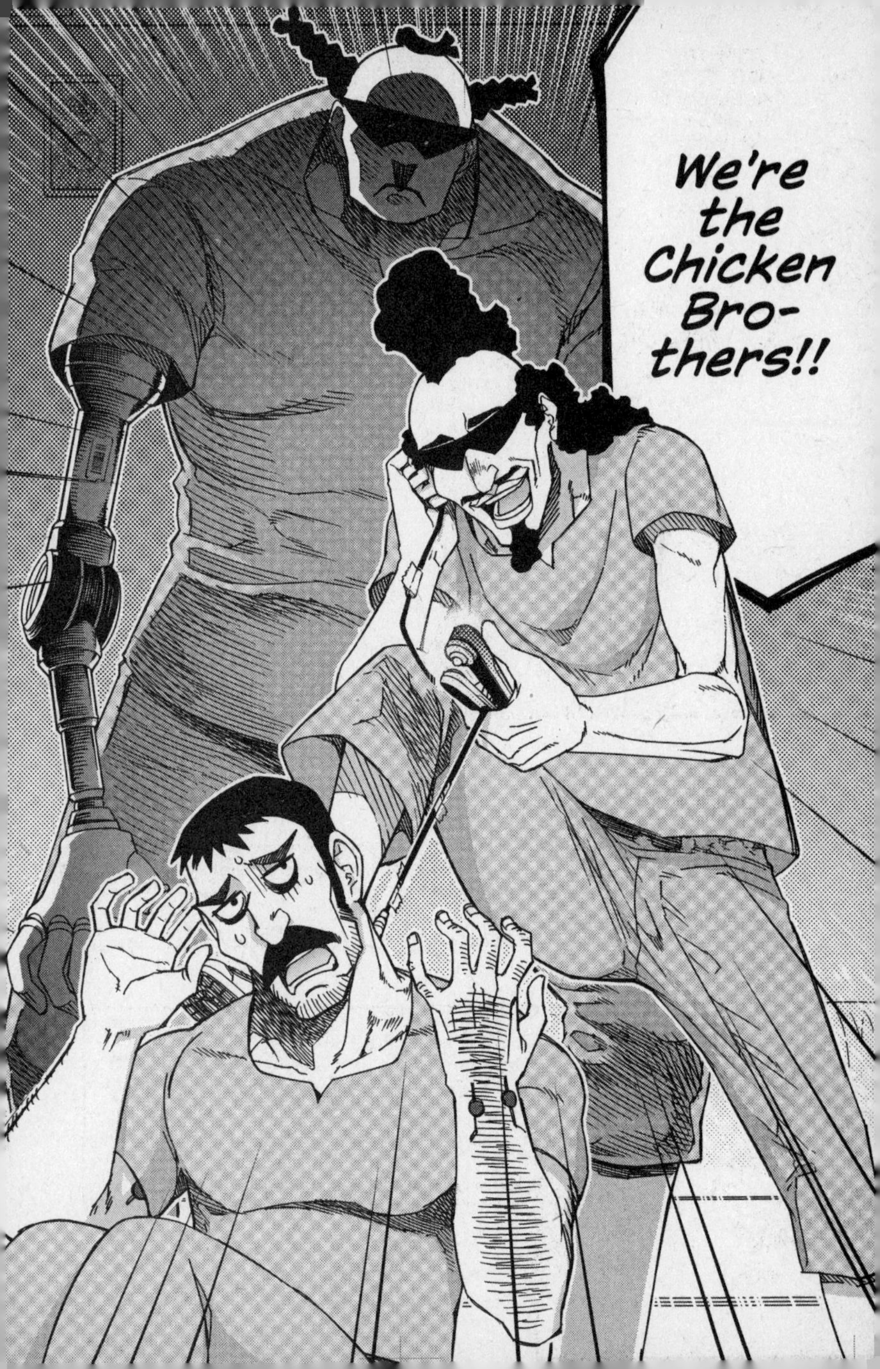
We're the Chicken Bro- thers!!

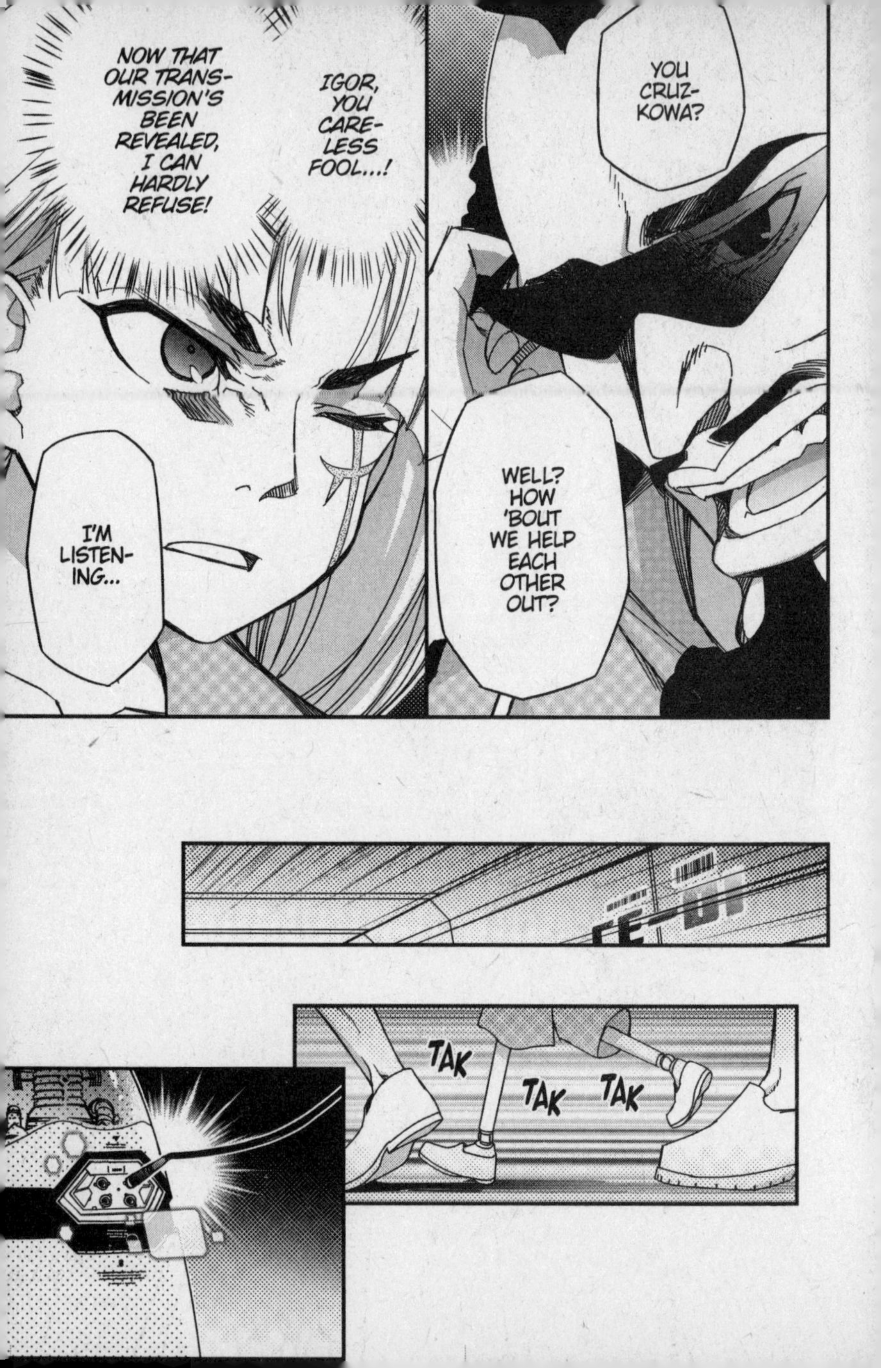
YOU CRUZKOWA?
WELL? HOW 'BOUT WE HELP EACH OTHER OUT?
IGOR, YOU CARELESS FOOL...!
NOW THAT OUR TRANSMISSION'S BEEN REVEALED, I CAN HARDLY REFUSE!
I'M LISTENING...
TAK
TAK
TAK

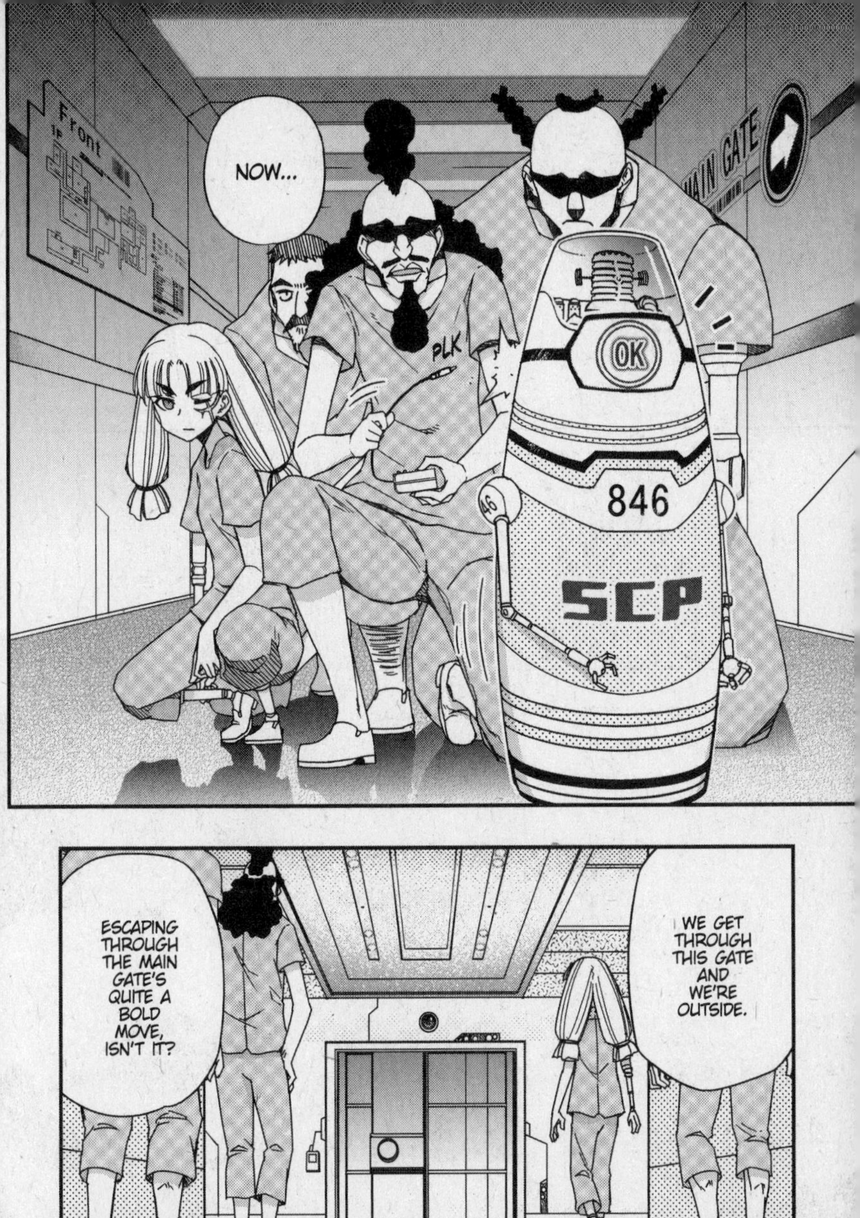
MAIN GATE
Front
1F
NOW...
PLK
OK
846
SCP
WE GET THROUGH THIS GATE AND WE'RE OUTSIDE.
ESCAPING THROUGH THE MAIN GATE'S QUITE A BOLD MOVE, ISN'T IT?

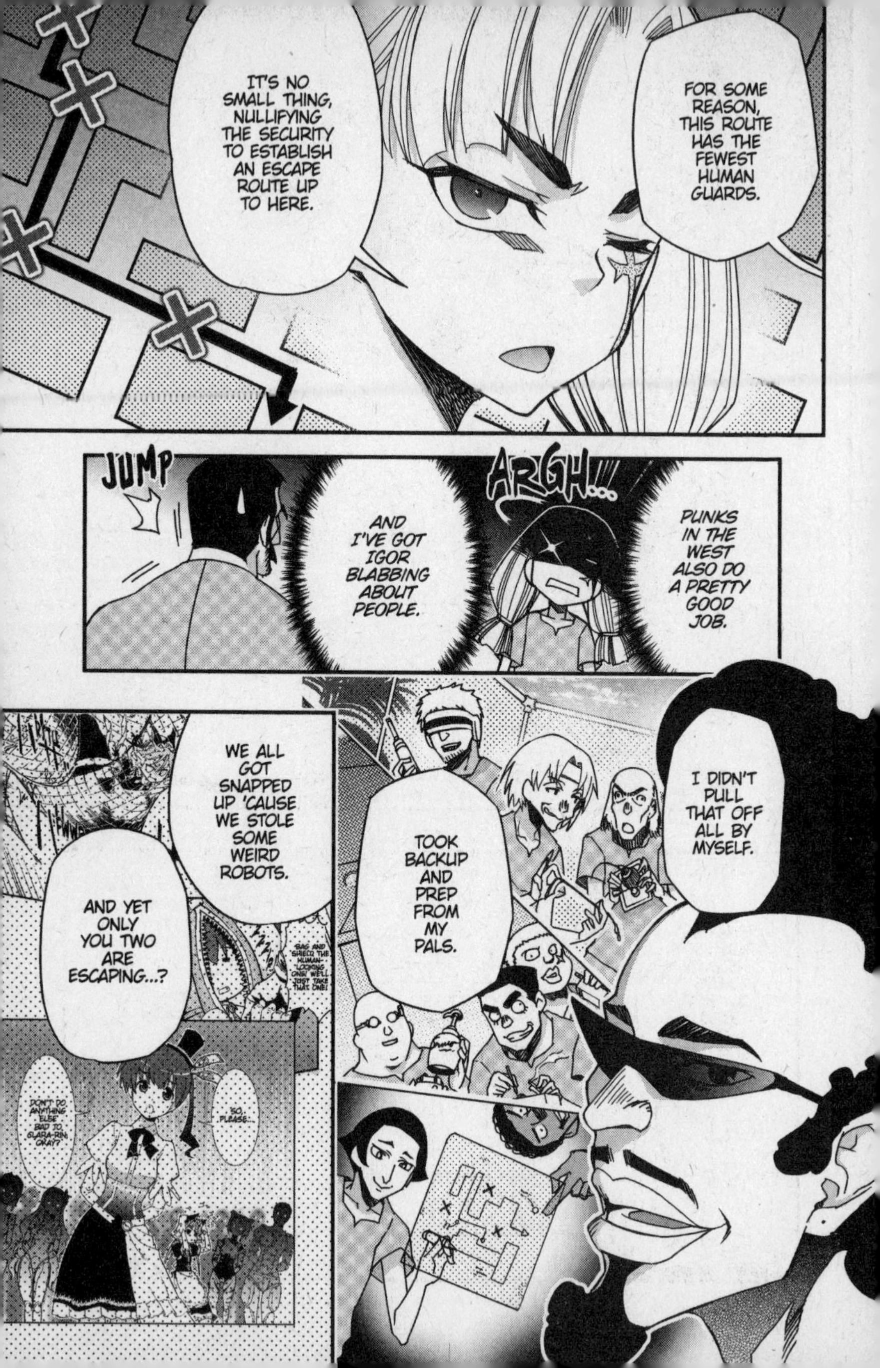
FOR SOME REASON, THIS ROUTE HAS THE FEWEST HUMAN GUARDS.
IT'S NO SMALL THING, NULLIFYING THE SECURITY TO ESTABLISH AN ESCAPE ROUTE UP TO HERE.
PUNKS IN THE WEST ALSO DO A PRETTY GOOD JOB.
ARGH...!!!
AND I'VE GOT IGOR BLABBING ABOUT PEOPLE.
JUMP
I DIDN'T PULL THAT OFF ALL BY MYSELF.
TOOK BACKUP AND PREP FROM MY PALS.
WE ALL GOT SNAPPED UP 'CAUSE WE STOLE SOME WEIRD ROBOTS.
"BAG AND SHIELD THE HUMAN-LOOKING ONE! WE'LL JUST TAKE THAT ONE!
AND YET ONLY YOU TWO ARE ESCAPING...?
"SO, PLEASE...
DON'T DO ANYTHING ELSE BAD TO GLARA-RIN, OKAY?"

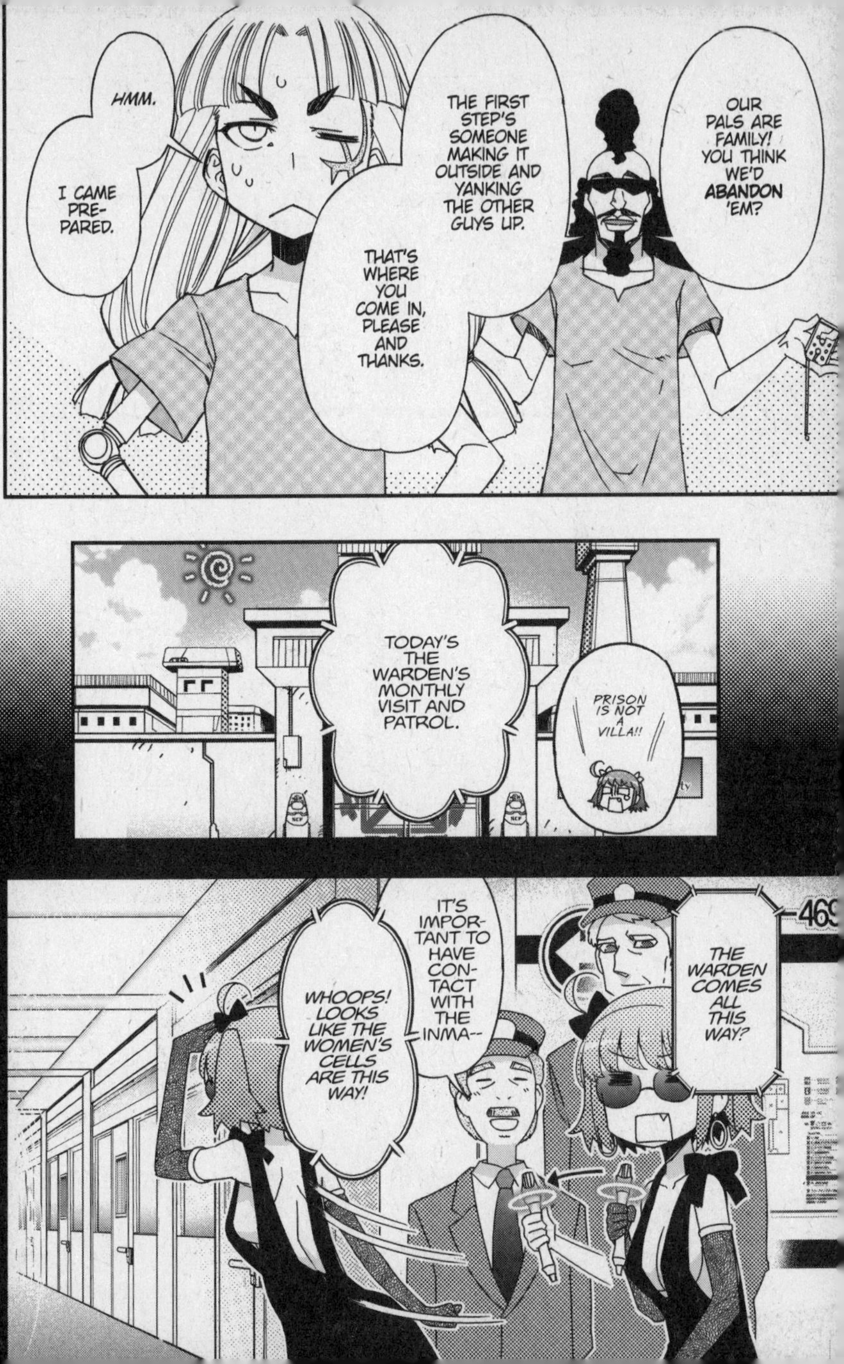
OUR PALS ARE FAMILY! YOU THINK WE'D ABANDON 'EM?
THE FIRST STEP'S SOMEONE MAKING IT OUTSIDE AND YANKING THE OTHER GUYS UP.
THAT'S WHERE YOU COME IN, PLEASE AND THANKS.
HMM. I CAME PRE-PARED.
TODAY'S THE WARDEN'S MONTHLY VISIT AND PATROL.
PRISON IS NOT A VILLA!!
THE WARDEN COMES ALL THIS WAY?
IT'S IMPOR-TANT TO HAVE CON-TACT WITH THE INMA--
WHOOPS! LOOKS LIKE THE WOMEN'S CELLS ARE THIS WAY!

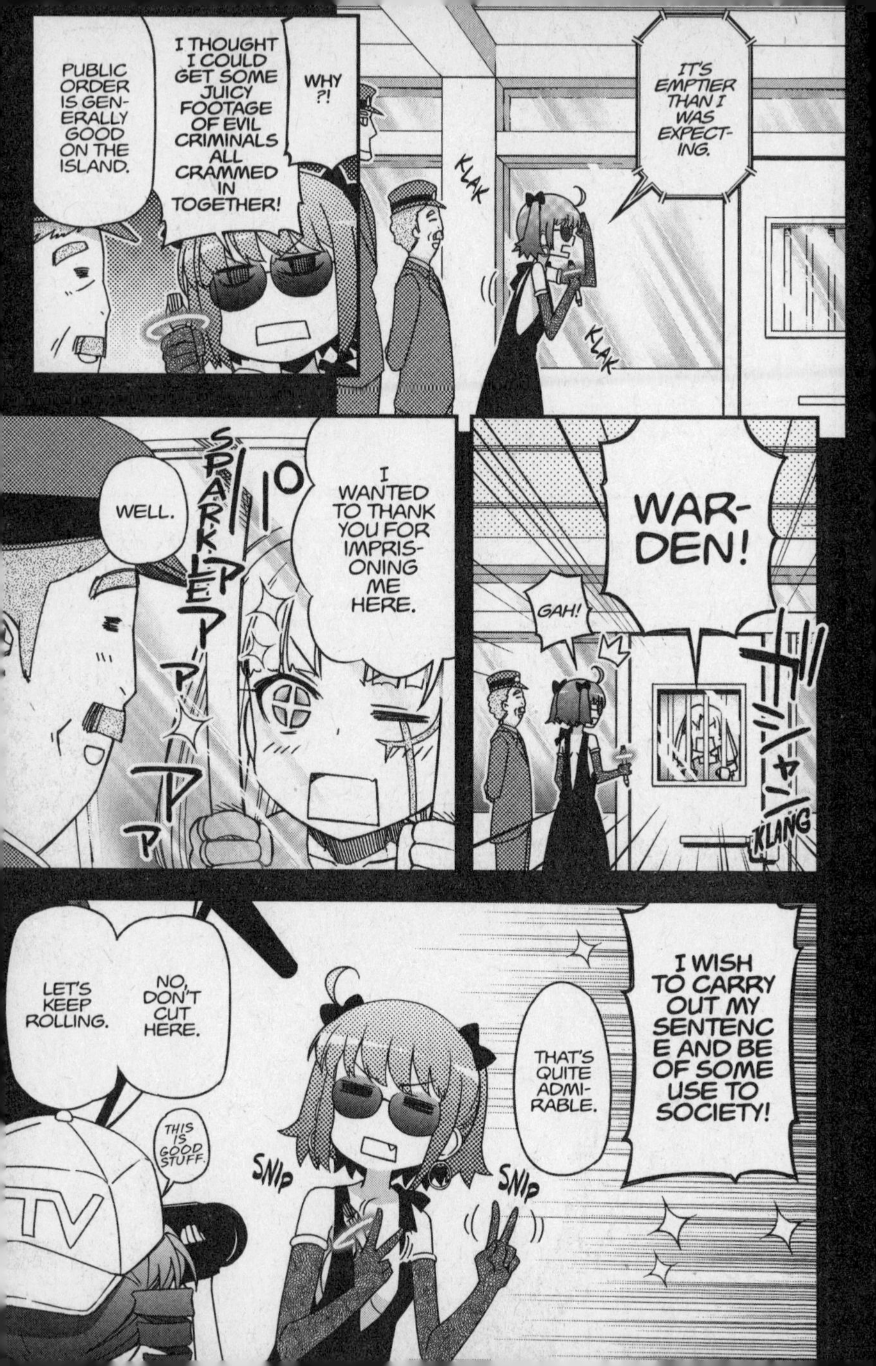
IT'S EMPTIER THAN I WAS EXPECTING.
KLAK
KLAK
WHY?!
I THOUGHT I COULD GET SOME JUICY FOOTAGE OF EVIL CRIMINALS ALL CRAMMED IN TOGETHER!
PUBLIC ORDER IS GENERALLY GOOD ON THE ISLAND.
WARDEN!
GAH!
KLANG
I WANTED TO THANK YOU FOR IMPRISONING ME HERE.
SPARKLE
WELL.
I WISH TO CARRY OUT MY SENTENCE AND BE OF SOME USE TO SOCIETY!
THAT'S QUITE ADMIRABLE.
NO, DON'T CUT HERE.
LET'S KEEP ROLLING.
THIS IS GOOD STUFF.
SNIP
SNIP
TV

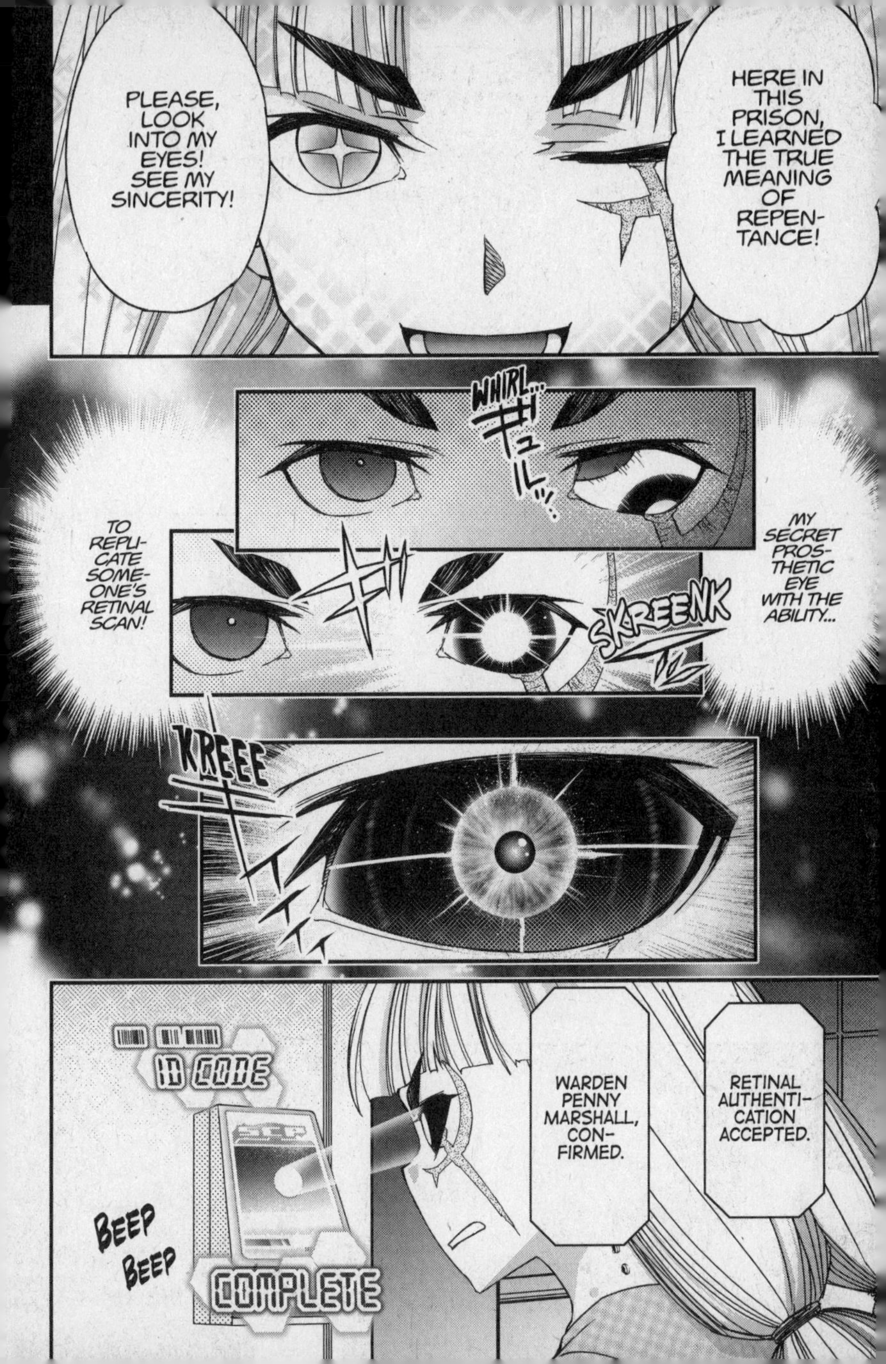
HERE IN THIS PRISON, I LEARNED THE TRUE MEANING OF REPENTANCE!
PLEASE, LOOK INTO MY EYES! SEE MY SINCERITY!
WHIRL...
ギュルッ...
MY SECRET PROSTHETIC EYE WITH THE ABILITY...
SKREENK
TO REPLICATE SOMEONE'S RETINAL SCAN!
KREEE
RETINAL AUTHENTICATION ACCEPTED.
WARDEN PENNY MARSHALL, CONFIRMED.
ID CODE
BEEP BEEP
COMPLETE

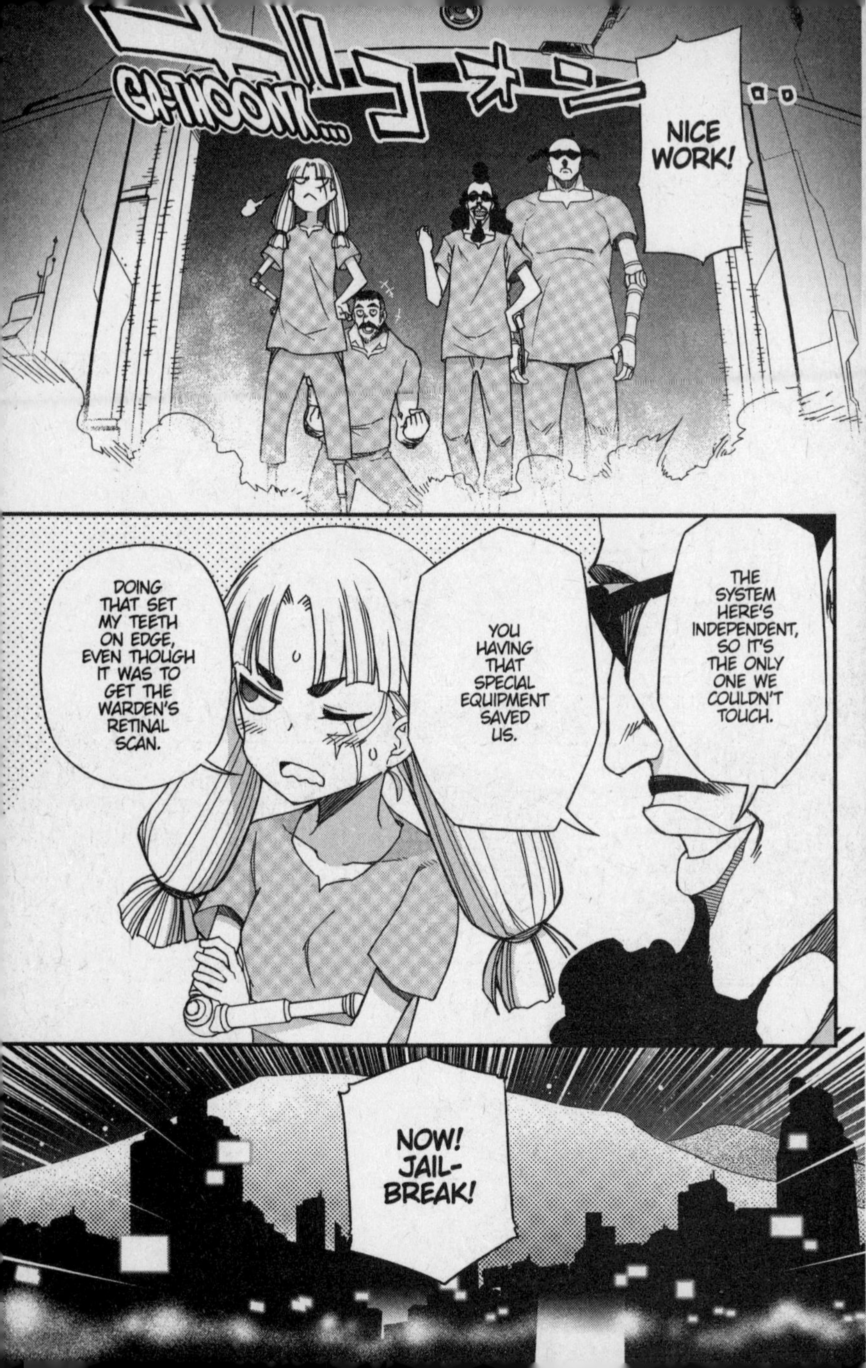
GA-THOONK...
NICE WORK!
THE SYSTEM HERE'S INDEPENDENT, SO IT'S THE ONLY ONE WE COULDN'T TOUCH.
YOU HAVING THAT SPECIAL EQUIPMENT SAVED US.
DOING THAT SET MY TEETH ON EDGE, EVEN THOUGH IT WAS TO GET THE WARDEN'S RETINAL SCAN.
NOW! JAIL-BREAK!

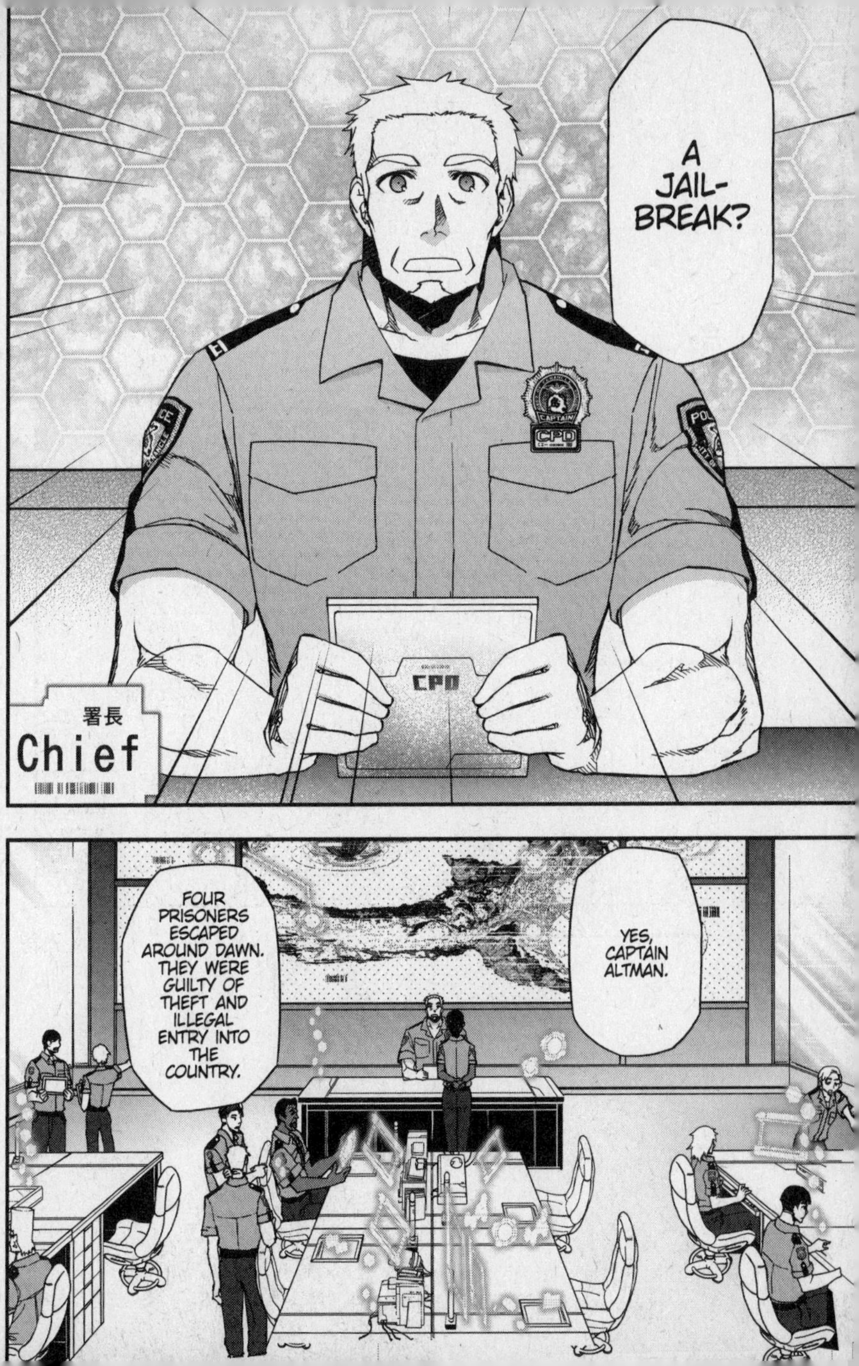
A JAIL-BREAK?
署長
Chief
YES, CAPTAIN ALTMAN.
FOUR PRISONERS ESCAPED AROUND DAWN. THEY WERE GUILTY OF THEFT AND ILLEGAL ENTRY INTO THE COUNTRY.

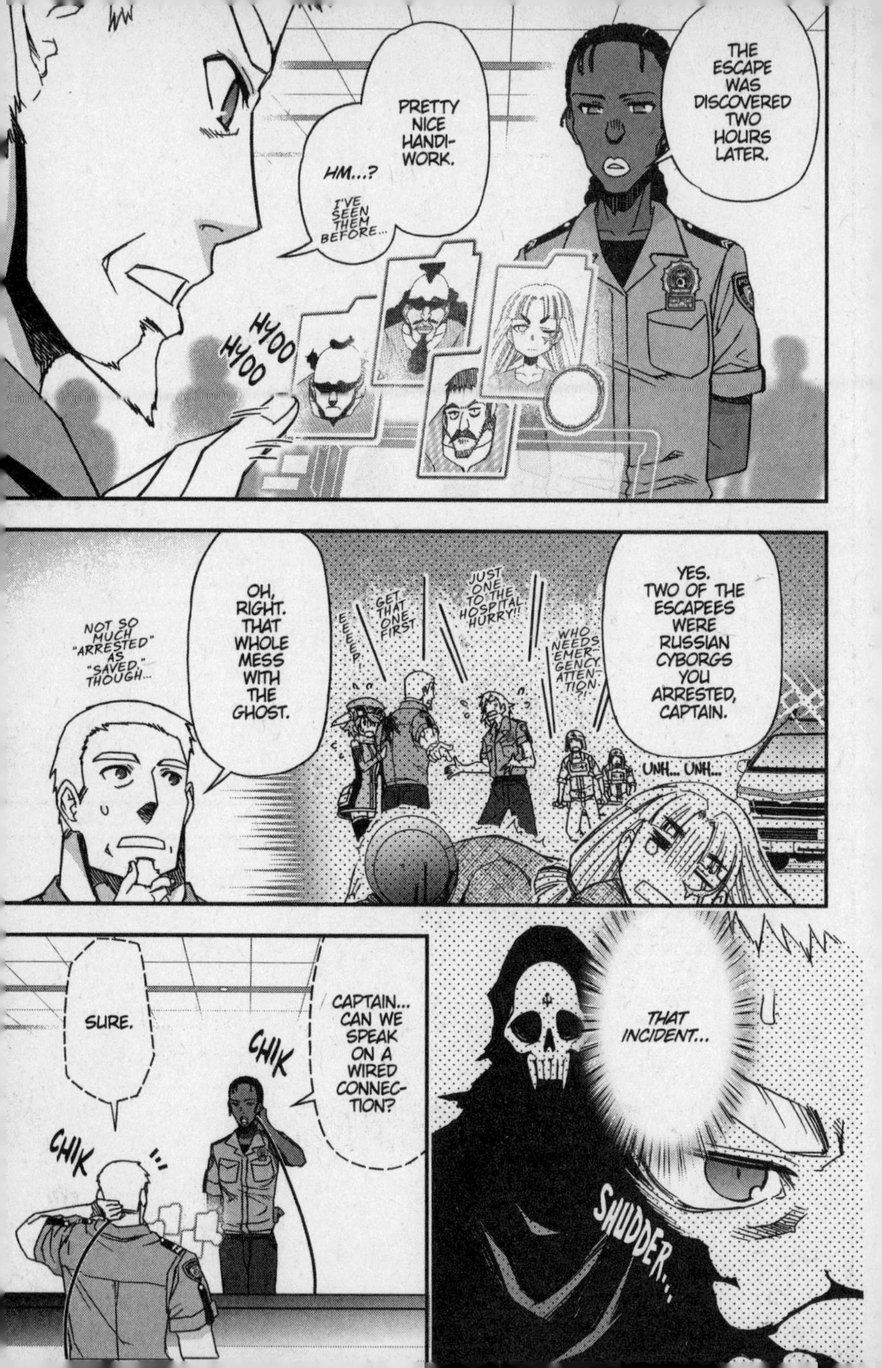
THE ESCAPE WAS DISCOVERED TWO HOURS LATER.
PRETTY NICE HANDIWORK.
HM...?
I'VE SEEN THEM BEFORE...
HYOO
HYOO
YES. TWO OF THE ESCAPEES WERE RUSSIAN CYBORGS YOU ARRESTED, CAPTAIN.
WHO NEEDS EMERGENCY ATTENTION?!
UNH... UNH...
JUST ONE TO THE HOSPITAL HURRY!!
GET THAT ONE FIRST.
EEEEEP!
OH, RIGHT. THAT WHOLE MESS WITH THE GHOST.
NOT SO MUCH "ARRESTED" AS "SAVED," THOUGH...
THAT INCIDENT...
SHUDDER...
CAPTAIN... CAN WE SPEAK ON A WIRED CONNECTION?
CHIK
SURE.
CHIK

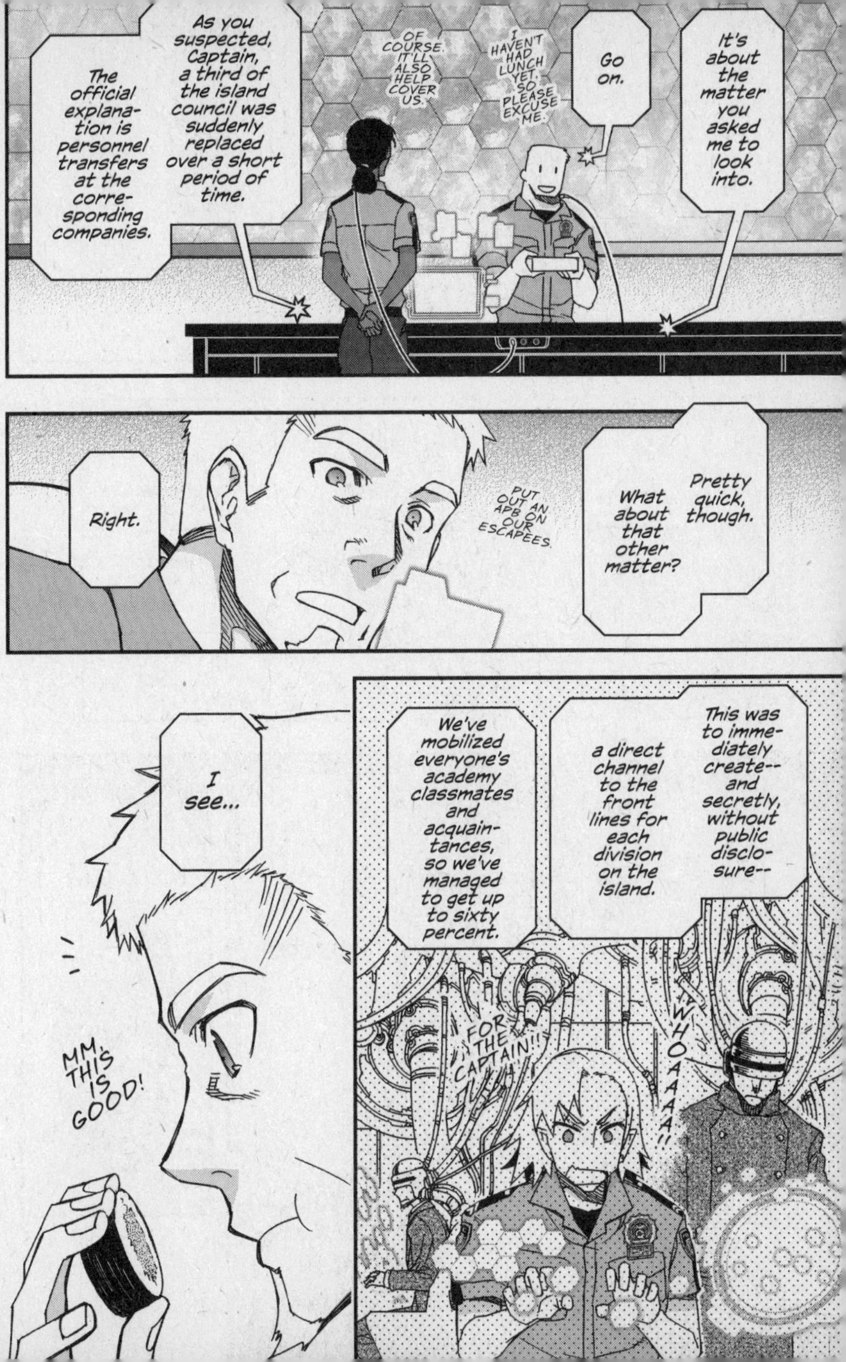
It's about the matter you asked me to look into.
Go on.
I haven't had lunch yet, so please excuse me.
Of course. It'll also help cover us.
As you suspected, Captain, a third of the island council was suddenly replaced over a short period of time.
The official explanation is personnel transfers at the corresponding companies.
Pretty quick, though.
What about that other matter?
Put out an APB on our escapees.
Right.
This was to immediately create--and secretly, without public disclosure--
a direct channel to the front lines for each division on the island.
We've mobilized everyone's academy classmates and acquaintances, so we've managed to get up to sixty percent.
WHOAAAA!!
FOR THE CAPTAIN!!
I see...
MM. THIS IS GOOD!

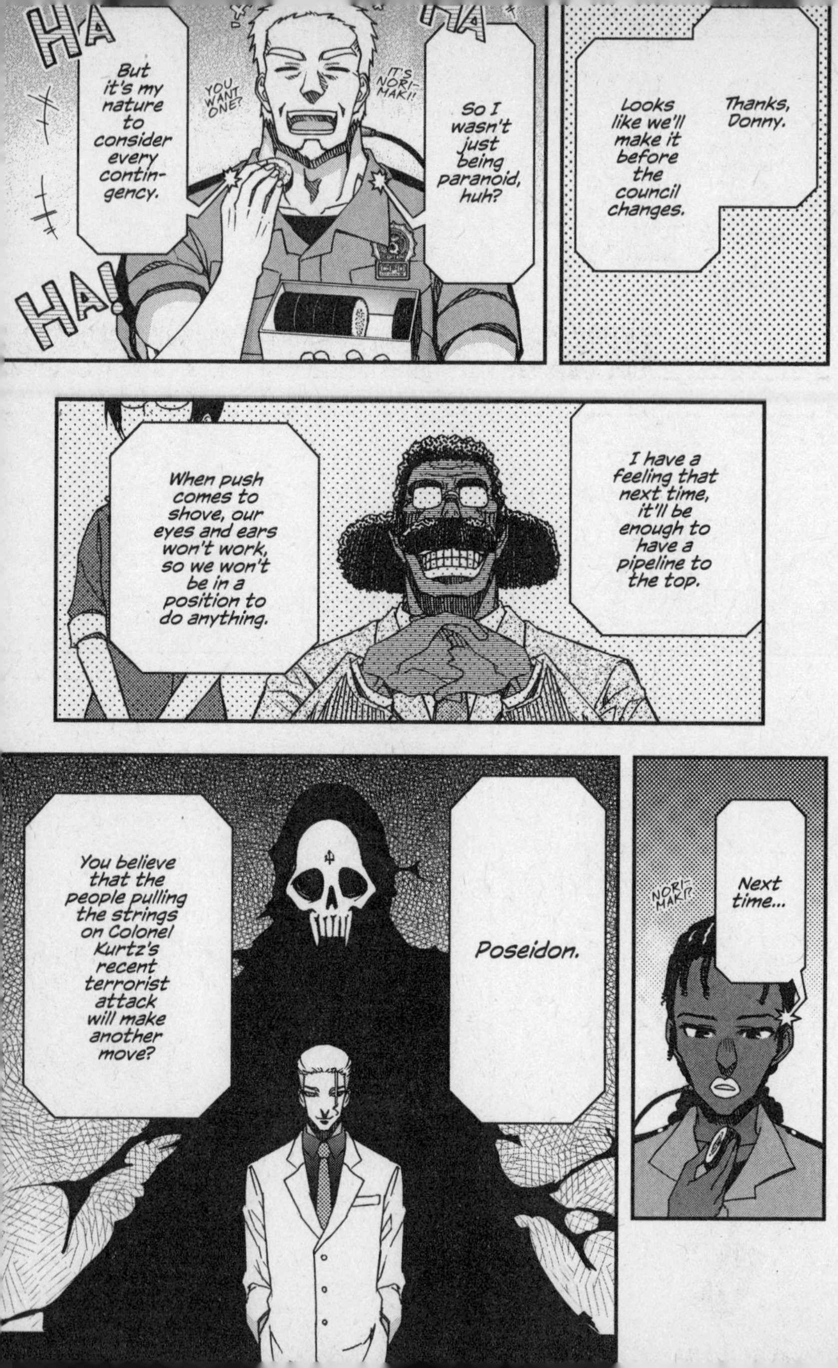
Thanks, Donny.
Looks like we'll make it before the council changes.
HA
IT'S NORI-MAKI!!
So I wasn't just being paranoid, huh?
YOU WANT ONE?
HA
But it's my nature to consider every contingency.
HA!
I have a feeling that next time, it'll be enough to have a pipeline to the top.
When push comes to shove, our eyes and ears won't work, so we won't be in a position to do anything.
Next time...
NORI-MAKI!?
Poseidon.
You believe that the people pulling the strings on Colonel Kurtz's recent terrorist attack will make another move?

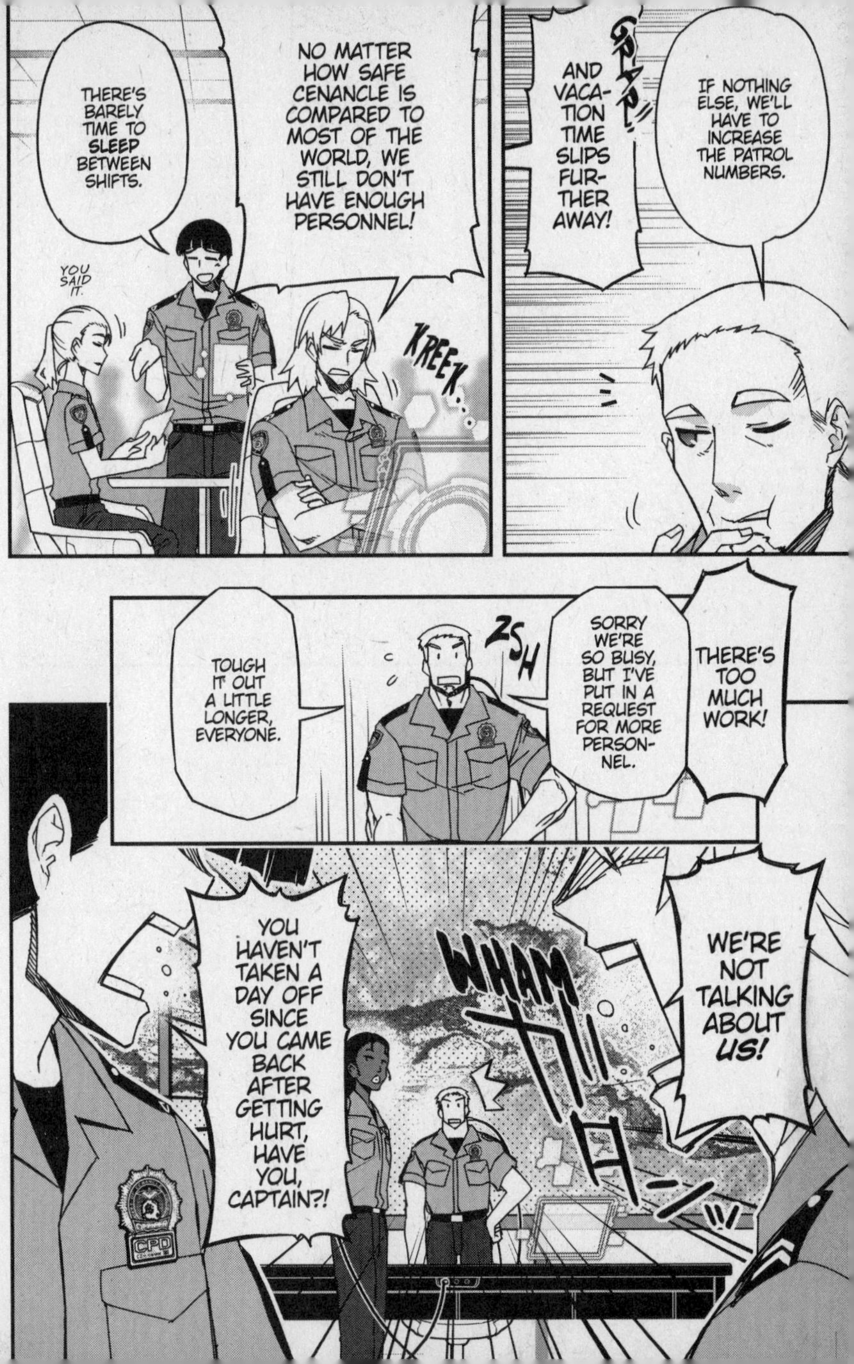
IF NOTHING ELSE, WE'LL HAVE TO INCREASE THE PATROL NUMBERS.
GRAP!!
AND VACATION TIME SLIPS FURTHER AWAY!
NO MATTER HOW SAFE CENANCLE IS COMPARED TO MOST OF THE WORLD, WE STILL DON'T HAVE ENOUGH PERSONNEL!
KREEK...
THERE'S BARELY TIME TO SLEEP BETWEEN SHIFTS.
YOU SAID IT.
THERE'S TOO MUCH WORK!
SORRY WE'RE SO BUSY, BUT I'VE PUT IN A REQUEST FOR MORE PERSONNEL.
ZSH
TOUGH IT OUT A LITTLE LONGER, EVERYONE.
WE'RE NOT TALKING ABOUT US!
WHAM!!
YOU HAVEN'T TAKEN A DAY OFF SINCE YOU CAME BACK AFTER GETTING HURT, HAVE YOU, CAPTAIN?!
CPD

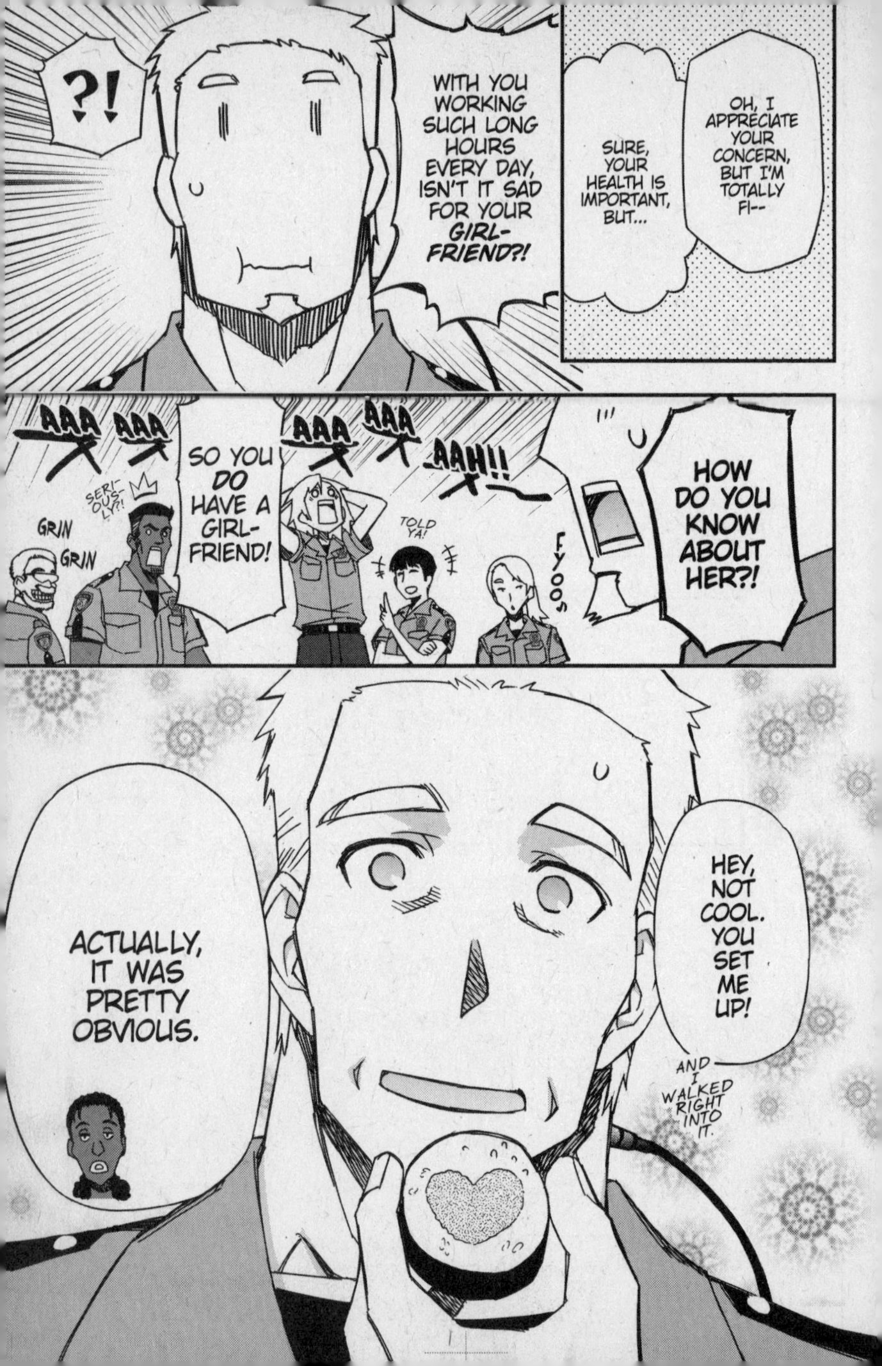
OH, I APPRECIATE YOUR CONCERN, BUT I'M TOTALLY FI--
SURE, YOUR HEALTH IS IMPORTANT, BUT...
WITH YOU WORKING SUCH LONG HOURS EVERY DAY, ISN'T IT SAD FOR YOUR GIRL-FRIEND?!
?!
HOW DO YOU KNOW ABOUT HER?!
FYOOS
TOLD YA!
AAA AAA AAA AAA AAH!!
SO YOU DO HAVE A GIRL-FRIEND!
SERI-OUS-LY?!
GRIN GRIN
HEY, NOT COOL. YOU SET ME UP!
AND I WALKED RIGHT INTO IT.
ACTUALLY, IT WAS PRETTY OBVIOUS.

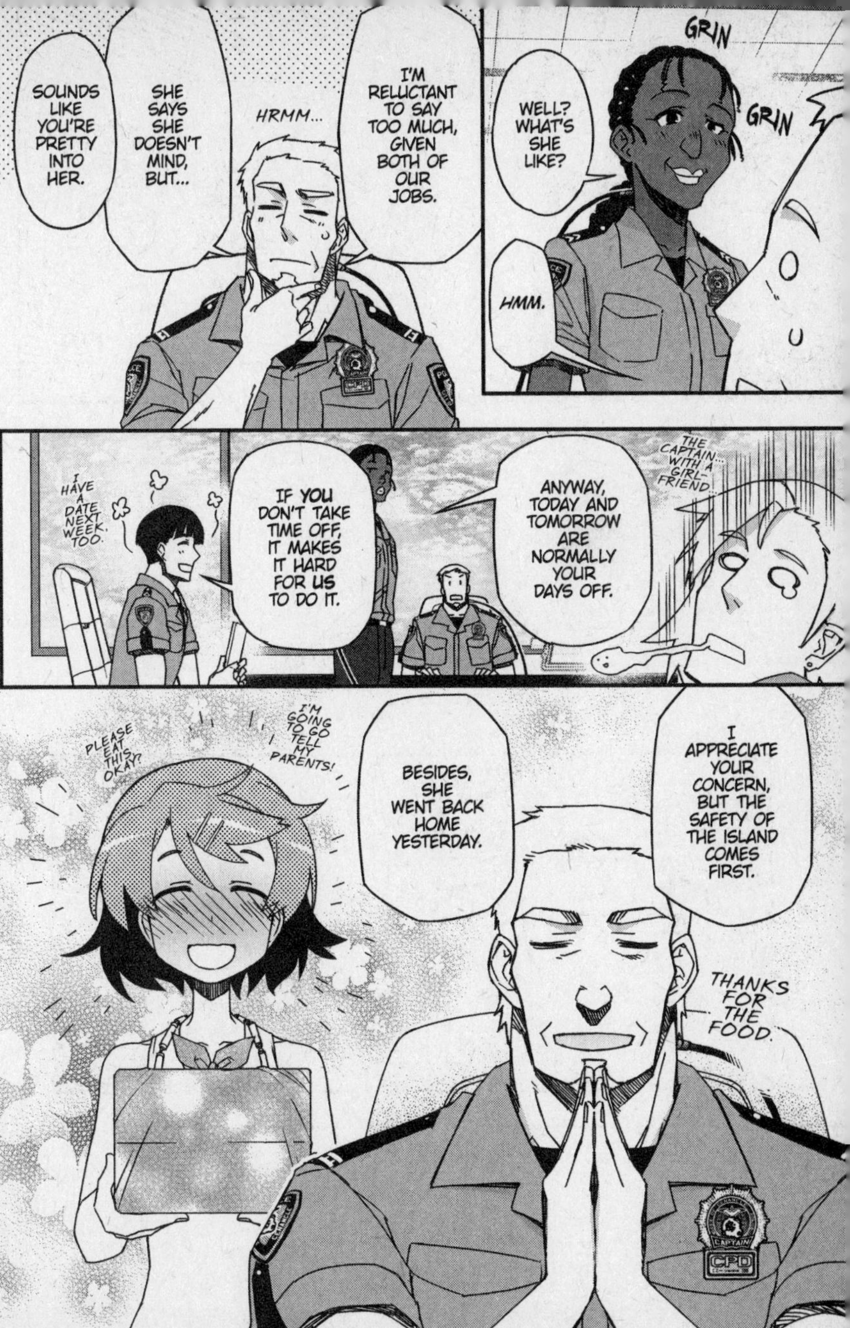
GRIN
GRIN
WELL? WHAT'S SHE LIKE?
HMM.
I'M RELUCTANT TO SAY TOO MUCH, GIVEN BOTH OF OUR JOBS.
HRMM...
SHE SAYS SHE DOESN'T MIND, BUT...
SOUNDS LIKE YOU'RE PRETTY INTO HER.
THE CAPTAIN... WITH A GIRLFRIEND...
ANYWAY, TODAY AND TOMORROW ARE NORMALLY YOUR DAYS OFF.
IF YOU DON'T TAKE TIME OFF, IT MAKES IT HARD FOR US TO DO IT.
I HAVE A DATE NEXT WEEK, TOO.
I APPRECIATE YOUR CONCERN, BUT THE SAFETY OF THE ISLAND COMES FIRST.
BESIDES, SHE WENT BACK HOME YESTERDAY.
THANKS FOR THE FOOD.
I'M GOING TO GO TELL MY PARENTS!
PLEASE EAT THIS, OKAY?

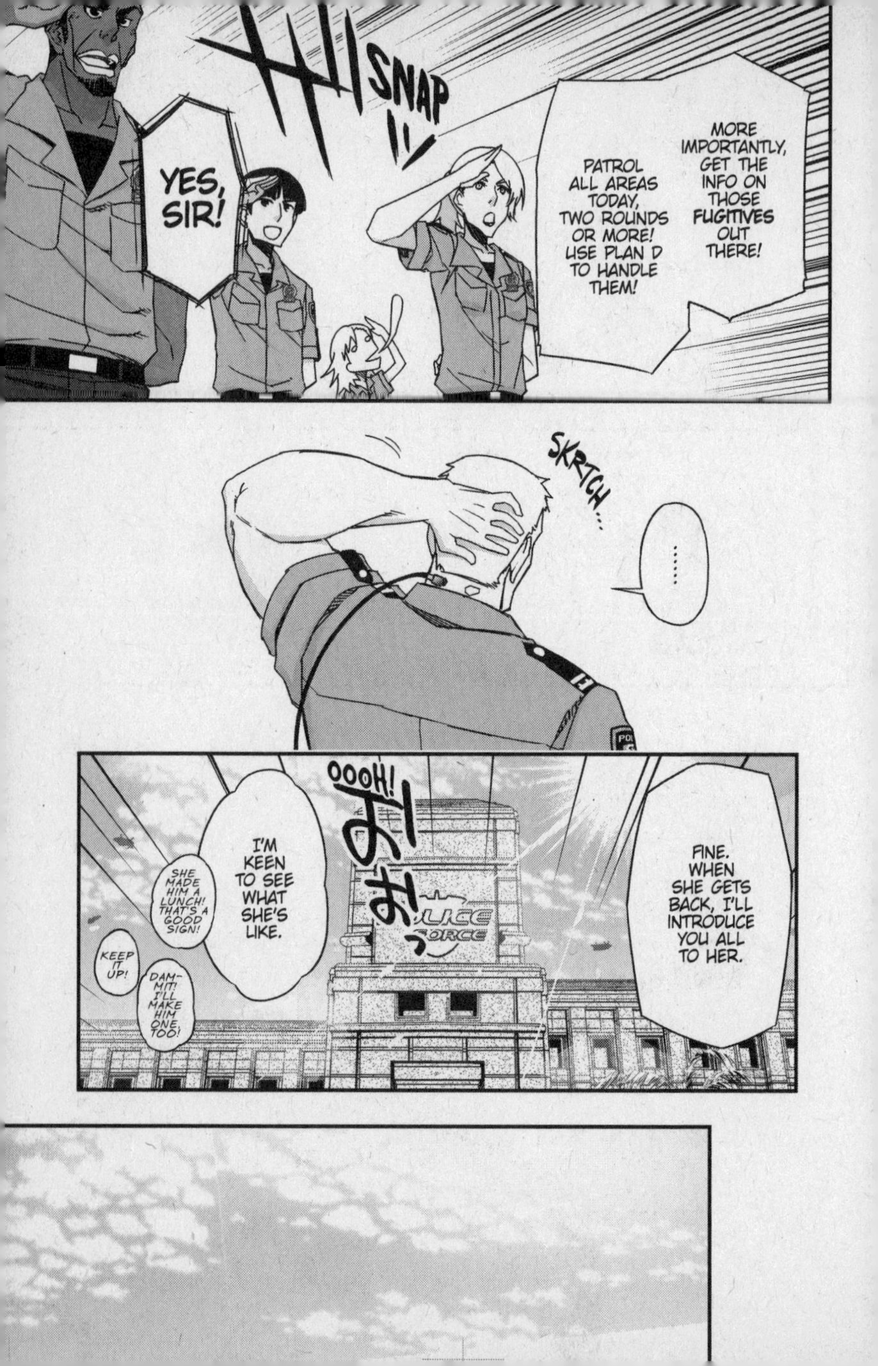
MORE IMPORTANTLY, GET THE INFO ON THOSE FUGITIVES OUT THERE!
PATROL ALL AREAS TODAY, TWO ROUNDS OR MORE! USE PLAN D TO HANDLE THEM!
SNAP
YES, SIR!
SKRTCH...
......
FINE. WHEN SHE GETS BACK, I'LL INTRODUCE YOU ALL TO HER.
OOOH!
おおっ
I'M KEEN TO SEE WHAT SHE'S LIKE.
SHE MADE HIM A LUNCH! THAT'S A GOOD SIGN!
KEEP IT UP!
DAMMIT! I'LL MAKE HIM ONE, TOO!

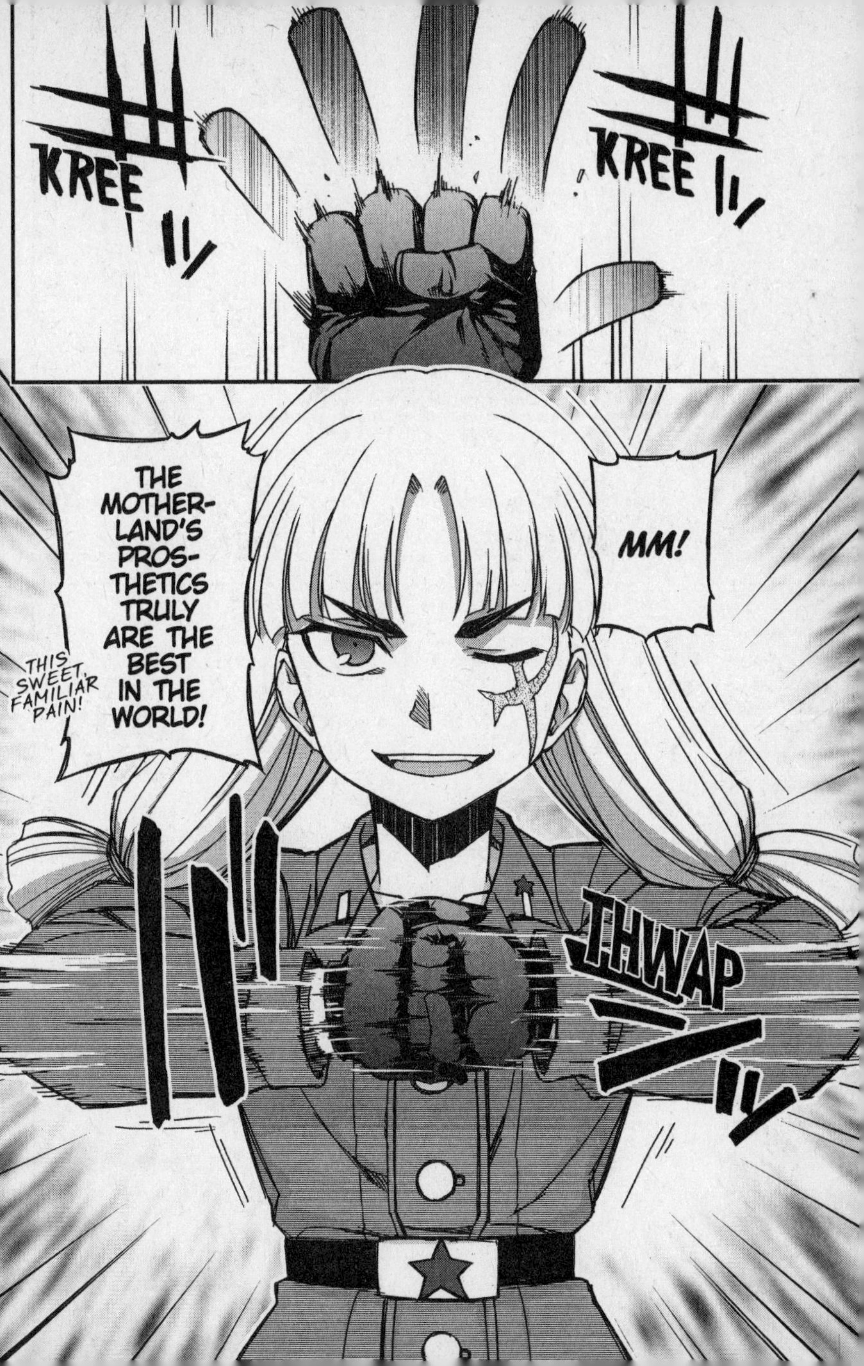
KREE
KREE
MM!
THE MOTHER-LAND'S PROS-THETICS TRULY ARE THE BEST IN THE WORLD!
THIS SWEET, FAMILIAR PAIN!
THWAP

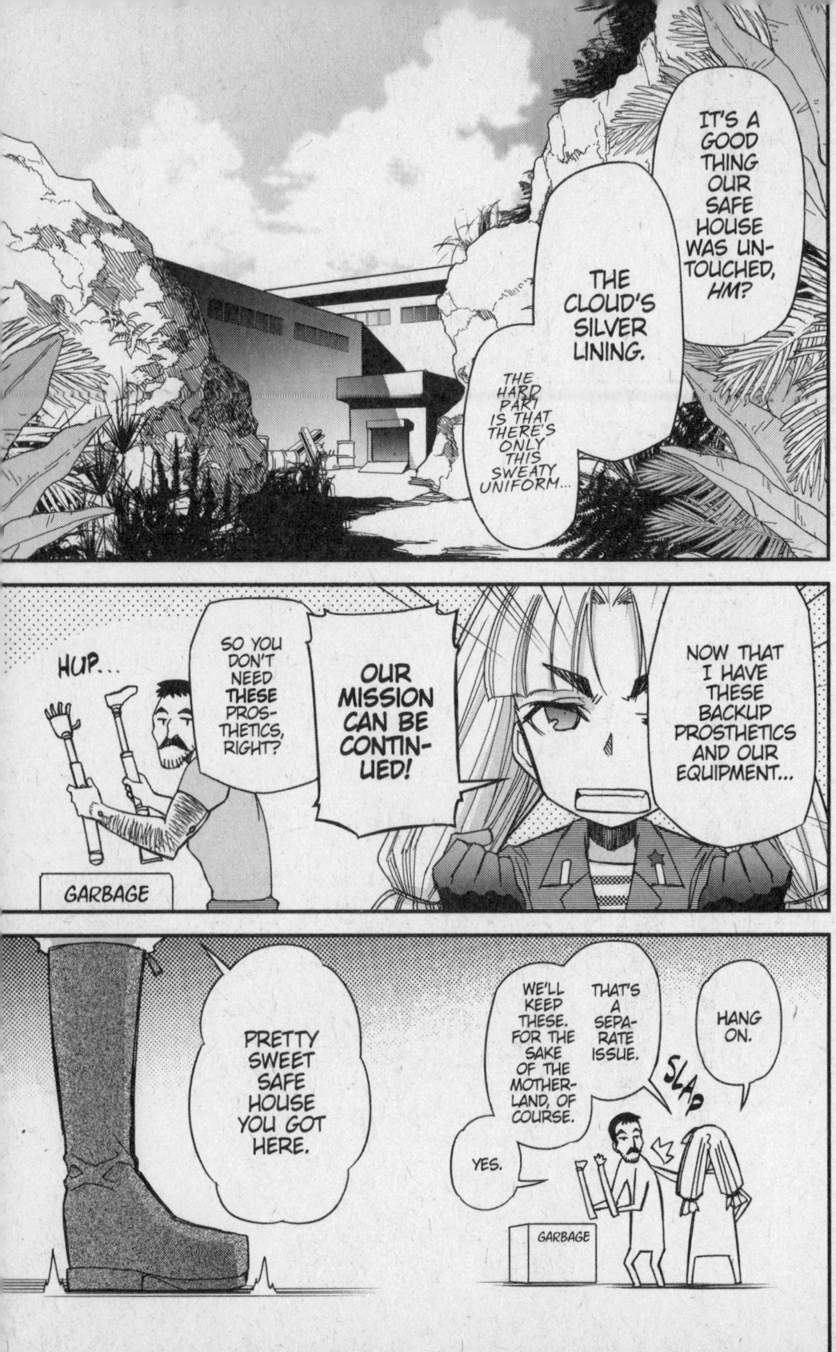
IT'S A GOOD THING OUR SAFE HOUSE WAS UN-TOUCHED, HM?
THE CLOUD'S SILVER LINING.
THE HARD PART IS THAT THERE'S ONLY THIS SWEATY UNIFORM...
NOW THAT I HAVE THESE BACKUP PROSTHETICS AND OUR EQUIPMENT...
OUR MISSION CAN BE CONTIN-UED!
SO YOU DON'T NEED THESE PROS-THETICS, RIGHT?
HUP...
GARBAGE
HANG ON.
SLAP
THAT'S A SEPA-RATE ISSUE.
WE'LL KEEP THESE. FOR THE SAKE OF THE MOTHER-LAND, OF COURSE.
YES.
GARBAGE
PRETTY SWEET SAFE HOUSE YOU GOT HERE.

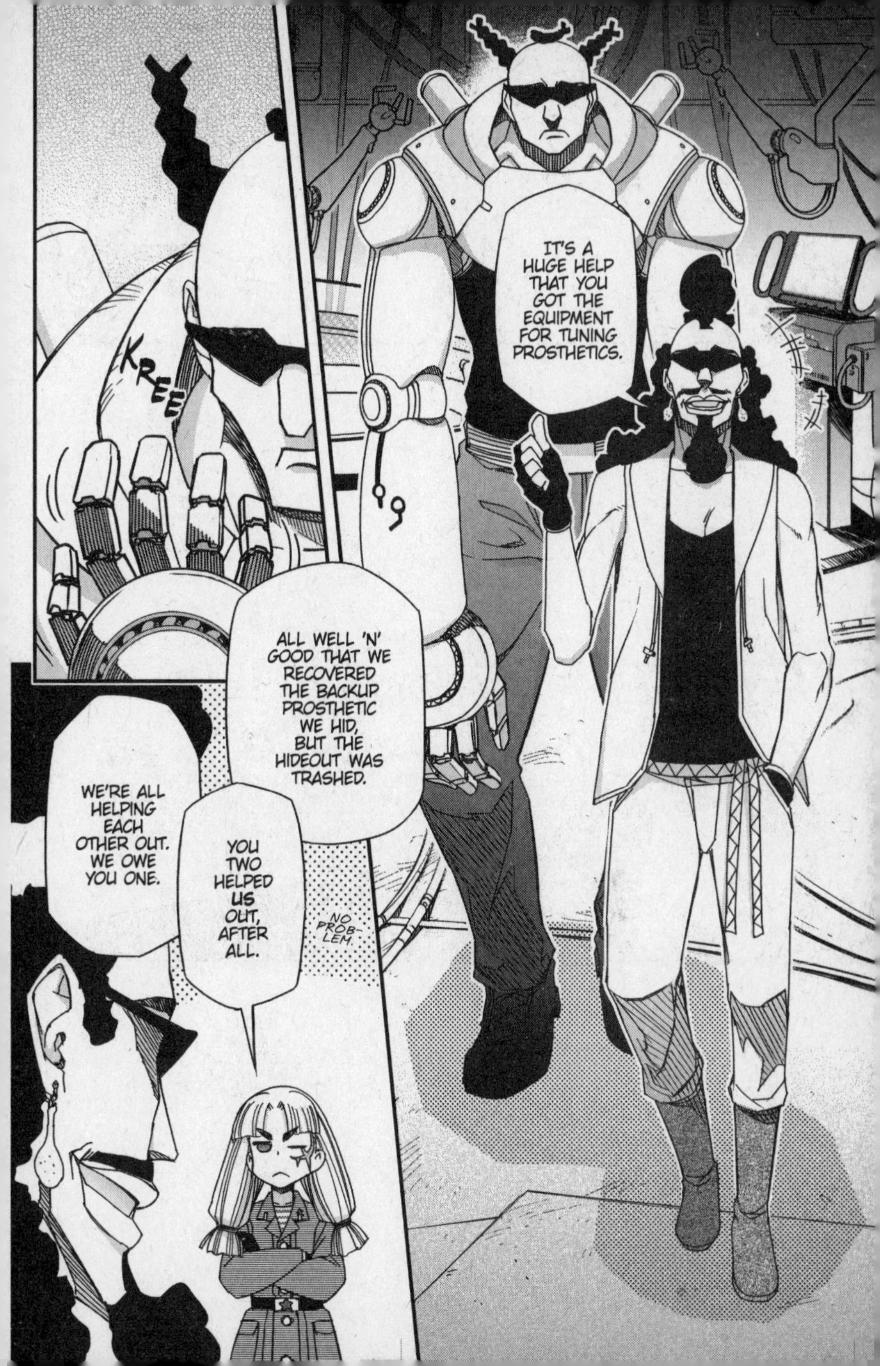
IT'S A HUGE HELP THAT YOU GOT THE EQUIPMENT FOR TUNING PROSTHETICS.
KREE
ALL WELL 'N' GOOD THAT WE RECOVERED THE BACKUP PROSTHETIC WE HID, BUT THE HIDEOUT WAS TRASHED.
NO PROB-LEM.
YOU TWO HELPED US OUT, AFTER ALL.
WE'RE ALL HELPING EACH OTHER OUT. WE OWE YOU ONE.

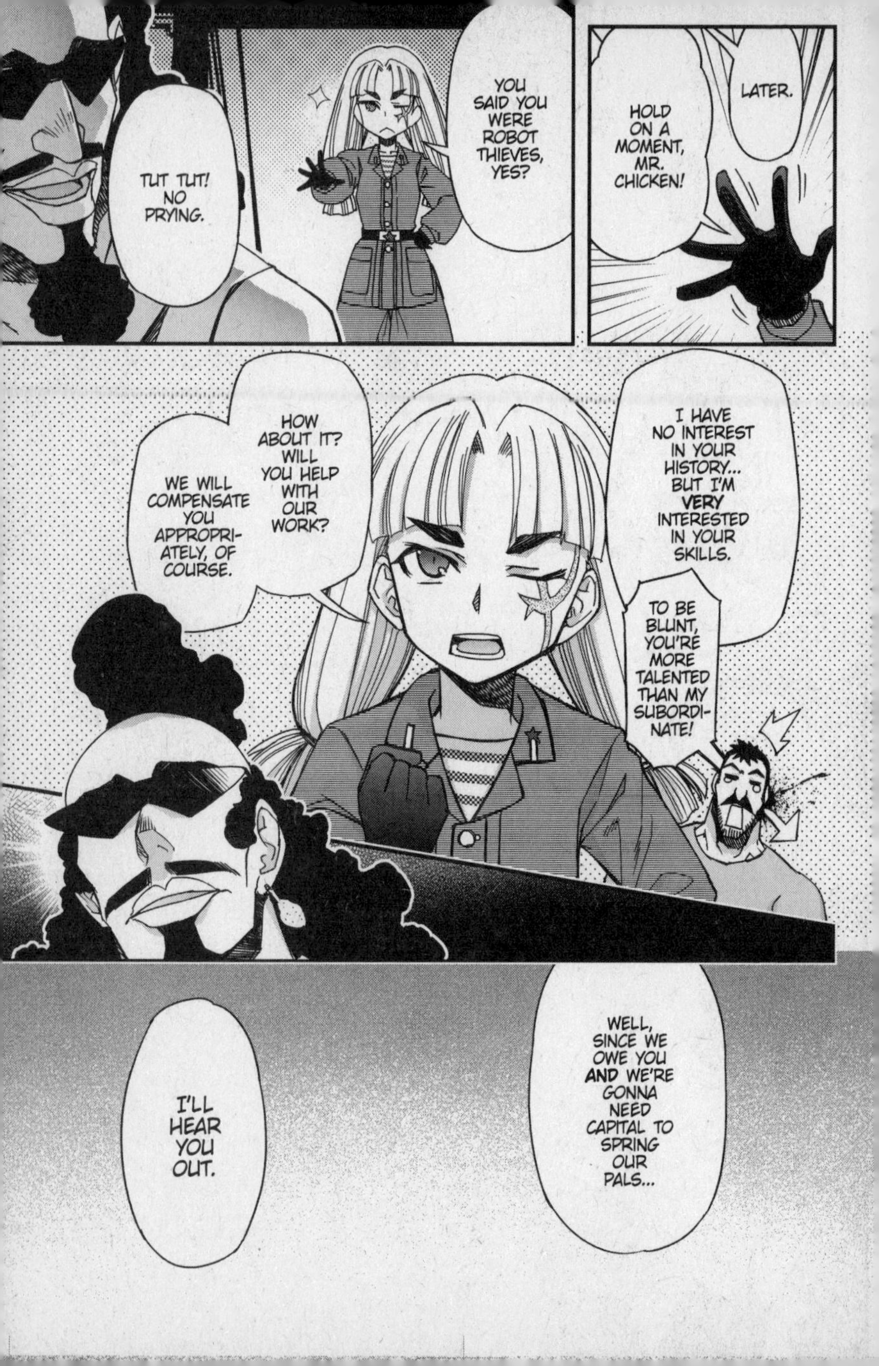
LATER.
HOLD ON A MOMENT, MR. CHICKEN!
YOU SAID YOU WERE ROBOT THIEVES, YES?
TUT TUT! NO PRYING.
I HAVE NO INTEREST IN YOUR HISTORY... BUT I'M **VERY** INTERESTED IN YOUR SKILLS.
TO BE BLUNT, YOU'RE MORE TALENTED THAN MY SUBORDINATE!
HOW ABOUT IT? WILL YOU HELP WITH OUR WORK?
WE WILL COMPENSATE YOU APPROPRIATELY, OF COURSE.
WELL, SINCE WE OWE YOU **AND** WE'RE GONNA NEED CAPITAL TO SPRING OUR PALS...
I'LL HEAR YOU OUT.

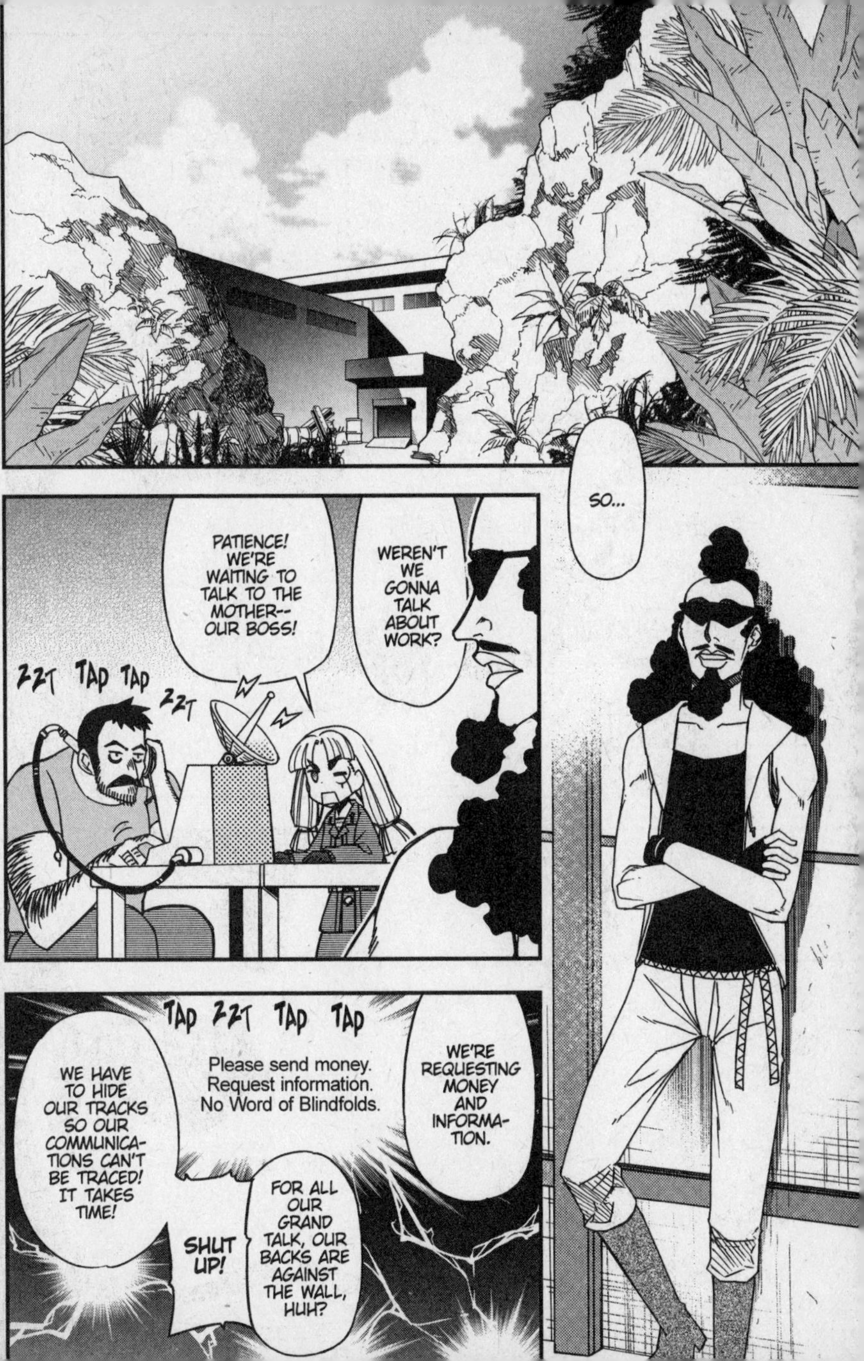
SO...
WEREN'T WE GONNA TALK ABOUT WORK?
PATIENCE! WE'RE WAITING TO TALK TO THE MOTHER-- OUR BOSS!
ZZT TAP TAP ZZT
TAP ZZT TAP TAP
WE'RE REQUESTING MONEY AND INFORMATION.
Please send money. Request information. No Word of Blindfolds.
WE HAVE TO HIDE OUR TRACKS SO OUR COMMUNICATIONS CAN'T BE TRACED! IT TAKES TIME!
FOR ALL OUR GRAND TALK, OUR BACKS ARE AGAINST THE WALL, HUH?
SHUT UP!

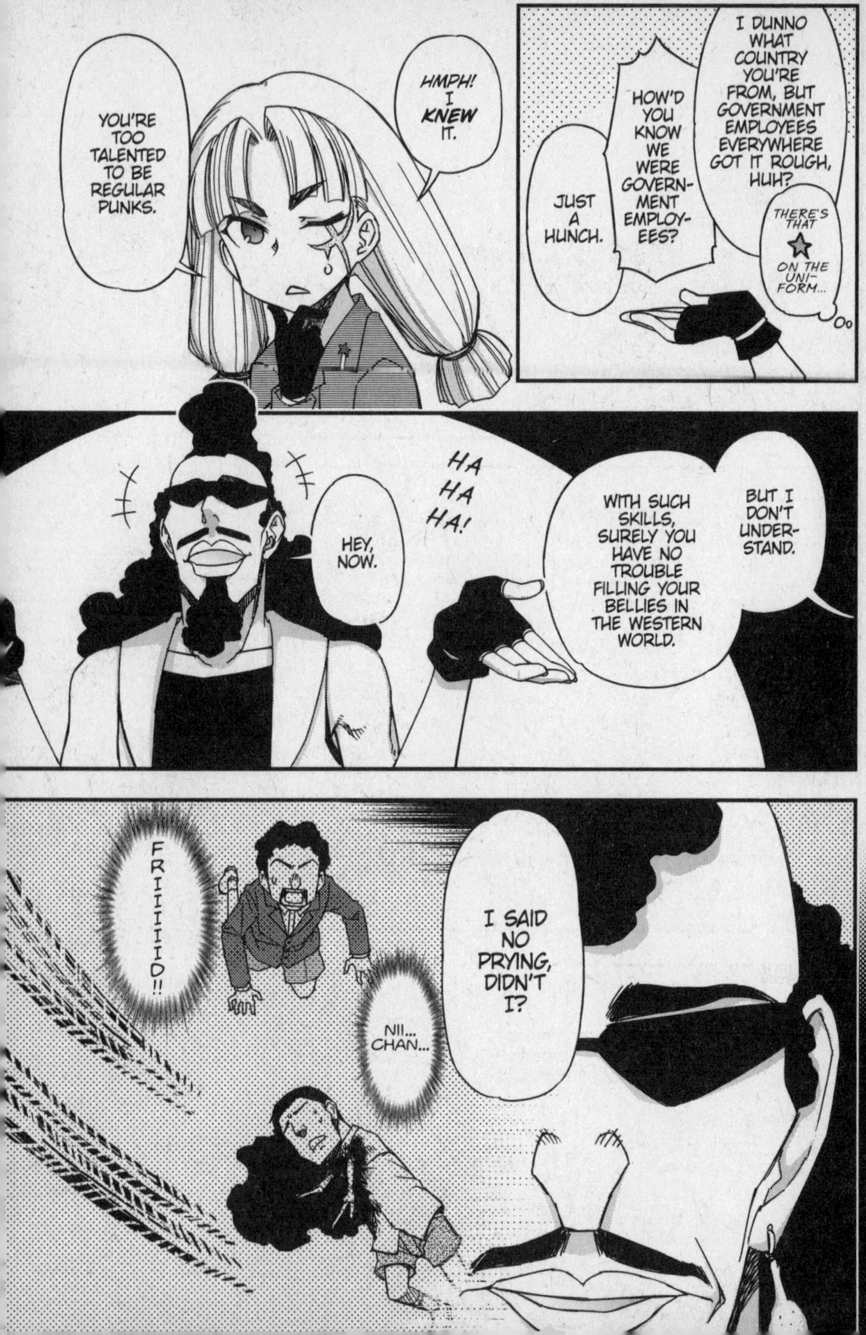
I DUNNO WHAT COUNTRY YOU'RE FROM, BUT GOVERNMENT EMPLOYEES EVERYWHERE GOT IT ROUGH, HUH?
THERE'S THAT ☆ ON THE UNI-FORM...
HOW'D YOU KNOW WE WERE GOVERN-MENT EMPLOY-EES?
JUST A HUNCH.
HMPH! I KNEW IT.
YOU'RE TOO TALENTED TO BE REGULAR PUNKS.
BUT I DON'T UNDER-STAND.
WITH SUCH SKILLS, SURELY YOU HAVE NO TROUBLE FILLING YOUR BELLIES IN THE WESTERN WORLD.
HA HA HA!
HEY, NOW.
I SAID NO PRYING, DIDN'T I?
FRIIIIID!!
NII... CHAN...

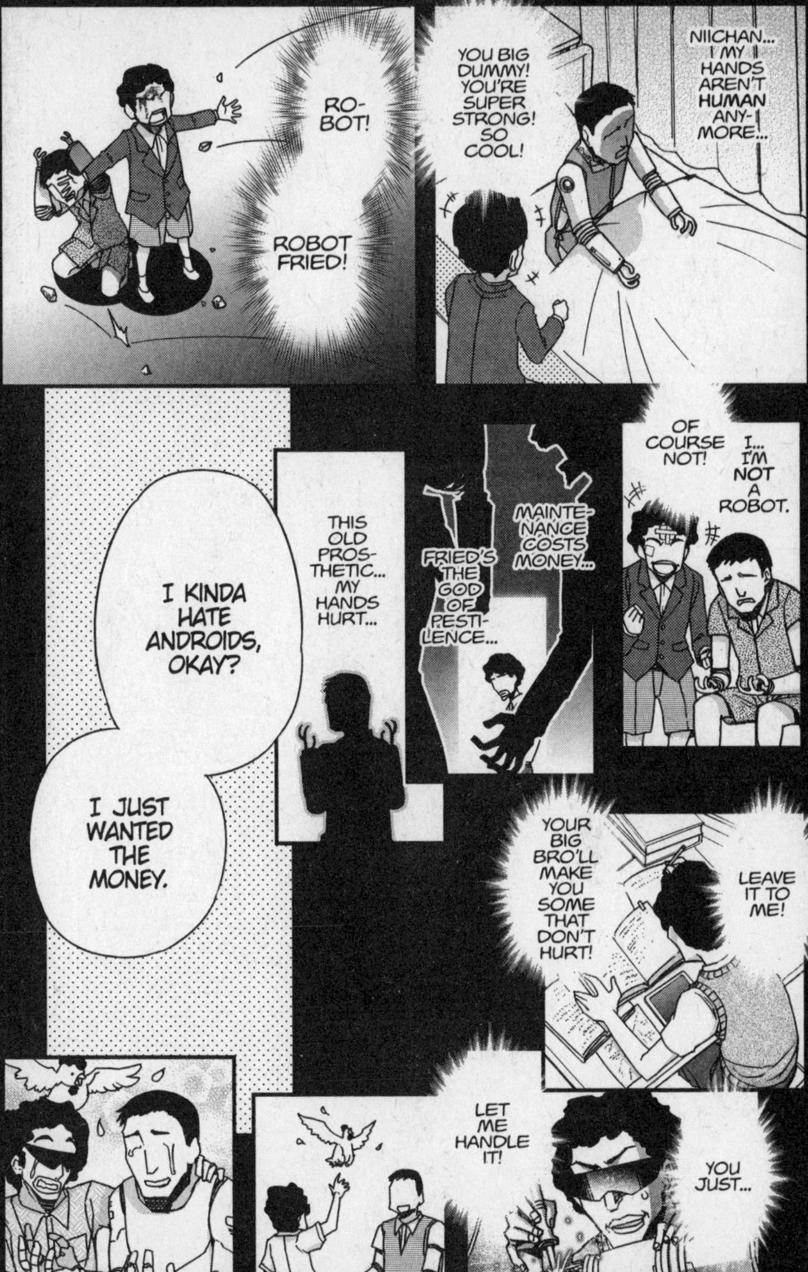
NIICHAN... MY HANDS AREN'T HUMAN ANYMORE...
YOU BIG DUMMY! YOU'RE SUPER STRONG! SO COOL!
RO-BOT!
ROBOT FRIED!
I... I'M NOT A ROBOT.
OF COURSE NOT!
MAINTE-NANCE COSTS MONEY...
FRIED'S THE GOD OF PESTI-LENCE...
THIS OLD PROS-THETIC... MY HANDS HURT...
LEAVE IT TO ME!
YOUR BIG BRO'LL MAKE YOU SOME THAT DON'T HURT!
I KINDA HATE ANDROIDS, OKAY?
I JUST WANTED THE MONEY.
YOU JUST...
LET ME HANDLE IT!

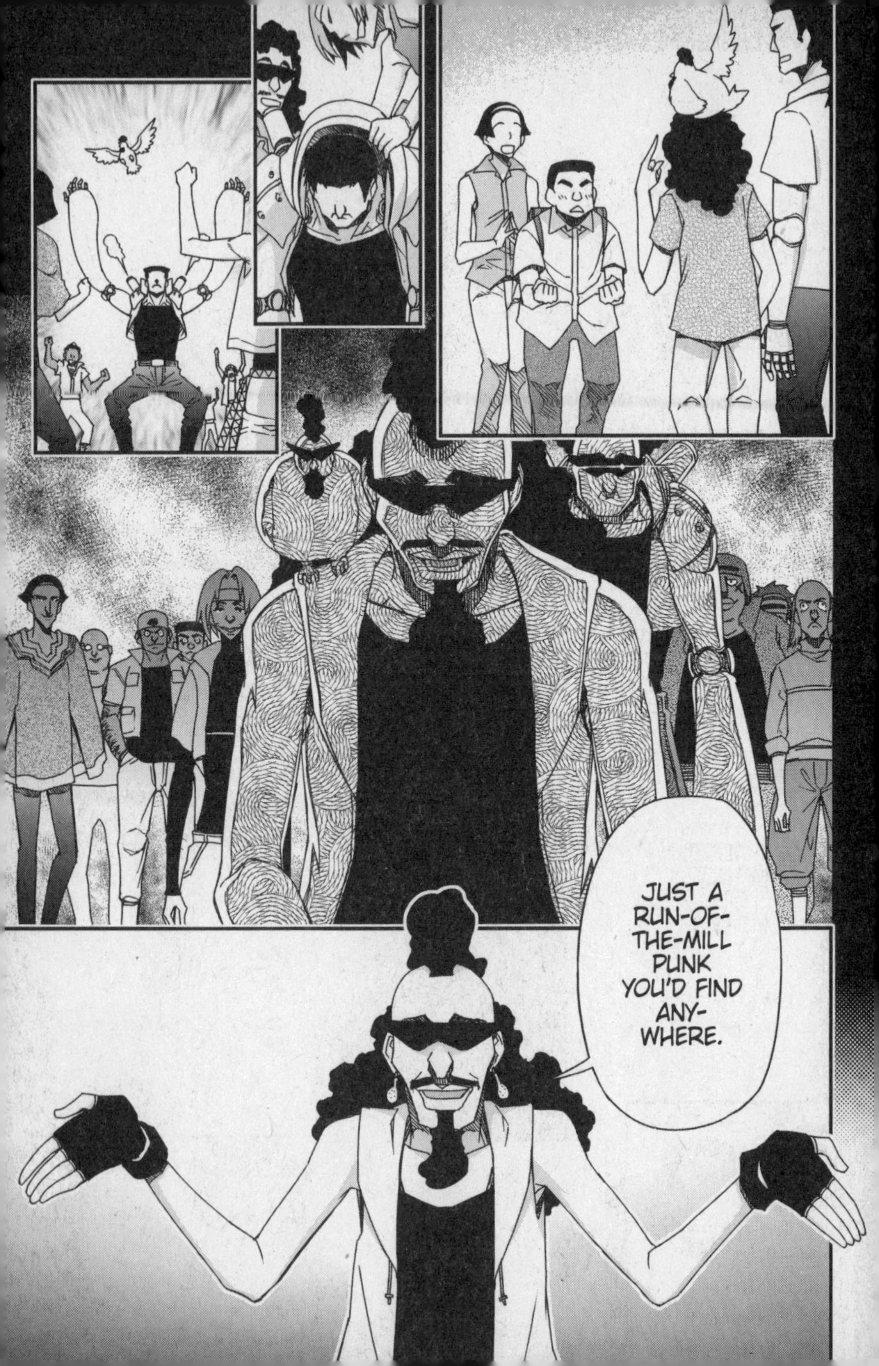
JUST A RUN-OF-THE-MILL PUNK YOU'D FIND ANYWHERE.

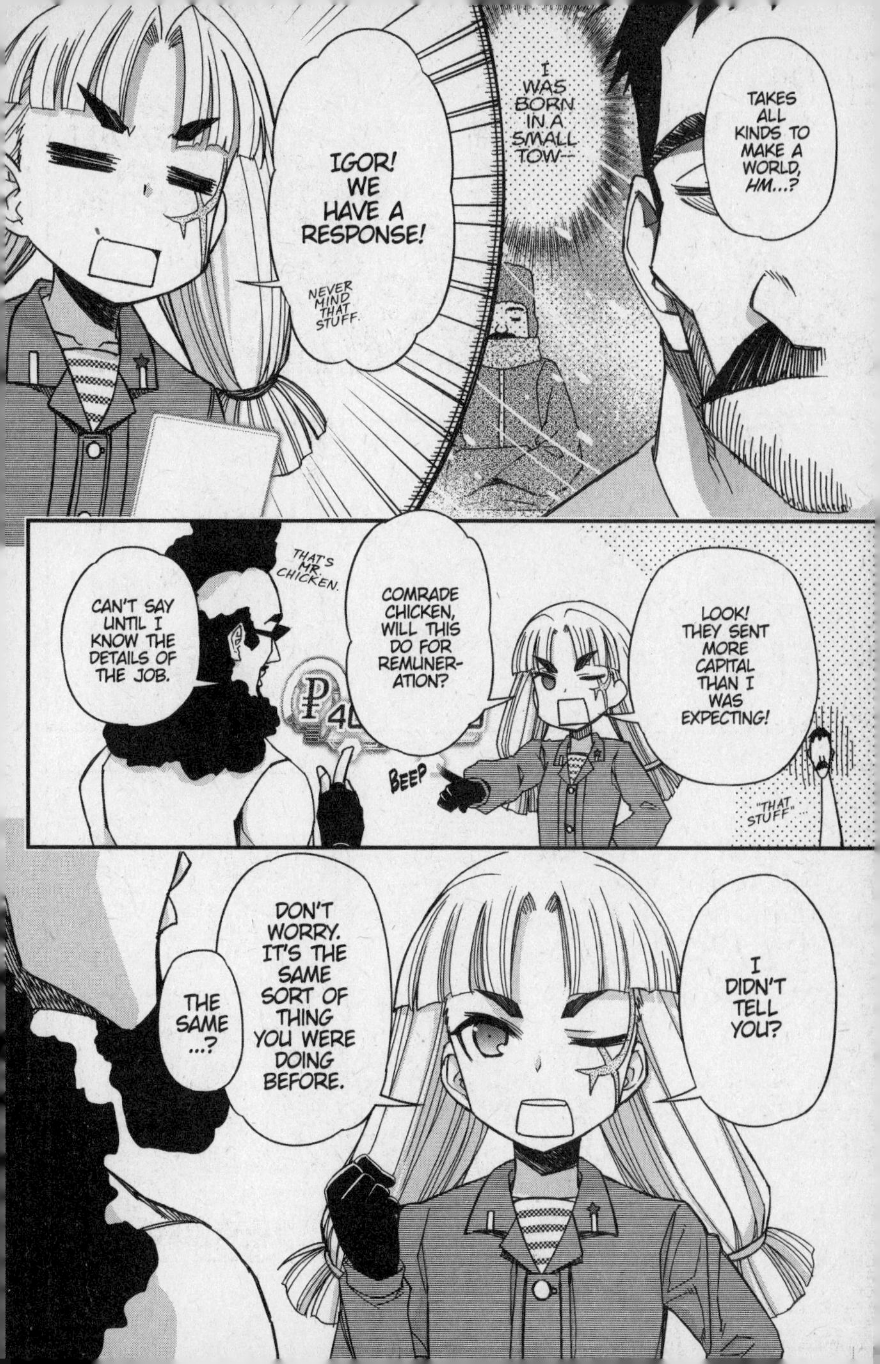
TAKES ALL KINDS TO MAKE A WORLD, HM...?
I WAS BORN IN A SMALL TOW--
IGOR! WE HAVE A RESPONSE!
NEVER MIND THAT STUFF.
LOOK! THEY SENT MORE CAPITAL THAN I WAS EXPECTING!
"THAT STUFF"...
COMRADE CHICKEN, WILL THIS DO FOR REMUNER-ATION?
BEEP
THAT'S MR. CHICKEN.
CAN'T SAY UNTIL I KNOW THE DETAILS OF THE JOB.
I DIDN'T TELL YOU?
DON'T WORRY. IT'S THE SAME SORT OF THING YOU WERE DOING BEFORE.
THE SAME ...?

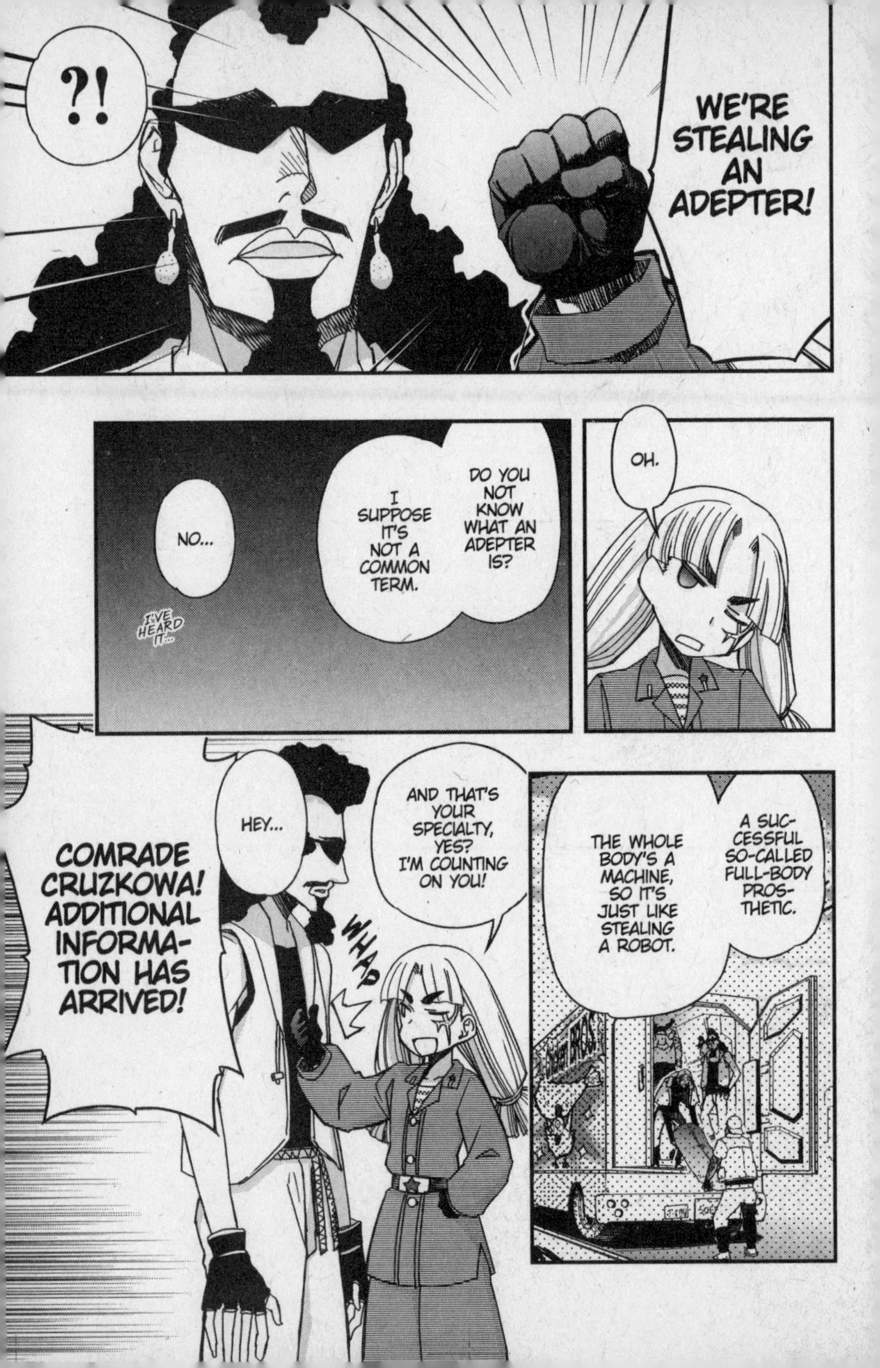
WE'RE STEALING AN ADEPTER!
?!
OH.
DO YOU NOT KNOW WHAT AN ADEPTER IS?
I SUPPOSE IT'S NOT A COMMON TERM.
NO...
I'VE HEARD IT...
A SUC-CESSFUL SO-CALLED FULL-BODY PROS-THETIC.
THE WHOLE BODY'S A MACHINE, SO IT'S JUST LIKE STEALING A ROBOT.
AND THAT'S YOUR SPECIALTY, YES? I'M COUNTING ON YOU!
WHA?!
HEY...
COMRADE CRUZKOWA! ADDITIONAL INFORMA-TION HAS ARRIVED!

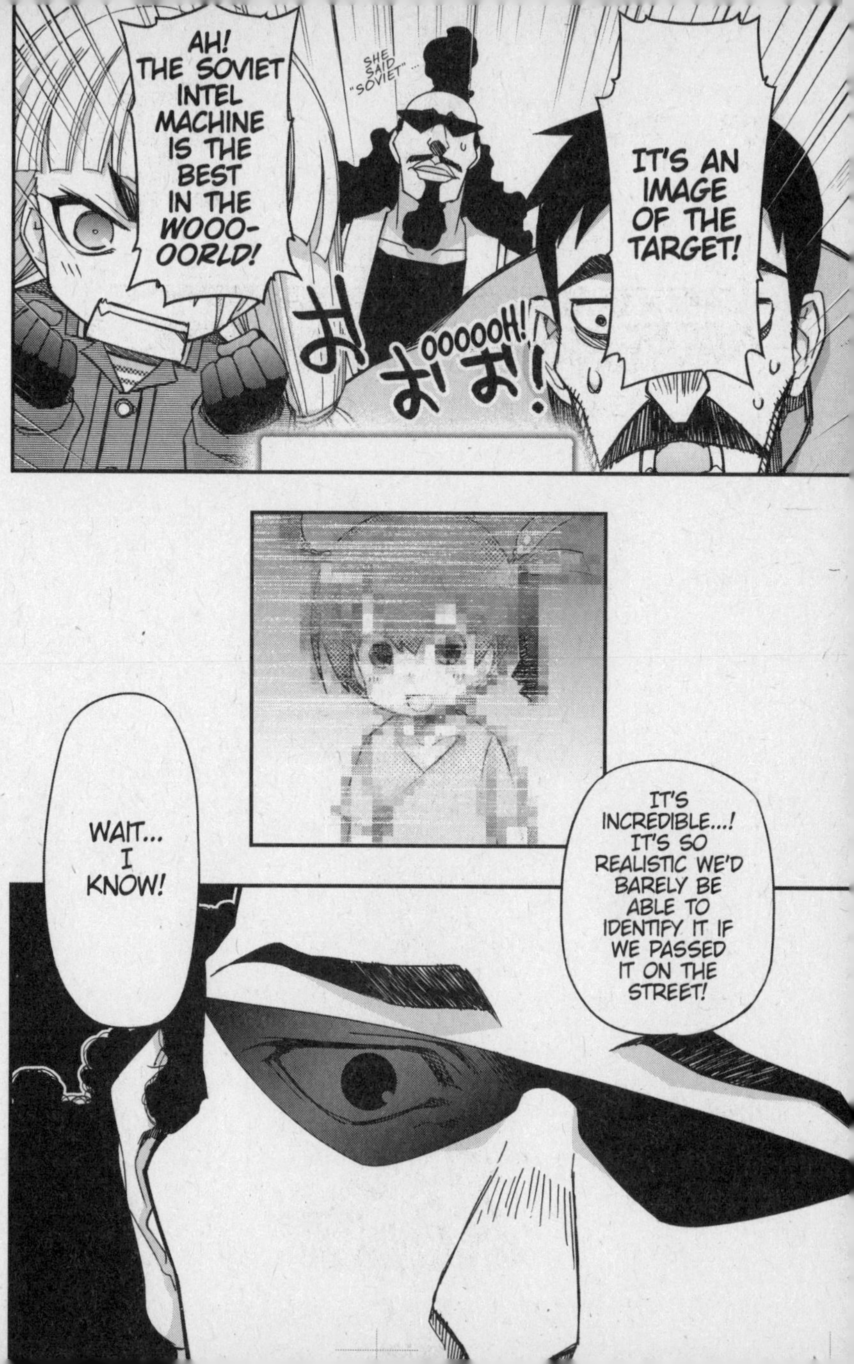
IT'S AN IMAGE OF THE TARGET!
SHE SAID "SOVIET"...
AH! THE SOVIET INTEL MACHINE IS THE BEST IN THE WOOO-OORLD!
OOOOOH!
お!お!お!
IT'S INCREDIBLE...! IT'S SO REALISTIC WE'D BARELY BE ABLE TO IDENTIFY IT IF WE PASSED IT ON THE STREET!
WAIT... I KNOW!

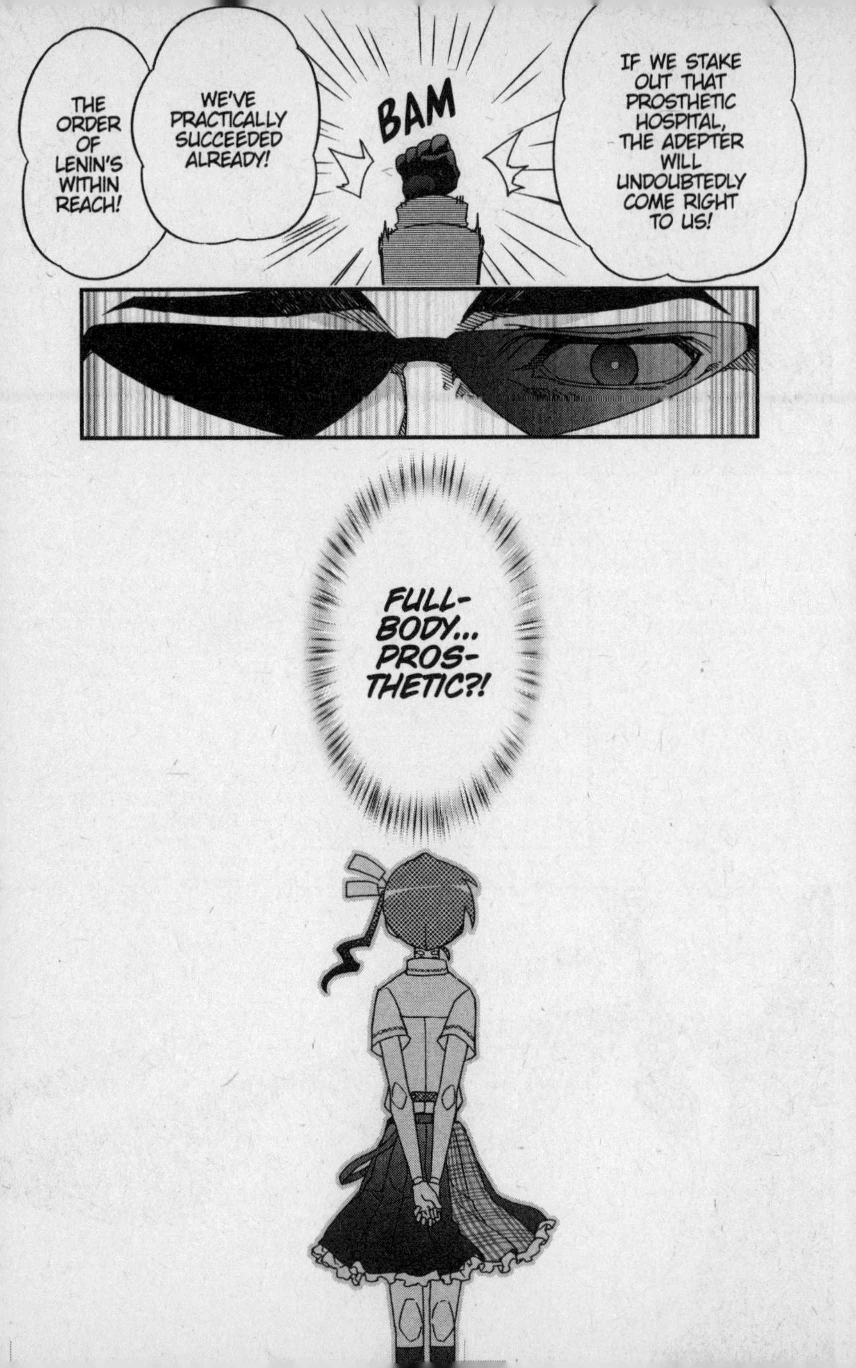
IF WE STAKE OUT THAT PROSTHETIC HOSPITAL, THE ADEPTER WILL UNDOUBTEDLY COME RIGHT TO US!
BAM
WE'VE PRACTICALLY SUCCEEDED ALREADY!
THE ORDER OF LENIN'S WITHIN REACH!
FULL-BODY... PROS-THETIC?!

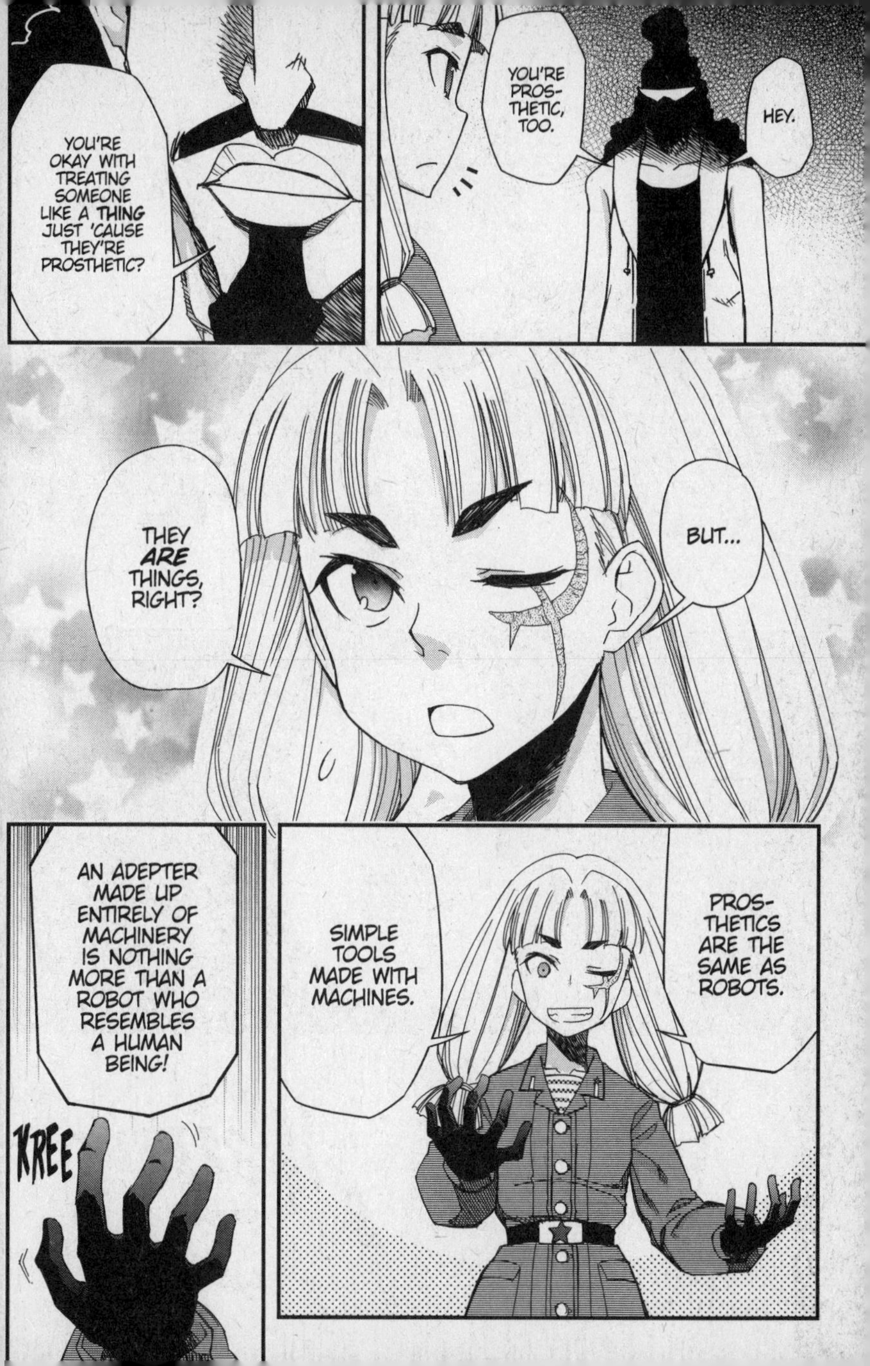
HEY.
YOU'RE PROS-THETIC, TOO.
YOU'RE OKAY WITH TREATING SOMEONE LIKE A THING JUST 'CAUSE THEY'RE PROSTHETIC?
BUT...
THEY *ARE* THINGS, RIGHT?
PROS-THETICS ARE THE SAME AS ROBOTS.
SIMPLE TOOLS MADE WITH MACHINES.
AN ADEPTER MADE UP ENTIRELY OF MACHINERY IS NOTHING MORE THAN A ROBOT WHO RESEMBLES A HUMAN BEING!
KREE

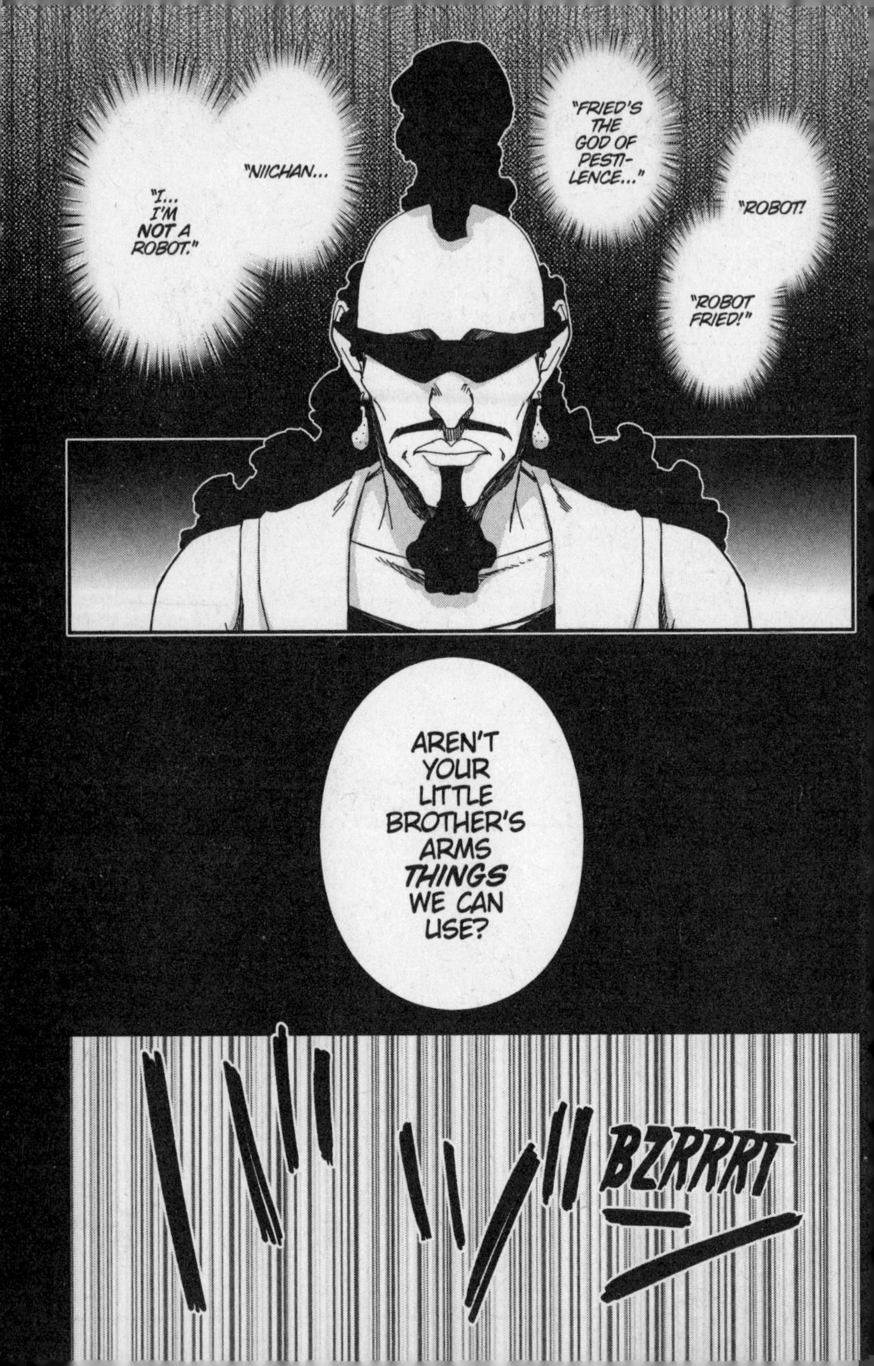
"ROBOT!
"ROBOT FRIED!"
"FRIED'S THE GOD OF PESTI-LENCE..."
"NIICHAN...
"I... I'M NOT A ROBOT."
AREN'T YOUR LITTLE BROTHER'S ARMS *THINGS* WE CAN USE?
BZRRRT

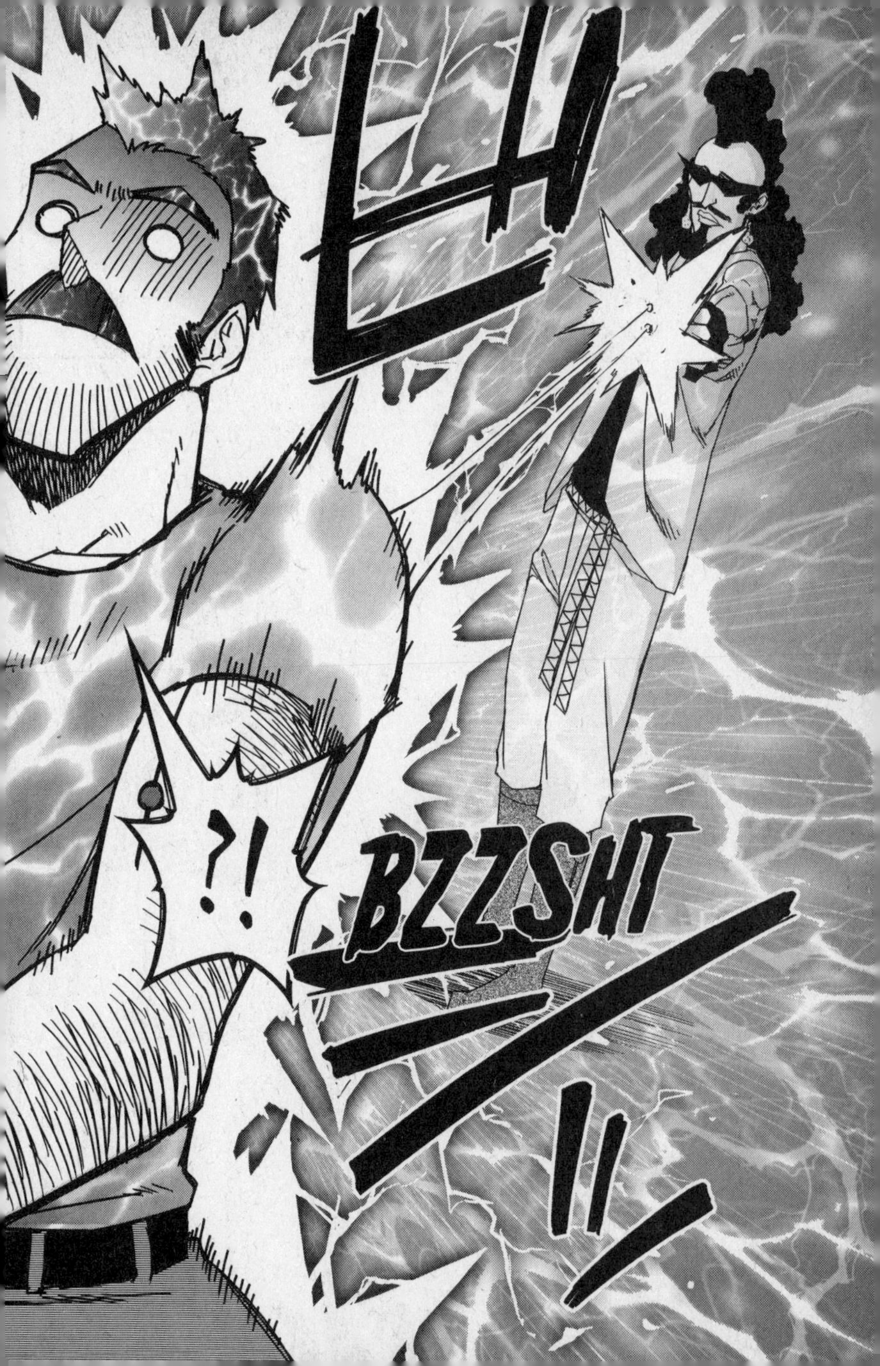
?!
BZZSHT

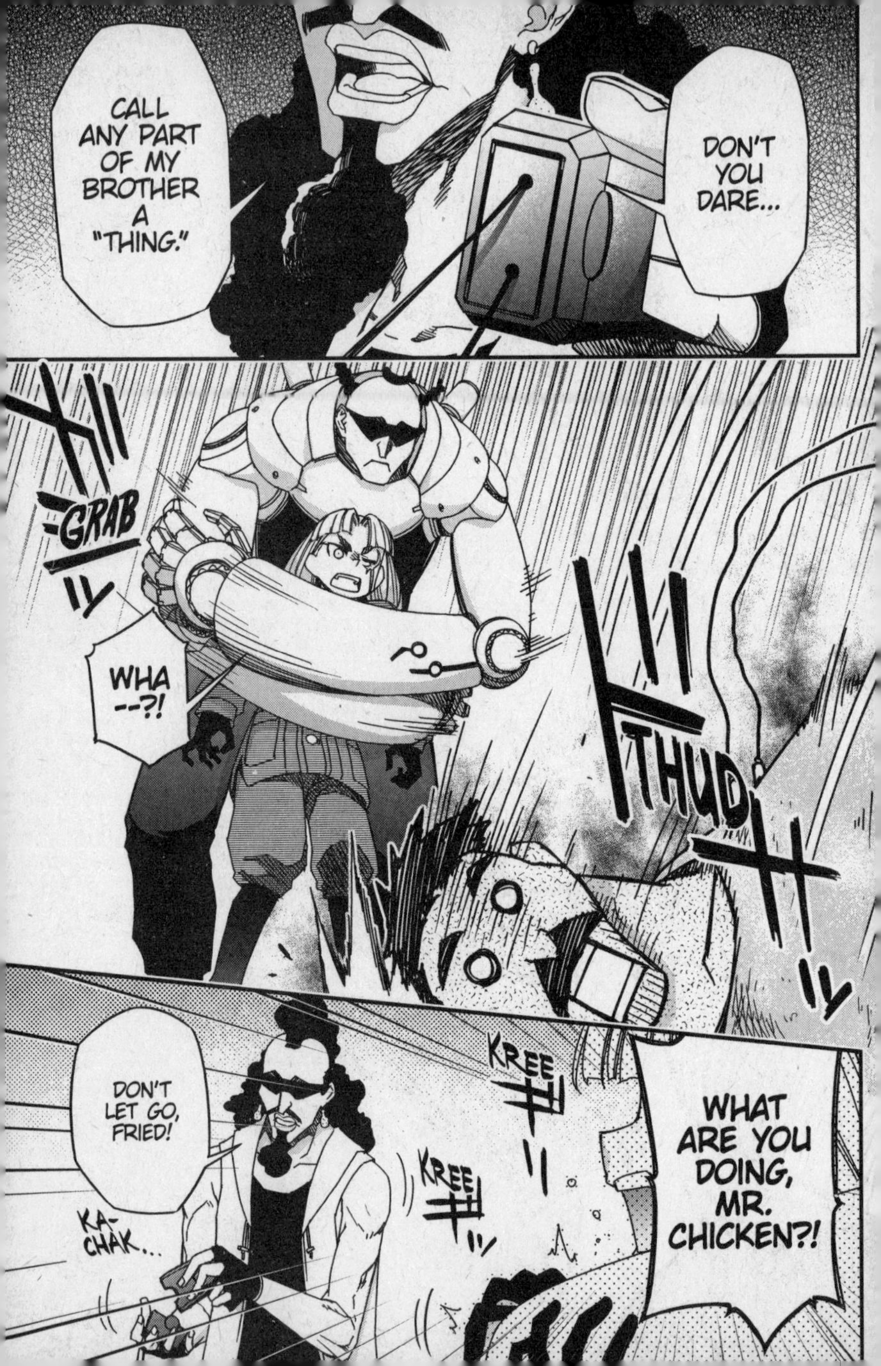
DON'T YOU DARE...
CALL ANY PART OF MY BROTHER A "THING."
THUD
GRAB
WHA--?!
WHAT ARE YOU DOING, MR. CHICKEN?!
KREE
KREE
DON'T LET GO, FRIED!
KA-CHAK...

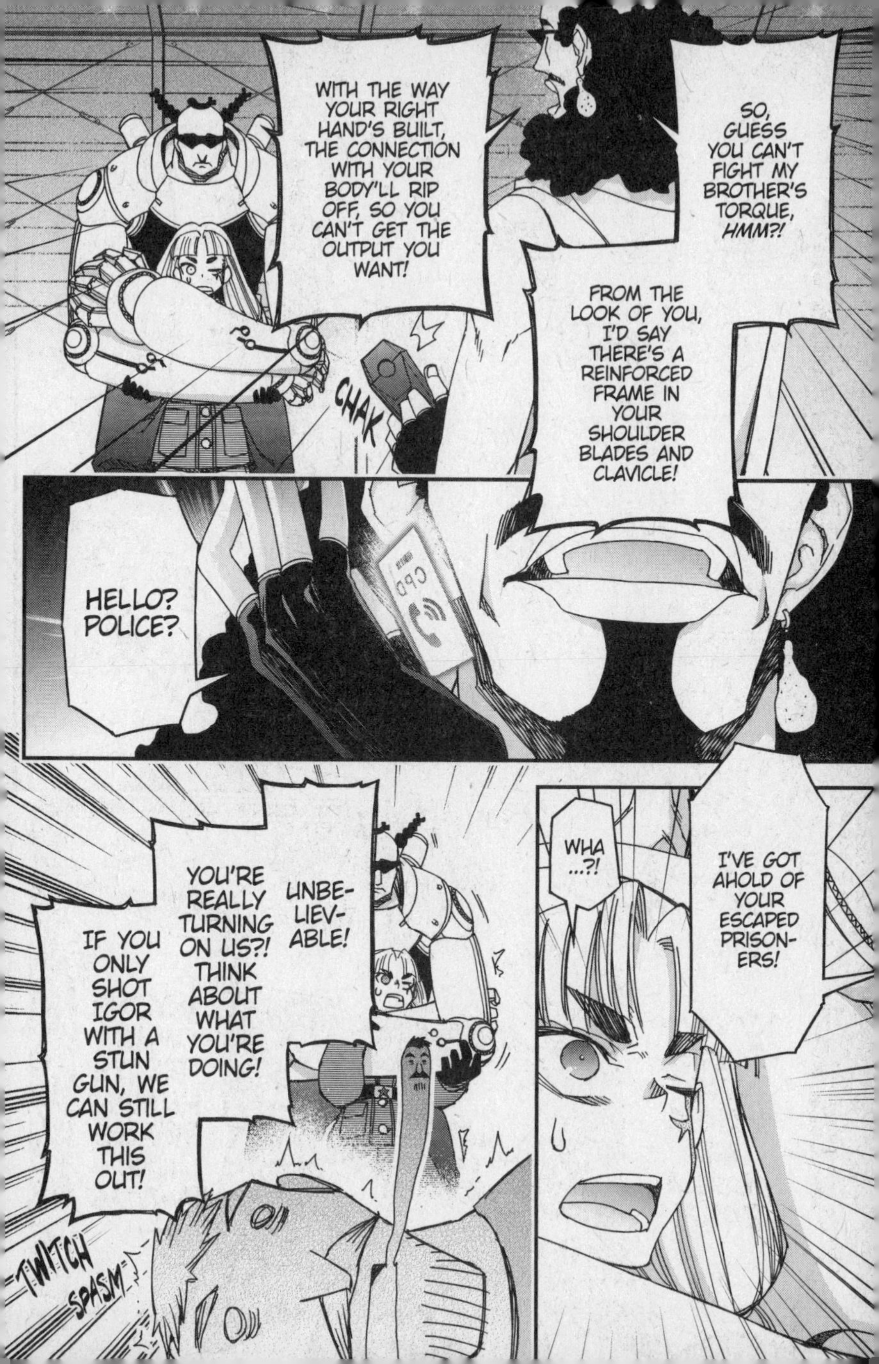

SO, GUESS YOU CAN'T FIGHT MY BROTHER'S TORQUE, *HMM?!*
WITH THE WAY YOUR RIGHT HAND'S BUILT, THE CONNECTION WITH YOUR BODY'LL RIP OFF, SO YOU CAN'T GET THE OUTPUT YOU WANT!
CHAK
FROM THE LOOK OF YOU, I'D SAY THERE'S A REINFORCED FRAME IN YOUR SHOULDER BLADES AND CLAVICLE!
CPD
HELLO? POLICE?
I'VE GOT AHOLD OF YOUR ESCAPED PRISONERS!
WHA ...?!
UNBE-LIEV-ABLE!
YOU'RE REALLY TURNING ON US?! THINK ABOUT WHAT YOU'RE DOING!
IF YOU ONLY SHOT IGOR WITH A STUN GUN, WE CAN STILL WORK THIS OUT!
TWITCH
SPASM

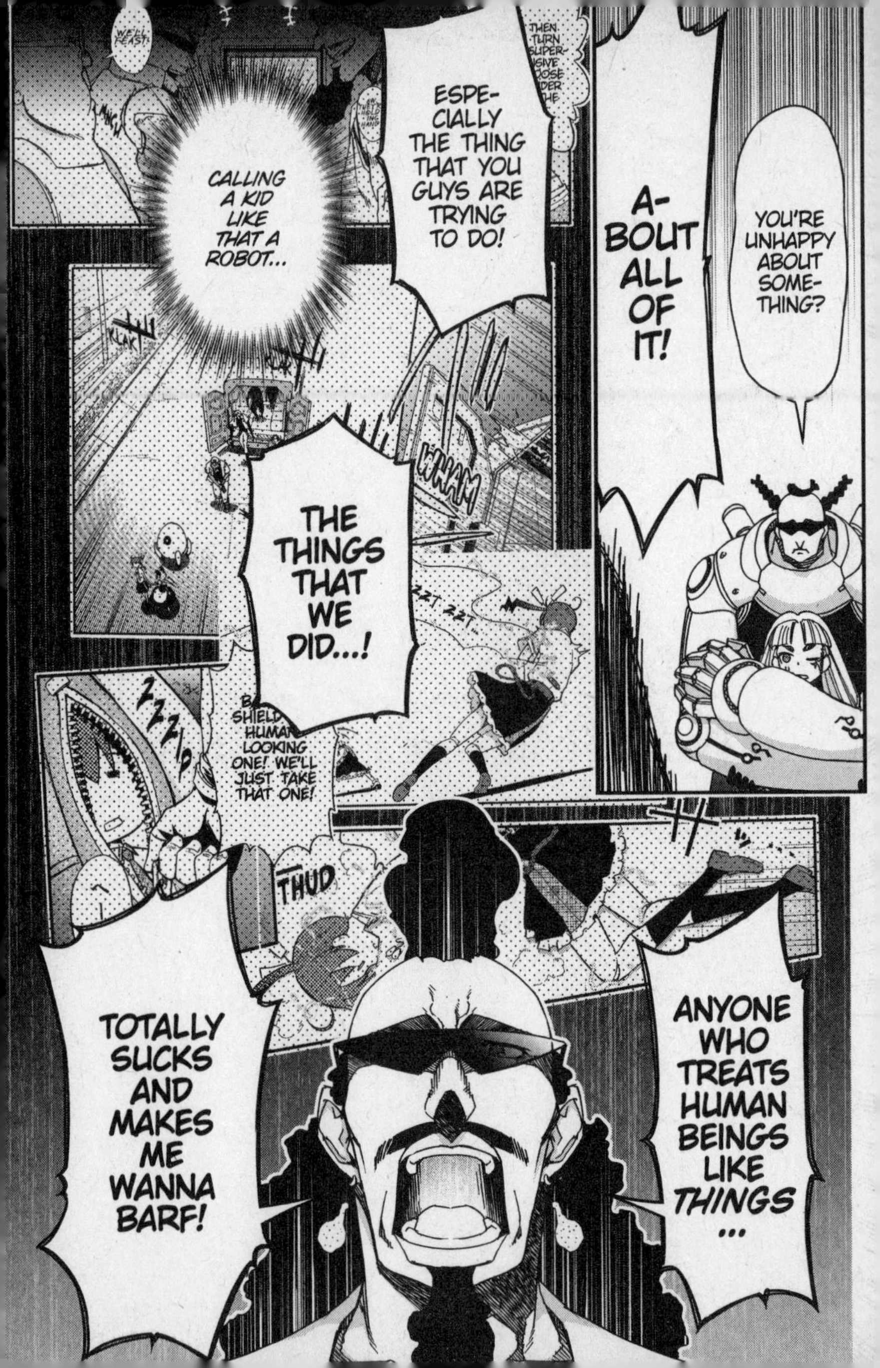

YOU'RE UNHAPPY ABOUT SOMETHING?
A-BOUT ALL OF IT!
ESPECIALLY THE THING THAT YOU GUYS ARE TRYING TO DO!
WE'LL FEAST!
CALLING A KID LIKE THAT A ROBOT...
KLAK
WHAM
THE THINGS THAT WE DID...!
ZZT ZZT...
LOOKING ONE! WE'LL JUST TAKE THAT ONE!
THUD
ANYONE WHO TREATS HUMAN BEINGS LIKE *THINGS*...
TOTALLY SUCKS AND MAKES ME WANNA BARF!

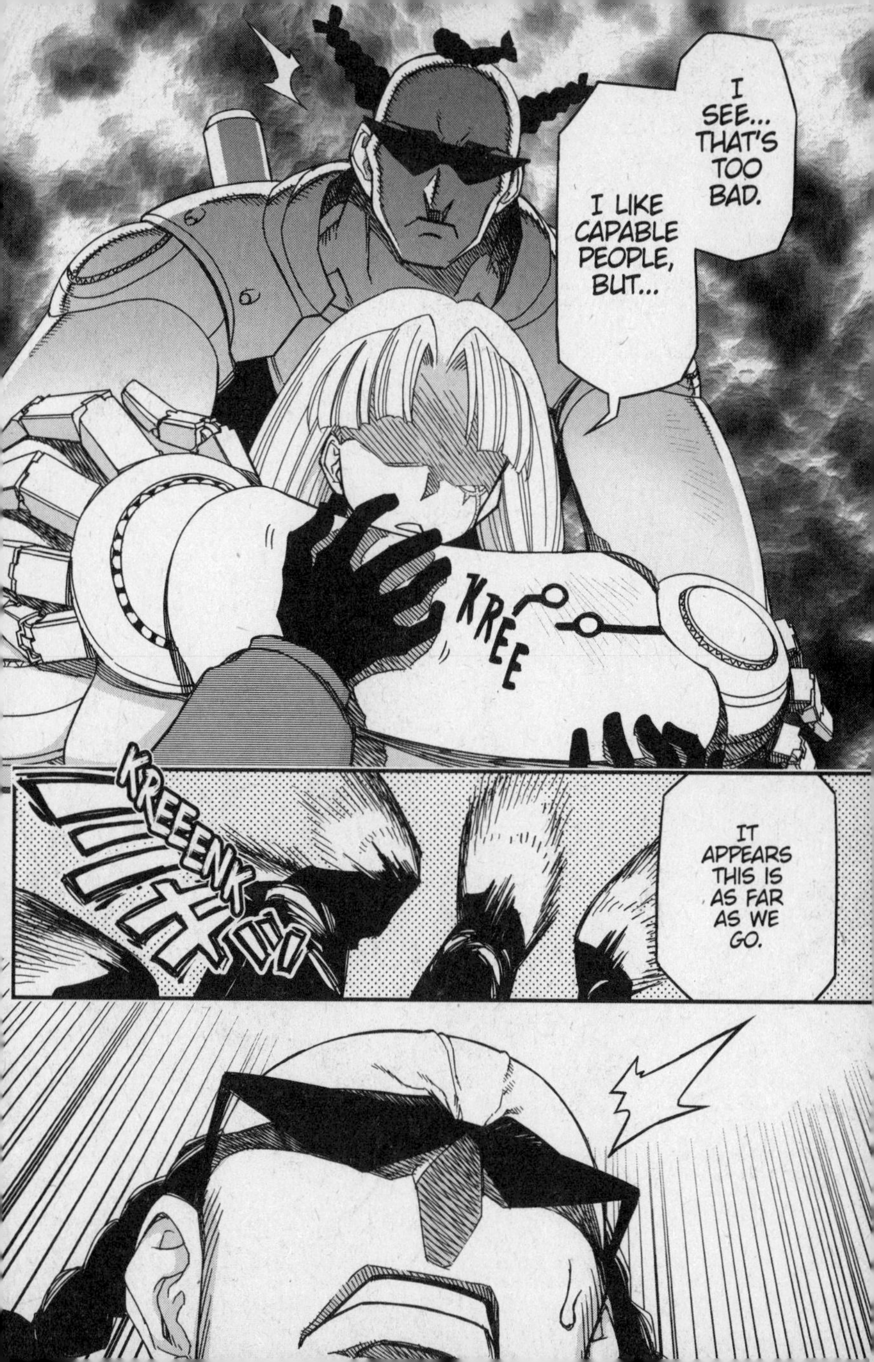
I SEE... THAT'S TOO BAD.
I LIKE CAPABLE PEOPLE, BUT...
KREE
IT APPEARS THIS IS AS FAR AS WE GO.
KREEENK

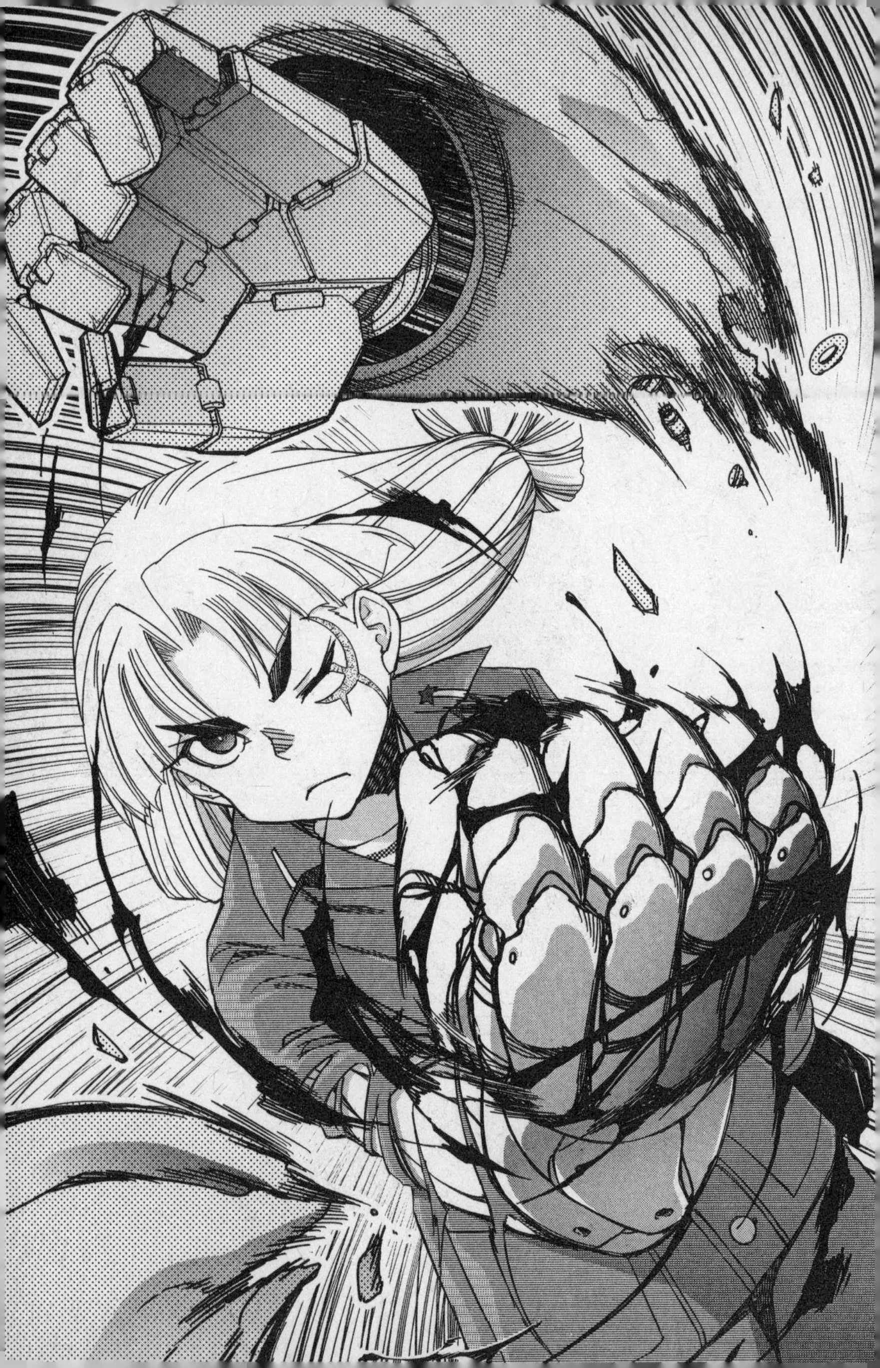

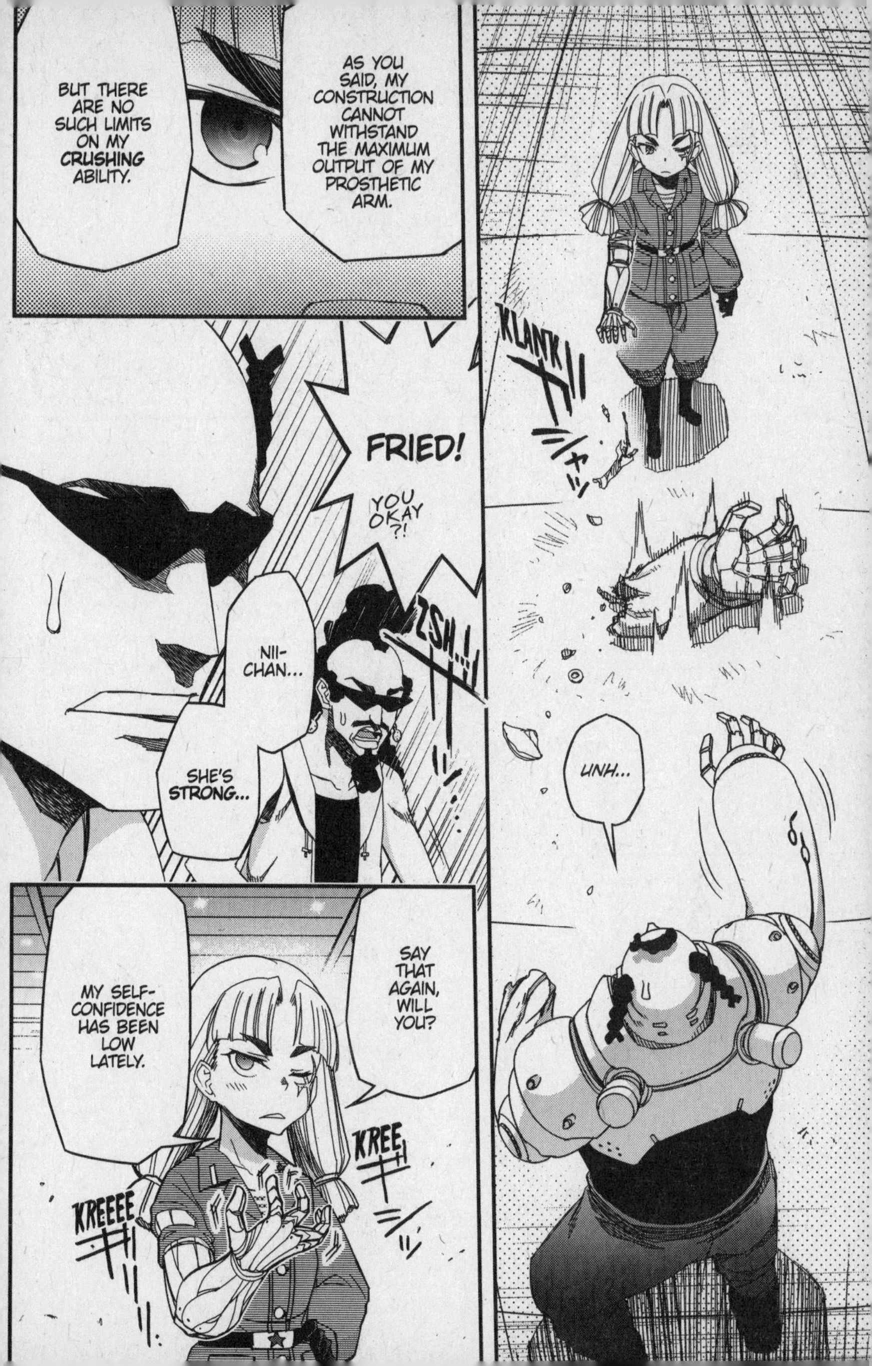
KLANK
UNH...
AS YOU SAID, MY CONSTRUCTION CANNOT WITHSTAND THE MAXIMUM OUTPUT OF MY PROSTHETIC ARM.
BUT THERE ARE NO SUCH LIMITS ON MY CRUSHING ABILITY.
FRIED!
YOU OKAY?!
ZSH
NII-CHAN...
SHE'S STRONG...
SAY THAT AGAIN, WILL YOU?
KREE
MY SELF-CONFIDENCE HAS BEEN LOW LATELY.
KREEEE

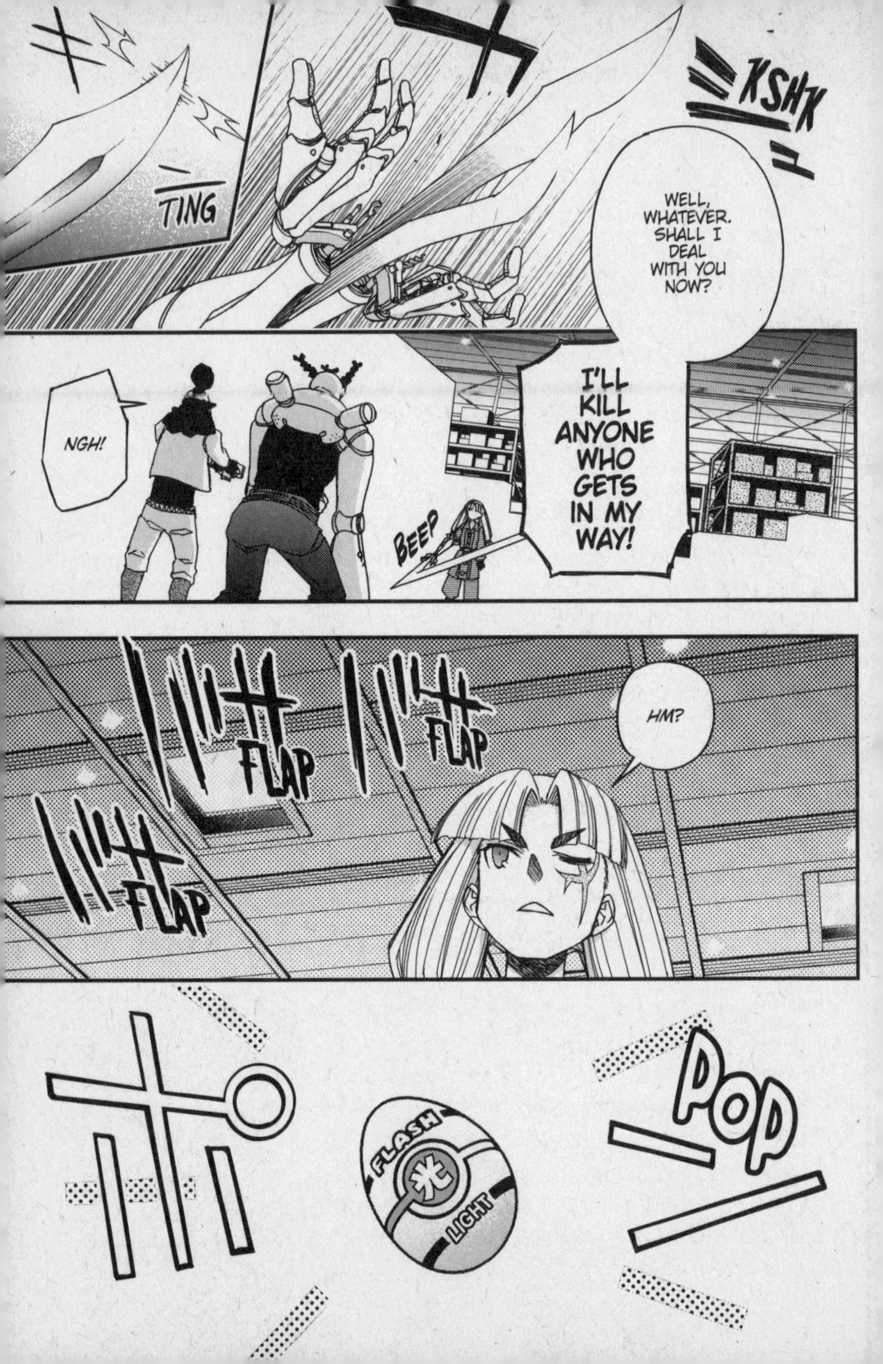
KSHK
WELL, WHATEVER. SHALL I DEAL WITH YOU NOW?
TING
I'LL KILL ANYONE WHO GETS IN MY WAY!
BEEP
NGH!
HM?
FLAP
FLAP
FLAP
POP
FLASH LIGHT

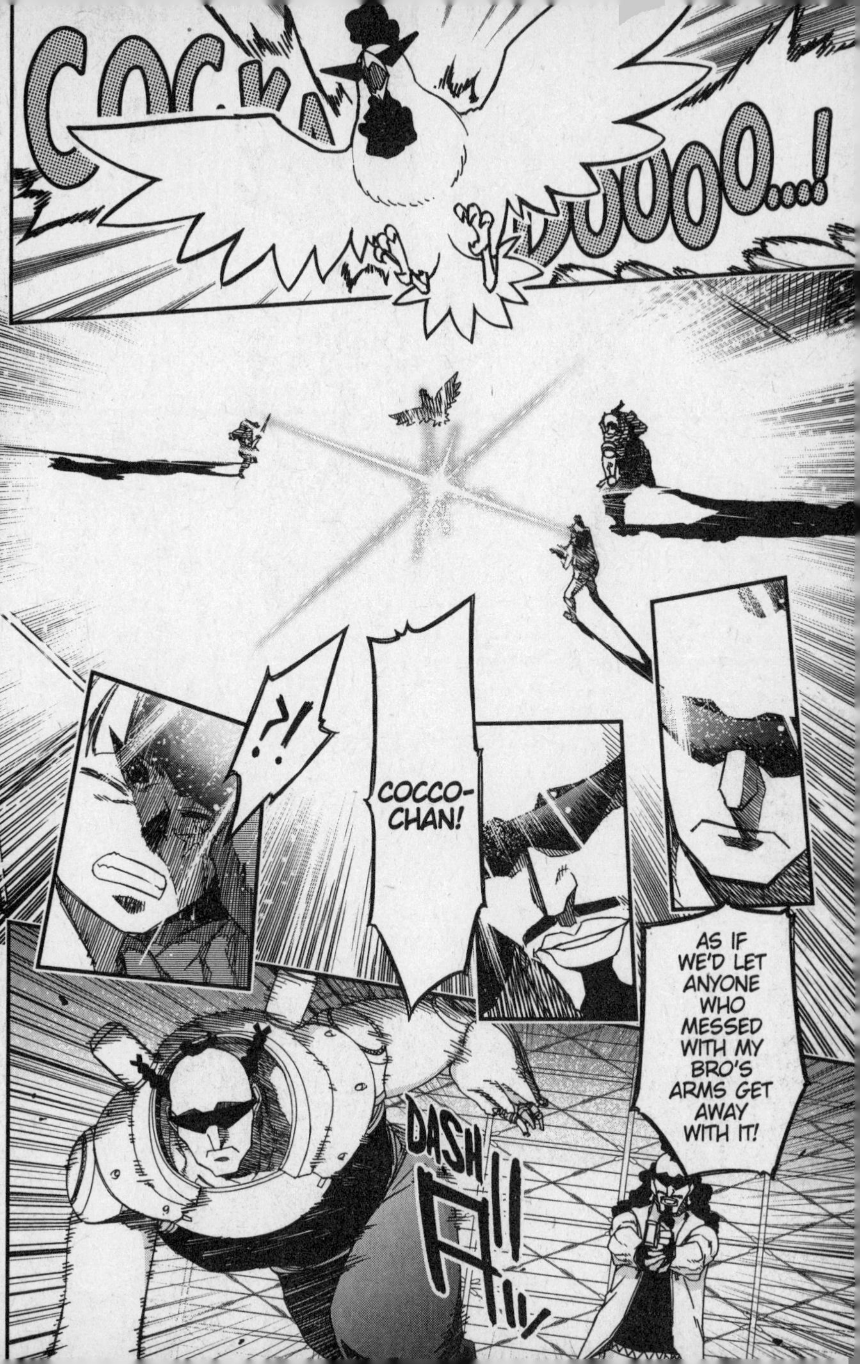
COCKA DOOOO...!
AS IF WE'D LET ANYONE WHO MESSED WITH MY BRO'S ARMS GET AWAY WITH IT!
COCCO-CHAN!
?!
DASH!!

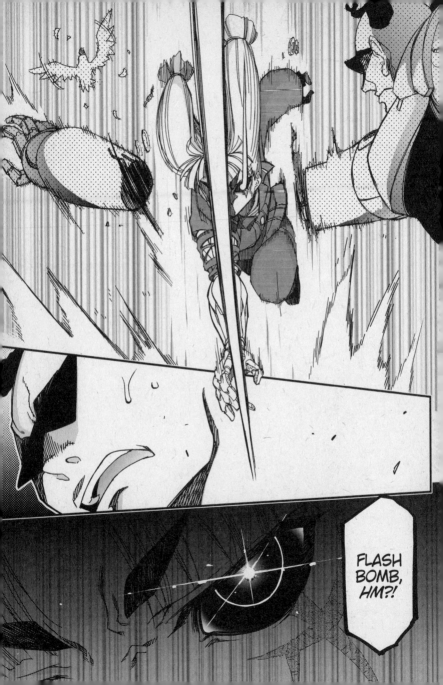

FLASH
BOMB,
HM?!

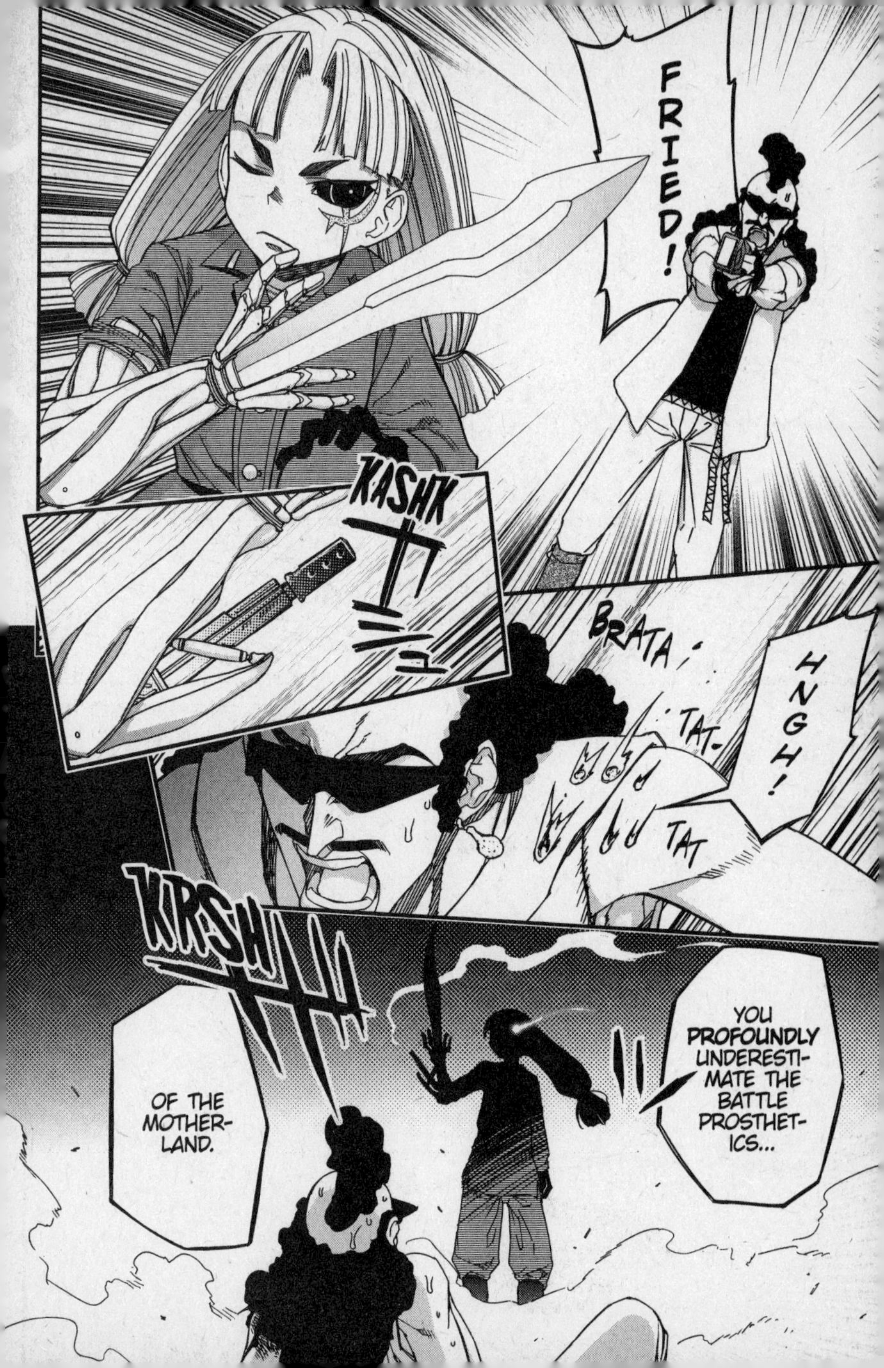
FRIED!
KASHK
BRATA
HNGH!
TAT-
TAT
KRSHH
YOU PROFOUNDLY UNDERESTI-MATE THE BATTLE PROSTHET-ICS...
OF THE MOTHER-LAND.

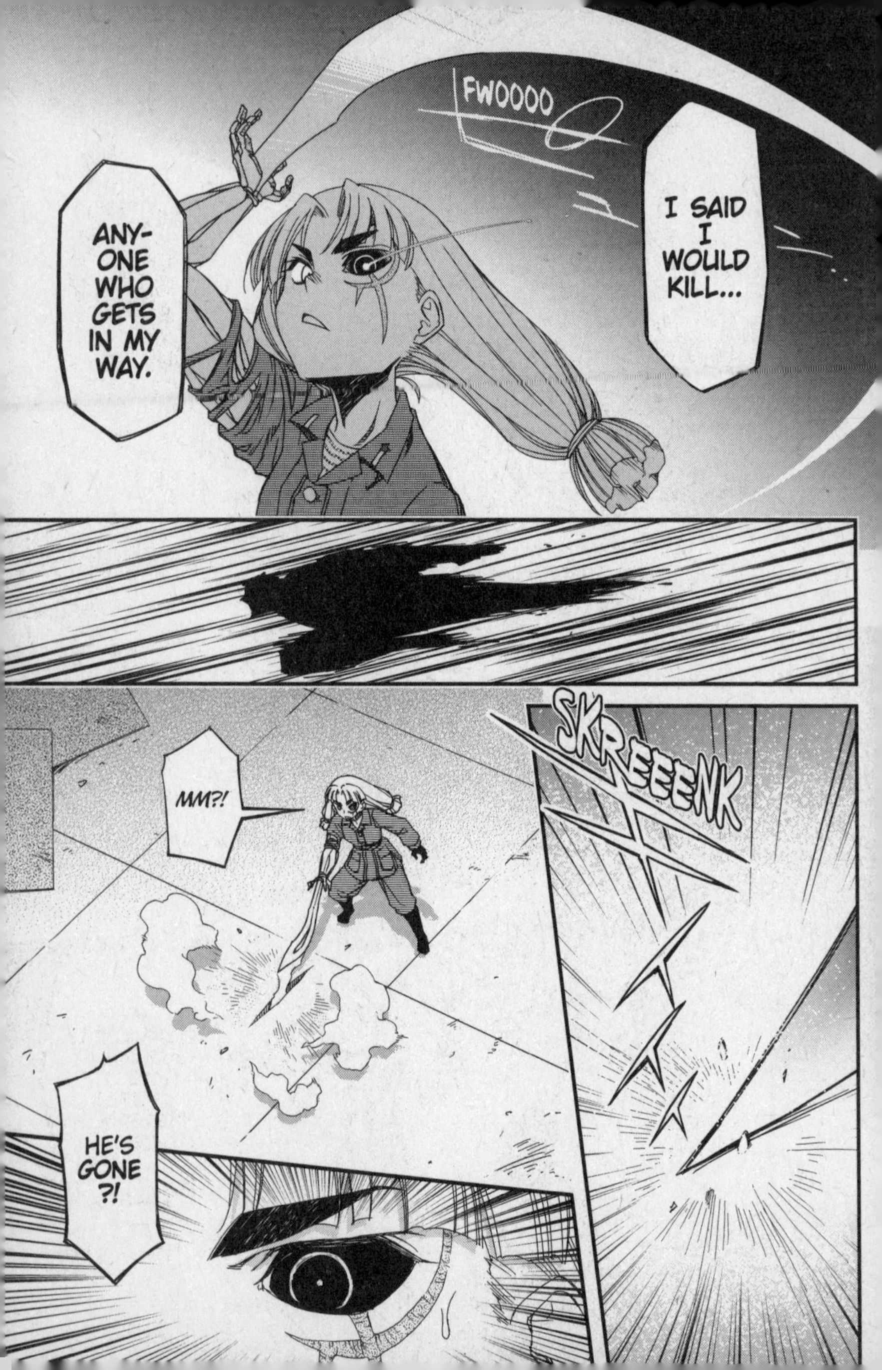
FWOOOO
I SAID I WOULD KILL...
ANY-ONE WHO GETS IN MY WAY.
SKREEENK
MM?!
HE'S GONE?!

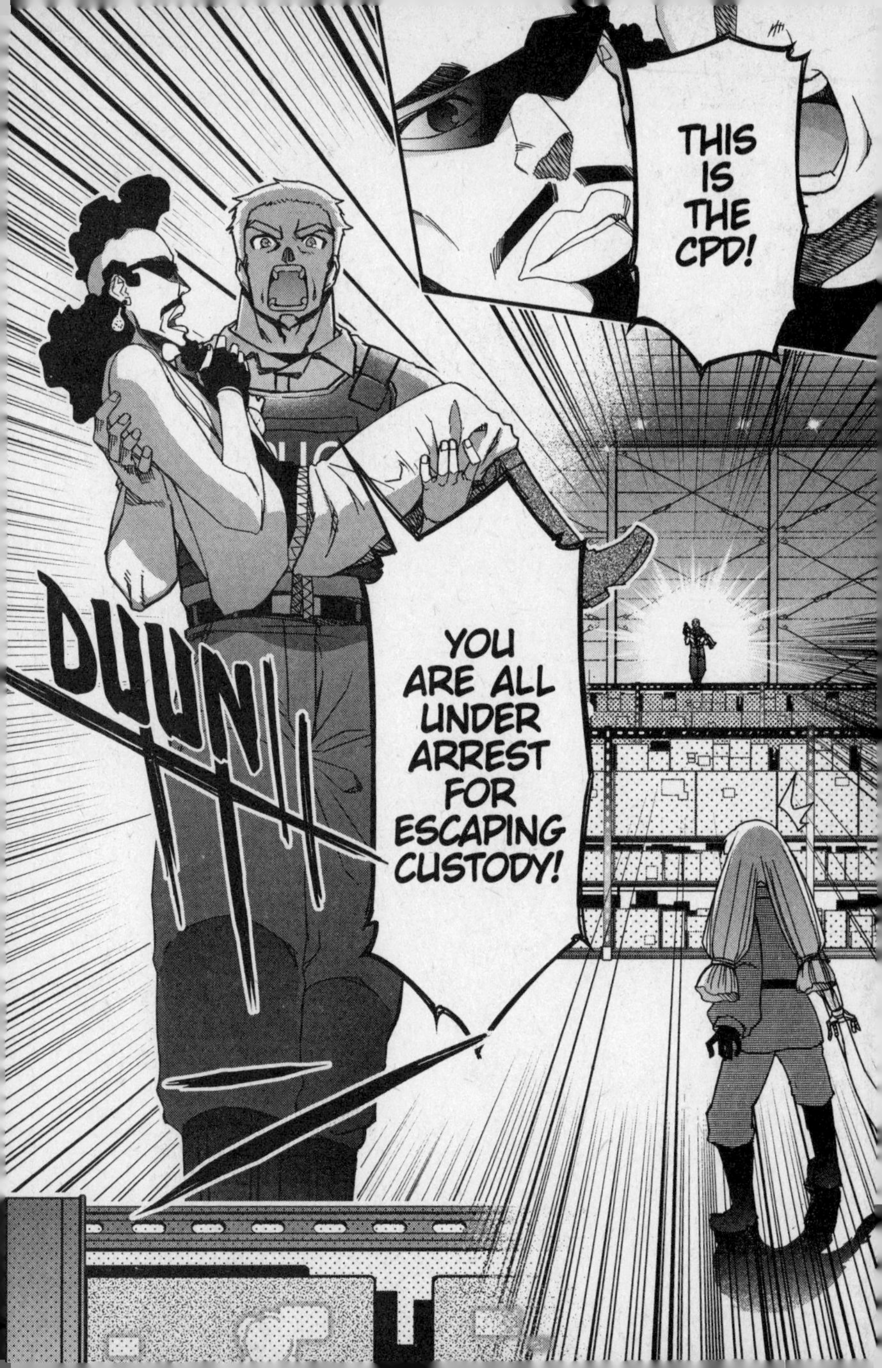
THIS IS THE CPD!
YOU ARE ALL UNDER ARREST FOR ESCAPING CUSTODY!
DUUN

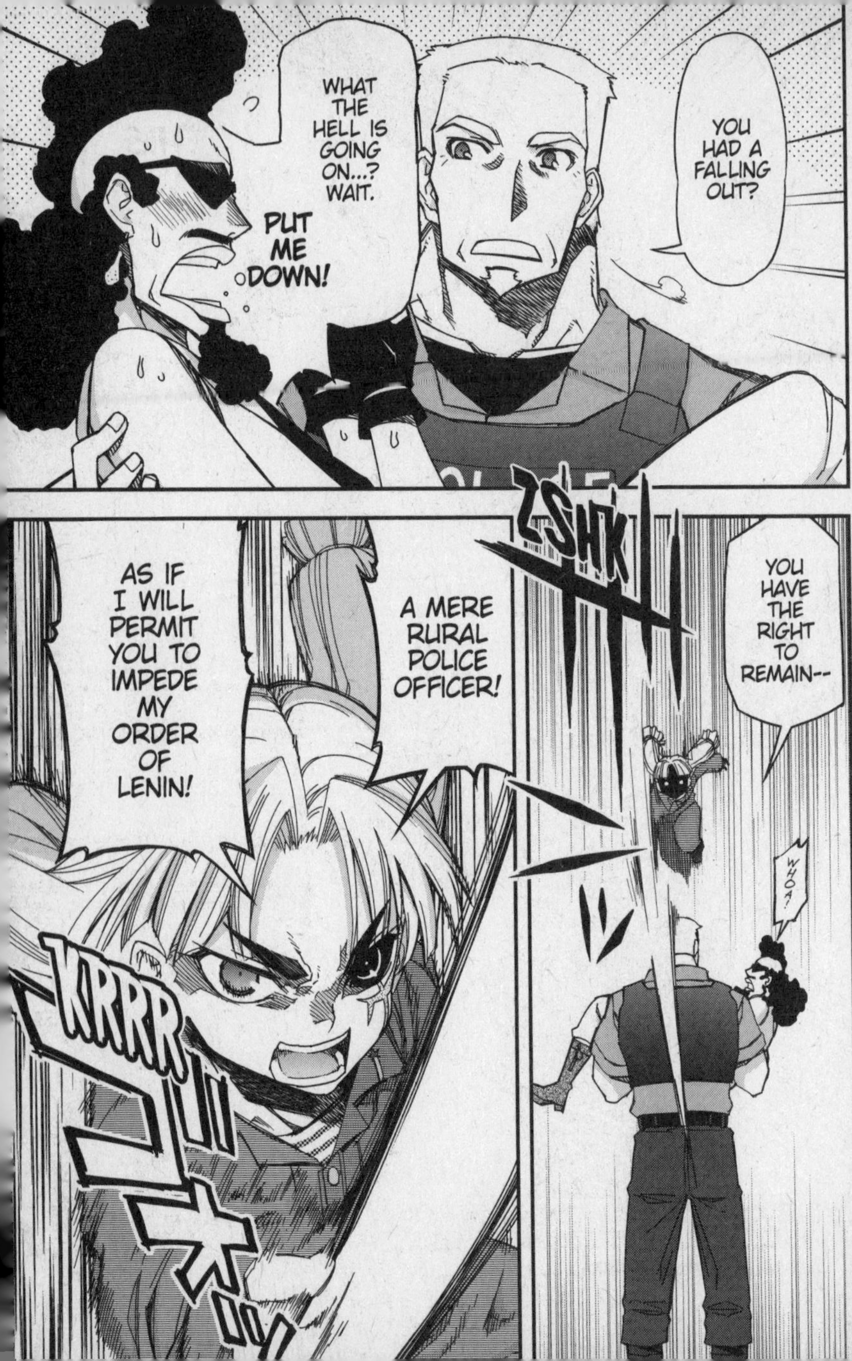
YOU HAD A FALLING OUT?
WHAT THE HELL IS GOING ON...? WAIT.
PUT ME DOWN!
ZSHK
YOU HAVE THE RIGHT TO REMAIN--
WHOA!
A MERE RURAL POLICE OFFICER!
AS IF I WILL PERMIT YOU TO IMPEDE MY ORDER OF LENIN!
KRRR

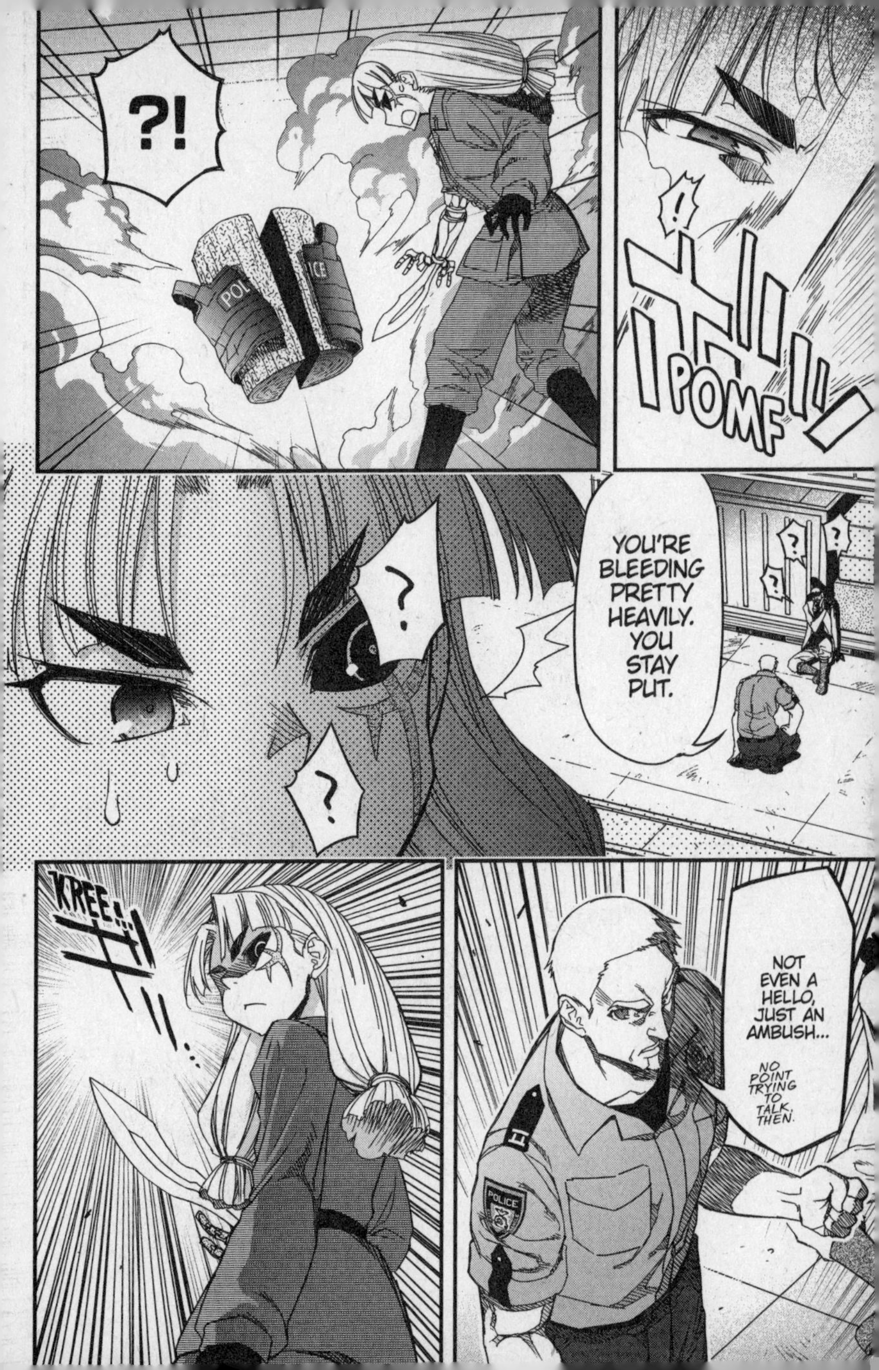
!
POMF
?!
?
?
?
YOU'RE BLEEDING PRETTY HEAVILY. YOU STAY PUT.
?
?
NOT EVEN A HELLO, JUST AN AMBUSH...
NO POINT TRYING TO TALK, THEN.
KREE...

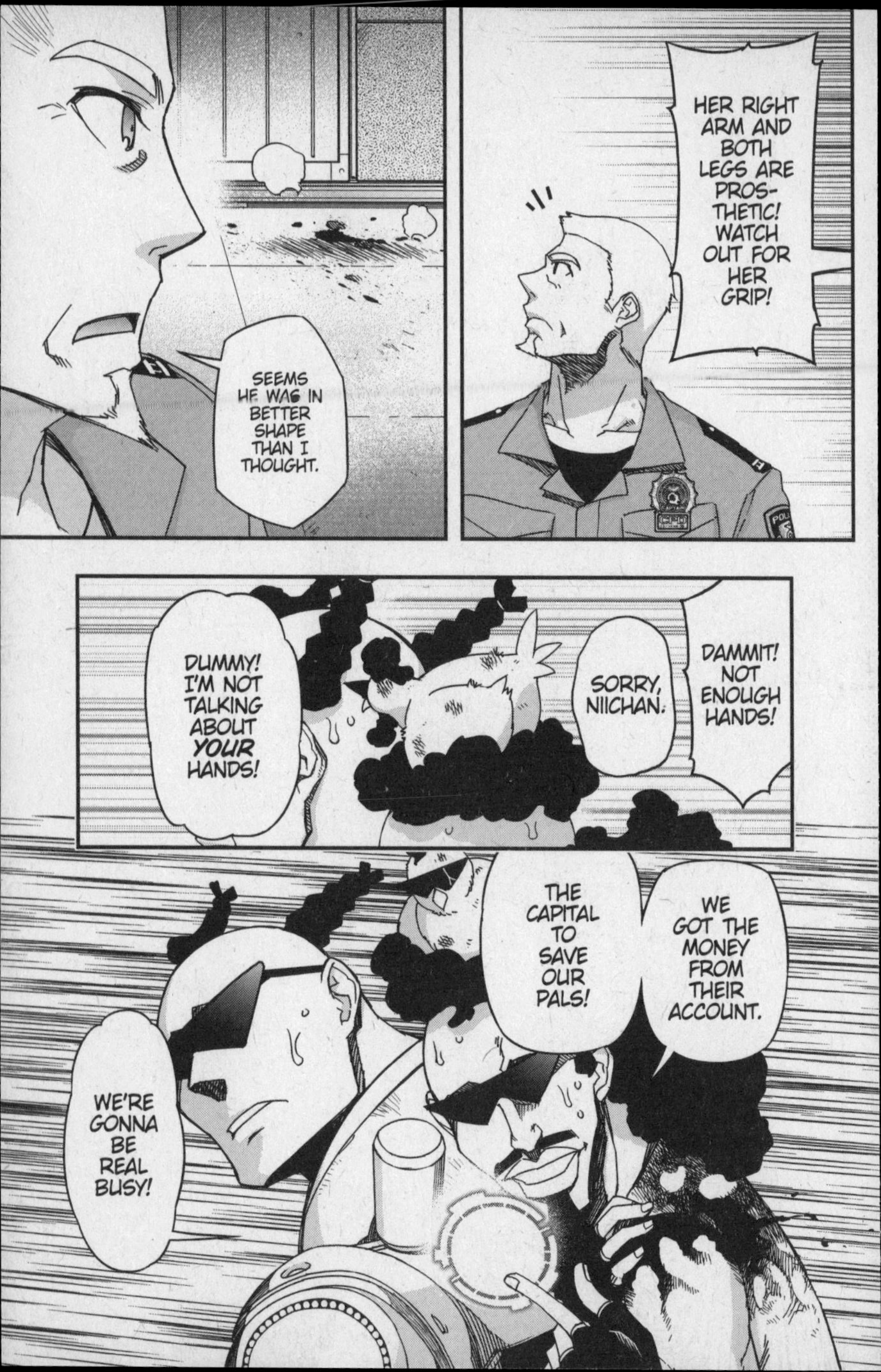
HER RIGHT ARM AND BOTH LEGS ARE PROS-THETIC! WATCH OUT FOR HER GRIP!
SEEMS HE WAS IN BETTER SHAPE THAN I THOUGHT.
DAMMIT! NOT ENOUGH HANDS!
SORRY, NIICHAN.
DUMMY! I'M NOT TALKING ABOUT *YOUR* HANDS!
WE GOT THE MONEY FROM THEIR ACCOUNT.
THE CAPITAL TO SAVE OUR PALS!
WE'RE GONNA BE REAL BUSY!

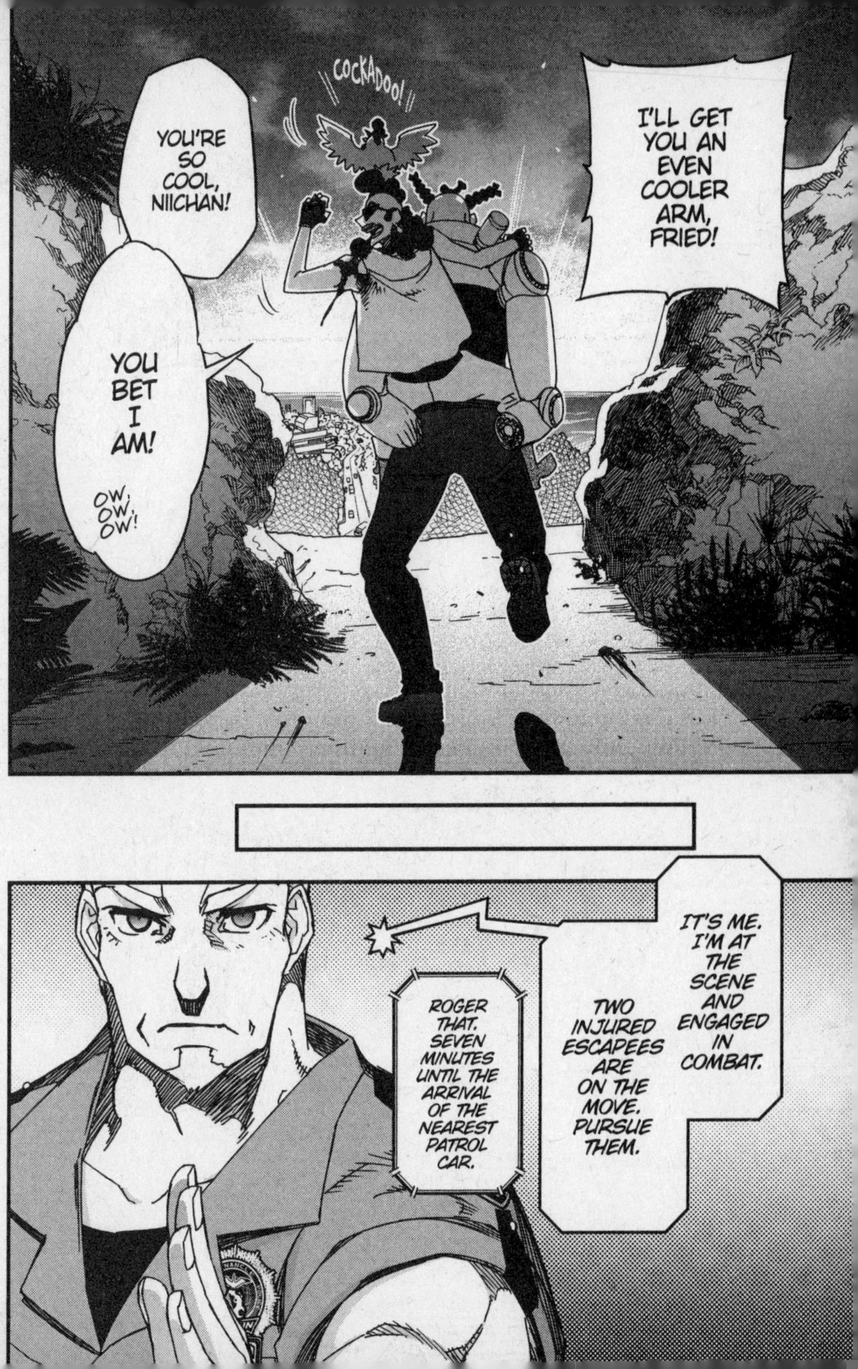
I'LL GET YOU AN EVEN COOLER ARM, FRIED!
COCKADOO!
YOU'RE SO COOL, NIICHAN!
YOU BET I AM!
OW, OW, OW!
IT'S ME. I'M AT THE SCENE AND ENGAGED IN COMBAT.
TWO INJURED ESCAPEES ARE ON THE MOVE. PURSUE THEM.
ROGER THAT. SEVEN MINUTES UNTIL THE ARRIVAL OF THE NEAREST PATROL CAR.

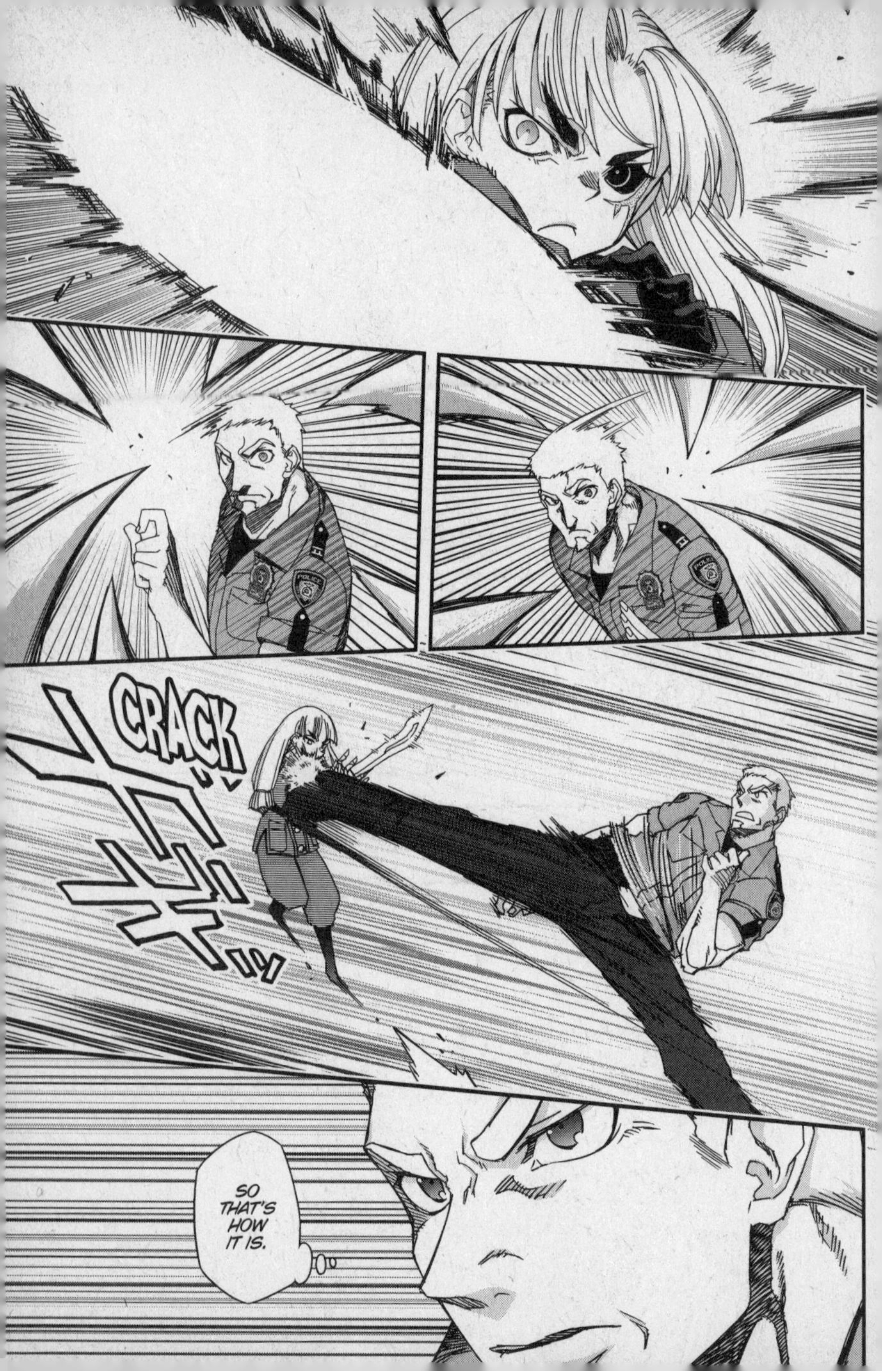
CRACK
SO THAT'S HOW IT IS.

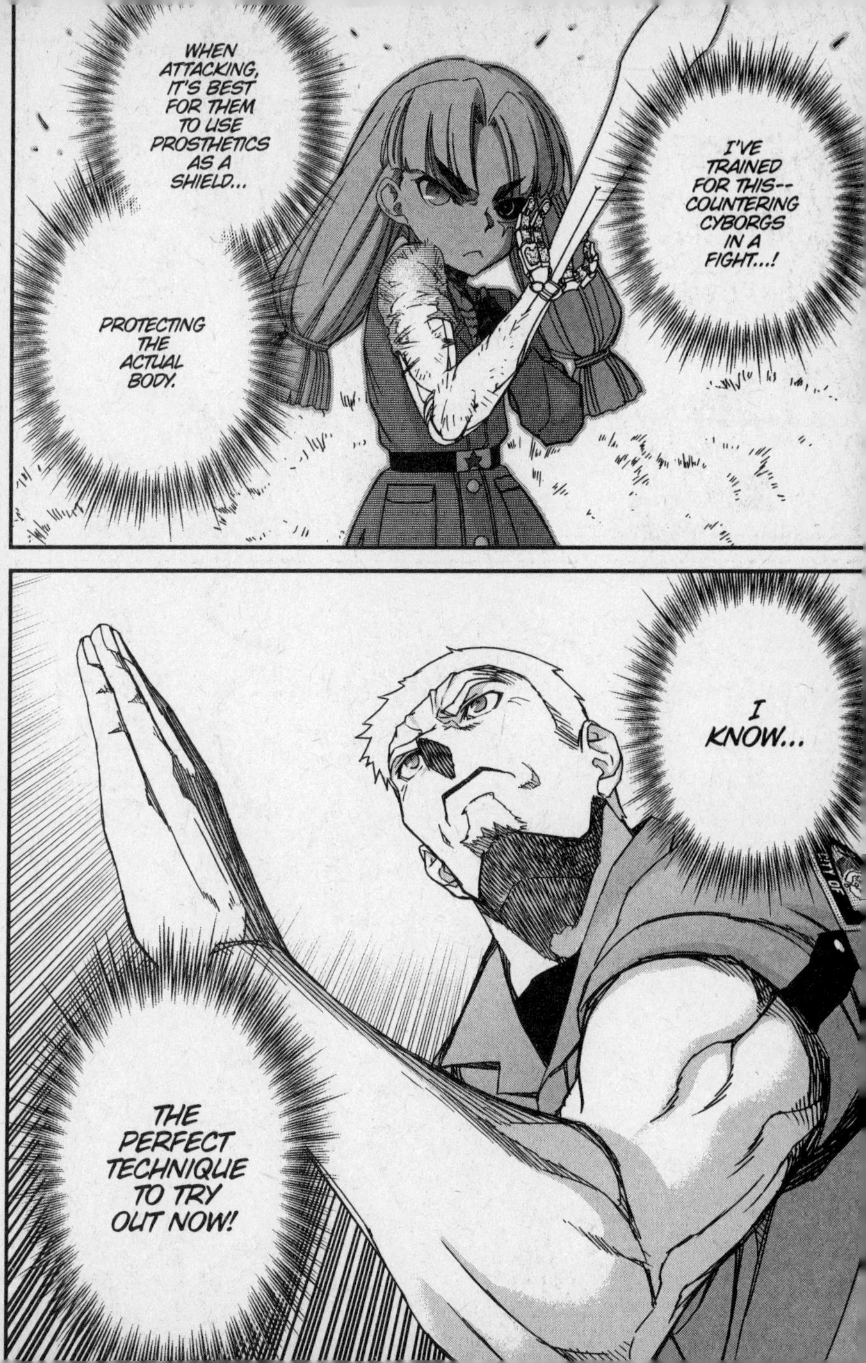
I'VE TRAINED FOR THIS-- COUNTERING CYBORGS IN A FIGHT...!
WHEN ATTACKING, IT'S BEST FOR THEM TO USE PROSTHETICS AS A SHIELD...
PROTECTING THE ACTUAL BODY.
I KNOW...
THE PERFECT TECHNIQUE TO TRY OUT NOW!

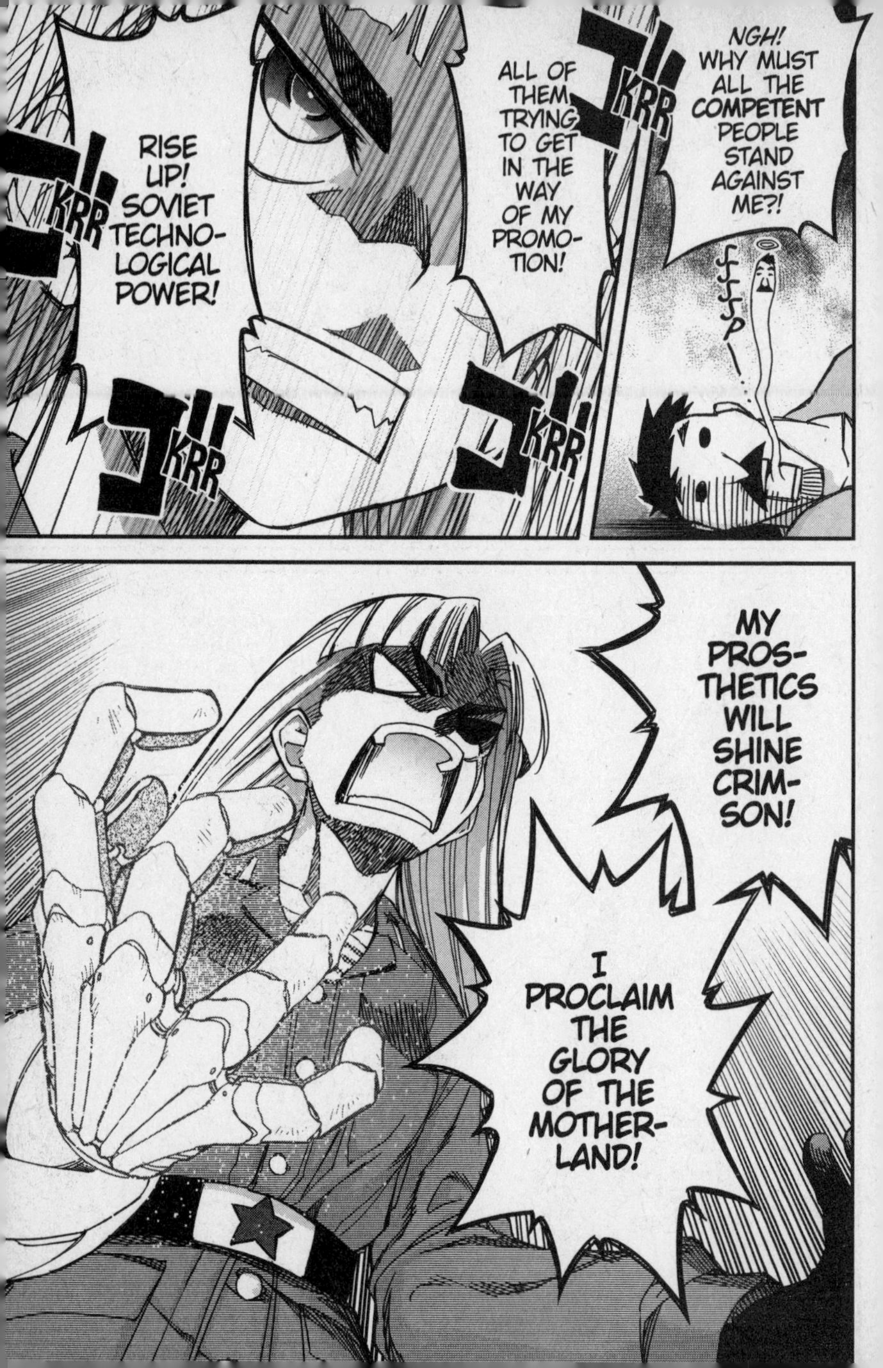
NGH! WHY MUST ALL THE COMPETENT PEOPLE STAND AGAINST ME?!
KRR
ALL OF THEM TRYING TO GET IN THE WAY OF MY PROMOTION!
KRR
RISE UP! SOVIET TECHNOLOGICAL POWER!
KRR
KRR
MY PROSTHETICS WILL SHINE CRIMSON!
I PROCLAIM THE GLORY OF THE MOTHERLAND!

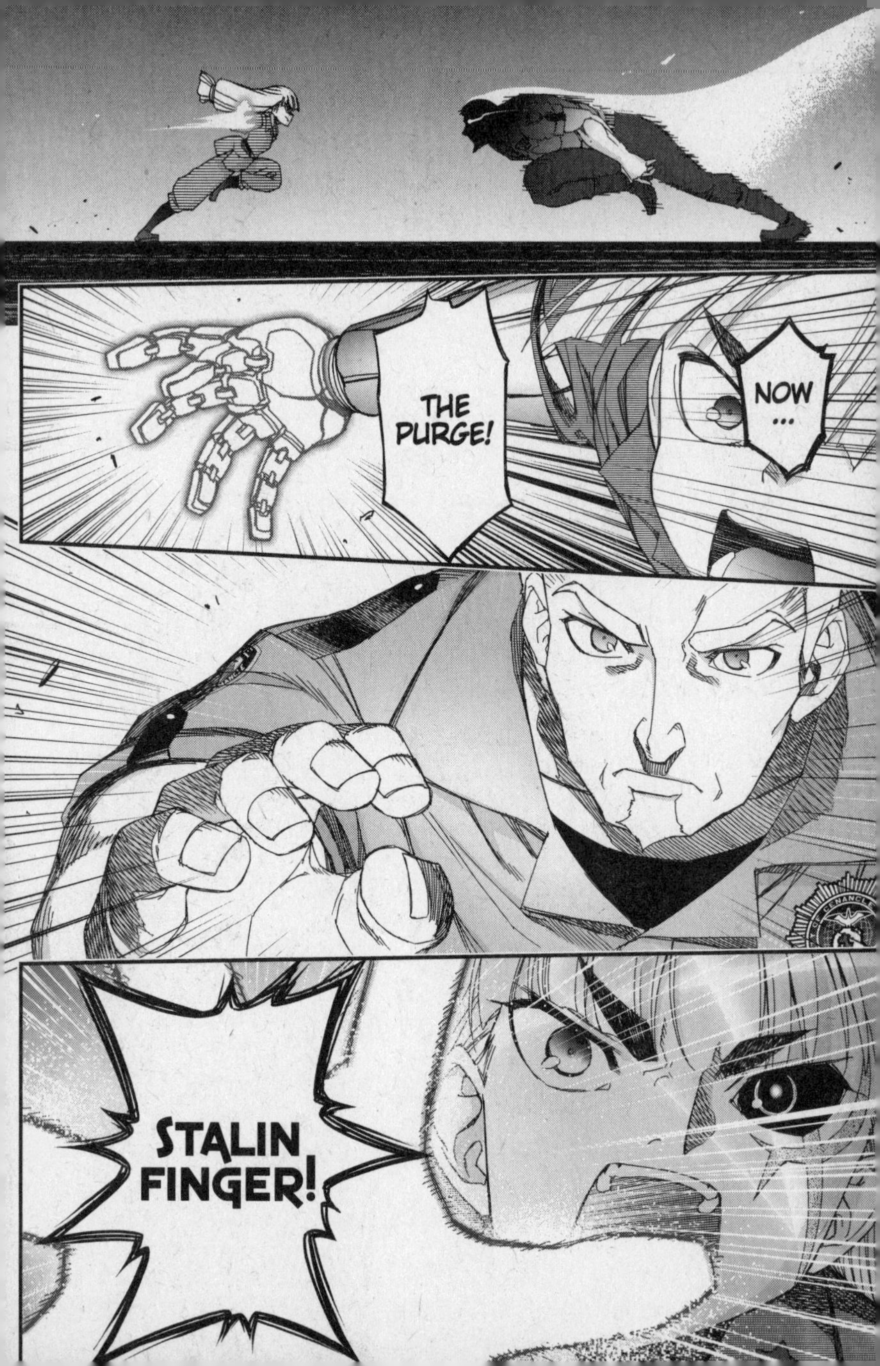
NOW ...
THE PURGE!
STALIN FINGER!

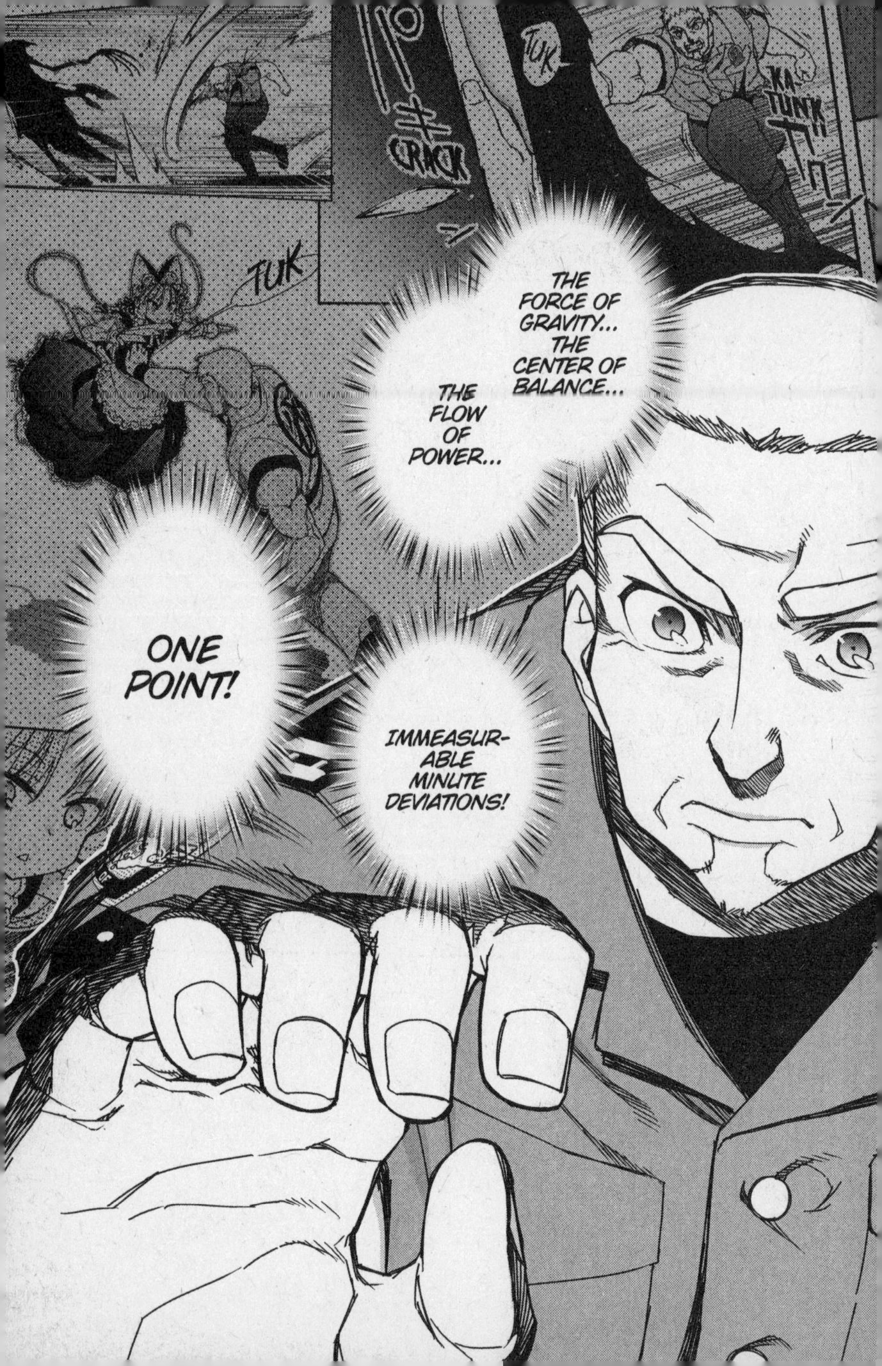
TUK
KA-TUNK
CRACK
TUK
THE FORCE OF GRAVITY... THE CENTER OF BALANCE...
THE FLOW OF POWER...
IMMEASUR-ABLE MINUTE DEVIATIONS!
ONE POINT!

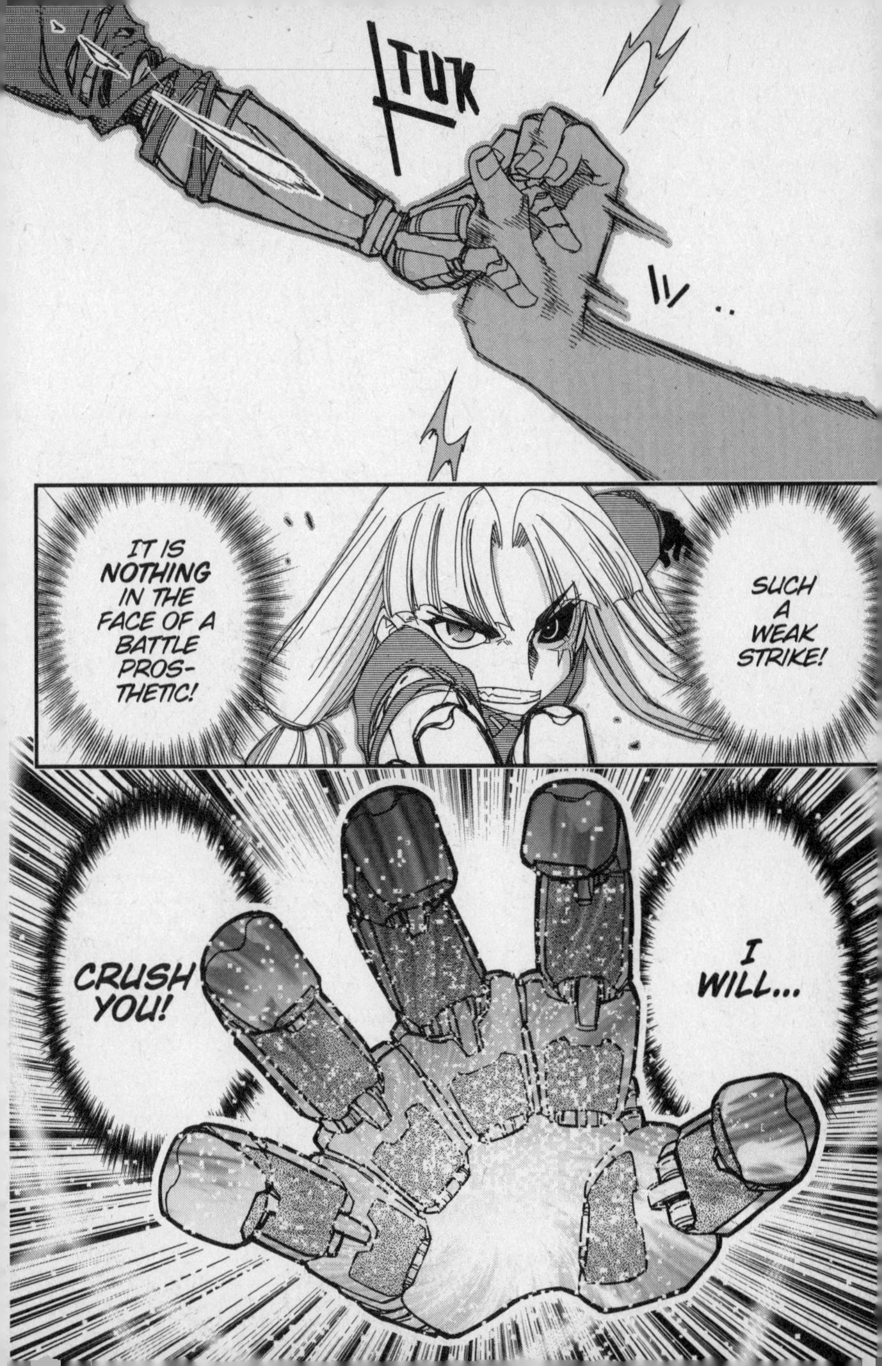
TUK
SUCH A WEAK STRIKE!
IT IS NOTHING IN THE FACE OF A BATTLE PROS-THETIC!
I WILL...
CRUSH YOU!

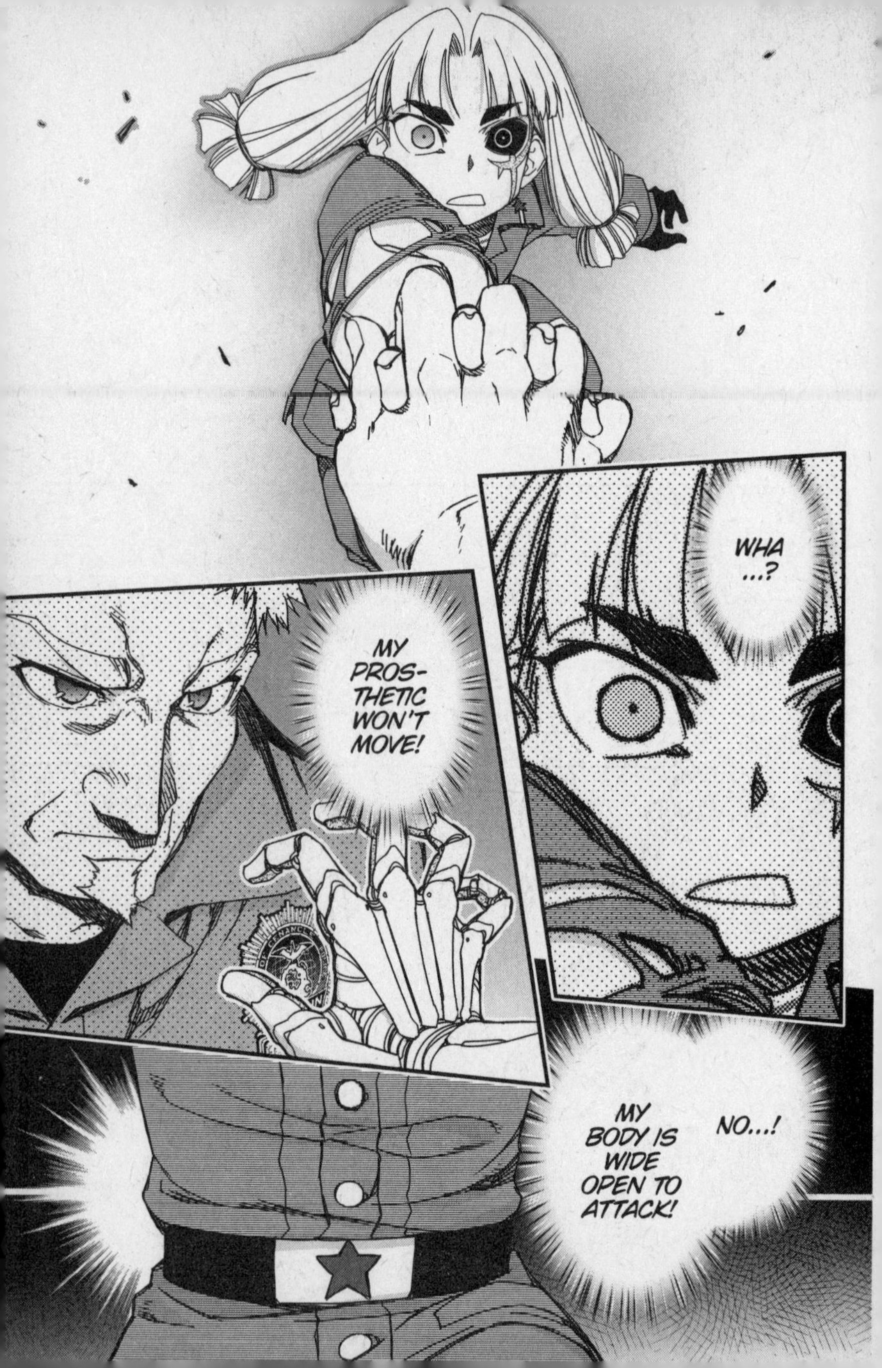
WHA ...?
MY PROS-THETIC WON'T MOVE!
NO...!
MY BODY IS WIDE OPEN TO ATTACK!

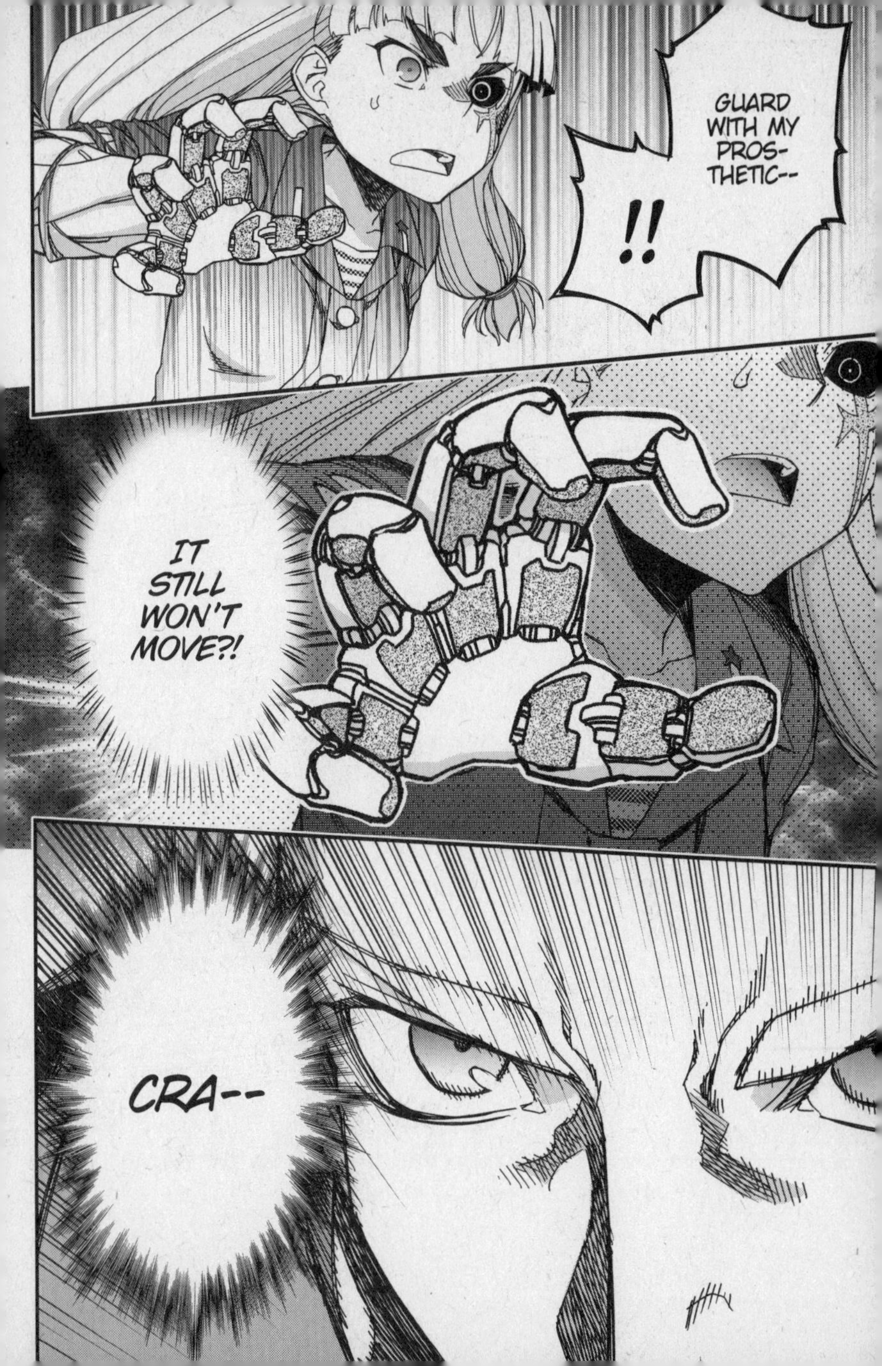
GUARD WITH MY PROS-THETIC--
!!
IT STILL WON'T MOVE?!
CRA--

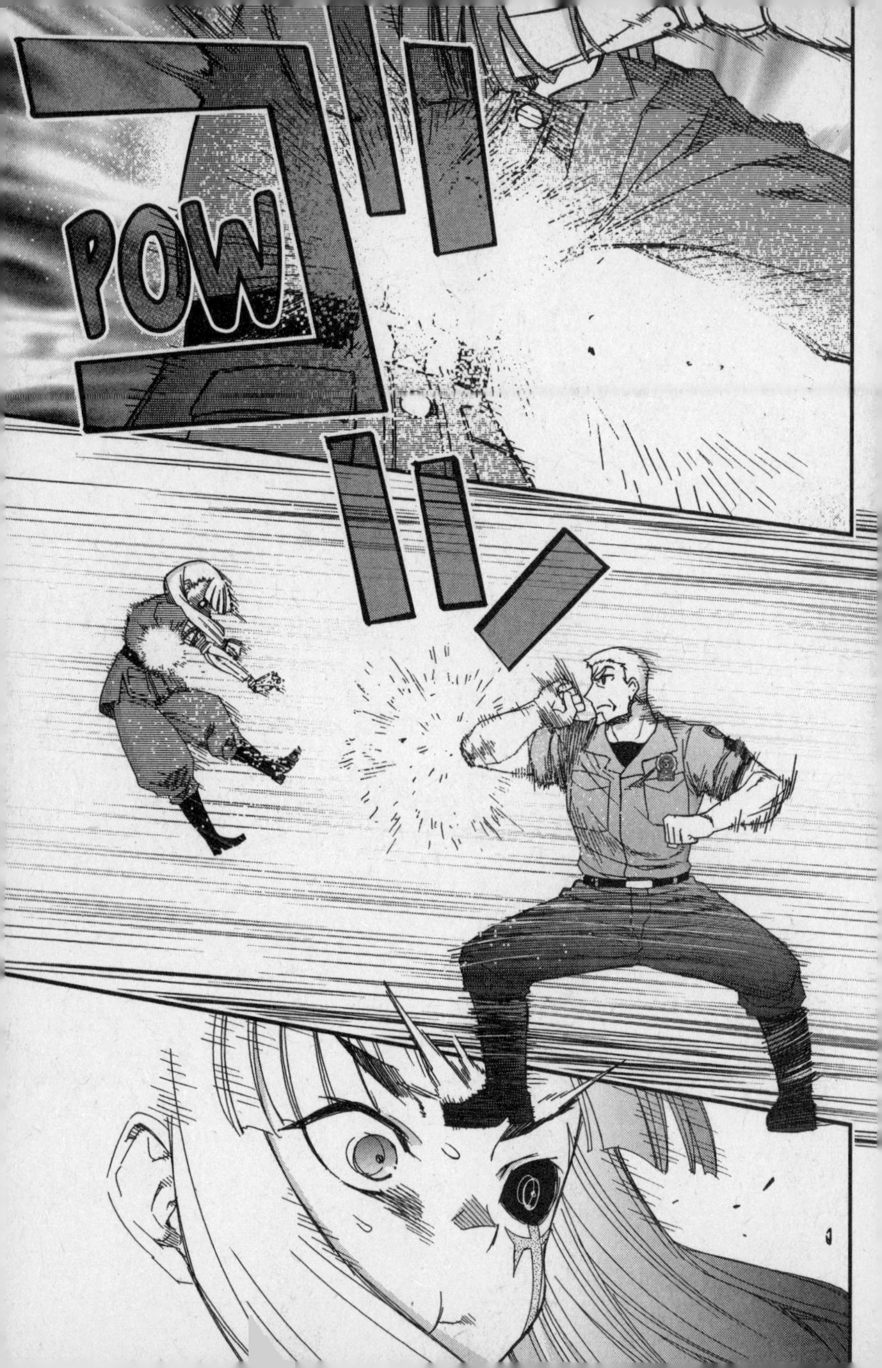
POW

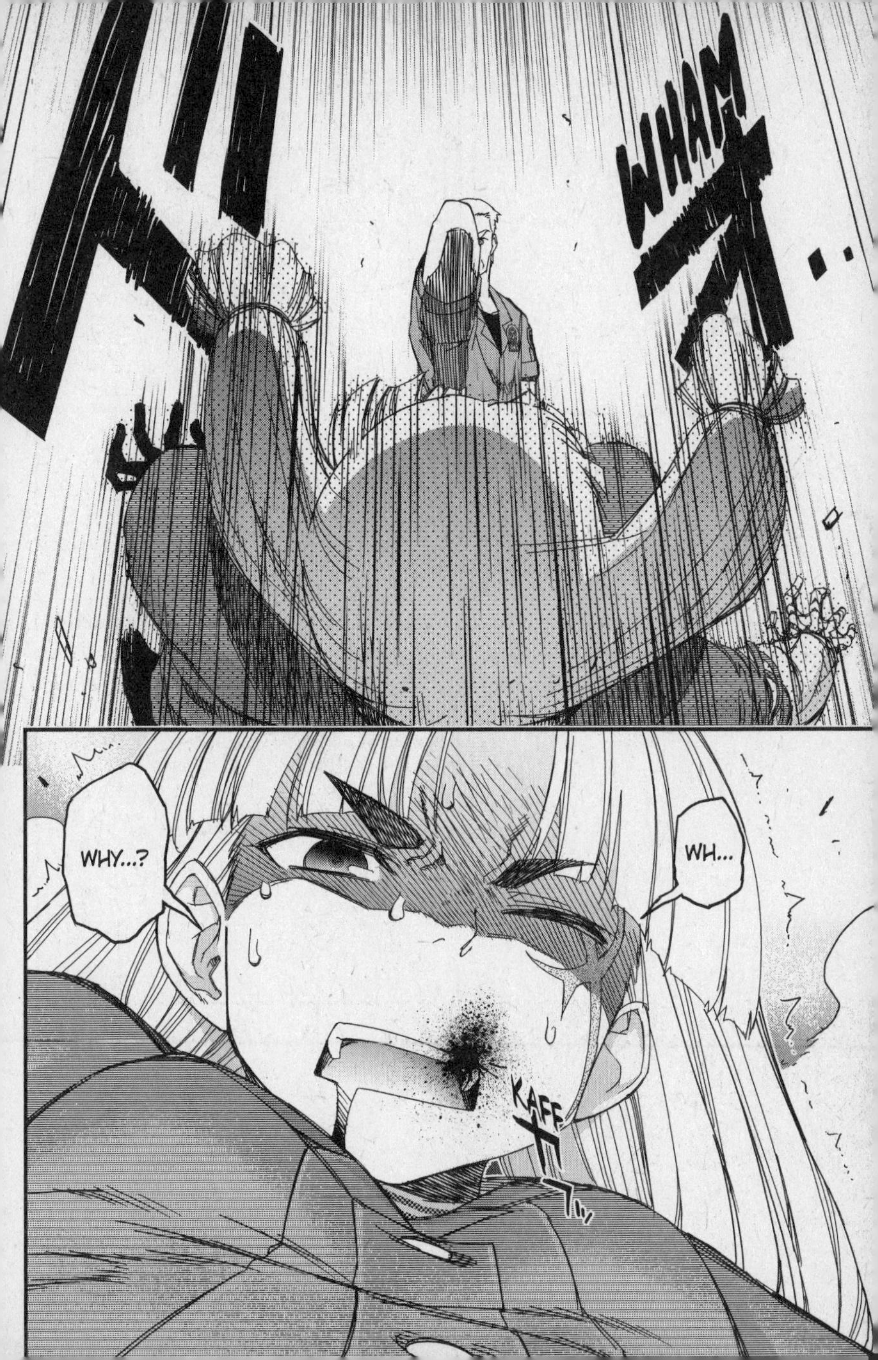
WHAM..
WH...
WHY...?
KAFF

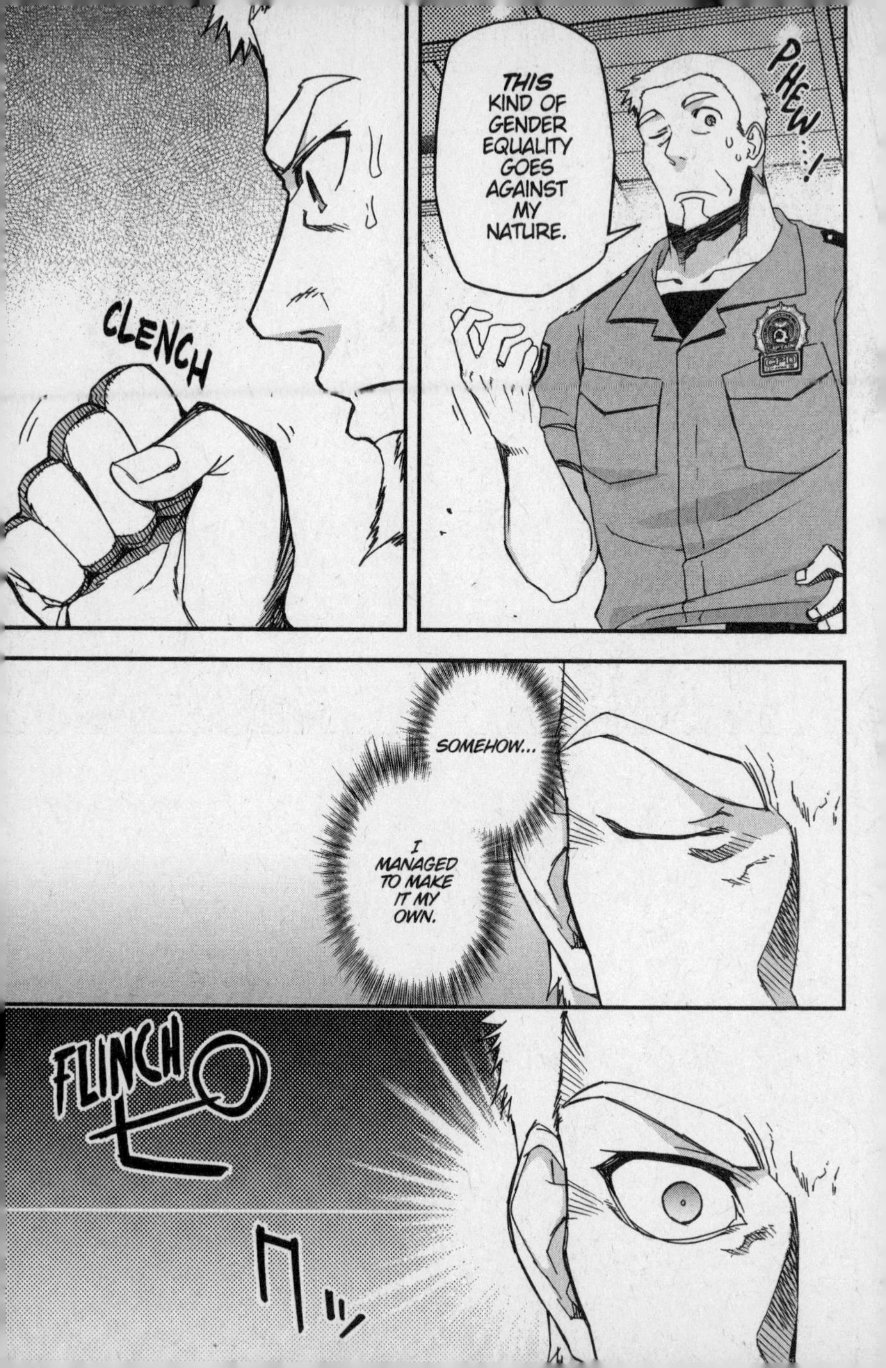
PHEW...!
THIS KIND OF GENDER EQUALITY GOES AGAINST MY NATURE.
CLENCH
SOMEHOW...
I MANAGED TO MAKE IT MY OWN.
FLINCH

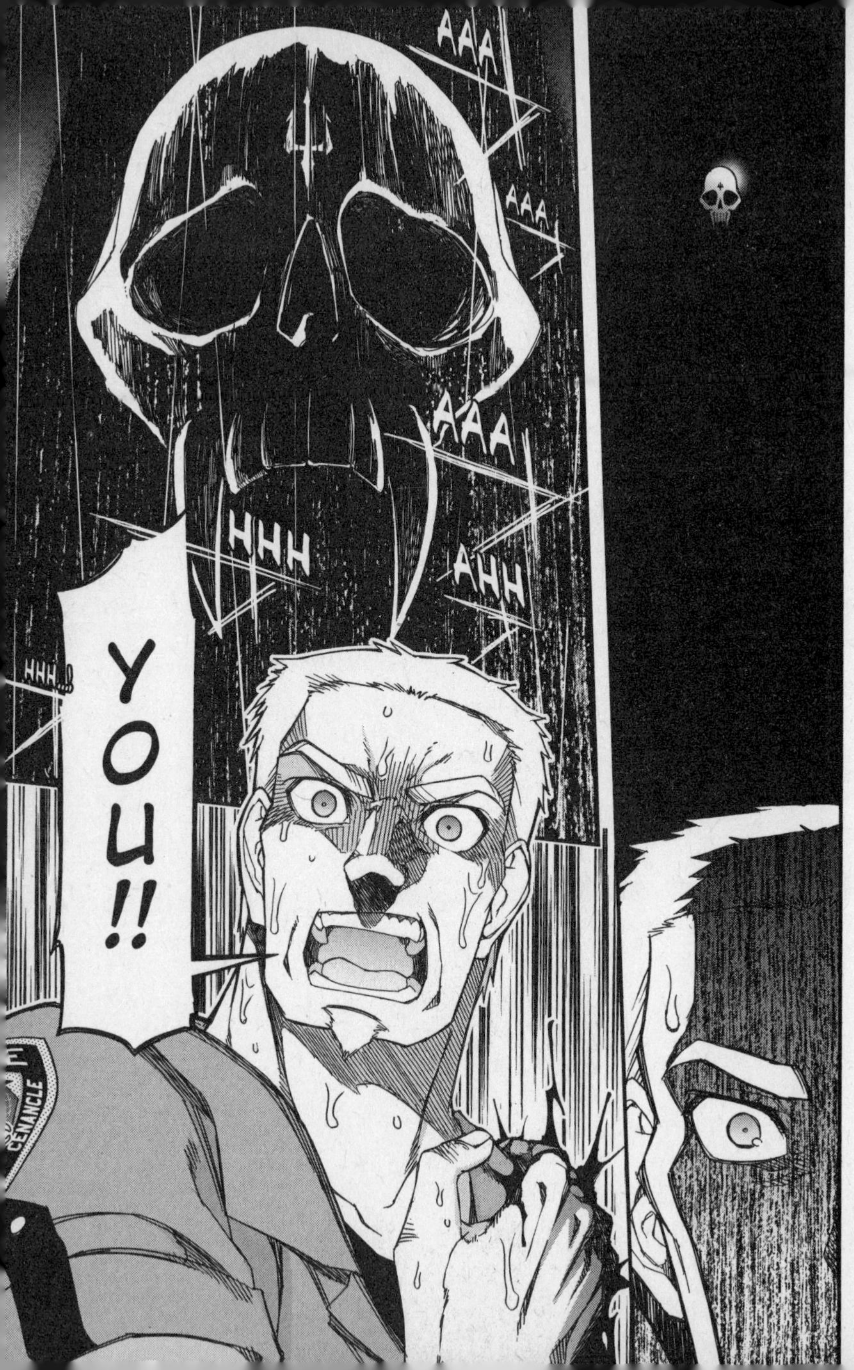
AAA
AAA
AAA
AHH
HHH
HHH...!
YOU!!
CENANCLE

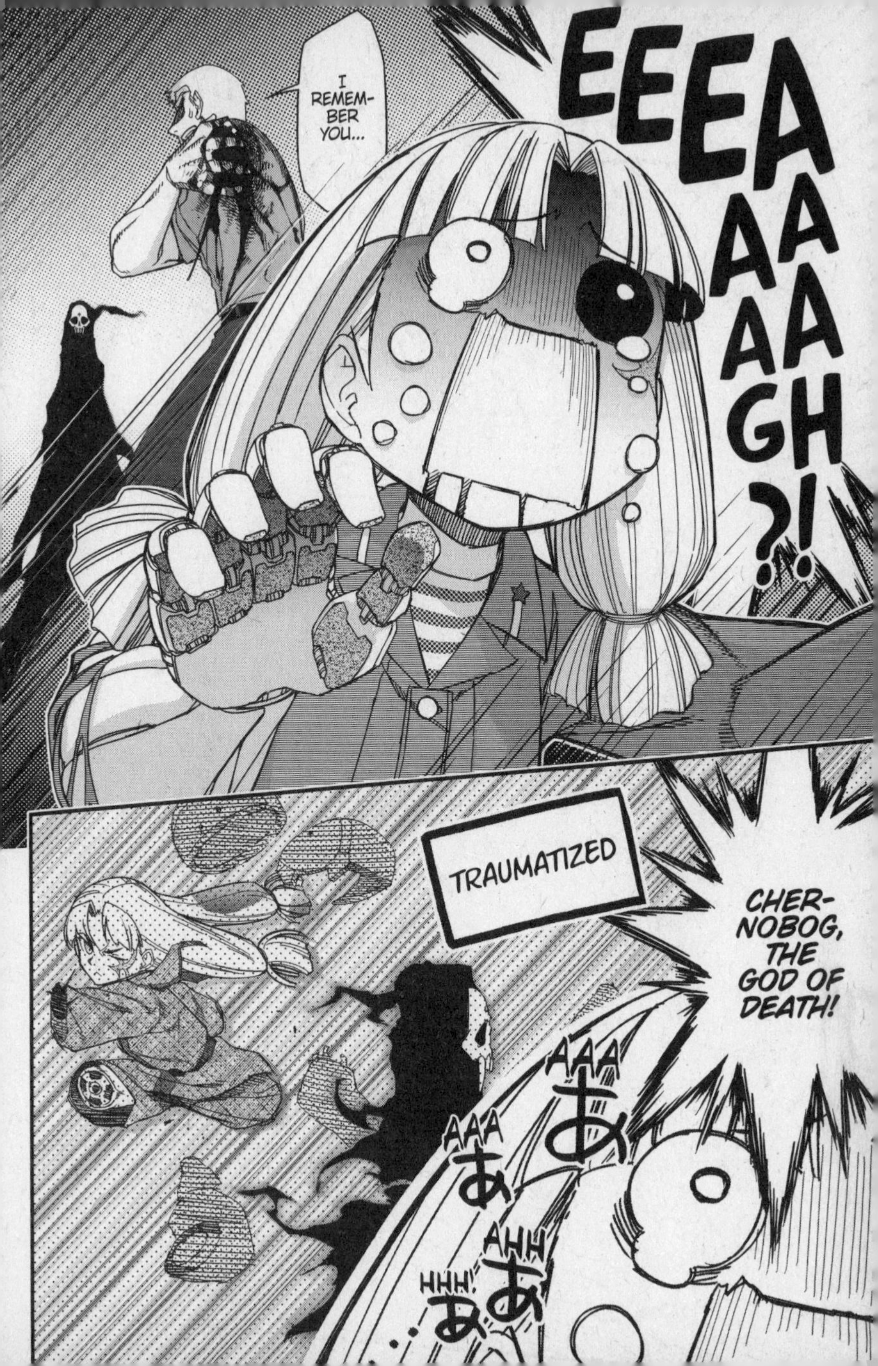
EEEAAAAAAGH?!
I REMEMBER YOU...
CHERNOBOG, THE GOD OF DEATH!
TRAUMATIZED
AAA あ
AAA あ
AHH あ
HHH! あ

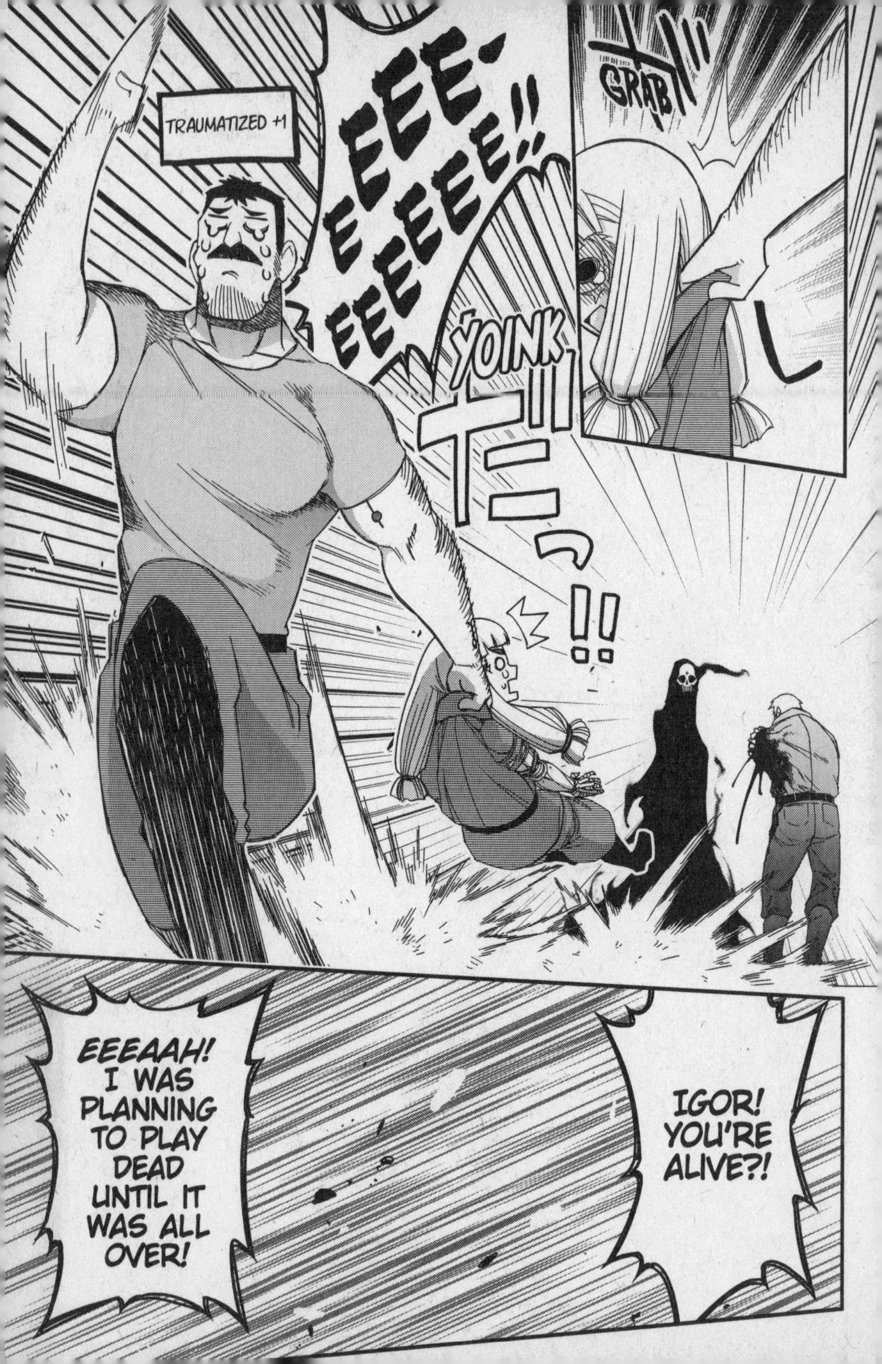
GRAB
EEE-EEEEEEEE!!
YOINK
TRAUMATIZED +1
IGOR! YOU'RE ALIVE?!
EEEAAH! I WAS PLANNING TO PLAY DEAD UNTIL IT WAS ALL OVER!

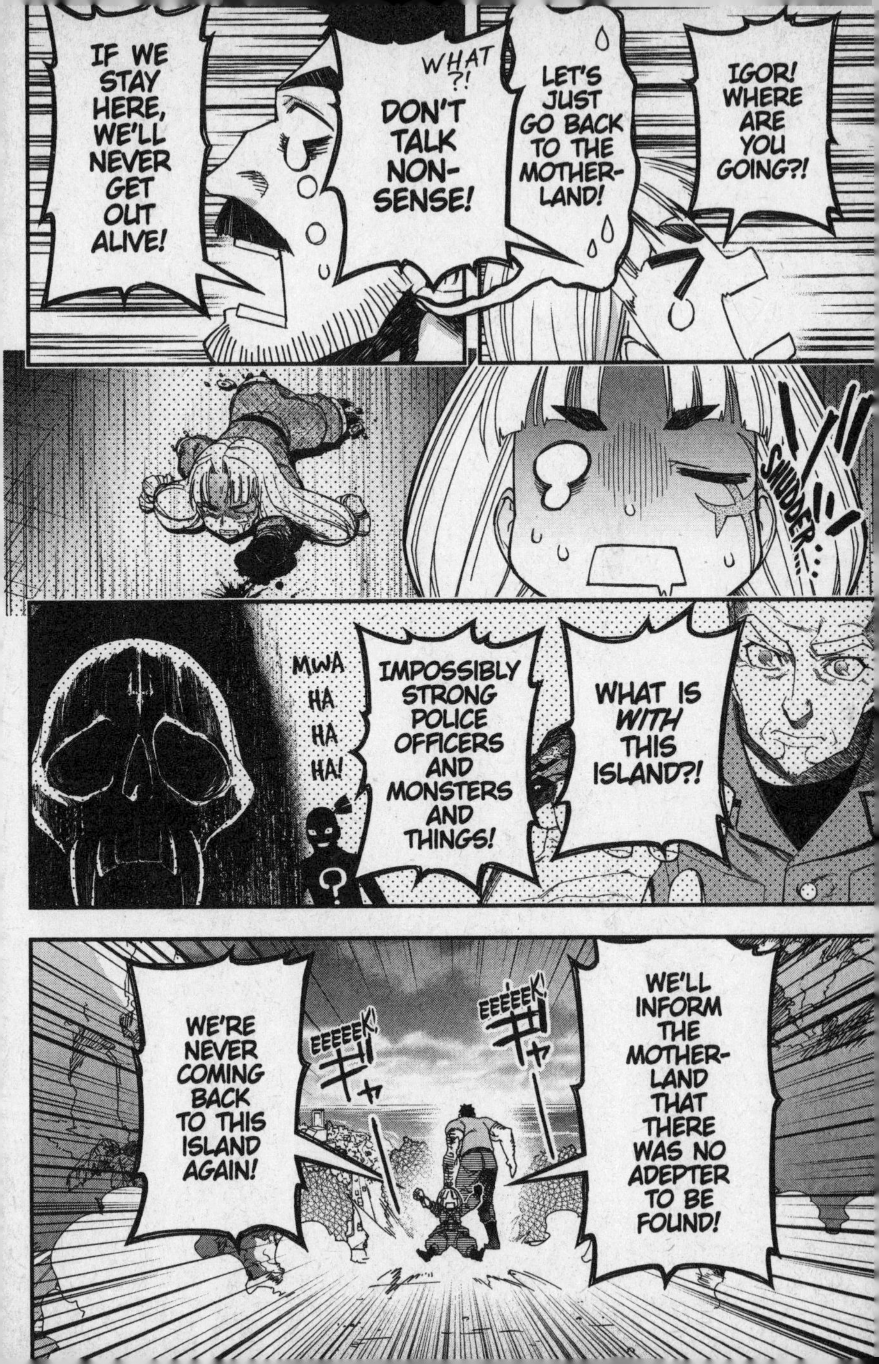
IGOR! WHERE ARE YOU GOING?!
LET'S JUST GO BACK TO THE MOTHER-LAND!
WHAT ?!
DON'T TALK NON-SENSE!
IF WE STAY HERE, WE'LL NEVER GET OUT ALIVE!
SHUDDER...
WHAT IS *WITH* THIS ISLAND?!
IMPOSSIBLY STRONG POLICE OFFICERS AND MONSTERS AND THINGS!
MWA HA HA HA!
WE'LL INFORM THE MOTHER-LAND THAT THERE WAS NO ADEPTER TO BE FOUND!
EEEEEK!
ギャー
EEEEEK!
ギャ
WE'RE NEVER COMING BACK TO THIS ISLAND AGAIN!

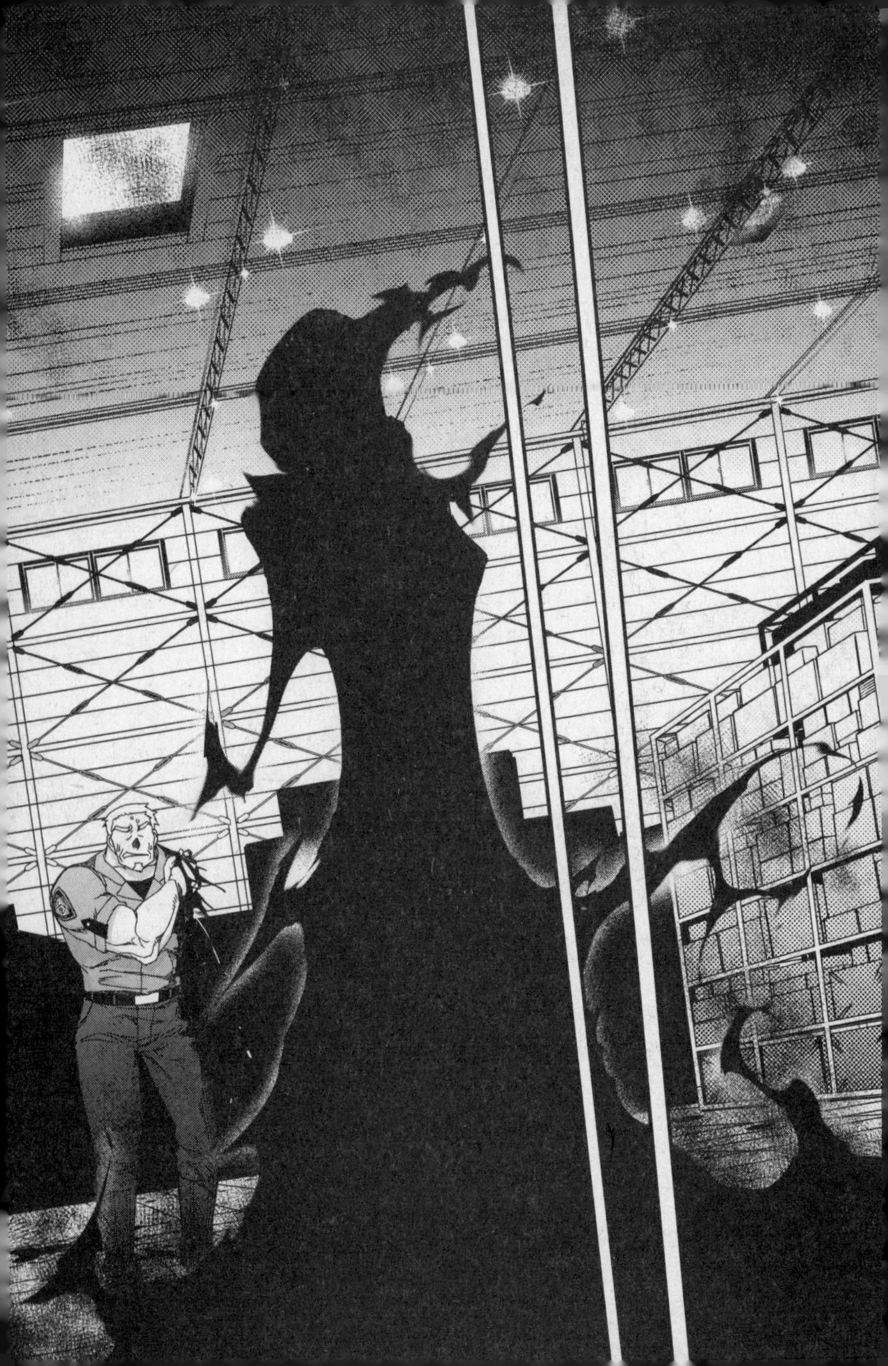

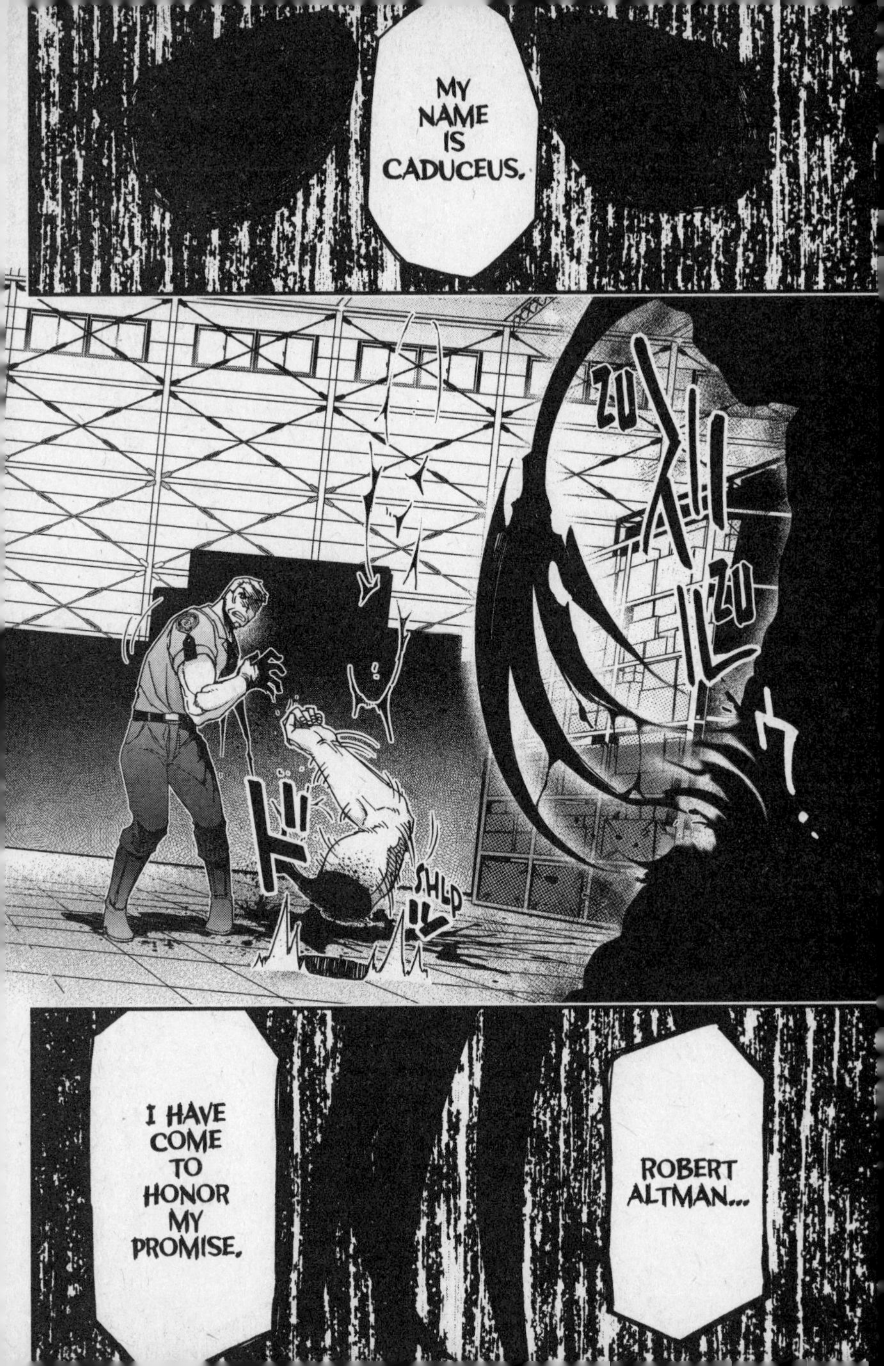
MY NAME IS CADUCEUS.
ZU
ZU
SHLP
ROBERT ALTMAN...
I HAVE COME TO HONOR MY PROMISE.

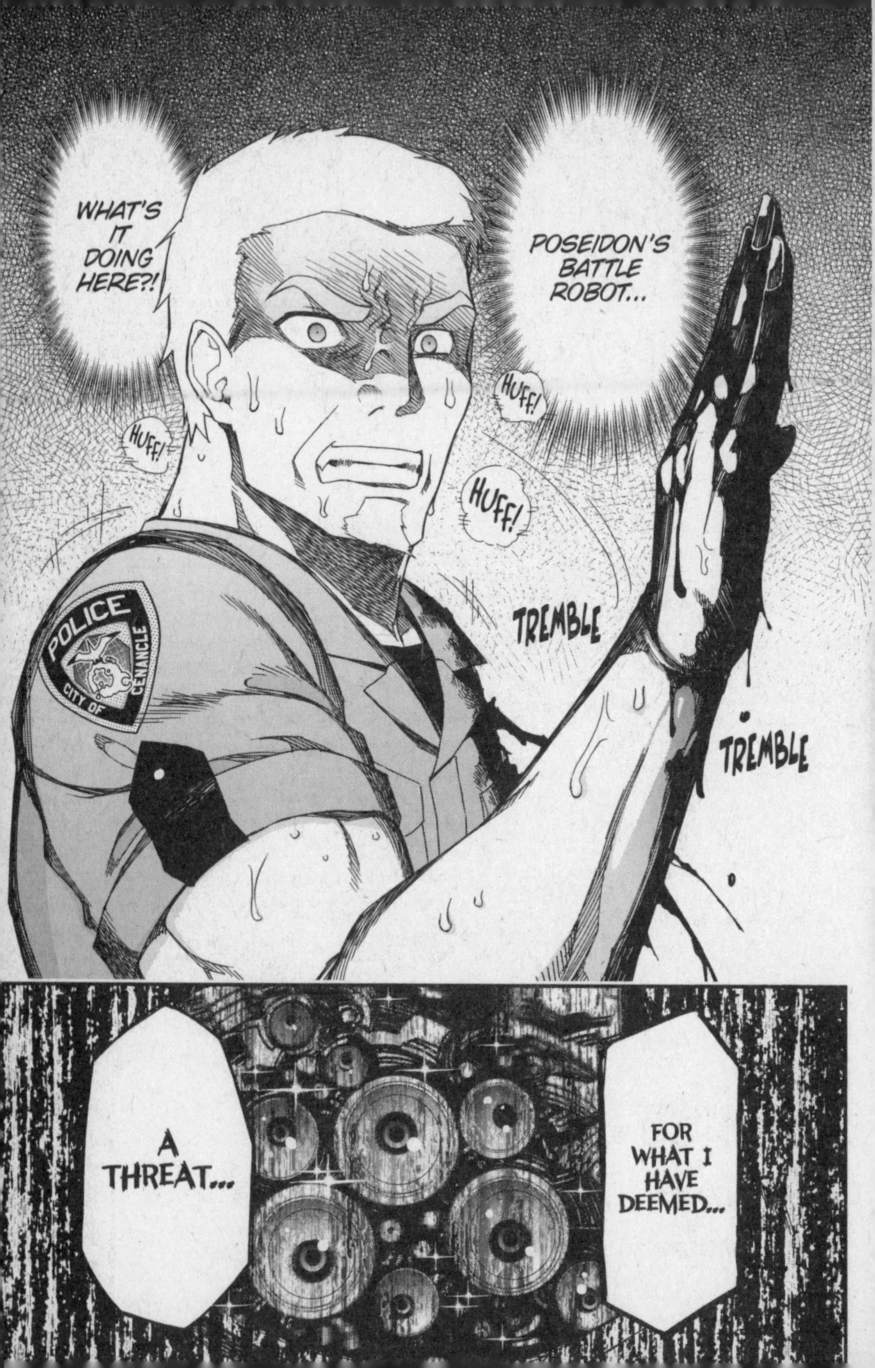
POSEIDON'S BATTLE ROBOT...
WHAT'S IT DOING HERE?!
HUFF!
HUFF!
HUFF!
TREMBLE
TREMBLE
FOR WHAT I HAVE DEEMED...
A THREAT...

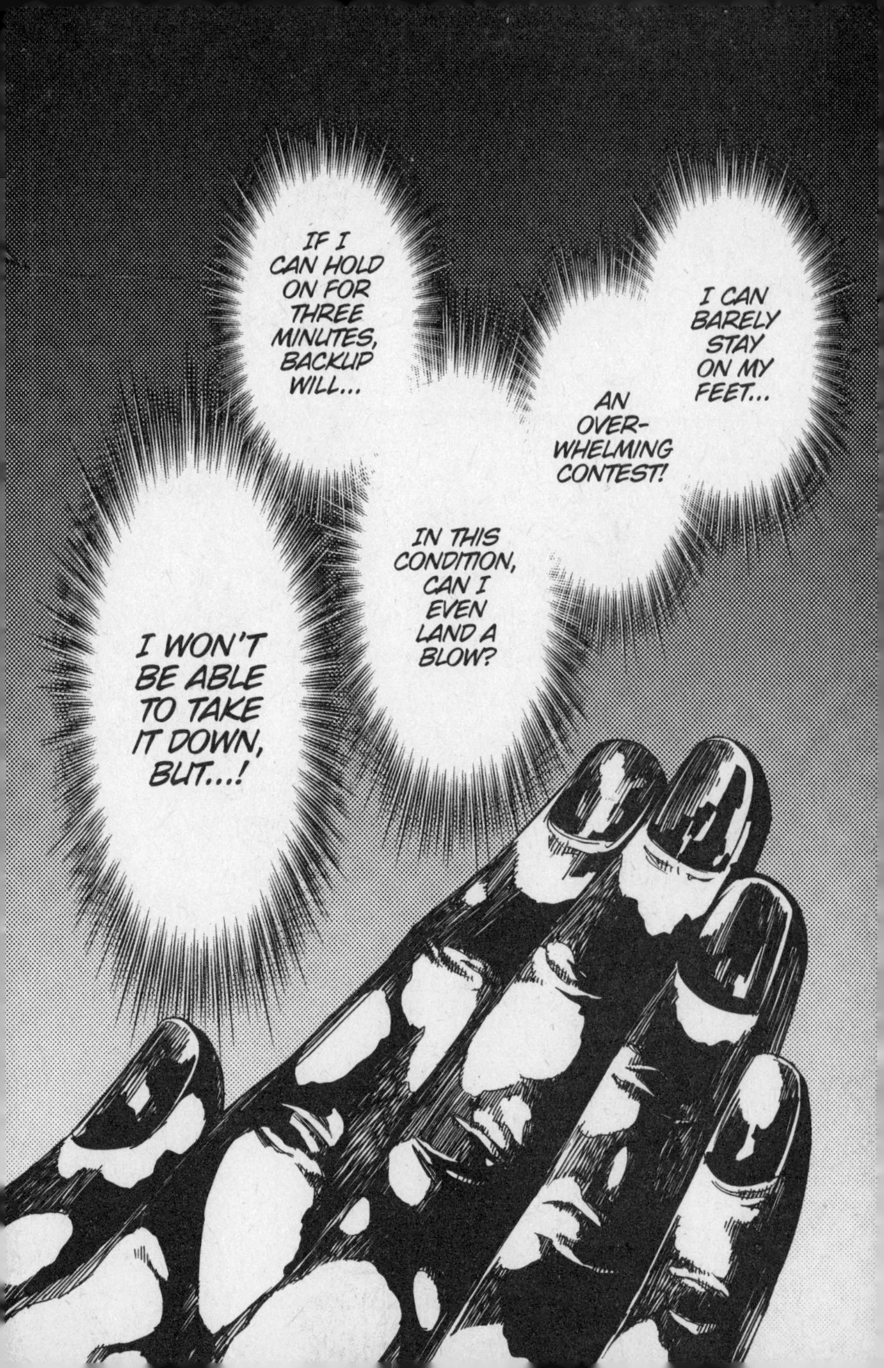
I CAN BARELY STAY ON MY FEET...
AN OVER-WHELMING CONTEST!
IF I CAN HOLD ON FOR THREE MINUTES, BACKUP WILL...
IN THIS CONDITION, CAN I EVEN LAND A BLOW?
I WON'T BE ABLE TO TAKE IT DOWN, BUT...!

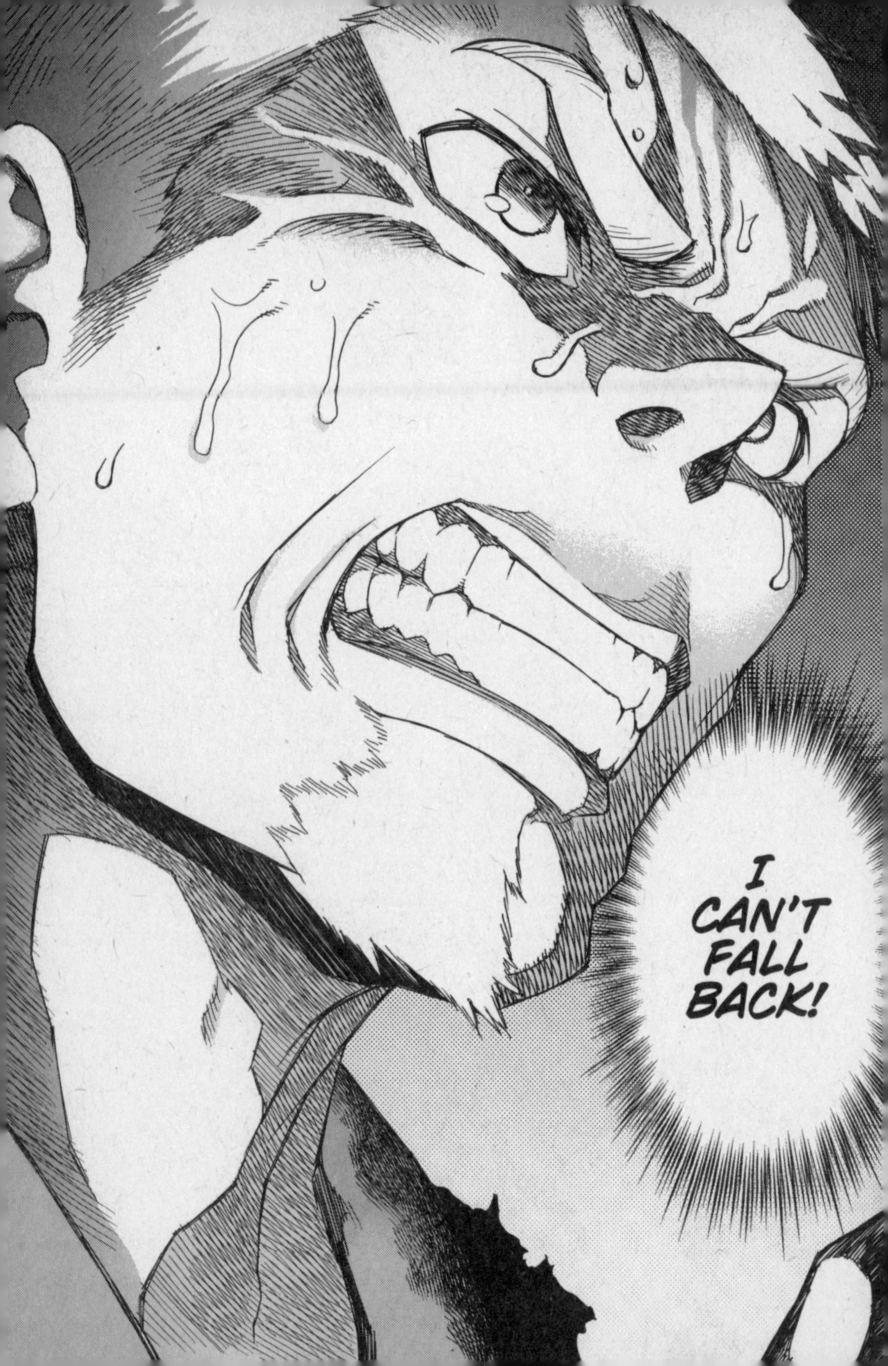
I CAN'T FALL BACK!

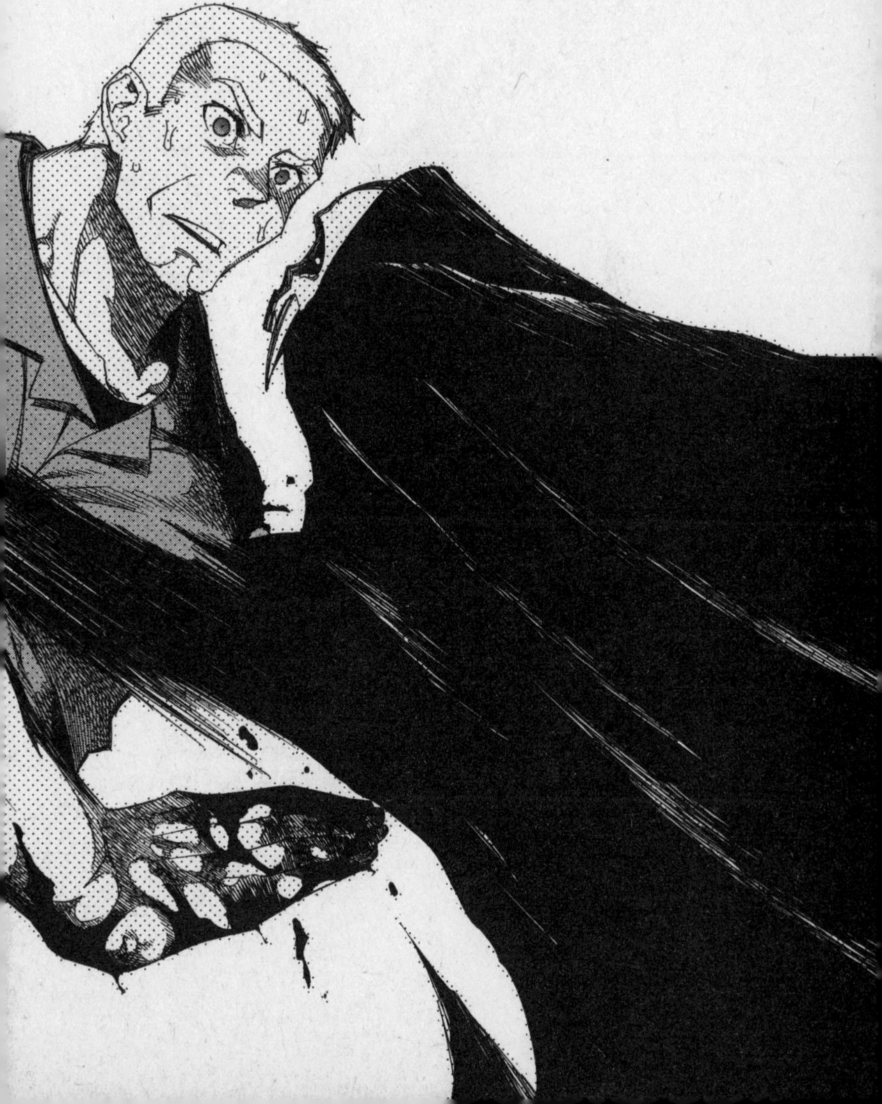

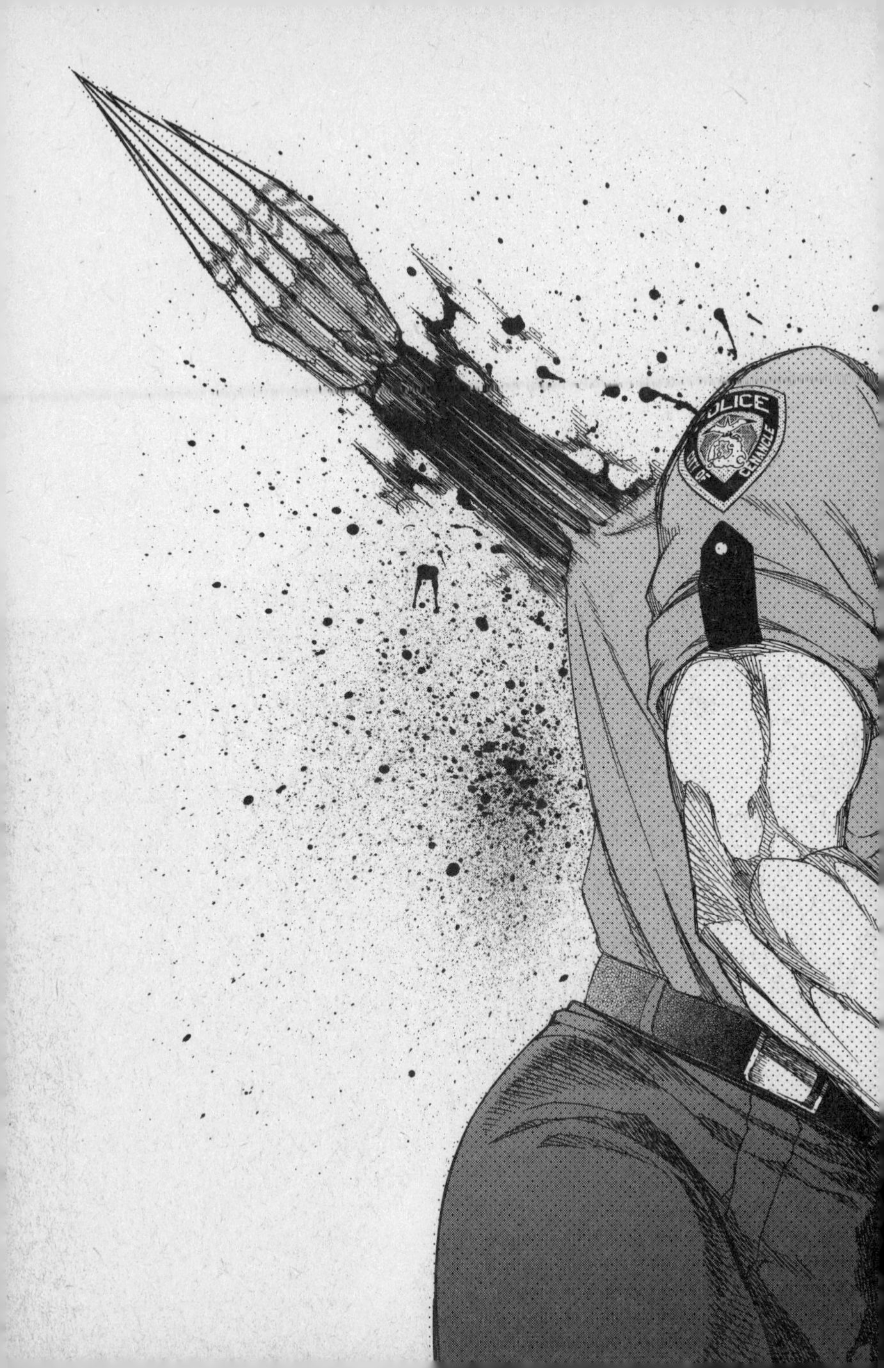
OLICE
CITY OF
CENANCLE

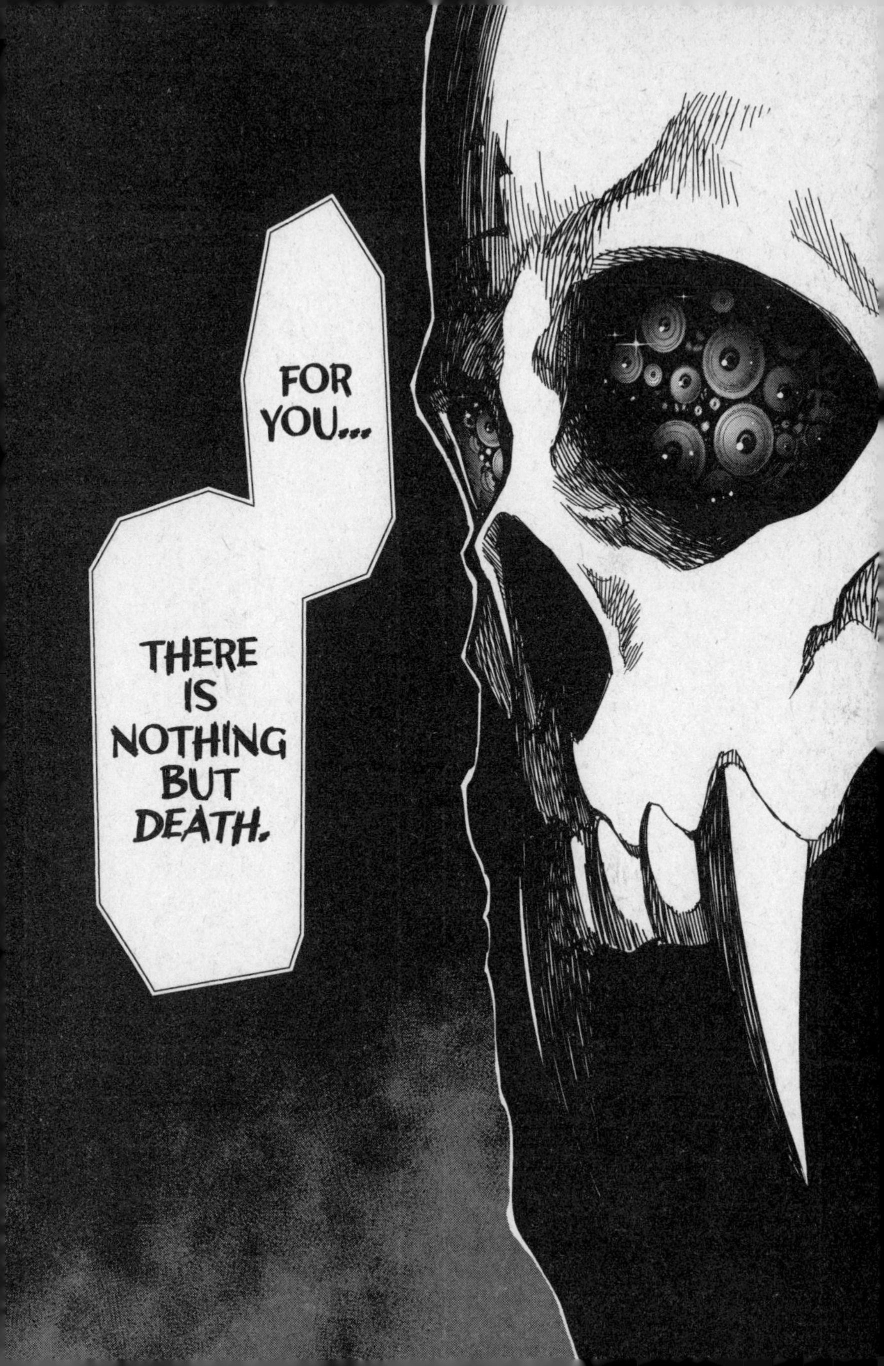
FOR YOU...
THERE IS NOTHING BUT DEATH.

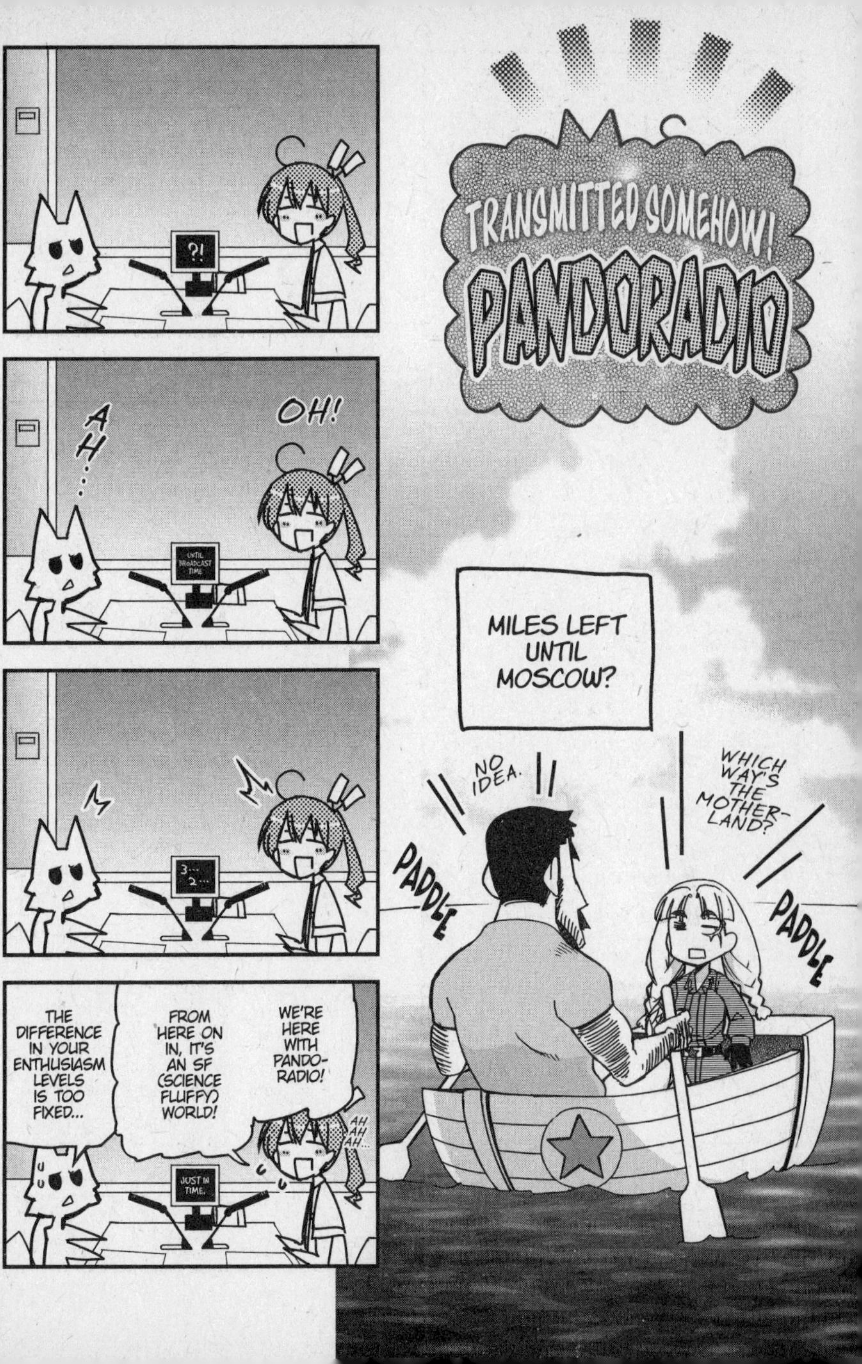
TRANSMITTED SOMEHOW!
PANDORADIO
MILES LEFT UNTIL MOSCOW?
WHICH WAY'S THE MOTHER-LAND?
NO IDEA.
PADDLE
PADDLE
?!
OH!
AH...
UNTIL BROADCAST TIME
3... 2...
WE'RE HERE WITH PANDO-RADIO!
FROM HERE ON IN, IT'S AN SF (SCIENCE FLUFFY) WORLD!
THE DIFFERENCE IN YOUR ENTHUSIASM LEVELS IS TOO FIXED...
AH AH AH...
JUST IN TIME.

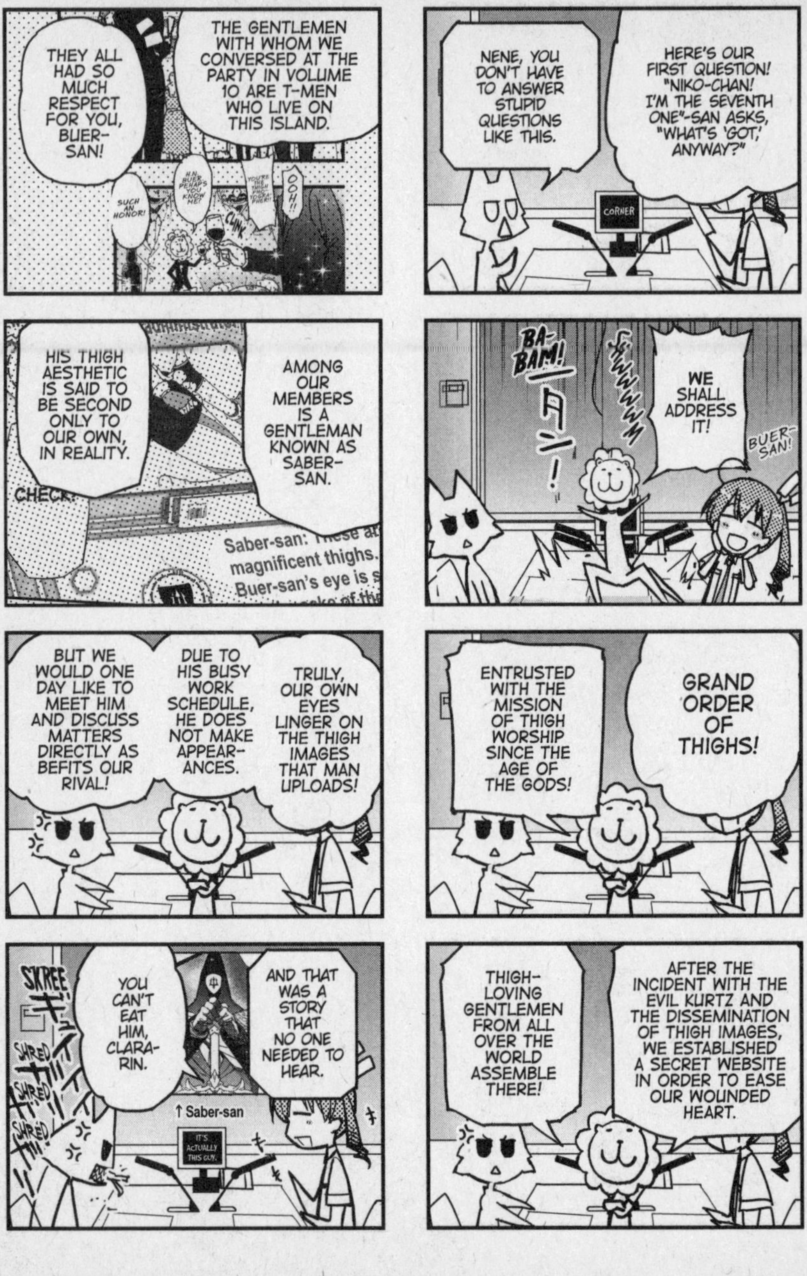
HERE'S OUR FIRST QUESTION! "NIKO-CHAN! I'M THE SEVENTH ONE"-SAN ASKS, "WHAT'S 'GOT,' ANYWAY?"
NENE, YOU DON'T HAVE TO ANSWER STUPID QUESTIONS LIKE THIS.
CORNER
WE SHALL ADDRESS IT!
BUER-SAN!
BA-BAM!
SHWWWWM
GRAND ORDER OF THIGHS!
ENTRUSTED WITH THE MISSION OF THIGH WORSHIP SINCE THE AGE OF THE GODS!
AFTER THE INCIDENT WITH THE EVIL KURTZ AND THE DISSEMINATION OF THIGH IMAGES, WE ESTABLISHED A SECRET WEBSITE IN ORDER TO EASE OUR WOUNDED HEART.
THIGH-LOVING GENTLEMEN FROM ALL OVER THE WORLD ASSEMBLE THERE!
THE GENTLEMEN WITH WHOM WE CONVERSED AT THE PARTY IN VOLUME 10 ARE T-MEN WHO LIVE ON THIS ISLAND.
THEY ALL HAD SO MUCH RESPECT FOR YOU, BUER-SAN!
OOH!!
YOU'RE THE THIGH PHOTOGRAPHER!!
H.N. BUER. PEHAPS YOU KNOW ME?
CLINK
SUCH AN HONOR!
AMONG OUR MEMBERS IS A GENTLEMAN KNOWN AS SABER-SAN.
HIS THIGH AESTHETIC IS SAID TO BE SECOND ONLY TO OUR OWN, IN REALITY.
CHECK
Saber-san:
magnificent thighs.
TRULY, OUR OWN EYES LINGER ON THE THIGH IMAGES THAT MAN UPLOADS!
DUE TO HIS BUSY WORK SCHEDULE, HE DOES NOT MAKE APPEARANCES.
BUT WE WOULD ONE DAY LIKE TO MEET HIM AND DISCUSS MATTERS DIRECTLY AS BEFITS OUR RIVAL!
AND THAT WAS A STORY THAT NO ONE NEEDED TO HEAR.
YOU CAN'T EAT HIM, CLARA-RIN.
SKREE
SHRED
SHRED
SHRED
↑ Saber-san
IT'S ACTUALLY THIS GUY.

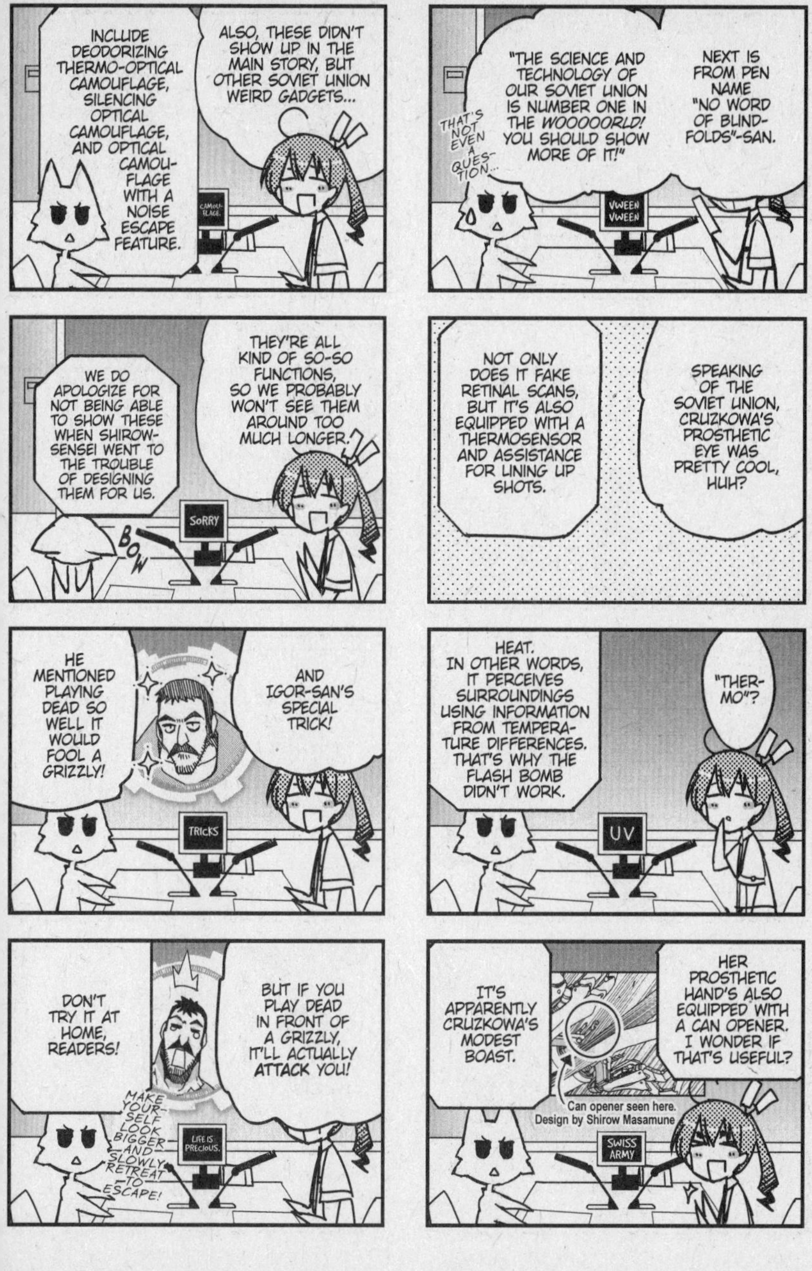
NEXT IS FROM PEN NAME "NO WORD OF BLIND-FOLDS"-SAN.
"THE SCIENCE AND TECHNOLOGY OF OUR SOVIET UNION IS NUMBER ONE IN THE *WOOOOORLD!* YOU SHOULD SHOW MORE OF IT!"
THAT'S NOT EVEN A QUES-TION...
VWEEN VWEEN
ALSO, THESE DIDN'T SHOW UP IN THE MAIN STORY, BUT OTHER SOVIET UNION WEIRD GADGETS...
INCLUDE DEODORIZING THERMO-OPTICAL CAMOUFLAGE, SILENCING OPTICAL CAMOUFLAGE, AND OPTICAL CAMOU-FLAGE WITH A NOISE ESCAPE FEATURE.
CAMOU-FLAGE.
SPEAKING OF THE SOVIET UNION, CRUZKOWA'S PROSTHETIC EYE WAS PRETTY COOL, HUH?
NOT ONLY DOES IT FAKE RETINAL SCANS, BUT IT'S ALSO EQUIPPED WITH A THERMOSENSOR AND ASSISTANCE FOR LINING UP SHOTS.
THEY'RE ALL KIND OF SO-SO FUNCTIONS, SO WE PROBABLY WON'T SEE THEM AROUND TOO MUCH LONGER.
WE DO APOLOGIZE FOR NOT BEING ABLE TO SHOW THESE WHEN SHIROW-SENSEI WENT TO THE TROUBLE OF DESIGNING THEM FOR US.
SORRY
BOW
"THER-MO"?
HEAT. IN OTHER WORDS, IT PERCEIVES SURROUNDINGS USING INFORMATION FROM TEMPERA-TURE DIFFERENCES. THAT'S WHY THE FLASH BOMB DIDN'T WORK.
UV
AND IGOR-SAN'S SPECIAL TRICK!
HE MENTIONED PLAYING DEAD SO WELL IT WOULD FOOL A GRIZZLY!
TRICKS
HER PROSTHETIC HAND'S ALSO EQUIPPED WITH A CAN OPENER. I WONDER IF THAT'S USEFUL?
IT'S APPARENTLY CRUZKOWA'S MODEST BOAST.
Can opener seen here.
Design by Shirow Masamune
SWISS ARMY
BUT IF YOU PLAY DEAD IN FRONT OF A GRIZZLY, IT'LL ACTUALLY ATTACK YOU!
DON'T TRY IT AT HOME, READERS!
MAKE YOURSELF LOOK BIGGER AND SLOWLY RETREAT TO ESCAPE!
LIFE IS PRECIOUS.

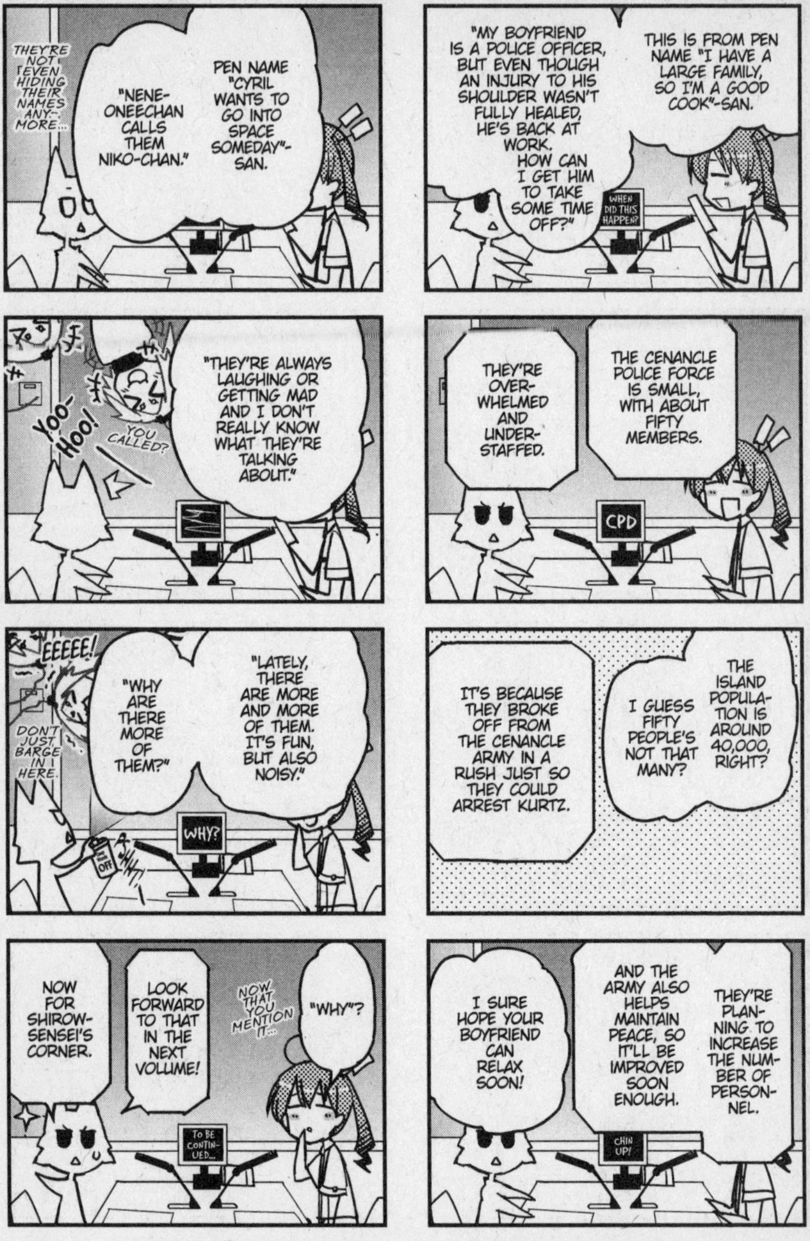
THIS IS FROM PEN NAME "I HAVE A LARGE FAMILY, SO I'M A GOOD COOK"-SAN.
"MY BOYFRIEND IS A POLICE OFFICER, BUT EVEN THOUGH AN INJURY TO HIS SHOULDER WASN'T FULLY HEALED, HE'S BACK AT WORK. HOW CAN I GET HIM TO TAKE SOME TIME OFF?"
WHEN DID THIS HAPPEN?
PEN NAME "CYRIL WANTS TO GO INTO SPACE SOMEDAY"-SAN.
"NENE-ONEECHAN CALLS THEM NIKO-CHAN."
THEY'RE NOT EVEN HIDING THEIR NAMES ANYMORE...
THE CENANCLE POLICE FORCE IS SMALL, WITH ABOUT FIFTY MEMBERS.
THEY'RE OVERWHELMED AND UNDERSTAFFED.
CPD
"THEY'RE ALWAYS LAUGHING OR GETTING MAD AND I DON'T REALLY KNOW WHAT THEY'RE TALKING ABOUT."
YOU CALLED?
YOO-HOO!
THE ISLAND POPULATION IS AROUND 40,000, RIGHT?
I GUESS FIFTY PEOPLE'S NOT THAT MANY?
IT'S BECAUSE THEY BROKE OFF FROM THE CENANCLE ARMY IN A RUSH JUST SO THEY COULD ARREST KURTZ.
"LATELY, THERE ARE MORE AND MORE OF THEM. IT'S FUN, BUT ALSO NOISY."
"WHY ARE THERE MORE OF THEM?"
EEEEEE!
DON'T JUST BARGE IN HERE.
WHY?
OFF
THEY'RE PLANNING TO INCREASE THE NUMBER OF PERSONNEL.
AND THE ARMY ALSO HELPS MAINTAIN PEACE, SO IT'LL BE IMPROVED SOON ENOUGH.
I SURE HOPE YOUR BOYFRIEND CAN RELAX SOON!
CHIN UP!
"WHY"?
NOW THAT YOU MENTION IT...
LOOK FORWARD TO THAT IN THE NEXT VOLUME!
NOW FOR SHIROW-SENSEI'S CORNER.
TO BE CONTINUED...

DESIGN NOTES

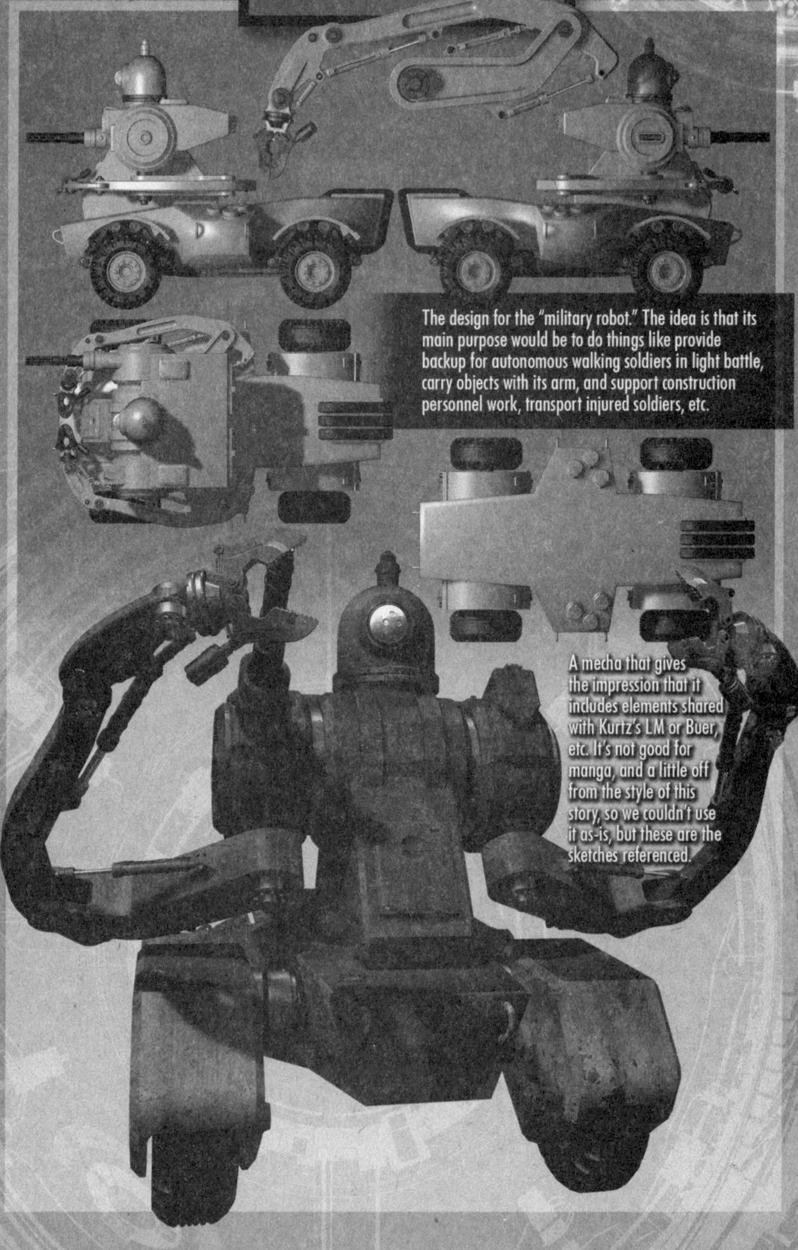

The design for the "military robot." The idea is that its main purpose would be to do things like provide backup for autonomous walking soldiers in light battle, carry objects with its arm, and support construction personnel work, transport injured soldiers, etc.

A mecha that gives the impression that it includes elements shared with Kurtz's LM or Buer, etc. It's not good for manga, and a little off from the style of this story, so we couldn't use it as-is, but these are the sketches referenced.

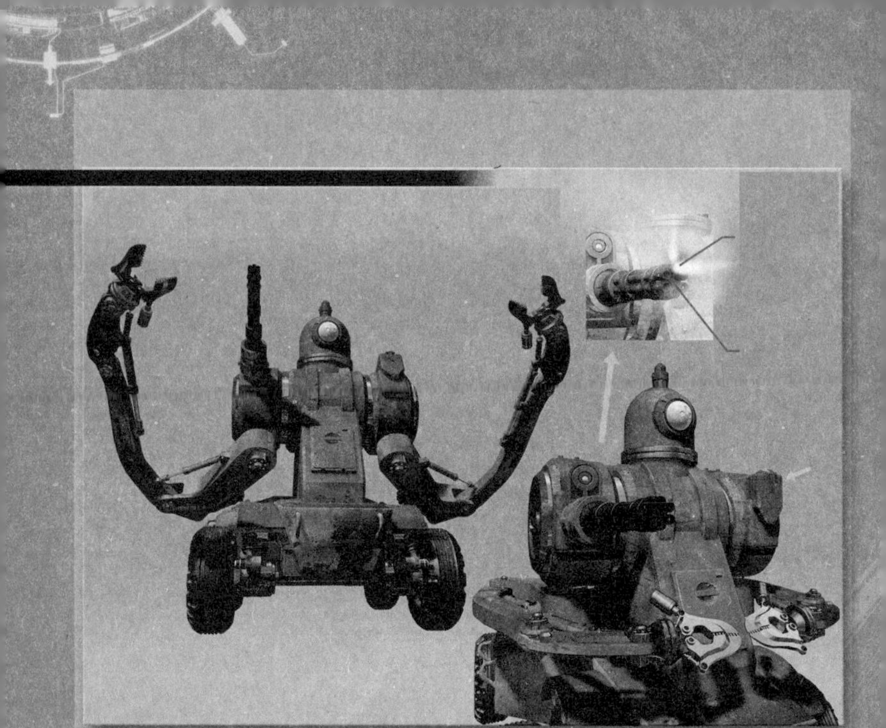

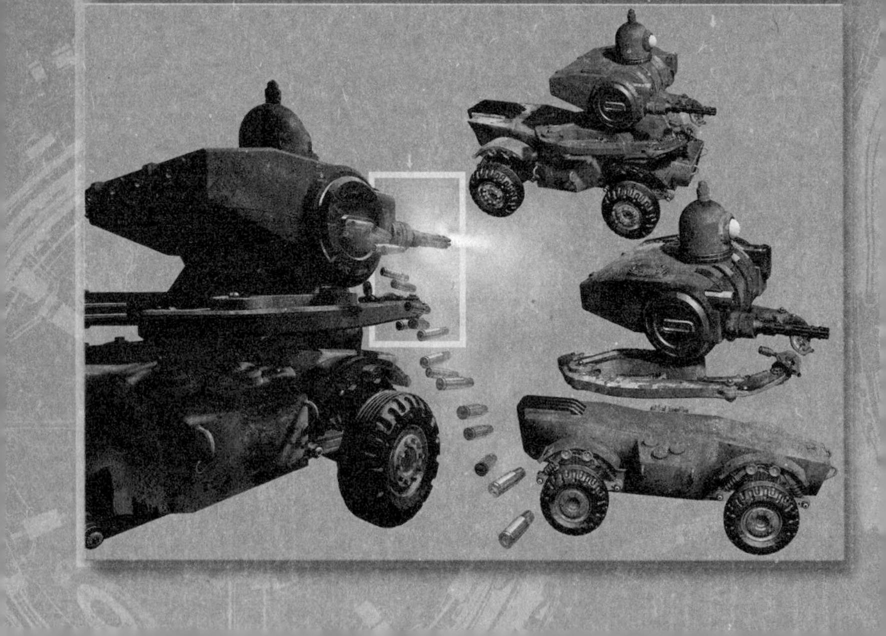

DESIGN NOTES

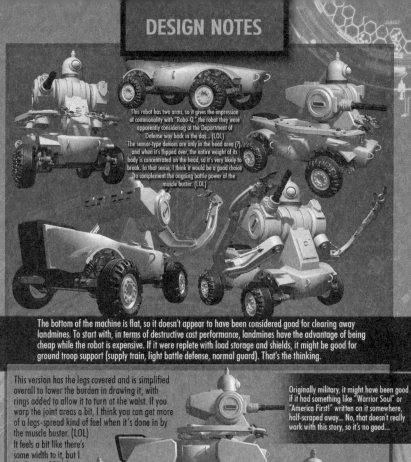

This robot has two arms, so it gives the impression of commonality with "Robo-Q," the robot they were apparently considering at the Department of Defense way back in the day... (LOL)
The sensor-type devices are only in the head area (?), and when it's flipped over, the entire weight of its body is concentrated on the head, so it's very likely to break. In that sense, I think it would be a good choice to complement the ongoing battle power of the muscle buster. (LOL)

The bottom of the machine is flat, so it doesn't appear to have been considered good for clearing away landmines. To start with, in terms of destructive cost performance, landmines have the advantage of being cheap while the robot is expensive. If it were replete with load storage and shields, it might be good for ground troop support (supply train, light battle defense, normal guard). That's the thinking.

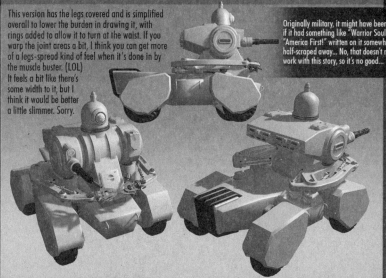

This version has the legs covered and is simplified overall to lower the burden in drawing it, with rings added to allow it to turn at the waist. If you warp the joint areas a bit, I think you can get more of a legs-spread kind of feel when it's done in by the muscle buster. (LOL)
It feels a bit like there's some width to it, but I think it would be better a little slimmer. Sorry.

Originally military, it might have been good if it had something like "Warrior Soul" or "America First!" written on it somewhere, half-scraped away... No, that doesn't really work with this story, so it's no good...

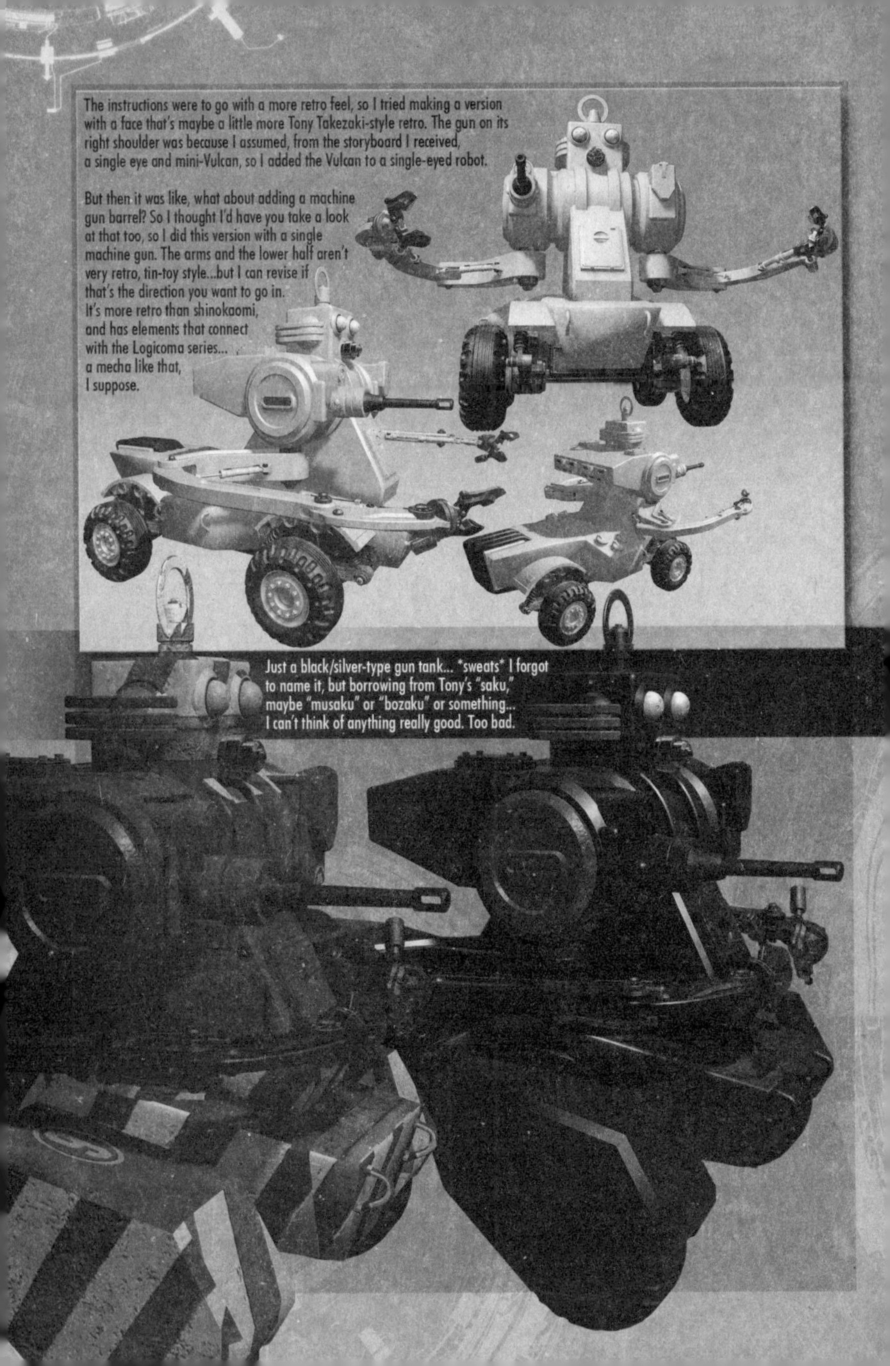
The instructions were to go with a more retro feel, so I tried making a version with a face that's maybe a little more Tony Takezaki-style retro. The gun on its right shoulder was because I assumed, from the storyboard I received, a single eye and mini-Vulcan, so I added the Vulcan to a single-eyed robot.
But then it was like, what about adding a machine gun barrel? So I thought I'd have you take a look at that too, so I did this version with a single machine gun. The arms and the lower half aren't very retro, tin-toy style...but I can revise if that's the direction you want to go in. It's more retro than shinokaomi, and has elements that connect with the Logicoma series... a mecha like that, I suppose.
Just a black/silver-type gun tank... *sweats* I forgot to name it, but borrowing from Tony's "saku," maybe "musaku" or "bozaku" or something... I can't think of anything really good. Too bad.

Greetings (for the twelfth time)!

So here we are at the milestone of Volume 12 of *Pandora in the Crimson Shell*! I'm grateful for the efforts of everyone involved, starting with Rikudou Koushi-shi and Hitotose Rin-shi, and including all the readers who have been kind enough to support us this far. Thank you so much, as always.

Even after going through the change in artist in Volume 9 and the change in editor in Volume 11, the project is currently right on track and maintaining a good pace; the work is in an extremely good place. Many thanks for that...although it also connects directly to the fact that the project has generated no special items to report to you readers or anything along the lines of, "You have to hear this!" (LOL)

One thing that's been bothering me, which they've been slow to amend, is the copy on the book cover. As of when I'm writing this, Hitotose Rin-shi's name is only shown on the back flap, which is an extremely regrettable situation for both Hitotose-shi and his fans. I don't know why it happened this way, but perhaps there's some rule about the logistics of book sales where only two names are allowed, or perhaps it's some sort of custom in the manga industry. Personally, I really think it should be amended.

With anime, it's quite normal to list all the people involved in the production who bear some responsibility for the work, such as the writer, director, animation director, sound director, and so on, so I think it would be preferable to note a manga work's production status similarly when the division of labor changes.

Incidentally, the Crossroad named on that same book cover flap is the company responsible for mediating between myself and the editorial department for *Pandora in the Crimson Shell*. With other projects, they sometimes also handle the proposals for manga and anime, but here they're only facilitating communication, so their credit is the vague "in cooperation with." When people who don't know specifics hear this, perhaps it sounds like they're not doing anything vital, but in a situation where people with very distinct idiosyncrasies are working together, it's critical to have other people who can step in and serve as a buffer as necessary. If that buffer were to weaken or lose its neutrality, frustrations could quickly become a problem.

Shirow Masamune
January 13, 2018

Caricature difficulty chart!

Easy to draw.

Hard to draw.

I hope you'll join us in the next volume!
Hitotose Rin

SEVEN SEAS ENTERTAIN...

PANDORA in the
CRIMSON SHELL

GHOST URN vol. 12

story by SHIROW MASAMUNE / art by RIKUDOU KOUSHI

TRANSLATION
Jocelyne Allen

ADAPTATION
Ysabet Reinhardt MacFarlane

LETTERING AND RETOUCH
Roland Amago
Bambi Eloriaga-Amago

COVER DESIGN
KC Fabellon

PROOFREADER

Shar...

PRODU...

M...

EDITOR-IN-CHIEF
Adam Arnold

PUBLISHER
Jason DeAngelis

KOUKAKU NO PANDORA Volume 12
© Koushi RIKUDOU 2018
© Shirow Masamune 2018
First published in Japan in 2018 by KADOKAWA CORPORATION, Tokyo.
English translation rights arranged with KADOKAWA CORPORATION, Tokyo,
through TOHAN CORPORATION, Tokyo.

Printed in Canada
First Printing: October 2019
10 9 8 7 6 5 4 3 2 1

FOLLOW US ONLINE: *www.sevenseasentertainment.com*

READING DIRECTIONS

This book reads from *right to left*, Japanese style.
If this is your first time reading manga, you start
reading from the top right panel on each page and
take it from there. If you get lost, just follow the
numbered diagram here. It may seem backwards at
first, but you'll get the hang of it! Have fun!!

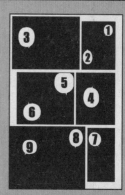

12 STAFF

Original story	Shirow Masamune (in cooperation with Crossroad)
Production/Composition	Rikudou Koushi
Art	Hitotose Rin
Direction assistance	Takepon G
Assistant	Unamu Kibayashida Mekabu Chashibu
Editing	Koichiro Ochiai (Kadokawa) Kinoshita Kosuke (Kadokawa)
Design	Noriyuki Jinguji (Zin Studio)
SPECIAL THANKS	Seishinsha Co., Ltd.